HUMAN MEMORY

An Introduction to Research and Theory

HUMAN MEMORY
An Introduction to Research and Theory

Eugene B. Zechmeister
Loyola University of Chicago

Stanley E. Nyberg
Barnard College

Brooks/Cole Publishing Company
Monterey, California

Brooks/Cole Publishing Company
A Division of Wadsworth, Inc.

Printed in the United States of America

10 9 8 7 6 5 4 3 2 1

Library of Congress Cataloging in Publication Data

Zechmeister, Eugene B., [date]
    Human memory, an introduction to research
and theory.

    Includes bibliographies and indexes.
      1. Memory   2. Memory—Research.
I. Nyberg, Stanley E., [date].   II. Title.
BF371.Z43   153.1'2   81-7640
ISBN 0-8185-0458-7   AACR2

Subject Editor: *C. Deborah Laughton*
Manuscript Editor: *Sylvia Stein*
Production Editor: *Patricia E. Cain*
Interior Design: *Otto Speck*
Cover Design: *Angela Lee*
Illustrations: *Lori Heckelman*
Typesetting: *Graphic Typesetting Service, Los Angeles, California*

To Kathy, Katie, Peter, Liz, and Danny
(E.B.Z.)
and
To My Family
(S.E.N.)

Preface

This book is intended to do more than merely present students with the facts known about human memory. Our goal is to draw students into the scientific process of research and theory construction—to engage students intellectually and perhaps directly in the scientific pursuit of knowledge about human memory, its nature, and its processes. Accordingly, the book's organization is somewhat unusual, both providing a broad introduction to research and theory and focusing at some length on particular problems and issues in the field. The chapter topics reflect this issue orientation.

The issues selected allow us to survey a wide range of questions. By examining these questions historically and by tracing the development of research and theory in important experiments, we can put students in a position to appreciate what is known and what is not yet known about human memory. Such a structure helps students find answers to the many questions they bring to the study of memory, such as: Why do we forget? How long does it take for a memory to be formed? How can memory be improved? Is memory reconstructive? The book shows where research has been and where it might be headed in the search for answers to these and other questions.

In keeping with our goal, nearly all the chapters include descriptions of experimental procedures that are adapted from important published experiments. The original experiments will be recognized by most instructors as having played pivotal roles in the development of research and theory about human memory. Using materials provided in the Appendix, instructors and students can actually perform these experiments. Although they are designed for individual testing, in most instances the experimental procedures can be easily modified to allow for group testing and, thus, for use in the classroom.

We have found that involving students, either as subjects for classroom demonstrations or as experimenters who use friends or classmates as subjects, adds a new dimension to their inquiry into human memory. For example, students who have participated in an experiment are better able to understand a particular interpretation or theoretical controversy surrounding the outcome of that experiment. Further, with their own data present, students who are otherwise silent have less difficulty expressing an interpretation or offering a theory for the experimental results. The explanations given by students are sometimes similar, if not identical, to published theoretical accounts of these experiments. Pointing out this fact to students draws them into the scientific enterprise. Not to be minimized is the fact that students usually enjoy participation in experiments.

Generally, the Appendix includes more than the minimum materials necessary to carry out each experiment. Therefore, instructors can modify the original demonstrations without having to turn to other sources. Instructors can even assign to students the task of modifying the procedures in order to answer alternative questions about human memory. None of the experimental tasks described in the book requires more than paper, pencil, and perhaps a watch with a second hand.

A wide variety of tasks and methodologies are represented in the experimental descriptions. Even if the memory experiments are not actually conducted, the reading of these descriptions will give students a feel for the particular experiment and will introduce to them many of the major paradigms used to investigate memory. Therefore, rather than appearing at the end of the chapter, each experimental description immediately follows discussion of the experiment on which it is based.

Because the book is issue-oriented and relatively free (we hope) from theoretical pontificating, it offers the instructor considerable flexibility. Although the chapters are basically independent, the later chapters build on methods and terms that are introduced in early chapters. Should an instructor wish to omit certain chapters or to rearrange the order of study, we suggest that this be done after the material in Chapters 1, 2, and 3 is presented. Chapter 1 provides an introduction to the text and a description of the plan of the book, which is necessary for the students' understanding of our approach. Chapters 2 and 3 set the stage for questions regarding different "types" of memory, including sensory memory, primary memory, and secondary memory. Chapter 3 contains a discussion (and experimental description) of the important Brown-Peterson task, which figures prominently in later chapters.

Although we have emphasized some issues over others, instructors will find that the appropriate foundation has been laid should they desire to include additional material. By ending each chapter with a list of recommended readings, we direct the reader to sources that present related or additional topics. We have not given extensive space to a discussion of theoretical models of memory or memory structure. Our experience has been that most instructors have their own views on such models and that textbooks sometimes get in the way of an instructor's presentation when the opinions in the textbook do not coincide with his or her particular theoretical orientation. Should additional theoretical material be desired, instructors will likely know of appropriate supplemental readings that can be incorporated into their teaching. The recommended readings identify a number of useful sources.

This book is written for students of psychology enrolled in courses that offer an introduction to the study of human memory. These courses are taught under various titles including human memory, memory and cognition, learning and memory, cognitive processes, and information processing. Although the book is intended primarily for a lecture course, its structure and organization are appropriate for courses that include classroom demonstrations of memory phenomena or that allow students the opportunity for experimental inquiry.

Finally, we have our acknowledgments to make, and we do so most gladly. We truly appreciate the help that was given by many people during the writing of this book. First on the list is our editor at Brooks/Cole, C. Deborah Laughton, who bought us breakfast more than two years ago and slipped us a book contract with our orange juice. We hope that her confidence in us and the attention she has paid to our progress these past years are justified in this book. She also corralled many fine reviewers to show us where we were right and where we had gone wrong during the writing process.

Investigators in the field of memory are naturally a critical bunch; given even the most modest inducement by a publisher to show their critical side, their response can be simply humbling. The book has benefited greatly from the reviewers' time and efforts. We want to mention specifically Richard Block (Montana State University), George Goedel (Northern Kentucky University), Richard Griggs (University of Florida, Gainesville), Lynn Hasher (Temple University), Richard Mayer (University of California, Santa Barbara), and John Shaughnessy (Hope College). Other reviewers to whom we owe thanks are Shahin Hastroudi (George Washington University), Tom Malloy (University of Utah), and Lawrence S. Meyers (California State University, Sacramento). In addition, we wish to thank several colleagues and friends who commented on portions of the manuscript, including Ira Appelman, Richard Bowen, and Dick Fay, all of Loyola University of Chicago. We also want to thank Henry

C. Ellis (University of New Mexico) for his review of the original outline of the book.

Many people at Brooks/Cole provided valuable support and assistance throughout this project. Our production editor, Patricia Cain, coordinated it all and worked the magic (and just plain worked) to make this book appear. Sylvia Stein edited the original manuscript and performed some magic herself when she changed words and in other ways improved the prose but left ideas intact. Marsha Baxter and, later, Carline Haga oversaw the difficult job of assembling permissions. Stan Rice and Angela Lee made us look good by their design work.

The secretarial staffs at Loyola University of Chicago, North Park College, and Barnard College not only contributed their typing skills but provided other assistance as well—their words of encouragement being the most appreciated. We want to thank Bernie Jaroch-Hagerman, Cheryl Sporlein, and especially Joyce Lambo for their help. The cooperation of many other people affiliated with these institutions, particularly the fine library staffs, is also gratefully acknowledged. A special word of thanks goes to Anne Delano-Dolan of Barnard College for her help in checking the references. Finally, we want to thank the students in our 1980 Spring semester classes at Loyola University and Barnard College who read and commented on earlier drafts of the manuscript.

We hope now to be able to pay more attention to the needs and concerns of our families and friends, who have given up much so that we could devote our time and energy to writing this book.

Eugene B. Zechmeister
Stanley E. Nyberg

Contents

1

Introduction   1

2

Sensory Registers:
Visual and Acoustic Stores   6

The Stimulus Suffix Effect   21

3

Primary Memory 28

4

The Role of Rehearsal 53

5

Memory Consolidation 77

6

Principles of Forgetting: Interference and Altered Stimulus Conditions 99

7

Evidence for Encoding on
Multiple Dimensions   128

8

Memory for Frequency of Events   148

9

Distribution of Practice   175

10

Recall, Recognition, and Relearning   198

11

Metamemory:
Knowing about Knowing   227

12

Levels of Processing   250

13

Mnemonics 275

14

Constructive and Reconstructive Processes in Memory 296

15

Individual Differences in Remembering   324

HUMAN MEMORY

An Introduction to Research and Theory

1

Introduction

Introduction to the Study of Human Memory
Getting Involved in Research
The Plan of This Book

INTRODUCTION TO THE STUDY OF HUMAN MEMORY

There is a game sometimes played with nursery school children that goes like this. A number of different common objects are displayed on a tray or small table for the children to see. Objects typically include such familiar items as a scissors, cup, spoon, and chalk. The exact number of objects can vary, but there are usually at least seven or eight. After the children view the objects, someone covers the objects with a cloth. The children are then invited to try to name the things under the cloth. They are usually quite good at this game and readily call out the names of objects they can no longer see. The game, of course, is a memory game. But what or where is the memory? If we were observing this game, we would likely speak of the children's memory *for* the objects or, more specifically, their memory *for* the names of the objects. But neither the objects nor their names are memories. Memory is nothing that can be seen or heard. We must assume that the memory resides *in* the child. Its existence is *inferred* on the basis of the children's performance. One researcher's definition of memory is as follows:

> [Memory is] ... some property or state of the organism which is assumed to have resulted from some experience and which has the consequence of altering the organism's potentialities for a response in any of an infinite number of new test situations to which it might be exposed [Estes, 1975, p. 10].

The goal of this textbook is to introduce you to research and theory about human memory. As you will see, memory research is often conducted in a

1

manner not unlike this children's game. The nature and quantity of the to-be-remembered material is planned by an investigator. The conditions under which a subject will experience the material are also carefully arranged. Finally, with the material no longer present, some type of memory "test" is given. What can be discovered about memory depends on the researcher's ingenuity in orchestrating these three phases of a memory experiment. For example, we might learn something about the limits of memory processing if, in the game described, the time the children spent viewing the objects or the number of objects was systematically varied among different groups of children.

A researcher often designs an experiment with some idea as to the nature of memory or the memory processes involved in a particular task. In other words, the researcher has a theory about human memory, and the results of an appropriately designed experiment can be used to evaluate this theory. Actual experimental results are contrasted with the results predicted by the theory. Successful prediction gains support for the theory; a discrepancy between the results predicted and those actually obtained calls for revision or even outright rejection of the theory. In reading this book you will find that psychologists often disagree about a particular theory of memory. Memory is not only abstract and necessarily inferred from behavior; it is also complex. Therefore you should not be surprised to find that not everyone agrees on what memory is or how it works. For example, what theory might you propose to explain the performance of children in the object memory game described? Undoubtedly, some people would suggest that the children create a mental picture (visual image) of the objects. It could be argued that a visual image is able to preserve the objects in memory. By scanning the contents of the image, much as they would scan a picture on the wall, the children could identify the objects. This sounds reasonable enough. But such a theory does not explain why all the objects may not be remembered, why some children may remember more than others, how a "picture" can be produced and then "called up" when it is needed, or how we are able to "stand back" in our minds to scan the contents. You can see that more research would be required to provide an adequate theory of memory even to explain retention in this simple children's game. Other experiments would have to be conducted to provide answers for the many questions this theory has raised. Additional research would also be needed to counter arguments made from opposing theories. Others, for example, might suggest that the children repeat the names of the objects over and over to themselves and thereby ensure retention. An experiment would have to be done to help choose between the "imagery" and "repetition" theories.

Obtaining evidence to support a particular theory or marshaling arguments against an alternative is often a complicated and slow process. Anyone associated with the scientific enterprise will quickly tell you that science progresses in small steps—a kind of detective work associated with carefully examining evidence, retracing steps, and gathering bits and pieces of a story from many sources. Major breakthroughs are few, and, when they do occur, they are more likely the result of many previous failures than the product of sudden insight. However, through this process we inch our way closer to a better understanding of the central core of human cognition—memory.

GETTING INVOLVED IN RESEARCH

An unusual feature of this textbook is that in every chapter except this and the final one there is a description of the procedures necessary to do a memory experiment. Materials required for the experiment are found in the Appendix. By reading these procedure sections, you will find out how to do an important, even "classic," experiment discussed in the text. We hope that your doing the experiments will make the experimental results we report come alive. And having conducted an experiment, you should find yourself in a better position to appreciate the theoretical arguments that surround its interpretation. Getting involved in research will also give you valuable experience in the methods and analysis of memory experiments. This will be useful should you want to do original research in this area. With only little modification, the experimental procedures described in this text can be arranged to test some of your own hypotheses about human memory. More than the minimal amount of materials is usually provided in the Appendix should you want to expand on the experimental procedures.

Table 1-1 provides a list of the experimental procedures described in the following chapters. If you are using this textbook as part of a course, your instructor probably has plans for how you should carry out these experiments. If not, don't hesitate to do all or some of these experiments by having a relative, friend, or spouse be your subject. It isn't always necessary to complete the experiment with a large number of subjects. Doing the experiment with only one or two people can provide important insight as to what the experiment was designed to reveal about memory. In fact, for those experiments you choose not to perform, you will find that reading through the procedure section will help you understand the original research.

THE PLAN OF THIS BOOK

In each chapter of this book we show how research and theory have developed around an important question about human memory. Some of these questions were first asked by philosophers many centuries ago as they speculated about memory and its contents. With the emergence of a scientific psy-

TABLE 1-1. List of Experimental Procedures Described in Text

Experiment	Chapter	Purpose
The Stimulus Suffix Effect	2	To demonstrate the effect on short-term serial recall of a redundant element at the end of the series.
Short-Term Retention of Individual Items	3	To examine forgetting of a single item over a short interval following one brief presentation of the item.
The Serial Position Effect in Free Recall	4	To demonstrate the characteristic serial position curve obtained in free recall and to show how the curve is affected by a delay between presentation and test.
Memory Consolidation	5	To determine whether an event experienced only one time and not rehearsed leaves a "permanent mark" in memory.
Unlearning of Associations	6	To investigate the "fate" of List 1 associations (A-B) after learning List 2 associations (A-C).
Release from PI	7	To demonstrate that cumulative proactive inhibition in the Brown-Peterson task can be lessened by shifting to a new class of to-be-remembered items.
Availability as a Heuristic for Judging Frequency	8	To demonstrate how an availability heuristic is used to judge frequency of an event's occurrence.
The Spacing of Repetitions in Free Recall	9	To observe the differential effect on retention of repeating items in either a massed or distributed fashion in a list presented for free recall.
The Word-Frequency Effect	10	To compare recognition memory for high-frequency (HF) and low-frequency (LF) words.
The "Feeling-of-Knowing" Phenomenon	11	To determine whether a "feeling of knowing" is a reliable predictor of what is stored in memory.
Recall as a Function of Semantic and Nonsemantic Orienting Tasks	12	To investigate differences in recall of unrelated words as a function of semantic and nonsemantic orienting tasks.
Imagery as a Mnemonic Device	13	To demonstrate the effect of instructions to use mental imagery on retention of simple associations.
The Effect of Prior Knowledge on Recall	14	To show how prior knowledge of the semantic context of a verbal passage can influence memory for that passage.

chology in the 19th century, psychologists sought answers to these same questions through experimentation and carefully controlled laboratory procedures. For instance, the nature of forgetting and the relationship between repetition of an event and memory for that event were among the first problems to be tackled by early memory researchers. Other questions are related to relatively recent theoretical proposals regarding the nature of memory and information processing. Questions, for example, about the possible differences between short-term and long-term memory processes or about the possible reconstructive nature of remembering are important issues in contemporary theories of human memory. Much has been learned about the answers to these and other questions, but, as you will see, the answers are far from complete.

Each of the experimental procedures listed in Table 1-1 is based on an experiment that has played a significant role in answering an important question about human memory. A description of these experimental tasks is found in each chapter immediately following discussion of the original experiment. Although the results of these critical experiments have given us important information about our memory, these experiments have often been the source of additional questions about memory and how it works. By emphasizing in each chapter a major problem confronting researchers in this field, we are in a position to show you where we have been and where we might be headed in our attempt to answer these important questions.

The arrangement of chapters is somewhat arbitrary, although the order of topics generally conforms to that found in most recent textbooks on human memory. In the initial chapters we treat the topics of brief sensory memory and memory for information over short intervals of time. In subsequent chapters we examine the conditions under which more permanent memories are formed. Topics in this section include questions about the time course of memory formation, the nature of forgetting, and how information stored in memory is used to remember new information. In the final chapter we discuss the important question of individual differences in remembering. Because each chapter emphasizes a particular contemporary issue in the field of memory research, the chapters are relatively independent. However, particular methodologies and experimental findings presented in early chapters are sometimes important for a complete understanding of topics discussed in later chapters. Therefore we encourage you to read the chapters in order. By reading all the chapters, you will gain a broad introduction to research in this field. You will also find answers to some of your questions about memory and information processing. Should you wish to pursue a topic further, "Recommendations for Further Reading" are found at the end of each chapter. And, as we mentioned, there are materials provided in the Appendix to aid you, should you decide to plan your own experiment investigating a question about human memory.

2

Sensory Registers:
Visual and
Acoustic Stores

Information Available in Brief Visual Presentations
Properties of the Visual Sensory Register
The Locus of Iconic Memory
Echoic Memory
The Stimulus Suffix Effect
The Suffix Effect Reconsidered

Introduction/overview

How much can you remember of something shown to you only briefly? To find out, in 1871 W. S. Jevons tossed beans in the air and tried to count them as they fell. Actually, Jevons's procedure was quite ingenious. He placed a flat white box in the middle of a black tray. Then he tossed handfuls of black beans into the air toward the box in such a way that some of them would land in the white box. Then, without hesitating, he estimated the number of beans falling in the white box. Jevons recorded both his estimates and the actual number of beans falling in the box for more than 1000 tosses. He found he was quite accurate when the number of beans falling in the white box was fewer than four or five. However, his accuracy, as measured by the percentages of times he estimated exactly, fell off dramatically as his tosses included increasing numbers of beans. When the number of beans falling in the box was more than nine, he was correct less than 50% of the time. Clearly, there are limits on the number of items that can be "apprehended" or to which we can pay attention at any one time. The nature of this limit, referred to as the span of apprehension, *has interested psychologists for many years because it raises important questions regarding the limits of human information processing.*

In this chapter we look at research directed toward finding out just how much information can be extracted from a briefly presented array. As you will see, this inquiry has revealed evidence for both visual and auditory sensory registers capable of holding information for very short intervals of time. Unless the information in these sensory registers is quickly attended to, it soon disappears. This kind of memory is apparently qualitatively different from the memory that contains such information as what you ate for breakfast today or who was the last president of the United States. Nevertheless, you will see that sensory memory plays an important role in cognitive processing and is perhaps the first stage in establishing a more permanent record of our experiences.

INFORMATION AVAILABLE IN BRIEF VISUAL PRESENTATIONS

Contemporary psychologists usually don't toss beans in the air in order to study the limits of visual information processing. Instead, they typically rely on a tachistoscope to present visual stimuli very briefly. A *tachistoscope* is an optical device that permits stimuli to be viewed for very brief times and allows precise control of both the duration and luminance (brightness) of the visual exposure. As testimony to Jevons's talents as an experimenter, modern tachistoscopic studies of the span of apprehension have tended to confirm his results. For example, Averbach (1963), working at Bell Telephone Laboratories, used a tachistoscope to show subjects displays of black dots on a white background. The number of dots varied randomly from trial to trial, with duration of the display also controlled. Dot displays were viewed for intervals that ranged from 40 milliseconds (a millisecond is a thousandth of a second) to 600 milliseconds. Subjects estimated the number of dots they saw after each visual presentation. Averbach himself was a subject in this experiment, and his accuracy of reporting the number of dots at three different exposure times is shown in Figure 2-1.

Exposure time affected the span of apprehension. With the briefest duration (40 milliseconds), accuracy of number estimates fell off rapidly as the number of dots in the display increased. For the longer durations (150 and 600 milliseconds), the drop-off in accuracy was not as dramatic. We can see in Figure 2-1 that, even when the number of dots was fewer than five, accuracy was greater at the longer duration. You might think that with very few stimuli one could do as well at short durations as at long ones. That one cannot suggests that, even when there are relatively few dots in a display, the ability to extract number information is time dependent.

If we assume that the longer durations in Averbach's experiment approximate the "exposure time" of Jevons's quick look at beans falling in a box, it is

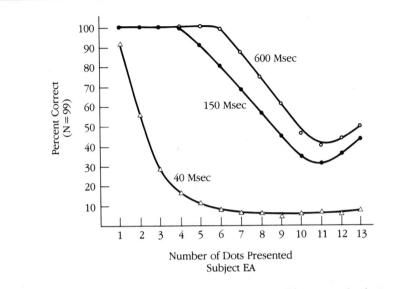

Figure 2-1. Span of apprehension as measured by E. Averbach. Percent correct estimates of black dots seen at three different exposure times given in milliseconds are displayed. *(From "The Span of Apprehension as a Function of Exposure Duration," by E. Averbach. In* Journal of Verbal Learning and Verbal Behavior, *1963, 2, 60–64. Copyright 1963 by Academic Press. Reprinted by permission.)*

seen that the point at which Averbach was correct 50% of the time corresponds very well with Jevons's estimate. Both experimenters found that they were accurate less than half the time when the number of stimuli (beans or dots) was greater than eight or nine. Numerous experiments have shown that the span of apprehension (defined as 50% accuracy) is about eight or nine when only the number of simple stimuli is to be judged (Woodworth & Schlosberg, 1954). On the other hand, when the stimuli are complex and must be named or otherwise identified as well as counted, the span of apprehension is likely to be less.

In a series of experiments now famous in psychology, Sperling (1960) investigated the span of apprehension for letter stimuli and in doing so revealed considerably more about this phenomenon than had been known before. He asked subjects to report what they saw immediately after viewing displays of letter stimuli for 50 milliseconds. The number of letters in the display was varied and, as you can see in Figure 2-2, the subjects were clearly limited as to the number of letters they could recall correctly. No more than four or five letters were recalled even when the display actually contained twice this number. The visual span of apprehension for letters did not change even when the

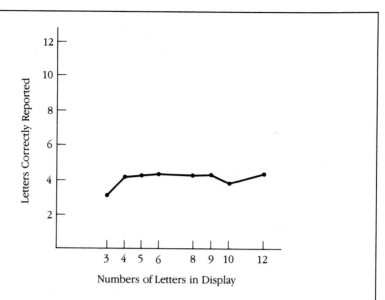

Figure 2-2.   The span of apprehension as measured by the number of letters that can be correctly recalled from a tachistoscopic display as a function of number of letters in the display. The figure shows the average number of letters correctly reported by all subjects. *(From "The Information Available in Brief Visual Presentations," by G. Sperling. In* Psychological Monographs, *1960, 74(Whole No. 11). Copyright 1960 by the American Psychological Association. Reprinted by permission.)*

exposure duration was increased to 500 milliseconds. As might be expected, the letter span is appreciably less than that found when merely the number of simple stimuli is estimated.

When subjects described their experience in the letter-span experiments, they almost universally claimed that they saw more than they could report. These subjective reports led Sperling and others to suggest that we are capable of briefly holding a rather large amount of information but that we are severely limited in our ability to extract information from what is there. This would be the case, for example, if the time required to report the letters exceeded the time the letters could be held.

Sperling devised a way to investigate the amount of information potentially available to an observer in a brief visual display. The technique is called the *partial report procedure.* To explain the logic behind this method, Sperling offered an analogy to the way students are frequently tested as part of a classroom examination. The instructor does not need to include everything presented in the time period covered by the examination. Rather, an exam typically is made up of questions that sample what has been covered in the course. On the basis of performance on this sample of questions, the instructor estimates what has been learned about all the material. Similarly, following a brief tachistoscopic presentation, Sperling argued that, if portions of the array were sampled, an estimate could be made of what the subject actually knew, or should we say saw.

Sperling asked subjects to view displays that contained consonants or consonants and numbers arranged in three rows of four. A typical display might look like this:

7	V	2	F
X	L	5	3
B	6	W	8

The subjects were informed that they did not have to recall all the letters (and numbers) but only those in one row of the display—that is, 4. (Following Sperling, we will hereafter use the word *letters* to refer to both letters and numbers.) The particular row to be recalled was signaled to the subject by one of three tones—of either high, medium, or low pitch—that corresponded to the top, middle, or bottom row of the display, respectively. A critical manipulation was the time at which the tone was presented to the subject. Subjects heard the tone either .10 second *before* the onset of the display (which lasted 50 milliseconds) or following intervals up to 1.0 second *after* the offset of the display. Because only 4 letters were to be recalled, this procedure did not exceed the subjects' previously determined span of apprehension. Most important, because all three rows were randomly tested, it was possible to estimate the total amount of information available to the subject by multiplying the subject's response by 3 (the number of rows). For example, if over a number of trials a subject correctly reported on the average 2 letters from a row, the total information available to the subject would be estimated as 6 letters, or 50% of the 12-letter display.

Using the partial report procedure, Sperling found that, if subjects heard the tone immediately before or immediately after the onset of the display, about 75%, or 9 letters, were available. As the interval between onset (and offset) of the display and the tone increased, the estimate of information available dropped off rather quickly. This is shown in Figure 2-3. When the tone was heard 1 second after display presentation, the estimate was about 4 letters, which was not different from the results obtained when subjects were required to recall all the letters in the display (the *whole report procedure*). Sperling's results strongly suggested that visually presented information is briefly registered and almost totally available to subjects but is quickly lost unless attended to.

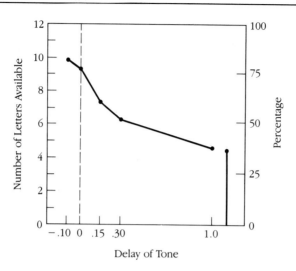

Figure 2-3. Letters available (in actual numbers and percentage equivalents) to a subject using the partial report procedure as a function of the delay between the presentation of the letter display and the tone signaling recall. The bar at right shows the average number of letters recalled when the whole report procedure was used. *(From "The Information Available in Brief Visual Presentations," by G. Sperling. In* Psychological Monographs, *1960, 74(Whole No. 11). Copyright 1960 by the American Psychological Association. Reprinted by permission.)*

PROPERTIES OF THE VISUAL SENSORY REGISTER

The sensory register revealed in Sperling's experiments has been at times called short-term visual storage, visual persistence, visual sensory memory, or, perhaps most frequently, *iconic memory* (Neisser, 1967). It is generally assumed to be memory for a rapidly fading visual icon (image) but is usually not considered the same as an afterimage. If you remember the last time that someone took your picture using a flash attachment, you likely also remember the colored spot you saw following the bright light from the flash. This spot was superimposed on everything you looked at for many seconds after the flash. This kind of visual image is called a *positive afterimage.* The visual system also produces *negative afterimages,* as when you stare for a while at a lighted window and then look toward a white or gray wall. An afterimage of the window will appear, with dark panes and a light frame, against the white background.

Superficially, afterimages display properties similar to those of iconic memory. However, there are several important differences indicating that the two kinds of images are not the same. For example, visual sensory memory is considered to be of very short duration (likely less than 500 milliseconds when the postexposure field is lighted). Afterimages, as you may recall from your own experience, often last much longer. Also, a visual sensory memory operates under low levels of luminance, which do not usually produce afterimages (Sperling, 1960).

The existence of a visual sensory memory has not gone unquestioned (for example, Holding, 1975). Students sometimes express some of the same concerns as researchers after first being introduced to the Sperling results, and these criticisms are worthy of brief mention. Two important considerations are *cue anticipation* and *output interference*. These represent alternative explanations for the results based on the partial report procedure. Cue anticipation refers to the possibility that subjects under the partial report technique are actually guessing which row will be tested and are therefore assuring themselves of a high level of recall. In fact, one of Sperling's subjects reported that he tried this strategy, especially when the interval between the display and tone was increased. Sperling, however, took great care to ensure that his subjects would not have any way of knowing which row would be tested. For example, although the three rows were tested the same number of times during the experiment, in any particular experimental session there was not necessarily an equal number of tests for a particular row. Therefore subjects could not likely learn from what had already been tested and draw conclusions as to which row was coming up next.

It has been argued that output interference may contribute to the differences obtained when results of the partial report method are compared with those of the whole report method. The problem arises from the fact that in the whole report procedure the subject must recall more letters than in the partial report procedure. It could be argued that the whole report underestimates the amount subjects have available, because trying to output that many items will produce interference and cause some items to be lost. However, an examination of experimental findings based on these methods does not generally support this view (Coltheart, 1975). Further, the output interference argument would be more serious if it were not for an important experiment investigating the visual sensory store that was performed shortly after Sperling's experiment.

Averbach and Coriell (1961) presented subjects with a 2 × 8 array of randomly chosen letters for 50 milliseconds. A typical display looked like this:

C	F	P	Y	C	A	X	N
L	F	T	J	M	Y	N	V

Unlike Sperling, they asked subjects to recall only one letter. The letter to be recalled was indicated by a bar presented either above one of the eight letters on the top row or directly beneath a target letter on the bottom row. Subjects did not know which letters would be in the array or which position was to be tested. Averbach and Coriell varied the time interval between the offset of the array and the appearance of the bar signaling the target letter. It is highly unlikely that output interference is a problem when a single letter is tested, so this criticism of Sperling's experiment is not justified in this study. Yet Averbach and Coriell (1961) obtained results that bore a striking resemblance to Sperling's.

When the bar cued a letter immediately before or immediately after the display was presented, Averbach and Coriell found that report accuracy indicated that about 12 letters, or 75%, were available. When the bar did not appear for 300 milliseconds or longer after the display, performance produced estimates of about 4 to 5.6 letters available, or about 25 to 35%. This latter finding apparently reflects what the subject is able to get into a more permanent memory system and is similar to what Sperling found when the whole report procedure was used. That performance was not 100% when the bar came on just before the display was attributed by Averbach and Coriell to the fact that, even though all letters were available, some of the letters were not legible in the array. This was confirmed by an analysis of recall according to the position in the array. Although some positions yielded close to 100% recall, other positions were near chance. Also, putting the bar too close to a letter served to affect the perception of the letter. Therefore, although the exact capacity of the visual sensory register is unknown, the possibility exists that, with increasing amounts of information in the store, there is a breakdown in the perceptibility of stimulus items.

A second experiment by Averbach and Coriell (1961) revealed another important characteristic of information in iconic memory—namely, that it can be erased. As these investigators pointed out, it would be hard to understand how we might possibly process visual information from the environment if everything we saw persisted for some time in a visual store. As we look around us, the environment is changing continually. Without some system of erasure, new visual input would get mixed up with the input already in the store. Averbach and Coriell showed that a stimulus presented after a target letter interfered with the visual icon of the letter. Interference with visual information due to a stimulus appearing *after* the target stimulus is called *backward visual masking*. Specifically, they found that, when the interval between the target and the mask was very short (under 100 milliseconds), the mask was superimposed on the letter. As the interval increased, the mask served to erase the previously stored information. At even longer intervals the mask no longer interfered, presumably because the target information had already gotten into a more permanent memory. These results support Sperling's original demonstration that we continue to "see" information beyond the time a stimulus is presented unless interfered with by new visual information.

The results of these and other experiments provide evidence of a visual register with the capability to store information for a brief period of time, probably no more than 500 milliseconds. Storage is generally considered to be *preattentive,* or outside our control. We apparently play a passive role in the process—for example, exhibiting an influence only to the extent that we fixate our eyes in the right direction to receive stimulation. However, by directing more sophisticated processing mechanisms, we can attend to information in the array and rescue it before it has a chance to decay. The nature of the relationship between this relatively passive visual sensory store and the more active components of memory processing has been of considerable importance to those seeking a complete theory of human information processing. The specific manner in which the sensory register contacts a more permanent memory system is a matter of considerable controversy. In the next chapter we will look at some representative models of this relationship.

THE LOCUS OF ICONIC MEMORY

There is significant disagreement as to where in the nervous system the icon is produced. Some investigators claim that the locus of iconic memory is the photoreceptors (rods and cones) in the retina. For example, Sakitt (1975, 1976; see also Sakitt & Long, 1978) has argued that information in the icon is based on activity of rod cells in the retina. Other researchers (for example, Banks & Barber, 1977; Meyer & Maguire, 1977) have presented evidence that the rod cells cannot play an exclusive role in producing iconic memory. The issue is complex yet very critical because it relates to the role of visual information storage in a complete theory of memory. For example, simple afterimages are known to result from processes arising in the retinal cells. A description of iconic memory in terms of rod cell activity would be difficult to distinguish from a description of activity associated with simple afterimages. As we previously noted, however, most researchers suggest that they are different phenomena. The weight of the evidence suggests that iconic memory is at least partially controlled by *central processes* (toward the brain) rather than *peripheral* ones (away from the brain).

An experiment by McCloskey and Watkins (1978) investigated an interesting phenomenon that appears to document central involvement in producing the icon. They examined a visual illusion first discovered some time ago in psychology, which they call the "seeing-more-than-is-there" phenomenon. In their experiment subjects were asked to view a narrow opening on an otherwise dark background. Several different stimulus figures were moved back and forth very quickly behind the slit. Examples of the figures are shown in the top part of Figure 2-4. Compare the size of the figures relative to the size of the slit through which the subjects saw them. The figures are wider than the slit, and therefore the complete figure could not possibly be seen when it was stationary behind the slit. As the figures were oscillating behind the slit at the rate of 64 cycles per minute, subjects were asked to draw what they saw. The reproductions in the lower part of the figure reveal what subjects claimed to see. There was an interesting seeing-more-than-is-there effect in that subjects reported seeing the complete figure sandwiched in the narrow slit. Subjects tended to see the figures

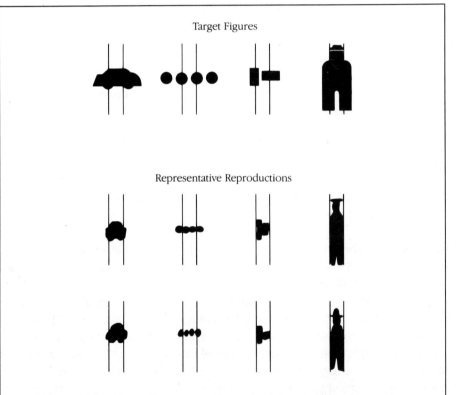

Figure 2-4. Target figures actually presented and subjects' reproductions of what they saw. The size of the target figures is shown relative to the size of the slit behind which they oscillated. In the experiment subjects could see only what is revealed in the space between the two lines. *(From "The Seeing-More-Than-Is-There Phenomenon: Implications for the Locus of Iconic Storage," by M. McCloskey and M. J. Watkins. In* Journal of Experimental Psychology: Human Perception and Performance, *1978, 4, 553–565. Copyright 1978 by the American Psychological Association. Reprinted by permission.)*

as narrower than the target figures and reportedly saw the whole figure even though the figure was larger than the slit through which it was viewed.

McCloskey and Watkins suggested that the illusion is based on iconic memory. The subjects perceived simultaneously parts of the figure that are never seen together, which implies that information is held in iconic memory until later-appearing information can be integrated with it. The effect does not seem to be explained by stimulation of the photoreceptors, because it is unlikely that a single set of photoreceptors could first hold part of the figure and then another. Further, the effect appears to be present even when subjects do not move their eyes—a behavior that would have the effect of spreading out the successive parts of the figure on the retina so that more than one set of photoreceptors is used. Therefore the illusion, and hence the icon, appears to be more centrally located rather than in the photoreceptors of the retina.

McCloskey and Watkins point out that the effect is quite strong and can be produced by simply passing a figure beneath a piece of cardboard in which you have cut a slit. To experience the illusion, the figure must be moved quickly back and forth and moved far enough that it clears the slit on both sides.

ECHOIC MEMORY

Consider for a minute how our visual system processes information. Objects in the environment reflect radiant energy (light waves) that strikes the photoreceptors of the retina simultaneously. Visual information, in other words, reaches us all at once, as in the flash of a tachistoscopic display. Now think about what happens when the auditory system is stimulated. The beginning of a spoken word, for example, is processed before the end of the word. We sometimes hear a noon whistle rise in pitch (frequency) before we hear it fall. Auditory information, unlike visual information, is processed sequentially. It is spread out in time. If information entering the auditory system disappeared immediately after it arrived, we could not put together information arriving first with that arriving later. Consider how impossible a task it would be to make sense of a sentence if we forgot its first half by the time we processed its second half. Auditory information processing requires us briefly to store sensory input so we can integrate it with input arriving later. Neisser (1967) proposed calling this acoustic sensory store *echoic memory*.

Initial evidence for echoic memory was obtained from *dichotic listening* experiments (Broadbent, 1958; Treisman, 1964). In this type of experiment, subjects are typically outfitted with a set of headphones so they can hear information presented to both ears (dichotic listening). In one such experiment, Broadbent (1958) presented subjects two lists of three digits simultaneously to both ears. For example, in one ear the subject might hear 7 2 3, and in the other ear, 9 4 5. Broadbent asked his subjects to report all the digits from both ears in any order. Subjects could, in fact, do this. However, their order of report was almost always such that all the digits from one ear were reported before the digits heard in the other ear. For example, subjects listening to the numbers just given would report either 7 2 3 9 4 5 or 9 4 5 7 2 3. They never mixed the digits when recalling the sequences successfully. Subjects apparently were able to attend to only one list of digits at a time. Because the digits were heard simultaneously, it can be assumed that digits presented in one ear were held briefly until the subject could attend to them. Digits in the "unattended" ear were presumably held in an auditory sensory register.

Additional evidence for an auditory sensory memory is found when subjects are asked to *shadow* information in one ear while information is presented to the other ear. Shadowing is the task of repeating information as soon as it is heard. It is generally assumed that shadowing completely occupies the attention of a subject so that anything reported from the nonshadowed ear must result from a shift in the subject's attention from the shadowed ear. Treisman (1964) examined how far a message presented to one ear could lag behind a message presented to the other ear and still be recognized by the subject as the same message. She presented verbal messages to both ears but out of synchrony so that the shadowed message either preceded or followed the nonshadowed message. When subjects shadowed the leading message, they detected that the two messages were identical when the nonshadowed message lagged as long as 4.5 seconds (up to 13 words) behind the shadowed message. When the shadowed message lagged behind the nonshadowed message, subjects did not recognize the two messages as being the same until they were within 2 seconds of each other (about 6 words apart). The longer interval obtained when the shadowed message was leading was presumably due to the fact that subjects were able to get some of this message into a more permanent memory. When the nonshadowed message led, it would have to be held briefly until the subject could shift attention from the shadowed message (see Crowder, 1976). These results provide evidence for the existence of a brief auditory sensory memory. Treisman's findings also appear to help explain a phenomenon we all have experienced. How many times have you had your attention on something—for instance, reading a book—only to be interrupted by someone saying something to you? Attention now shifts to this new source of information, and frequently you find yourself responding immediately with "What did you say?" But almost before the words are out of your mouth, you "hear" what was said to you. We can assume that the unattended spoken message was held briefly in echoic memory until attention was directed to it.

Darwin, Turvey, and Crowder (1972) adapted Sperling's partial report procedure to the study of echoic memory. Subjects in their experiment listened to

three different lists of letters and numbers that had been recorded on stereo-
phonic equipment. As you likely know from listening to stereo records or tapes,
with the proper placement of speakers it is possible to experience sounds
coming from several directions. In this experiment subjects simultaneously
heard one list on their left, one on their right, and a third in front of them. The
three lists heard from three directions are analogous to the three rows of letters
subjects saw in Sperling's tachistoscopic array.

After hearing the last items from the three lists, subjects saw a line projected
on a screen either to their left, right, or in front of them that was a cue to recall
the left, right, or middle lists. As in Sperling's experiment, the delay between
stimulus presentation and the signal for recall was varied. Delays were 0, 1, 2,
or 4 seconds. The results were similar to Sperling's in that the partial report
procedure produced better recall than the whole report procedure. In this task
the whole report method required subjects to attempt recall of items from all
three lists. The results of this experiment are summarized in Figure 2-5. The
span of auditory apprehension as estimated by the whole report procedure was
similar to that found with visual displays—namely, between four and five items.
As in the visual experiments reviewed earlier, the advantage of the partial report

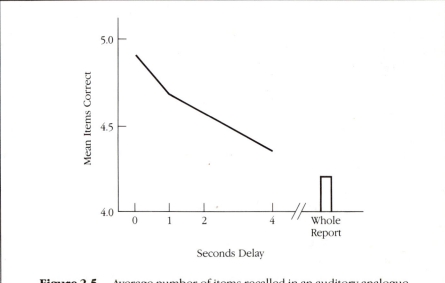

Figure 2-5. Average number of items recalled in an auditory analogue
of the Sperling partial report and whole report procedures. *(From "An
Auditory Analogue of the Sperling Partial Report Procedure: Evidence
for Brief Auditory Storage," by C. J. Darwin, M. T. Turvey, and R. G.
Crowder. In* Cognitive Psychology, *1972, 3, 255–267. Copyright 1972 by
Academic Press, Inc. Reprinted by permission.)*

method decreased as the interval between stimulus presentation and the cue for recall increased. However, there was one important difference. The advantage of the partial report procedure in a visual memory experiment disappears in a fraction of a second (see Figure 2-3). With auditory presentation, partial report was superior to whole report even when the interval between presentation and cue was as great as 4 seconds. Echoic memory apparently holds information for several seconds.

The greater storage time for auditory than visual sensory memories provides an explanation for a well-known difference in retention that is observed when presentation modality is varied. If a list of items—for example, words—is presented to subjects for learning with the requirement that they recall the words in the order of presentation, recall errors are related to the position of the items in the list. Specifically, recall errors are least for items from the beginning of the list, only slightly greater for items presented at the end of the list, and greatest for items from the middle of the list. The generally better retention for early list items is called the *primacy effect;* the relatively good performance for last-presented items is known as the *recency effect.* When modality of presentation is varied, recall of items from lists presented auditorily is often superior to recall of items from lists presented visually (see Penney, 1975). However, the difference in recall between the two modalities is generally found only for the recency part of the list; that is, more items are remembered from the end of the list following auditory presentation than following visual presentation. Idealized serial position curves illustrating the difference in recall between auditory and visual presentation are shown in Figure 2-6.

Crowder and Morton (1969) argued that the greater recency effect seen with auditory presentation is due to the fact that information in the auditory sensory memory is held longer than is comparable information in visual sensory memory. Note that in experiments leading to the results portrayed in Figure 2-6, items from a list are presented one at a time—that is, sequentially. The only difference is that in one case subjects see the individual items, whereas in the other case they hear the list presented. Given the difference in storage times for the two registers, when recall is signaled after the last list items, there would be more items from the end of the list in the auditory sensory register than in the visual sensory register. There is, in other words, more recent information still in the auditory store.

THE STIMULUS SUFFIX EFFECT

Evidence for an auditory sensory register also comes from the analysis of an interesting memory phenomenon called the *stimulus suffix effect* (Crowder, 1967; Dallett, 1965). The effect is quite simple to demonstrate, and we will

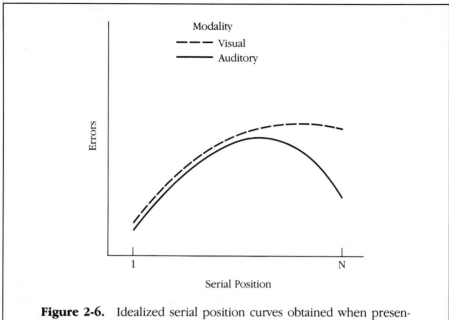

Figure 2-6. Idealized serial position curves obtained when presentation modality (auditory and visual) is varied and serial recall is requested.

introduce it to you by referring to an experiment carried out by Morton, Crowder, and Prussin (1971). In most suffix experiments the task is that of *serial recall*. Subjects must remember items from short lists in the exact order in which they were presented. The to-be-remembered items are often digits, although letters or words can be used. In the experiment performed by Morton and his associates, subjects learned lists of eight digits that were, of course, presented auditorily.

There were three conditions in the experiment. In the control condition the instructions requested serial recall of eight digits read to subjects at the rate of two digits every second. In the other two conditions something was added to the end of the list. For some subjects the first digit from the list was repeated after the eighth digit, and subjects were told that this would help their recall by getting them started right. In the third condition "zero" was said after the last digit. Subjects were told to ignore the zero and to begin recalling the eight other digits when they heard it. An item appearing at the end of the list is a *suffix*.

The effect on serial recall of adding a suffix is shown in Figure 2-7. The extra item at the end of the list led to an increase in the number of errors made on the final list items. This occurred whether the suffix was the first digit in the list repeated or the zero, which subjects were told to ignore. The disruption of

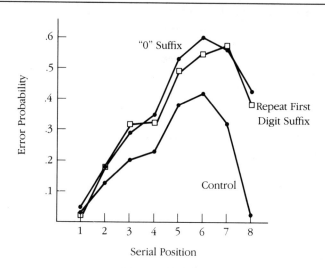

Figure 2-7.   The effect of adding a suffix on serial recall of digits. The suffix was either zero or the first digit in the list repeated. *(From "Experiments with the Stimulus Suffix Effect," by J. Morton, R. G. Crowder, and H. A. Prussin. In* Journal of Experimental Psychology, *1971, 91, 169–190. Copyright 1971 by the American Psychological Association. Reprinted by permission.)*

the usually strong recency effect due to the additional item is called the *stimulus suffix effect*.

The stimulus suffix effect

Purpose
To demonstrate the effect on short-term serial recall of a redundant element at the end of the series.

Materials
Use a table of random numbers (see Table A in the Appendix) to construct 11 different strings of eight digits. Each eight-digit string is formed by randomly selecting eight different digits between 1 and 9, inclusive. Consecutive sequences of more than two digits are prohibited (for example, 3 4 5). An example of an appropriate series is 8 7 2 5 1 6 9 4. Next prepare an additional 11 strings of nine digits by simply adding zero to the end of each of the previously constructed strings (for example, 8 7 2 5 1 6 9 4 0). Each set of 11 digit strings (those with a zero and those without) is randomly ordered and listed in a manner so as to be easily read by the experimenter. Responses can

be recorded on quarter sheets of standard-sized paper or on 3 × 5-inch cards on which eight squares appear in a row.

Procedure

Half the subjects to be tested are presented the 11 strings with the zero added (Suffix Condition), and half are tested without the zero (No-Suffix Condition). The first series in each set serves as a practice series to familiarize the subject with the task requirements and with the rate at which the digits will be presented. Each series of digits is read to the subject at the rate of two digits per second. The experimenter should practice reading the digits at this rate. Immediately after the last digit is read, the subject is to attempt recall of the eight digits in the exact order of presentation. The subject is to write down the digits in the eight boxes on the data sheet. Approximately 10–20 seconds is given for recall of each series. Subjects are encouraged to guess when not sure.

Instructions to Subjects

NO-SUFFIX CONDITION

This is a test of your memory for short lists of digits. In this test I am going to read to you a series of eight digits at a rather fast rate. There will be a number of such series. Immediately after I read the last digit, I want you to try to recall the digits in the exact order I read them to you. You can use the row of eight squares on the answer sheet to write down the digits. I will give you a new response sheet for each series. To be correct, a digit must be placed in the exact position in which it was read. For example, if you do not remember the second digit but you do remember the third digit, you must write the third digit in the third square in order to be correct. You are correct only when you can remember the digits in the exact position in which they were read. Before we begin I will give you a practice series to give you a better idea of the task. (If there are no questions after the practice series, the remaining ten digit strings can be presented.)

SUFFIX CONDITION

This is a test of your memory for short lists of digits. In this test I am going to read to you a series of nine digits at a rather fast rate. There will be a number of such series. The last digit in every series will be a zero, and this zero is your signal for recall. However, I do not want you to recall the zero. Please ignore it for purposes of recall. When you hear the zero, you are to try to recall the first eight digits in the exact order I read them to you. You can use the row of eight squares on the answer sheet to write down the digits. I will give you a new response sheet for each series. To be correct, a digit must be placed in the exact position in which it was read. For example, if you do not remember the second digit but do remember the third digit, you must write the third digit in the third square in order to be correct. You are correct only when you can remember the digits in the exact position in which they were read. Before we begin I will give you a practice series to give you a better idea of the task. (If there are no questions after the practice series, the remaining ten digit strings can be presented.)

Summary and Analysis

The practice series is not scored. For each of the remaining ten series, determine the number of errors made by each subject at each of the eight serial positions. Each subject provides you with eight scores, which can range from 0 to 10. Data are summarized by constructing a separate serial position curve for each of the experimental conditions. To do this, find the total number of errors made by all subjects in a condition at each serial position. Multiply the number of subjects by 10, and divide this into the total number of errors for each serial position. These results are then presented graphically. A *t* test for independent groups may be used to compare recall of the eighth item.

Recommended Minimum Number of Subjects

Total of 24; 12 in each of two conditions.

Based on an experiment by Morton, Crowder, and Prussin (1971).

Crowder and Morton (1969) suggested that the stimulus suffix effect is evidence for a *precategorical acoustic storage* (PAS). The PAS is a theoretical model of the auditory sensory register. Although there are other models, this one has received considerable attention in the psychological literature. A major assumption of the PAS theory is that information is held in acoustic storage before it can be attended to—that is, before it can be categorized. You can think of *categorization* as the process by which you make sense out of something, as in recognizing that you heard a letter, not a number, spoken. In this respect PAS is similar to iconic memory in that information decays from this sensory storage unless given additional processing.

According to Crowder and Morton, the stimulus suffix effect occurs because the suffix either displaces (knocks out) or otherwise interferes with the information currently held in the sensory store. Items from the end of the list would be in the store when the suffix is heard, so the processing of these items is disrupted. Telling subjects to ignore the item does not help, because the disruption occurs preattentively, before the subject can disregard it. The suffix does its damage, in other words, before we realize it is there. Because Crowder and Morton suggest that new information can displace information already in PAS, their model assumes that the acoustic store has a limited capacity. Although we know little about the capacity of a visual sensory register, most investigators have assumed that it is relatively large (however, see Chow & Murdock, 1975). Therefore the PAS has been assumed to have a more limited capacity than is generally assumed for a visual sensory store.

Morton, Crowder, and Prussin (1971) found that varying the acoustic properties of the suffix decreased the magnitude of the disruption, whereas changing the "meaning" of the suffix did not reduce the suffix effect. For example, simply adding a noise to the end of the list, such as a tone, does not produce the stimulus suffix effect. If the suffix is spoken in a voice different from the voice that spoke the list items, the suffix effect is again reduced. However, varying semantic aspects of the suffix did not reduce the effect. For example, in one experiment the to-be-remembered items were words from the same semantic class (for example, the names of utensils: fork, spoon, and so forth). The suffix was a word from either the same class or a different semantic class (for example, the name of an animal). Both kinds of suffix produced interference, and there was no difference in the magnitude of the effect for the same- or different-class suffix.

These findings supported Crowder and Morton's assumption that information entering PAS is screened according to its acoustic properties before receiving conscious attention. In other words, a suffix that differs acoustically will not interfere, because it has undergone screening and has been channeled elsewhere. You may have noticed at parties that it is more difficult to follow a conversation if the voices of two people speaking at once sound similar than if they sound dissimilar. On the other hand, acoustically dissimilar stimulation, such as music or moving chairs, can easily be ignored. These observations tend to support Crowder and Morton's model. Changes in the suffix meaning do not alter the effect, because disruption is assumed to occur before the meaning is processed; that is, disruption is precategorical.

THE SUFFIX EFFECT RECONSIDERED

Recent experimental findings have questioned major assumptions underlying the PAS model of echoic memory. Specifically, investigators have reported that semantic variations of the suffix do affect the size of the stimulus suffix effect (for example, Harris, Gausepohl, Lewis, & Spoehr, 1979; Salter & Colley, 1977) and that a suffix that is acoustically dissimilar to other list items can produce a stimulus suffix effect (Spoehr & Corin, 1978). It has also been shown that a suffix effect is produced when the stimuli are presented visually (Hitch, 1975; Spoehr & Corin, 1978) or when a suffix occurs as long as 20 seconds after the list of to-be-remembered items (Watkins & Todres, 1980). It is not clear what procedural differences may be responsible for the discrepancy between these results and those reported earlier (for example, by Morton, Crowder, &

Prussin, 1971). However, taken as a whole they seriously weaken important assumptions of the PAS model, and modification of the original theory appears to be necessary (see also Penney, 1979).

One of the more interesting experiments providing evidence to challenge the PAS interpretation of the suffix effect was conducted by researchers at the University of Michigan (see Ayres, Jonides, Reitman, Egan, & Howard, 1979). They tested whether the magnitude of the suffix effect depends on how the subject interprets the suffix. As we have seen, the PAS model is clear on this point. The suffix effect occurs precategorically—before any meaningful interpretation is possible. What makes the Michigan experiment unique is that the researchers found a way to hold the acoustic properties of the suffix constant while varying its interpretation by the subjects.

There were three conditions in the experiment. The to-be-remembered items for all subjects were lists of seven one-syllable words (for example, bed, car, hat). Subjects recalled the words in serial order after listening to them at the rate of two words per second. One group of subjects did not hear a suffix; they served as a control group. In each of the other two groups, a suffix was presented. In one condition subjects were told that, following each list of to-be-remembered words, they would hear a musical sound; the suffix was either a tone, a plucked violin string, a bowed violin string, or a "plunger-muted trumpet note sounding like a nasally spoken syllable, *wa.*" In the third condition subjects were told to expect one of four speech sounds at the end of the to-be-remembered list of words. Speech sounds were the syllables *da, pin, wing,* and *wa.* The *wa* sound was exactly what subjects heard in the music suffix condition. Perhaps you can see the point of the experiment. Because the to-be-remembered words and the *wa* suffix are the same in the two conditions, the PAS model predicts the same suffix effect. To the extent that the *wa* suffix produces different results in the two conditions, it can be argued that the suffix effect depends on the subjects' interpretation of the *wa* sound.

The results of this clever experiment are shown in Figure 2-8. Note first that a suffix effect was obtained in both the speech and music conditions relative to the control condition. For the suffix conditions the effect produced by the *wa* sound is shown separately in Figure 2-8 from the other music and speech sounds. It is clear that the suffix effect due to the *wa* sound was not the same in the two suffix conditions. When subjects thought they were hearing musical sounds, the *wa* sound produced an effect like other musical sounds. When subjects expected speech sounds, the *wa* sound acted like a speech sound. That the suffix effect is greater overall for the speech sounds than for the musical sounds is to be expected given that the to-be-remembered items were also speech sounds. What is important to realize is that the effect of the *wa* sound depended on the context in which it appeared. These results, in addition to

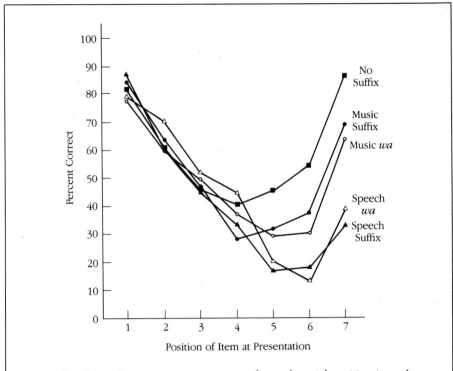

Figure 2-8. Percent correct responses for each serial position in each of the suffix conditions and the control (no-suffix) condition. Data for the *wa* suffix are shown separately in the two suffix conditions. *(From "Differing Suffix Effects for the Same Physical Stimulus," by T. J. Ayres, J. Jonides, J. S. Reitman, J. C. Egan, and D. A. Howard. In* Journal of Experimental Psychology: Human Learning and Memory, *1979, 5, 315–321. Copyright 1979 by the American Psychological Association. Reprinted by permission.)*

those previously mentioned, raise problems for an interpretation of the suffix effect in terms of the PAS model of echoic memory. Apparently, the suffix effect cannot be explained completely by what happens in the auditory sensory register unless we assume that some type of meaningful interpretation of a stimulus can occur at this stage of memory processing. This raises the interesting possibility that echoic memory is not as "precategorical" as some would believe.

Summary

There are distinct limits on the amount of information we can attend to at any one time. This limit, the span of apprehension, is about eight items when we are asked to report the number of simple stimuli seen in a brief *visual presentation. It is less than eight when we must identify and recall more complex items. Using a partial report procedure, Sperling (1960) showed that we actually remember more than we can report. This brief visual memory is called iconic memory. Storage of information in iconic memory is not under our control, and information decays in about 500 milliseconds unless attended to.*

The analogue to iconic memory in the auditory system is called echoic memory. Unlike its visual counterpart, however, information in echoic memory can last for several seconds. We reviewed four sources of evidence for echoic memory: dichotic listening experiments, an auditory partial report procedure, modality effects in serial recall, and the stimulus suffix effect. The stimulus suffix effect has been interpreted as evidence for a particular model of echoic memory referred to as precategorical acoustic storage (PAS). The PAS model assumes that the suffix effect occurs prior to recognition and interpretation of the stimulus; that is, it is precategorical. Results of recent experiments have questioned this assumption and have indicated that some form of meaningful analysis of a stimulus occurs very early in auditory information processing.

The existence of both iconic and echoic memory appears to be widely accepted by memory researchers. Current research is aimed at understanding the kinds of processes that contribute to a brief sensory memory and at investigating how information storage is affected by task demands.

Recommendations for further reading

Major findings by Sperling and others regarding a visual sensory register are reviewed in articles by Coltheart (1975) and Holding (1975). The articles should be read together because they represent somewhat different views on this issue. Coltheart (1980) reviews evidence for the distinction between iconic memory and other forms of visual persistence, such as afterimages. Possible capacity limitations of iconic memory are investigated in an interesting experimental report by Chow and Murdock (1975). An excellent review of the literature dealing with echoic memory has been given by Crowder (1976). In addition, Crowder (1978) has also elaborated on his original PAS model of the suffix effect in a theoretical article. Numerous experiments investigating the suffix effect have recently been reported in the major experimental psychology journals. Many of these have been referenced in this chapter, and the reader is invited to consult these research reports for additional information on this interesting phenomenon.

3

Primary Memory

Introduction/overview

Consider for a minute an age-old memory problem, that of remembering names of people we meet at a party, meeting, or other large gathering. For example, imagine you are at a party and are engaged in earnest conversation with an acquaintance, the one who dragged you to this place filled with strangers. As you are talking, a woman approaches the two of you. Your friend knows her and he introduces you to her, "Stan, this is Kathy O'Keane." You say hello, smile, and comment on what a nice party it is. Within seconds you are tapped on the shoulder by a person who it turns out has mistaken you for someone else. After straightening things out, you turn around only to find that the woman you just met has moved on. Your friend asks what you thought of her. If you are like many of us, your reaction is likely to be, "She seemed nice, but what was her name?"

The fact that we momentarily attend to something does not guarantee we will be able to recall it later. In the previous chapter we saw that information is most likely held first in some preattentive state (sensory register) for a very brief time. By directing attention to the information, we keep it from fading or being interfered with by other incoming information. Attending to something makes it part of our conscious experience. Now we have "hold" of it. At this moment we have no trouble remembering it because the information is still "there." It has never not been attended to. Yet as we saw in our example of the party situation, we sometimes have trouble keeping new information. How different this is from the memories we apparently have no trouble holding onto for years. For example, most of us can still recall the name of our favorite high school teacher or the presents we got on our last birthday.

William James (1890, pp. 646–647) discussed this important difference:

> An object which is recollected, in the proper sense of that term, is one which has been absent from consciousness altogether, and now revives again. It is brought back, recalled, fished up, so to speak, from a reservoir in which, with countless other objects, it lay buried, and lost from view. But an object of primary memory is not thus brought back; it was never lost; its date was never cut off from that of the immediately present moment.

As you see, James gave the name primary memory to the conscious experience that results from our attention to something. He distinguished primary memory from that represented by the "reservoir" of information that, once part of the present moment, was dropped from consciousness and now must be called back. This kind of memory James called secondary memory. For James, secondary memory was "memory proper," by which he meant that this type of memory is generally what we associate with the term memory. You, too, are likely to think of memory mainly in terms of your ability to recall things experienced some time ago—that is, in terms of secondary memory.

Until the 1950s, memory research was mainly identified with the study of secondary memory. However, a unique combination of events occurred about that time, leading researchers to concentrate a significant amount of their time and effort on understanding the nature of primary memory and in particular its relation to "memory proper." For example, where should primary memory fit in the complete picture of our memory system? Many, if not most, psychologists think a distinction should be made between two different memory systems (Broadbent, 1971; Craik & Levy, 1976). According to this view, primary and secondary memory represent two kinds of memory; that is, there is something different about the way we remember information over short intervals of time as opposed to the way we remember information over long intervals. Not all psychologists accept this dual nature of memory (for example, Melton, 1963), nor do those psychologists who wish to make such a distinction always agree on how to describe theoretically the dual nature of memory. We will review the evidence for a distinction between primary and secondary memory in this and the subsequent two chapters. In this chapter we will first describe events that recently caused psychologists to converge on this issue and then review some of the results of their investigations. Three aspects of memory processing have been particularly *important in attempting to distinguish between primary and secondary memory: the nature of forgetting, capacity limitations, and memory coding. We will discuss each of these in relation to the possible dual nature of memory. We will also look at some of the ways psychologists have attempted to represent primary memory in a complete theory of memory.*

Clearly, primary memory is something that must be studied when the retention interval is on the order of seconds, only a fraction of a minute. On the other hand, the study of secondary memory will necessarily involve much longer retention intervals—for example, many minutes, hours, days, or even years. In the memory literature, the terms short-term memory *and* long-term memory *are often used to describe studies of memory involving relatively short or relatively long retention intervals, respectively. That is, short-term memory and long-term memory need refer only to the procedures used to investigate memory, specifically the length of time that intervenes between study and a test of retention. However, researchers have also used these terms when distinguishing between two different memory systems. In other words, although these terms need refer only to the length of the retention interval in a memory experiment, "short-term memory" and "long-term memory" are frequently used in the same sense as primary and secondary memory—namely, when referring to different kinds of memory. As you can imagine, this is sometimes confusing. It is not always possible to know whether someone using these terms is indicating a particular kind of memory or simply describing the length of the retention interval used in a memory experiment. Following a distinction made by Waugh and Norman (1965), we will reserve the terms* primary *and* secondary memory *for a theoretical description of the dual nature of memory. And because the terms short-term memory and long-term memory must inevitably be present in any discussion of memory, we will endeavor to make it clear when we mean these terms to refer to the memory task, as when we refer to a short-term memory experiment, or when we mean to characterize the nature of memory itself, as when we refer to a short-term memory system, process, or store.*

THE BROWN-PETERSON PARADIGM

There are few experiments in the history of memory research that have had as great an impact as the ones carried out by Brown (1958), a British psychologist, and Peterson and Peterson (1959), from Indiana University. The experiments were deceptively simple. Their procedure is often called the *Brown-Peterson paradigm* because of their nearly simultaneous and independent use of this technique. The Petersons' findings have figured more prominently in later discussions in this area, and therefore we will refer mainly to their task and results.

Peterson and Peterson (1959) systematically investigated the retention of information over very short intervals of time. Specifically, they asked subjects to attempt recall of a single trigram after either 3, 6, 9, 12, 15, or 18 seconds. A *trigram* is a combination of three letters. In this case it was three consonants— for example, *F B M*. The experimenter pronounced the trigram once for the subject and then spoke a three-digit number. The subject was instructed to begin counting backward by threes from the number until signaled to recall. The purpose of backward number counting was to keep the subject from rehearsing the trigram during the brief retention interval. Each subject was tested 48 times, 8 times at each of the 6 retention intervals.

Figure 3-1 shows the results of the Peterson and Peterson experiment as well as the results of an experiment published a couple of years later by Murdock (1961). Murdock used the Brown-Peterson paradigm to test subjects' retention

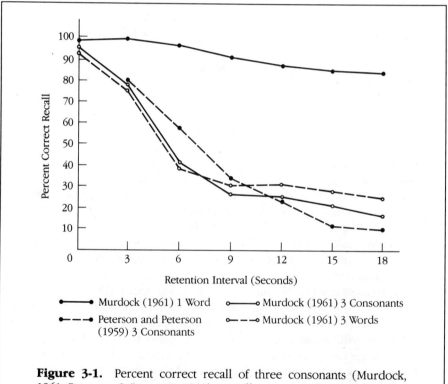

Figure 3-1. Percent correct recall of three consonants (Murdock, 1961; Peterson & Peterson, 1959) as well as one-word and three-word units (Murdock, 1961) in the Brown-Peterson paradigm. *(From "Implications of Short-Term Memory for a General Theory of Memory," by A. W. Melton. In Journal of Verbal Learning and Verbal Behavior, 1963, 2, 1–21. Copyright 1963 by Academic Press. Reprinted by permission.)*

of three words or one word as well as a single trigram. The results of both these experiments were quite striking. The Petersons demonstrated that a trigram was almost completely forgotten after 18 seconds if subjects were not permitted to rehearse it. Murdock showed that this was true even when three words were used rather than three letters. This is important because it points out that the number of units, not the number of letters, is critical. Further, Murdock's results showed that there was forgetting even of a single word if, due to number counting, subjects could not continue active processing. Remember our example of first hearing and then forgetting a name at a party? These results reveal how difficult it is to remember something when information processing is interrupted. In our example, the intrusion of that person tapping on our shoulder would act like backward number counting. Without a chance to continue processing the name, we forget it.

Short-term retention of individual items

Purpose
To examine forgetting of a single item over a short interval following one brief presentation of the item.

Materials
The stimulus material consists of 26 low-association, consonant trigrams (CCCs) (see Table B in the Appendix) and 26 three-digit numbers selected from a table of random numbers (see Table A in the Appendix). Each CCC is typed or printed on an individual 3 × 5-inch card. The 26 cards are then randomly arranged (shuffled) and a different three-digit number assigned to each CCC. The number should be printed next to the CCC so the experimenter can easily read the CCC and the number. Two cards should be set aside to be used as practice items. No two successive trigrams should contain letters in common.

The remaining set of 24 trigrams is divided into four blocks of six items (1–6, 7–12, 13–18, 19–24). Because three retention intervals will be used (3, 9, and 15 seconds), each CCC is randomly assigned one of the three intervals with the restriction that in each block an interval appears twice (that is, there are two items tested at intervals of 3, 9, and 15 seconds in the first six items, the second six, and so forth). The interval should be noted on the 3 × 5 card. For example, a card might have written on it: XQR – 381 – 3 seconds.

Procedure
The experiment is best performed with the experimenter sitting at a table across from the subject. The experimenter first reads aloud a CCC and then immediately says a three-digit number. The experimenter takes note of the

retention interval and watches a clock (a wristwatch with a second hand will do) for either 3, 9, or 15 seconds. The subject counts backward by threes from the three-digit number until the experimenter signals (for example, by raising a hand from the table) for the subject to attempt recall of the trigram. Ten seconds is allowed for recall. After that time a new trial begins with another trigram and three-digit number. (All subjects should be rehearsed before the experiment on counting backward by threes so as to count at about a 1-second rate.) This procedure continues until all 24 items have been tested. Recall must be recorded after each trial and a record kept of all responses, including partial ones.

Instructions to Subjects

This is an experiment involving a test of your memory for short sequences of letters. When we begin, I will read aloud three letters. Immediately after the letters are read, I will say a three-digit number. You are to repeat the number to me and then begin counting backward by threes. I will signal to you to stop by raising my hand from the table. For example, I might read XQR – 309. You would then say 309, 306, 303, until you see me raise my hand. At that time try to say back to me the letters you heard. Guess if you are not sure. It is important that you start counting backward immediately and that you count so that you say a number about every second. Let us practice that for a few minutes. . . . Now, before we begin, let me give you two practice trials so you'll know what to expect when we actually begin the experiment. (The practice trials should include the longest [15 second] and shortest [3 second] intervals.) Now we are ready to start the experiment. Do you have any questions?

Summary and Analysis

An item is recalled correctly only if all three letters are recalled in the original order. The total number of items (of a possible eight) recalled for each subject at each of the three retention intervals is determined. Data can be summarized by finding the mean number of items recalled at each interval across all subjects participating in the study. (Recall can also be expressed as a proportion of the possible number of items recalled at each interval across all subjects. For example, if ten subjects participated, there would be 80 possible correct responses at each interval.) Statistical analysis requires a within-subjects analysis of variance. The independent variable is retention interval. It has three levels—3, 9, and 15 seconds. The dependent variable is the number of trigrams correctly recalled at each retention interval.

Recommended Minimum Number of Subjects

Total of 12.

Based on an experiment by Peterson and Peterson (1959).

Why was the Peterson and Peterson experiment so important? In reviewing these findings, Melton (1963) called the Brown-Peterson paradigm the key to integrating data from short-term and long-term memory experiments. In other words, it was the procedural technique necessary to examine the functional relationship between retention over short and long intervals. Now psychologists could get down to the task of linking knowledge gained from the study of long-term memory to the study of memory over brief intervals. However, there was another important reason, a theoretical one, that made the demonstration of rapid forgetting over short intervals so critical. The reason arose from an information-processing approach to the study of memory.

BROADBENT'S MODEL OF INFORMATION PROCESSING

In the late 1950s, important changes took place in the field of human memory that were to alter the way psychologists approached the task of understanding the learning and memory process. Possibly the most important of these changes occurred not in psychology but in the field of computer science. The computer age was taking off, and it greatly influenced how psychologists thought about memory (Estes, 1975; Tulving & Madigan, 1970). Many researchers abandoned (or at least temporarily set aside) a traditional viewpoint based on principles of associative learning. This view of memory emphasized the continuity of stimulus-response (S-R) relationships established in the animal conditioning laboratory with those discovered in the human learning and memory laboratory.

The dominant theme of the traditional associative learning approach to the study of memory is that forgetting is based on the interference of verbal associations. Time per se is rejected as an explanation of forgetting (McGeoch, 1932). According to the interference theorist, it is what happens in time that produces forgetting. Such an approach makes no distinction between the forgetting that occurs over brief intervals, as in a short-term memory experiment, and the forgetting that occurs over longer intervals. There is just one principle of forgetting—interference.

For many psychologists a more appropriate model of memory is one that attempts to analyze the flow of information within the organism. This approach often uses as an analogy the electronic computer and describes the processing of information through registers, loops, memory stores, and retrieval routines. This general view of human memory is called an *information-processing approach*. Perhaps the most influential of the early information-processing approaches was that of Broadbent (1958), a British psychologist working at Cambridge University.

Broadbent's model of the human processor charted the flow of information through general memory "systems." Input from the senses is received into a preattentive sensory store (the "s system"). (In the previous chapter we discussed characteristics of both visual and acoustic sensory stores.) From the sensory store, or s system, information is filtered and arrives in a limited capacity store ("p system"). The p system is the site of conscious awareness. We may assume that in Broadbent's theory primary memory represents a combination of the s and p systems. (Broadbent referred to the combination of these systems as "immediate memory.") In order for information to be maintained in primary memory, however, it has to be rehearsed. Rehearsal allows information to be circulated through the sensory store and back into the p system. Without this active processing, information is assumed to decay. (We will look closely at rehearsal mechanisms in the next chapter.) Secondary or long-term memory is assumed to be a third and more permanent memory system. Information enters the long-term memory system from primary memory. Information is lost quickly from primary memory, but comparatively little forgetting is assumed to occur in the long-term memory system.

Broadbent's model influenced practically every information-processing model that followed it. It contained three important assumptions about memory processing: (1) Primary and secondary memory involve separate memory systems. (2) Primary memory has a limited capacity. (3) Primary memory holds information only to the extent that the human processor actively rehearses it; otherwise information decays.

As we have noted, at the time of the Brown-Peterson experiments, the major explanation for forgetting was based on interference theory. Information acquired either before or after the to-be-remembered material was presented disrupted retention of that material. However, the rapid forgetting obtained in the Peterson and Peterson experiment when subjects were prevented from rehearsing suggested that decay might be responsible for forgetting over short intervals of time. Broadbent's information-processing model provided a theoretical framework within which to place an explanation of forgetting based on decay. However, it did not take long for interference theorists to offer an explanation other than decay for the results of the Peterson and Peterson experiment. In order to appreciate these theorists' arguments, you must have a brief introduction to interference theory.

THE INTERFERENCE THEORY OF FORGETTING

Interference is of two types: *retroactive* and *proactive*. Retroactive interference (also called *inhibition*) is memory loss brought about by activity that occurs *after* we learn something but before our retention is tested. For example, suppose you have a psychology test coming up but also have homework from a biology class to finish. If you study psychology first and then do your biology homework, the activities associated with doing your biology homework may interfere with your retention of psychology. We would not know for sure, however, without a comparison group that does not study biology. In order to study retroactive inhibition, the situation would have to look like this:

	A	B		Test A
Experimental Group:	Study Psychology	Study Biology	Retention Interval	Test on Psychology
Comparison Group:	Study Psychology	———		Test on Psychology

Everything else being equal, if the experimental group did more poorly on the psychology test than the comparison group, we could argue that this was due to interference caused by studying biology. The difference in retention between the experimental and comparison groups defines the amount of retroactive inhibition.

A second major source of interference is from activities carried out *before* learning the critical to-be-remembered material. This is called proactive inhibition. We can illustrate this kind of forgetting by doing some rearranging in the previous example. Look closely at the following situation:

	A	B		Test B
Experimental Group:	Study Biology	Study Psychology	Retention Interval	Test on Psychology
Comparison Group:	———	Study Psychology		Test on Psychology

Note that now the difference between the two groups is the presence or absence of an activity (studying biology) prior to the learning and test of the critical material (psychology). Again, all things being equal, if the experimental group does more poorly on the psychology test than the comparison group, we can attribute this to interference produced by the presence of the prior activity in the experimental group. Proactive inhibition is generally greater the longer the retention interval between study of the to-be-remembered material and the test (Underwood, 1957).

Although forgetting due to retroactive inhibition (interpolated learning) is often easily understood by students, they sometimes find it more difficult to get a feel for forgetting due to proactive inhibition. Therefore let us refer to one example from the psychology literature to illustrate this phenomenon. Greenberg and Underwood (1950) required subjects to learn four lists of ten adjective pairs over more than a week's time. On the first day the subjects learned a list of word pairs and then, after a retention interval of 48 hours, were tested for their memory of the word pairs. The subjects were then presented a different ten-pair word list to learn, and this list was tested following an additional 48 hours. This was repeated two more times so that subjects learned and were tested on four different lists. Retention of the word pairs got progressively poorer with each successive list. The results are shown in Figure 3-2. Proactive inhibition was a direct function of the number of previous lists subjects had learned. Be sure to note that the *retention,* not the acquisition, of successive lists is interfered with. Learning rate is likely to increase across lists, although retention decreases (for example, see Keppel, Postman, & Zavortink, 1968).

The descriptions we have provided of retroactive and proactive inhibition say nothing about the specific mechanisms believed to produce forgetting. That is, although we have described the procedures necessary to reveal forgetting, we have not identified the particular way interference operates to produce forgetting in these situations. For example, how does it happen that biology studied before psychology disrupts the later retention of psychology? In Chapter

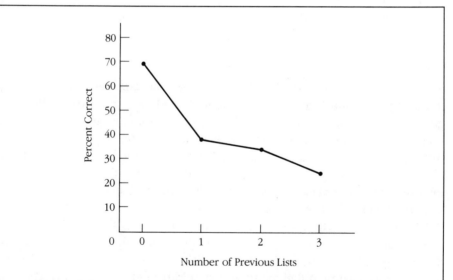

Figure 3-2.   Percent recall of ten-pair word lists as a function of number of previous lists studied and tested in an experiment by Greenberg and Underwood (1950). *(From "Interference and Forgetting," by B. J. Underwood. In* Psychological Review, *1957, 64, 49–60. Copyright 1957 by the American Psychological Association. Reprinted by permission.)*

6 we will review carefully the whole story of interference theory and discuss in detail the processes thought to be involved in retroactive and proactive inhibition. At that time we will provide information to help resolve a dilemma you may have spotted—namely, if interference yields forgetting by learning something *before* the critical material as well as by learning something *after* it, just when should we study biology?

CHARACTERISTICS OF PRIMARY MEMORY

The forgetting observed in the Peterson and Peterson experiment, along with Broadbent's theory of information processing, strongly reinforced the idea William James had originated—that the memory of the moment (primary memory) was somehow different from memory for information experienced some time previously (secondary memory). This made the topic of primary memory especially crucial if a complete theory of memory was to be had. In the years that followed, researchers directed their attention to examining the evidence for possible differences between primary memory and secondary memory. Three major characteristics have been suggested to distinguish these two memory systems: (1) the nature of forgetting, (2) capacity, and (3) the nature of information coding. In the following sections we will examine the evidence for these possible differences or distinctions between primary and secondary memory.

Forgetting

Although, to many, decay looked like a possible explanation for forgetting in the Peterson and Peterson experiment, Keppel and Underwood (1962) argued that forgetting was actually due to proactive inhibition. You may recall that each subject in the Petersons' experiment was tested on 48 different trigrams. In fact, there were two additional practice items, or a total of 50 items. These interference theorists argued that this provided plenty of room for proactive interference to operate. In their view, the learning of earlier trigrams likely interfered with memory for subsequent trigrams.

As we indicated, proactive inhibition increases as the interval between learning and a retention test increases. It is also greater the more prior learning there is (see Greenberg & Underwood, 1950). Therefore Keppel and Underwood (1962) suggested that two things should happen in the Brown-Peterson paradigm if proactive inhibition is operating. First, retention should decrease as the number of previous syllables tested increases. Second, the increase in forgetting as a function of the number of previous syllables learned should be greater for long retention intervals (for example, 12 and 18 seconds) than for short retention intervals (for example, 3 and 6 seconds).

Keppel and Underwood repeated the Petersons' experiment with several important changes. Subjects were tested on only two retention intervals, either 3 or 18 seconds, and on only six trigrams. Each subject was tested three times at each of the two retention intervals. By using a large number of subjects and counterbalancing the order of testing, these investigators were able to look at retention of trigrams after 3 and 18 seconds as a function of 0, 1, 2, 3, 4, or 5 previous tests.

The results of the Keppel and Underwood (1962) experiment are shown in Figure 3-3. There were three important findings. First, with no previous items tested (that is, when the trigram was the first one tested) there was virtually no forgetting even after 18 seconds. Second, retention of the trigrams became poorer as the number of syllables previously tested increased. Finally, forgetting as a function of number of previous items tested was greater for the 18-second condition than for the 3-second condition. As had been shown in previous long-term memory experiments, proactive inhibition was a more potent source of forgetting with long than with short retention intervals. Keppel and Underwood (1962) interpreted these results as evidence that interference produced forgetting over short intervals just as it did over longer intervals.

Other studies have shown that retroactive inhibition also plays a role in the forgetting seen in the Brown-Peterson paradigm (Reitman, 1971, 1974; Shif-

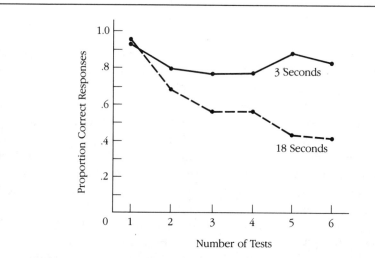

Figure 3-3. Retention of trigrams in the Brown-Peterson paradigm as a function of number of prior trigrams tested and length of the retention interval. *(From "Proactive Inhibition in Short-Term Retention of Single Items," by G. Keppel and B. J. Underwood. In* Journal of Verbal Learning and Verbal Behavior, *1962, 1, 153–161. Copyright 1962 by Academic Press, Inc. Reprinted by permission.)*

frin, 1973; Waugh & Norman, 1965). An important experiment in this regard was that of Reitman (1971). Consider the fact that retroactive inhibition, like proactive inhibition, is affected by the similarity of the interfering material. Is it possible that numbers (used in backward number counting) are similar enough to consonant trigrams to produce retroactive interference? They may very well be, if you think of the two kinds of material as consisting of verbal sounds. Reitman argued that the only way to investigate whether retroactive inhibition played a role in short-term forgetting was to employ a distractor task that would prevent subjects from actively processing the to-be-remembered items but would yield little or no verbal interference. Further, if the effect of proactive inhibition could be eliminated, and if forgetting still occurred under these conditions, then decay would still be a viable explanation of short-term forgetting.

Reitman designed a signal detection distractor task that required subjects to listen for a tone in the midst of white noise (white noise sounds like static on your radio). In another distraction condition subjects were required to detect the verbal sound "toh" in the midst of a background of "doh's." Subjects pressed a button whenever they heard the signal (tone or syllable) in the two conditions. The to-be-remembered items were three four-letter nouns. The retention interval was 15 seconds. Tone detection was assumed to provide virtually an interference-free interval but at the same time keep subjects occupied so they could not rehearse the three words. On the other hand, syllable identification was expected to produce verbal interference.

Reitman (1971) found that 13 out of 18 subjects performing the tonal task showed 100% retention after 15 seconds. There was no forgetting for these subjects, and the overall mean retention for subjects in this condition was 92%. However, word recall following the syllable detection task averaged 77%. Performance was even lower in a third condition that had required subjects to say the syllables aloud when they detected them. These results argued strongly that not only may retroactive inhibition be present in this situation, but, when no verbal task is present (tone detection), there is no forgetting.

It would seem that decay, as an alternative to interference, had pretty well been eliminated as an explanation for forgetting in primary memory. However, the decay explanation was not quite dead. Subsequent studies by Watkins, Watkins, Craik, and Mazuryk (1973) as well as a second and more extensive study by Reitman (1974) provided evidence for forgetting over an interval filled with nonverbal distraction—that is, when retroactive inhibition supposedly could not operate. For example, Watkins and his colleagues asked subjects to remember five nouns over retention intervals of 1, 3, 6, 9, and 20 seconds. The activities required of subjects during the retention intervals were (1) no activity, subjects were free to rehearse; (2) listening to four musical tones presented at a 1-

second rate, but with subjects also encouraged to rehearse the nouns during the interval; or (3) keeping track of which tone was played and at the same time humming the musical notes as they were heard. Subjects in this last condition had four keys in front of them that they pressed as they identified each tone.

The results of the experiment by Watkins and his associates are shown in Figure 3-4. There was little difference in retention between the silent rehearsal group (no activity) and the group trying to rehearse while listening to the tones. However, when subjects had to press the four keys identifying the tones while humming each tone, there was appreciable forgetting over the 20-second retention interval. These investigators argued that forgetting occurred because of "diversion of attention" from the items in primary memory. Diverting attention prohibited rehearsal and thus permitted the items to be lost. Diversion of attention, like decay, as an explanation for forgetting does not depend on interference from other learning. As we will see later, it is difficult to distinguish between decay and diverting attention as explanations of forgetting. For now let us treat them similarly. These investigators argued that previous results by Reitman (1971) and Shiffrin (1973) did not reveal memory loss in the absence of verbal interference because of the procedures used in these studies. For example, if the nonverbal distractor task was not sufficiently demanding of the subjects, they could still sneak in rehearsals and prevent forgetting. When Reitman

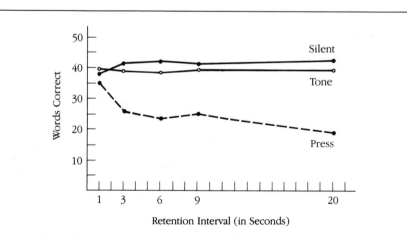

Figure 3-4. Number of words correctly recalled in a Brown-Peterson task as a function of retention interval and nature of interpolated activity. *(From "Effect of Nonverbal Distraction on Short-Term Storage," by M. J. Watkins, O. C. Watkins, F. I. M. Craik, and G. Mazuryk. In* Journal of Experimental Psychology, *1973, 101, 296–300. Copyright 1973 by the American Psychological Association. Reprinted by permission.)*

(1974), in a subsequent study, made important changes in her procedure, she obtained results similar to those of Watkins and his associates—namely, that there was forgetting when the retention interval was filled with a nonverbal task. Decay (or its close relative, diversion of attention) seemed possible again.

We wish we could say that the issue of decay (diverted attention) versus interference as explanations of forgetting in primary memory has been finally resolved and that, more than 20 years after the introduction of the Brown-Peterson task, conclusive evidence as to the nature of forgetting in this paradigm has been obtained. Unfortunately, the issue is not completely settled. For example, as Watkins and his associates point out, it is very difficult to rule out the possibility that "task-induced covert verbal activity" occurred even when subjects were faced with a demanding nonverbal distraction task. Such activity might be present if subjects monitor their own behavior in a detection task. This might take the form of a covert discussion with oneself about the task. The use of a nonverbal distractor task creates an interesting paradox (see also Roediger, Knight, & Kantowitz, 1977). The more similar the distractor activity is to a verbal memory task, the greater is the likelihood that retroactive inhibition will result and thereby cause forgetting. Yet the more *dissimilar* the distractor activity is from the memory task, the greater is the likelihood that subjects can do two things at once. For example, you have probably found yourself thinking about something else while driving your car. This covert verbal activity went on while you were detecting oncoming cars, staying in the right lane, and so forth. The choice of a highly dissimilar, nonverbal, distraction task in the Brown-Peterson paradigm may permit subjects to engage in covert verbal activity that produces retroactive inhibition. Finally, it is likely that interference theorists will not be satisfied until forgetting is demonstrated on the very first trial of a Brown-Peterson task or, in other words, when proactive inhibition is not operating. As others have pointed out, not all experimenters have chosen to analyze their data for the effects of proactive inhibition (Hintzman, 1978). Therefore the forgetting observed in some of these experiments may be due at least partially to proactive inhibition. Although a great deal has been learned about the effects of interference in primary memory, the question of whether decay might also operate to produce forgetting has not been definitely answered.

Capacity

Primary memory is frequently described as having a limited capacity. However, it is not always clear what is meant by capacity limitations in primary memory (for example, see Craik & Lockhart, 1972). *Storage* capacity usually refers to how much information a memory system can hold. For example, in the previous chapter we suggested that the capacity of the visual sensory register is relatively large—capable of holding more information than we can attend to at one time. *Processing,* or *attentional,* capacity refers to our ability to perform certain operations. For example, you might have heard someone say that a certain industrial plant is working "at capacity." This generally means that the company is processing material and creating products as fast as the machines and employees can work. Similarly, in our company the machine that is our memory must have physical limits on its capacity to process information. As we saw in the previous chapter, there is a limit to how much we can attend to at one time, and there are no doubt limits to how fast we can throw the cognitive levers that process to-be-remembered information. It is likely that both storage and processing limitations contribute to the limited capacity of primary memory.

Whatever the eventual definition of capacity, it is not difficult to demonstrate the limitations of primary memory. A common technique is to measure *immediate memory span.* Memory span is defined as the number of items that can be recalled immediately in their original order. For example, as a test of memory span you might be read a series of digits one at a time at the rate of one per second. After testing with both short and long digit series, you would likely find you could repeat somewhere between seven and nine digits, the approximate digit span for a college-age person. Memory span varies with age and as a consequence is usually part of tests to measure mental age (intelligence). In the last chapter we will discuss individual differences in remembering, including differences in memory span performance.

The unit used to measure primary memory capacity is usually a *chunk.* A chunk is a unit of information organized according to a rule or corresponding to some familiar pattern. We saw one example of chunking when we reviewed Murdock's experimental finding using the Brown-Peterson task (see Figure 3-1). Murdock showed that three words were forgotten at the same rate as three letters and that a single word showed only slight forgetting in this situation. If letters were the important units, we would expect a three-letter word to exhibit the same forgetting as three unrelated letters. Or because three words have many more than three letters, we might expect even greater forgetting. Murdock's results indicate, however, that the relevant unit in primary memory is a chunk. When three unrelated letters were used, the individual letters were chunks, whereas when words were used, the words became chunks.

In an insightful analysis of the chunking process, the Nobel-prize-winning economist and psychologist Herbert Simon (1974) was his own subject in a memory span experiment. Simon presented himself the following list of words to recall after only one quick reading (you might try it also):

Lincoln
milky
criminal

differential
address
way
lawyer
calculus
Gettysburg

Simon found he could not recall the words correctly after only one presentation. The number of items was greater than his immediate memory span. However, he then rearranged the words as follows:

Lincoln's Gettysburg Address
Milky Way
Criminal Lawyer
Differential Calculus

He then had no trouble remembering all nine words. When the words were presented singly, each was treated as a separate chunk to be learned. When the words were fitted into well-known phrases, each phrase became a chunk. Simon then moved on to longer phrases (for example, "Four score and seven years ago"); in fact, he tested himself with various kinds of materials. His findings are summarized in Table 3-1. Note that, when one-syllable words were used, the number of chunks was assumed to be seven. Similar results were obtained for two-syllable words. However, number of syllables in the to-be-remembered words had an effect on memory span; a lower memory span (six chunks) was found for three-syllable words. That chunk size influences memory span was also shown by the fact that when eight-word phrases were used, he could remember only three chunks (24 words). In other words, with an increase in the amount of information in the chunk, there was some decrease in the number

TABLE 3-1. Immediate Memory Span for Recall of Various Words and Phrases for a Single Subject

Words and phrases	Span			Syllables (chunk)
	Syllables	Words	Imputed chunks	
1-syllable	7	7	7	1.0
2-syllable	14	7	7	2.0
3-syllable	18	6	6	3.0
2-word	22	9	4	5.5
8-word	26	22	3	8.7

From "How Big Is a Chunk?" by H. A. Simon. In *Science*, 1974, *183*, 482–488. Copyright 1974 by the American Association for the Advancement of Science. Reprinted by permission.

of chunks that could be remembered. However, there are important factors to be considered in such a statement. First, the organization of information into chunks depends greatly on familiarity with the material. That is, "Lincoln's Gettysburg Address" is a chunk only because we recognize it as a familiar phrase. There are undoubtedly differences between our familiarity with two-syllable words and with multiword phrases that would contribute to decreasing recall with increasing chunk size. Further, as Simon pointed out, as the chunk size grows, it takes longer to rehearse the chunks. This time factor may also put limits on what we can remember.

After taking these factors (familiarity, length, and time) into consideration, Simon argued that the chunk is a meaningful way to describe capacity limitations in primary memory. Moreover, he fixed primary memory capacity at about five chunks. Note that this number is substantially lower than the average digit span for a college-age adult (about eight digits). Simon's estimate is also lower than that suggested by Miller (1956), who argued that "seven, plus or minus two" was an appropriate estimate of adult memory span performance. However, Simon argued that the larger estimates of digit span found with adults reflect years of learning digits and that adults naturally form chunks even when given a string of random digits. Therefore a test of memory span using single digits will overestimate the size of the span. He proposed that single digits would equal single chunks only at an age when the digits are familiar but when there has not been extensive practice with numbers. Simon figured this to be about the age we begin school, or about 7. The average digit span of a 7-year-old is, in fact, about five digits. Nevertheless, the number of units or chunks that reflect the capacity of primary memory is a major source of dispute (see Postman, 1975b, for interesting comments on this issue). For example, other researchers have provided estimates of capacity limitations as low as two to three items (Glanzer, 1972). Therefore, although the capacity limitations of primary memory undoubtedly are reflected in adult memory span performance, the size of an individual's memory span should not be considered equivalent with primary memory capacity. Performance in a memory span task likely reflects the contribution of both primary and secondary memory processes.

Assuming there are some capacity limitations in primary memory, the possibility exists that memory loss (forgetting) can occur through displacement. By this we mean that one item (chunk) literally knocks out another. Displacement may happen either because storage capacity is limited (for example, an item is lost to make room for another) or because processing capacity is limited (for example, an item is bumped away from a processing channel). Waugh and Norman (1965) have argued that retroactive inhibition occurs in primary memory by displacement of information from a limited-capacity memory system.

Although there is still considerable debate over the nature of capacity limitations in primary memory, such limitations are an important way to distinguish primary from secondary memory. Secondary memory has no known limitations. As far as we know, no one has yet exceeded the capacity of that vast reservoir James designated as "memory proper."

Coding

A *memory code* refers to the way an external event is represented in memory. Memory codes can only be inferred from subjects' behavior in memory experiments. An early study that investigated possible memory codes in primary memory was designed by Wickelgren (1965). He asked students to recall lists of letters presented auditorily—for example, $TCAJKZPL$. In addition to recording how many letters the subjects remembered, Wickelgren observed the types of errors made in recall. He found that when one letter was substituted for another, the substitutions tended to be letters that were acoustically similar to the missing letter. A Z might replace a $P,$ or an A might replace a $K,$ and so forth.

As part of a study conducted at Cambridge, England, Conrad (1964) performed an experiment similar to Wickelgren's but used both visual and auditory presentation of lists of letters. He was interested in comparing systematically the types of errors made by subjects in immediate recall as a function of the presentation modality of the letters. Would the errors subjects made following visual presentation of the letters tend to be letters that *look* like the to-be-remembered letters, as in substituting V for $X,$ or would the errors *sound* like the memory letters, as in substituting V for $C?$ Conrad found that, whether subjects had been listening to the letters or had seen them presented, the errors made in this immediate memory task tended to *sound* like the memory letters.

The results of these experiments suggested that the memory code for information in primary memory was an acoustic one. In contrast, it is generally assumed that information in secondary memory is coded in terms of the meaning or semantic aspects of the information. These findings suggested that primary memory could be differentiated from secondary memory in terms of the nature of the information coding: primary memory depended on acoustic codes, secondary memory, on semantic codes. Although recent research has not questioned these earlier findings, it has suggested that we look at them in a different way. Specifically, although corroborating the fact that acoustic coding is frequently used in primary memory, recent evidence does not confirm the once-maintained notion that *only* acoustic coding occurs in primary memory. Let us look at one important experiment in this regard.

Shulman (1972) designed a probe-recognition experiment to demonstrate that semantic information may be represented in primary memory. In a *probe-recognition task* a list of to-be-remembered items is presented followed by the presentation of a single item (the probe). The probe may or may not be an item from the list. Subjects are generally instructed to say whether the probe was one of the items in the original list. Speed of responding to the probe is often measured in a probe-recognition task. In Shulman's task, ten-word lists were presented visually, one word every 500 milliseconds. Subjects had two types of recognition decisions to make. In one condition they were to say whether the probe was a synonym (word meaning the same) of a word in the list. In a second condition they were to say whether the word was identical to a word in the list. The type of decision was signaled to the subjects by the letters *M* (meaning) or *I* (identity), which were flashed on a screen immediately before the probe. Subjects did not know which type of recognition decision they would have to make until after the list was presented, so this made it likely that they coded items according to their semantic characteristics on each trial. Subjects were instructed to respond quickly "yes" or "no" in both conditions by pressing one of two buttons.

Shulman was interested not only in whether subjects could quickly and accurately make recognition decisions based on the semantic relationship between the probe and a list item; he was also interested in the kinds of errors subjects might make in this type of task. Therefore in a third condition of the experiment, although subjects were signaled that their response should be based on the identity of the probe as a list item, sometimes a synonym of a list item appeared as the probe. A correct recognition decision in this case would be to respond "no," indicating that the item was not identical to any in the list. However, to the extent that the synonym probe resulted in a large number of errors, this would suggest that subjects had coded semantic information in this primary memory task.

Figure 3-5 shows the results of Shulman's experiment for the three conditions we have discussed. Subjects were most accurate when recognizing an item that had actually been in the list (identity match); however, they were also very accurate when recognizing a synonym (meaning match). The relationship between accuracy and serial position of the probe in the list was similar for both identity and meaning matches. Finally, the bottom line in the graph shows that at all serial positions there was a marked tendency to mistakenly say that an item was identical when in fact it was a synonym of one of the recently presented words. The overall proportion of these semantic errors was .19, which differed significantly from the proportion of errors made when an identity match was requested and the probe was an item semantically unrelated to the list items (.11).

The type of memory code a subject forms apparently depends on task requirements and not on whether information is processed in primary or secondary memory. In many short-term memory experiments a premium is placed

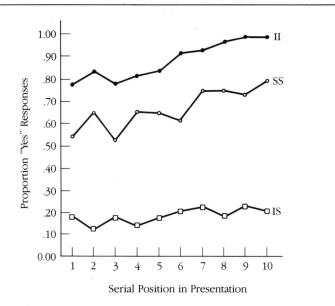

Figure 3-5. Proportion of correct identity matches (II) and synonym matches (SS) as well as proportion of times subjects mistakenly said "yes" to a synonym when an identity match was requested (IS) as a function of serial position. *(From "Semantic Confusion Errors in Short-Term Memory," by H. G. Shulman. In* Journal of Verbal Learning and Verbal Behavior, *1972, 11, 221–227. Copyright 1972 by Academic Press, Inc. Reprinted by permission.)*

on quickly recalling information that has just been presented—for example, in the measurement of memory span. It may be to our advantage to perform only minimal (or low-effort) coding in such tasks in order to perform efficiently. This minimal coding may take the form of representing an item only in terms of its acoustic features (see Craik & Lockhart, 1972). However, in other tasks that require a decision to be made on the basis of semantic information, as in the task designed by Shulman, we seem to be capable of modifying our coding activities and responding on the basis of the semantic features of the item. We cannot therefore adequately distinguish primary from secondary memory in terms of the type of memory code used. What must be determined is under what conditions we are likely to code information in one way or another.

THEORETICAL CONCEPTUALIZATIONS: STRUCTURE VERSUS PROCESS

It is probably safe to say that the most important question facing researchers in the field of human memory is how best to conceptualize memory. Despite the enormous progress made in our understanding of sensory memories and of primary and secondary memory, as yet there is no complete theory of memory with which all, or even most, psychologists can agree. An important distinction found among various theoretical approaches is between those approaches emphasizing the *structure* of human memory and those emphasizing memory *processes*. This distinction is by no means clear-cut; process theorists often speak about memory structures, and structural theorists, about memory processes. Theorists of both points of view acknowledge the difficulty in meaningfully defining "process" and "structure." Generally speaking, structural aspects of a memory system are considered fixed, whereas processes are flexible and under the subject's control (see Craik & Levy, 1976). Structure and process theorists tend to differ in their approach to primary memory.

The defining characteristic of a structural theory of memory is the division of memory into two or more memory "stores." As we mentioned earlier, one of the most influential of these theories has been that of Atkinson and Shiffrin (1968, 1971). This theory is outlined in Figure 3-6. It closely resembles Broadbent's information-processing model, described previously. The major goals of a structural memory theory are to describe the various memory structures, to show how information is lost from these structures, and to explain how information gets from one structure to another. To do this, Atkinson and Shiffrin distinguished between the structural components of our memory (for example, memory stores) and the control processes that determine how information is processed. *Control processes* are the cognitive activities that direct the flow of information. One of the more important control processes is rehearsal, a topic we will consider at length in the next chapter. Another important control process is *coding,* the activity by which we elaborate or transform to-be-remembered

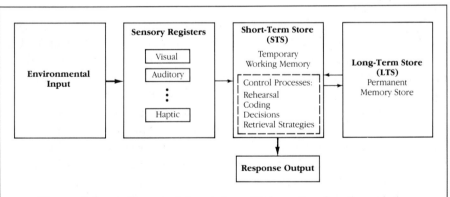

Figure 3-6. A theoretical description of information flow through the human processor. *(From "The Control of Short-Term Memory," by R. C. Atkinson and R. M. Shiffrin. In* Scientific American, *1971, 225, 82–90. Copyright © 1971 by Scientific American, Inc. All rights reserved. Reprinted by permission.)*

information in order to place it more effectively in the long-term memory store. For example, in order to remember a short list of words, we might make up a meaningful story using the words in the list or attempt to create a visual image incorporating objects to which the words refer.

Control processes are deployed within the short-term store; consequently, this structure is frequently called *working memory*. The short-term store apparently is also equivalent to William James's memory of the moment—that is, primary memory. Consider how Atkinson and Shiffrin (1971, p. 83) describe the short-term store: "In our thinking we tend to equate the short-term store with 'consciousness,' that is, the thoughts and information of which we are currently aware and can be considered as part of the contents of the short-term store." Retrieval of information from the short-term store is practically automatic because it is what we are currently attending to. But retrieval from the long-term store depends on the selection of an appropriate retrieval strategy and a successful search of the contents of the long-term store. For example, you will likely remember automatically the last few words you read, but remembering the contents of the last chapter requires a retrieval effort. According to the model, information from the short-term store can be lost relatively easily, perhaps through decay or displacement. Information can be "lost" from the long-term memory store because our retrieval strategy failed to locate it. That is, forgetting in secondary memory can result from an unsuccessful retrieval attempt. Although the model described in Figure 3-6 depicts information flowing from a short-term store to a long-term store, more recent multistore models have depicted this relationship differently. For example, Shiffrin (1976) describes the short-term store as an activated portion of the long-term store. That is, although functionally separate, the two stores are formed from the same psychological structure.

A process theory of memory (for example, Craik & Jacoby, 1975; Craik & Lockhart, 1972) does not divide memory into different stores but instead describes the kinds of cognitive processes that are important in information processing and their relation to memory performance. Memory processes are assumed to be a continuation of the cognitive processes governing perception (Craik & Lockhart, 1972). In this view information processing is not limited by memory structure but by the limitations of a hypothetical "limited capacity central processor" (Craik & Jacoby, 1975). The activity of the central processor is identified with primary memory. As we have seen, capacity limitations are one of the most striking features of primary memory. Consider the definition of primary memory given by Craik and Jacoby (1975, p. 175): "rather than viewing primary memory as a structure in which items are placed, this type of memory is seen as the activation of some part of the perceptual analyzing system by the processes of conscious attention."

Activities of the central processor also explain how information is lost from memory. For example, diverting attention from an item is assumed to be responsible for loss from primary memory. We previously reviewed evidence for this assumption (see Watkins, Watkins, Craik, & Mazuryk, 1973, and Figure 3-4). Differences between the multistore approaches, such as that of Atkinson and Shiffrin, and explanations of memory emphasizing the nature of processing activities will be discussed further in the following chapter.

Summary

Close to one hundred years ago William James (1890) speculated on the difference between our memory for the moment—primary memory—and our memory for information that was dropped from consciousness—secondary memory. However, possible differences in these two kinds of remembering were systematically investigated only after the publication of experiments by Brown (1958) and Peterson and Peterson (1959). Their findings suggested that information, if not actively rehearsed, would decay from primary memory. This idea was also present in Broadbent's (1958) influential model of information processing. The model separated memory into distinct memory systems, including those we might call primary and secondary memory.

Evidence for the dual nature of our memory has been sought by contrasting the nature of forgetting, capacity limitations, and information coding in primary and secondary memory. Interference is a major cause of forgetting in primary memory, although the door is still open to the possibility that some information is lost due to decay. It is in terms of capacity that primary and secondary memory appear to be most clearly differentiated. Only primary memory is generally judged to have a limited capacity, but there is disagreement as to the nature of capacity limitations. This is partly due to the contribution of secondary memory processes in tasks designed to measure primary memory capacity. The original evidence that information coding in primary memory was strictly acoustic has been subsequently interpreted to be related more to specific task demands than to the nature of the memory system.

Theoretical conceptualizations of primary memory often differ in terms of whether structures or processes are emphasized. These distinctions are not always clear, and research is needed to understand more fully the relationship between our memory for the moment and secondary memory. A view of this relationship that appears theoretically promising is one that considers primary memory to be an activated subset of secondary memory.

Recommendations for further reading

In the last 20 years, there has been a deluge of articles, chapters, and even books devoted to the topic of short-term memory and, in particular, to the theoretical construct of primary memory. Included are the excellent book *Short-Term Memory,* edited by Deutsch and Deutsch (1975), and several chapters in the six volumes edited by Estes under the general title *Handbook of Learning and Cognitive Processes*. Of particular importance is the chapter "The Concept of Primary Memory" in Volume 4 by Craik and Levy (1976). They present an informative overview of this concept and discuss the many different theoretical approaches to describing this aspect of our memory. Insightful comments by Postman regarding the distinction between primary memory and secondary memory are found in his article "Verbal Learning and Memory" (1975b). Significant theoretical contributions are also found in Broadbent (1971), Baddeley and Hitch (1974), and Shiffrin (1976).

4

The Role of Rehearsal

Introduction/overview

What kinds of mental activities are good for memory? What should we do, in other words, when we want to "memorize" something?

For centuries philosophers have speculated on possible answers to such questions, and many reached the same conclusion. Repetition is good for memory. Aristotle told Alexander the Great and his other students: to learn something, you must repeat it. In the Middle Ages the famous philosopher and theologian Thomas Aquinas said it was necessary to "meditate frequently" on what we wish to remember (see Yates, 1966). Through the 18th and 19th centuries, philosophers known as the British Associationists taught that frequency or repetition was a major factor in the acquisition of associations.

Is it any wonder that the first psychologists should consider repetition essential to memory formation? When William James (1890) discussed ways

53

to improve memory in his well-known Principles of Psychology, he described first the "mechanical" methods. These were methods, James said, that consisted of the "intensification, prolongation, and repetition of the impression to be remembered" (p. 668). The famous German psychologist Herman Ebbinghaus, in his monograph Memory (1885/1964), stated that repetition was indispensable for remembering. In fact, the effect of repetition on memory was the focus of Ebbinghaus's most famous research, which began psychology's attack on understanding the processes of learning and memory.

Ebbinghaus's interest in the relationship between repetition and memory was no doubt influenced by his reading of the philosophical works of the British Associationists (Boring, 1950). However, to scientifically investigate repetition as a factor influencing memory, Ebbinghaus needed to arrange experimental conditions so that repetition was isolated from all the other factors that might influence memory. There were two important considerations. First, the material to be remembered had to be something subjects had never experienced. Ebbinghaus wanted to study the formation of memory "from scratch," without the confounding influence of prior learning. So he formed nonsense syllables by arranging the consonants and vowels of his native German language into random three-letter units, with the restriction that a vowel always be between two consonants (CVC). After discarding any three-letter combinations that formed words, he had the raw material for his investigation.

The second consideration necessary to isolate the variable of repetition was to control the manner in which the nonsense syllables were learned. Ebbinghaus was both experimenter and subject. During more than two years of investigation, he first studied and then tested his retention for thousands of series of nonsense syllables. He took great care to read and recite the syllables at a constant rate, avoiding even the stressing of his voice, and struggling continually to keep his attention on the task at hand. Most important, Ebbinghaus tried to avoid any "meaningful" analysis of the material. As he described it, "there was no attempt to connect the nonsense syllables by the invention of special associations. . . . Learning was carried on solely by the influence of the mere repetitions on the natural memory" (1885/1964, p. 25).

Psychologists frequently refer to Ebbinghaus's methods as rote verbal learning. This is learning due to the sheer repetition of something with little contribution from any meaningful or semantic analysis. The study of rote verbal learning characterized much of the research on memory during the first half of this century. Psychologists emphasized both frequency of occurrence and contiguity of items (in space and time) as major factors in associative learning. Less attention was paid to the effect that meaningful analysis or semantic elaboration might have on retention. Yet, as a tribute to Ebbinghaus's insight into the processes governing memory, the topic of repetition, including rote repetition, is very much an important issue today. In this *chapter we will look at the effect of one particular form of repetition, re-hearsal, upon memory. You will see that psychologists have looked for lawful relationships between amount of rehearsal and amount remembered. One such relationship was expressed as the "total-time hypothesis," which posits a direct relationship between time spent studying and amount remembered. How this hypothesis has fared in the face of recent discoveries about re-hearsal will be discussed. Rehearsal has played an important role in multi-store views of memory—for example, as a mechanism by which information is transferred from one memory store to another. We will also look at this aspect of rehearsal in light of recent research. A major issue yet to be re-solved is whether there are different kinds of rehearsal.*

WHAT IS REHEARSAL?

Before going further, we would like to suggest that you perform the fol-lowing task. Take a few seconds to memorize this nine-digit number: 8 6 1 4 9 3 0 2 5.

Most likely you began by repeating the number over and over to yourself. You might even have found yourself turning your head away from the page or closing your eyes so you couldn't see the number while you repeated it, then looking back to see if your repetition was accurate. Perhaps you formed "chunks" by separating the number into three series of three digits, 8 6 1-4 9 3-0 2 5. Nevertheless, to accomplish this task, it appears we must repeat the digits to ourselves. With sufficient repetition the number becomes part of our memory. The mental activity associated with repeating an item is called *rehearsal*. It may be either *overt* (aloud) or *covert* (silent).

If in rehearsing the number you did not try to form any special associations or elaborate on the number in any way, then your approach was not that different from Ebbinghaus's. One of the ideas to be discussed in this chapter is that there are different kinds of rehearsal. Therefore let us begin by defining one kind of rehearsal (the method you likely just used, as Ebbinghaus might have done)—repeating an item in the form it was presented with no attempt to "add anything." We will refer to this type of mental activity as *rote* or *simple rehearsal*.

Learning to rehearse

As you just saw, it is very natural to start rehearsing when asked to remem-ber something. However, this is a strategy you have learned. Young children do not rehearse more, nor do they remember more, when instructed to memorize material for a later recall test than when they are instructed merely to look at the material (Appel, Cooper, McCarrell, Sims-Knight, Yussen, & Flavell, 1972). Appel and her associates showed colored pictures of common objects to pre-schoolers, first graders, and fifth graders with instructions either to look at the pictures or to remember the names of the pictures for a later test. To make the "look" instructions believable, they simultaneously engaged the children in a task involving identification of pictures from partial cues and told them that looking at the pictures would help them in the identification task.

Each of the children was seated at a table in front of a one-way mirror, behind which two experimenters were positioned in order to observe their overt study behaviors. The experimenters observed any naming of the objects by the child, and watched for lip movements, head movements, or facial expressions that indicated rehearsal activity. When they were instructed only to look at the pictures, the percentage of children showing signs of rehearsal activity was zero or very close to zero for all three groups (0, 3, and 5% for the preschoolers, first graders, and fifth graders, respectively). However, under memory instructions, as grade in school increased, there was a clear increase in the proportion of children showing signs of rehearsal activity. For the three grades the percentages were 5, 15, and 58, respectively. Note that the youngest children, the preschoolers, really did not behave very differently under the two instruction conditions. Also, on a subsequent test of retention the preschoolers did not remember more following the "memory" than the "look" instructions, whereas the fifth graders did. Therefore, when asked to memorize something, the older children knew what to do and the younger children did not.

On the basis of findings like these, Flavell and Wellman (1977) have argued that commonly seen differences in memory performance between younger and older children are not due to differences in the basic mechanisms governing learning and memory. They suggest that differences across age groups are likely due to the fact that children have learned different kinds of activities to employ when trying to memorize. One important activity is rehearsal. We will have more to say about our knowledge concerning what is good for memory and what should be done in a particular learning situation when we discuss the topic of "metamemory," or the knowledge we have about the knowing process, in Chapter 11. But for now let us inquire whether rehearsal is an activity restricted to the processing of verbal material or whether we are capable of rehearsing pictures as well.

Verbal versus visual rehearsal

Nearly everything we have to say about rehearsal is related to the processing of verbal material. Does this mean that only words or other verbal units can be rehearsed? Not necessarily. Frequently discussed but less frequently investigated is the hypothesis that we have the capability for nonverbal as well as verbal rehearsal. This would suggest that we can rehearse a picture just presented as we might a word just presented or that we are capable of reviewing in our "mind's eye" an image we have produced. Let's look at some of the evidence.

Several investigators have now shown that increasing the time available for subjects to rehearse pictures leads to an increase in their memory for the pictures (Graefe & Watkins, 1980; Tversky & Sherman, 1975; Weaver, 1974). For example, Tversky and Sherman asked subjects to view 60 "dictionary-type drawings of familiar objects" (television, teakettle, fish, and so forth) that were presented for various study times (ranging from .25 to 2.00 seconds). For half the subjects each picture was followed by an unfilled interval of 1.50 seconds; for the other half the interval was 3.00 seconds. If pictures can in fact be rehearsed following their presentation, then more rehearsal time would be available following a long than a short interval. Indeed, picture names were better recalled and the pictures were better recognized when the unfilled interval was 3.00 seconds than when it was 1.50 seconds. These investigators concluded that the "processing" of a picture, like that of a word, continues into the unfilled interval. We have no way of knowing, however, the nature of this processing. It is even possible that rehearsal takes the form of verbal descriptions of the pictures, although similar results have been obtained with pictures that are obviously difficult to describe, such as random shapes (for example, Graefe & Watkins, 1980).

There is also evidence that subject-generated images can be rehearsed. Peterson, Thomas, and Johnson (1977) tested students for their memory of numbers placed in an imaginary mental matrix. To understand the task, try to imagine for yourself a square matrix that has four rows and four columns, 16 "boxes" within a square. Now mentally put the number 1 in the box that marks the intersection of the second row and the second column. Got it? Now suppose you were given in consecutive numerical order the numbers 2 through 8 to add to your mental matrix. This was the kind of task confronting the students in this experiment.

Instructions directed students to place the numbers in the matrix beginning with a square adjacent to the first number and moving in one of four directions (up, down, right, or left). For example, having fixed 1 in a square, you might next be asked to place a 2 in the square to the right of the 1, then put a 3 in the adjacent square up from the 2, and so on until you have placed all eight digits in the matrix. Memory for the location of numbers in the matrix was tested either by having students write down the numbers in a matrix provided by the experimenter or by asking them to use a response sheet to record the direction the numbers took beginning with the second number (for example, right-up).

A memory test was given either immediately or after 30 seconds. Further, subjects in a "visual rehearsal" condition were told that during the 30-second interval they should try to focus the matrix clearly in their mind's eye so they could use this image to make their response. Another group of subjects was given verbal rehearsal instructions and was told to use the interval to repeat the messages quietly to help memory. When asked to remember by putting numbers in an actual matrix, memory was better following visual than verbal rehearsal instructions. The reverse was found when retention was tested by having subjects record the directions for the numbers. Apparently, the images could be rehearsed, and visual rehearsal aided memory when the response format (for example, placing the numbers in the matrix) was compatible with the rehearsal process.

The evidence from these few studies suggests that some type of "rehearsal" can take place with pictures or subject-generated images. However, it is not clear at this time exactly how similar we should consider this process to that of verbal rehearsal.

THE TOTAL-TIME HYPOTHESIS

In the previous chapter we saw that, in order to investigate whether information decays from memory, researchers often go to great lengths to prevent their subjects from rehearsing. Backward number counting or difficult signal detection tasks are commonly used to inhibit rehearsal activity. But suppose subjects are not prevented from rehearsing. Suppose they could rehearse as much or for as long as they wanted. Would we be able to predict performance on a memory test by knowing how much time a person spent rehearsing? Some psychologists say we can. The notion that memory performance can be best predicted from a knowledge of the time spent studying the material is called the *total-time hypothesis.*

Formally stated, the total-time hypothesis says "that a fixed amount of time is necessary to learn a fixed amount of material regardless of the number of individual trials into which that time is divided" (Cooper & Pantle, 1967, p. 221). It is basically very simple. Suppose you were asked to remember 50 facts for a biology test. According to the total-time hypothesis, you will end up knowing the same number of facts whether you study each fact once for 10 seconds (a total of 500 seconds of study time) or whether you study each fact two times for 5 seconds each time (again, making 500 seconds of total study time). If the total time is the same, then the amount remembered will be the same. Note we didn't say you would remember all 50 facts, only that the number of facts learned would be the same given that the time spent studying was the same.

Cooper and Pantle (1967) reviewed a large number of studies that provided data relevant to the total-time hypothesis and showed that the total-time hypothesis was supported if two conditions were met. First, the hypothesis was approximated when, as part of a learning and memory task, subjects engaged only in simple or rote rehearsal. Simple rehearsal, as we defined it previously, is the act of repeating an item in the form in which it was presented. The total-time hypothesis did not hold for those situations in which subjects engaged in what Cooper and Pantle called "active rehearsal." Active rehearsal involves developing associations or "adding to" an item. For example, we saw that Ebbinghaus tried to avoid active rehearsal when he studied his nonsense syllables.

The second condition required for the total-time hypothesis to work was that subjects actually engaged in rehearsal in the time allotted them. This may seem so obvious that it hardly needs mentioning, but this assumption has been an important source of misunderstanding regarding the hypothesis. If total time is clocked at 10 seconds but a subject spends only 5 seconds actually rehearsing an item and the other 5 seconds daydreaming, thinking about other items in the list, or just wondering what this task is all about, the total *effective* or *functional time* for that item is only 5 seconds, not 10 seconds. In situations where the total-time hypothesis was not supported, Cooper and Pantle argued that functional time did not correspond with *nominal* (clock) *time*. For example, the total-time hypothesis is frequently not supported when study times are fairly long. Subjects in laboratory studies of memory are not, as you can imagine, as devoted as Ebbinghaus was. They frequently have trouble keeping their minds on the task, especially when the presentation times are long. We can reasonably assume that subjects often use a relatively lengthy presentation time to think about other things or to do nothing.

The total-time hypothesis has been important to psychologists in their thinking about the role of rehearsal and its effect on memory. When the conditions stated by Cooper and Pantle are met, the hypothesis often provides a useful index of how much will be remembered. Of particular interest to psychologists have been those situations where the hypothesis is not supported, even when the conditions stated by Cooper and Pantle apparently have been met. Later in this chapter we will examine some of those situations.

REHEARSAL IN A MULTISTORE VIEW OF MEMORY

In Chapter 3 we described the memory theory of Atkinson and Shiffrin (1968, 1971). It is a representative model for the multistore models of memory that flourished in the early 1970s. Much of the research on rehearsal was designed to test certain assumptions of this model. According to this theory, there are two major memory stores—short-term (STS) and long-term (LTS). It was therefore necessary to describe how information gets from one memory store to another. In this respect, Atkinson and Shiffrin (1968) and others who have advocated multistore approaches were quite clear on the role of rehearsal: it keeps information "alive" in the short-term store. Without rehearsal, information was assumed to decay or to be displaced by new information. This is the conclusion that researchers have tried to draw from the results of the Peterson and Peterson (1959) study but that is still a matter of debate.

Besides temporarily holding information in the STS, rehearsal was also assumed to be an important mechanism for transferring information to a more permanent state. According to Atkinson and Shiffrin (1968, p. 115), "any information in STS is transferred to LTS to some degree throughout its stay in the short-term store." For example, consider your earlier attempt to memorize the nine-digit number. According to the original Atkinson and Shiffrin model, as you repeated the number to yourself, the number was gradually deposited in the long-term store. Eventually, you would be able to keep it (in LTS) without further rehearsal.

The analysis of performance in a free-recall task has been particularly important in examining the role of rehearsal in multistore approaches, such as that of Atkinson and Shiffrin. Therefore we will now turn to a description of this particular memory task and describe some experiments using free recall that were designed to investigate the role of rehearsal in establishing a memory.

FREE RECALL

Free recall and the serial position curve

The first use of the free-recall task is credited to E. A. Kirkpatrick (1894), a researcher who, as part of a developmental study of memory, asked "the pupils of a typical school and college in all grades from the third primary up" (p. 602) to learn the names of ten common objects when the object names were either spoken or written or the objects were displayed. The students were asked to write down, immediately after the last item was presented, all the names they could remember. No instructions were given as to the order of recall. Kirkpatrick observed that few of the pupils "gave the words in order, and it was quite noticeable that the first and last words were less frequently omitted than any others" (p. 606). Kirkpatrick also found that showing the objects led to better memory than speaking or writing their names, something that has been of theoretical importance in theories of memory stressing imagery (see Chapter 13).

In a free-recall task the items to be remembered are usually presented one at a time with the subject "free" to recall the items in any order. As Kirkpatrick observed, most individuals do not recall the items in the order in which they were presented. Further, there is a definite tendency for items at the beginning (primacy effect) and end (recency effect) of the list to be recalled better than items in the middle. This relationship between the position of an item during study and its probability of recall in a test produces a serial position curve of the type shown in Figure 4-1. To construct a serial position curve, plot the percentage of times (or probability) an item is correctly recalled at each of the serial positions in the list. In Chapter 2 we examined serial position curves based on errors made when subjects attempted ordered recall of short lists of digits. Traditionally, serial position curves following free recall are based on number correct at each serial position, not on the number of errors.

The particular shape of the serial position curve changes slightly depending on such variables as the length of the lists, whether subjects are tested on more than one list, the modality of presentation (for example, auditory versus visual), and presentation rate. For instance, the curve in Figure 4-1 best describes recall when subjects have had experience with many lists of the same length. Recall following only one list is not likely to exhibit such a dramatic recency effect. Some of the variables affecting the serial position curve have figured prominently in discussions of a multistore view of memory. An extensive discussion of these factors has been given by Glanzer (1972).

The free-recall task was not often used during the first part of this century, chiefly because the analysis of verbal learning and memory was dominated by a stimulus-response (S-R) theory of associative learning. For example, the task Ebbinghaus used to study memory was that of serial learning, in which subjects learn to anticipate the next item in serial order. Serial learning, as well as paired-

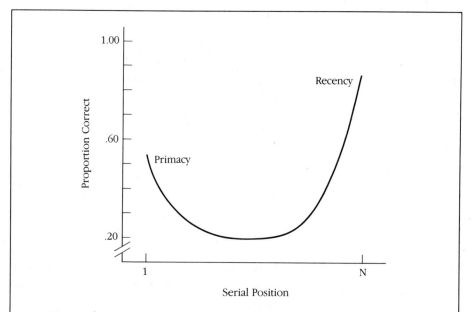

Figure 4-1. Idealized serial position curve—percent correct as a function of list position—in situations where subjects have had experience with more than one list.

associate learning, in which subjects learn an association between pairs of items (see Chapter 6), was considered to be more conducive to the study of associative learning than was free recall. This is not to say that free recall has escaped the analysis of S-R theorists; it hasn't. But it has been relatively recently, partly under the pressure of an information-processing approach to memory, that S-R theorists have turned their attention to free recall in an attempt to show how the principles of associative learning might explain performance in this task (for example, see Postman, 1972).

A multistore theory of free recall

Multistore theories, such as that of Atkinson and Shiffrin, had a ready explanation for the serial position curve seen in Figure 4-1. Remember that, in this view, as information is rehearsed in STS, it is deposited in LTS. Therefore, as items are presented to subjects in a free-recall task, they are placed in the STS, where they are rehearsed until new items displace them. (STS is presumed to have a limited capacity.) New items are continually being exchanged with previously presented items, but items experienced earlier are recirculated through the STS whenever possible for additional rehearsal. The primacy effect in free recall logically follows from such a description, because items from the first part of the list necessarily have the most opportunity for rehearsal. Therefore items presented early in the list have the greatest chance of being in LTS.

The recency effect can be understood by considering the subject's strategy when the signal for recall is given. Several new items have just been presented and are being rehearsed in STS, but they have had little opportunity for substantial rehearsal. If, when the signal for recall is given, the subject immediately "dumps" these items from the STS, recall is guaranteed. The recency effect, as you might have observed by looking at Figure 4-1, rarely extends more than three or four items back into the list. Examination of subjects' response output tends to confirm this strategy because subjects often recall first the items that were presented last.

This analysis of the serial position curve based on a multistore model can be tested rather simply by imposing a delay between the final item and the signal for recall, a delay that is filled with some kind of rehearsal-preventing activity (for example, number counting). Following a sufficient delay (say about 30 seconds), there should be a significant reduction in the probability of recall for the final items in the list. Why? Remember, these items have just been put into memory and have had little opportunity for rehearsal. Therefore they should have little chance to get into a long-term memory store. We know from the research reviewed in Chapter 3 that if items are only briefly registered and rehearsal is prevented, these items are likely not to be available for recall after 30 seconds.

Glanzer and Cunitz (1966) performed such an experiment. Their results are shown in Figure 4-2. They engaged subjects in number counting for 0, 10, or 30 seconds before the signal for free recall was given. Fifteen 15-word lists were presented to each of the subjects; the three delay conditions were presented five times each. As you can see, the results were as predicted. The recency effect was eliminated when recall was attempted after 30 seconds of number counting. Because such a short delay presumably would not be expected to have much of an effect on items in a long-term store, the primacy portion of the curve was relatively unaffected.

The serial position effect in free recall

Purpose

To demonstrate the characteristic serial position curve obtained in free recall and to show how the curve is affected by a delay between presentation and test.

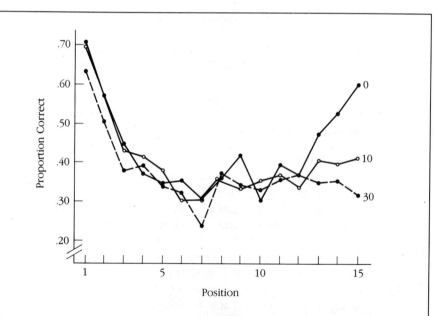

Figure 4-2. Serial position curves for free recall following 0-, 10-, and 30-second delays between presentation of the last item and the signal for recall. *(From "Two Storage Mechanisms in Free Recall," by M. Glanzer and A. R. Cunitz. In* Journal of Verbal Learning and Verbal Behavior, *1966, 5, 351–360. Copyright 1966 by Academic Press, Inc. Reprinted by permission.)*

Materials

Materials required are 15 monosyllabic nouns of Thorndike and Lorge (1944), frequency A or AA (see Table C in the Appendix), and one three-digit number. Several different random orders of the 15 words are needed. In fact, if it is possible, each subject serving in the experiment should be presented a different random order of words for recall.

Procedure

The task is free-recall learning. The 15 nouns are read aloud to subjects, who are instructed to try to remember the words in anticipation of a memory test. After reading instructions to the subject, the experimenter reads aloud the 15 words at the rate of one word about every 2 seconds. Half the subjects are signaled to recall the words immediately after the 15th word is read. The other half are given a number and asked to count backward by threes until they are signaled to stop (30 seconds). Then recall is requested. Therefore there are two conditions: immediate free recall and free recall after a 30-second delay. The several random orders should be used equally often in each condition.

Instructions to Subjects

This is a memory experiment involving free recall. I will read to you a list of words, one word at a time, approximately one word every 2 seconds. I cannot tell you exactly how long the list is. However, I want you to try to remember as many of the words I read as possible because later I will ask you to write them down for me. You may recall the words in any order you want. Simply try to remember as many as you can. Please have a pencil and paper ready, but do not begin to write down the words until I signal you by saying "OK, write." Do you have any questions? Ready?

(After reading the list of 15 items, subjects in the no-delay group are signaled to recall immediately after the 15th word is read. Subjects in the 30-second-delay group are told at the end of the list: "Now, please start counting backward by threes from this number until I ask you to stop." The number is read aloud and the sign for recall is given after 30 seconds of counting.)

Summary and Analysis

To plot a serial position curve, you must determine the proportion of words recalled at each of the 15 serial positions across all the subjects. This is done separately for each condition. That is, for each item recalled, you determine the serial position the item occupied during presentation of the list. Adding across all subjects, calculate the number of words recalled from the first, second, third, ... and fifteenth serial positions. Then divide each of the 15 totals by the total number of subjects in the condition. For example, if there are ten subjects and five of them recalled the word presented in the second serial position, the proportion recalled for that serial position is .50. For each condition plot a serial position curve by graphically showing the proportion recalled at each presentation position. If statistical analysis is desired, you may compare the two groups by obtaining two scores for each subject in both the no-delay and the 30-second-delay conditions. These scores could be the number recalled in serial positions 1–7 and 9–15 for each subject. A 2 × 2 analysis of variance can be performed with delay (zero and 30-second) as a between-subjects variable and serial position (1–7 and 9–15) as a within-subjects variable.

Recommended Minimum Number of Subjects
Total of 24; 12 in each of two conditions.

Based on an experiment by Glanzer and Cunitz (1966).

Although the results shown by Glanzer and Cunitz are in line with predictions from a multistore view (as well as some other views), is it reasonable to assume that subjects are actually rehearsing and recalling items in the way described by the theory? As you have seen, unless we resort to looking through one-way mirrors and trying to read lips (something that is highly unreliable with adults), the mental activity of rehearsal is generally not open to inspection. More certain evidence of the role played by rehearsal in producing the serial position curve comes from studies designed by Rundus and Atkinson (1970; Rundus, 1971) that required subjects to rehearse aloud. This *overt rehearsal task* has been very important to our understanding of rehearsal processes.

Overt rehearsal in free recall
In the first of several important studies using a free-recall task, Rundus and Atkinson (1970) asked eight Stanford University students to remember several lists of 20 common nouns. Each item was shown for 5 seconds. The restriction placed on the students was that they fill the presentation interval by repeating aloud items from the current list. The particular items chosen by the students to repeat were up to them. However, because presentation was visual, there was always one item in front of them. Rehearsals were recorded, and the mean number of rehearsals as well as the probability of recall for each list item were compared. The results of this analysis are seen in Figure 4-3. Early items in the list (primacy items) received the most rehearsals, and, as expected, recall was high for them. Items at the end of the list (recency items) were also well recalled, but these items had the fewest numbers of rehearsals. Clearly, the relationship Rundus and Atkinson obtained between rehearsal and recall offered substantial support for the multistore analysis of free recall.

Two questions are frequently asked about the overt rehearsal technique. First, people question whether subjects under instructions to rehearse aloud

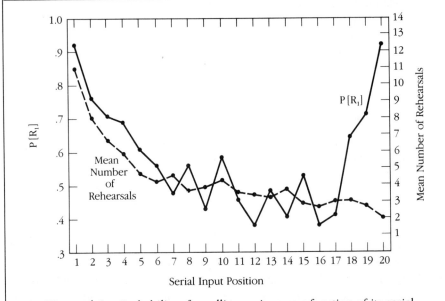

Figure 4-3. Probability of recalling an item as a function of its serial position and the mean number of rehearsals given each item at each serial position. *(From "Rehearsal Processes in Free Recall: A Procedure for Direct Observation," by D. Rundus and R. C. Atkinson. In* Journal of Verbal Learning and Verbal Behavior, *1970, 9, 99–105. Copyright 1970 by Academic Press, Inc. Reprinted by permission.)*

are in fact rehearsing the way they do when they are on their own and rehearsal is silent. It would be an unhappy state if theories of rehearsal were worked out on a task that was not representative of the way information is usually processed. Studies on this question, however, have failed to find any substantial differences when silent and aloud rehearsal instructions are varied and memory performance is analyzed (for example, Murdock & Metcalfe, 1978). Another frequently heard question is whether primacy effects are due solely to rehearsal. The primacy effect in free recall is not necessarily explained completely by differential numbers of rehearsals. Although this is certainly a factor, there appear to be factors other than rehearsal that may contribute to this effect. A slight primacy effect remains even when subjects are instructed to rehearse all the items in the list the same number of times (Fischler, Rundus, & Atkinson, 1970).

REHEARSAL TYPES

If you have gotten the idea that things so far look pretty good for the multistore theory of free recall and, in particular, for the role rehearsal plays in this task, you are right with us. These studies helped to strengthen the argument, introduced in the previous chapter, that primary and secondary memory involve different memory systems. However, part of the fun in this science game (and clearly part of the frustration) is that a theoretical rug can often be pulled out from under a theory on the basis of a simple experiment. It is to this rug-pulling show that we will now turn.

Craik (1970) reasoned that, if after a series of free-recall tests an additional recall test was given for items in all the lists, the recency items would be the worst recalled of all the items. As we have seen, these items, because they were rehearsed the least, should have the least opportunity to get into a long-term memory system. A retention test for all the list items, because it came after several lists had been studied and tested, would presumably tap only secondary memory processes. In Craik's study students were presented ten different lists of words, each followed by an immediate free-recall test. Each list had 15 words, and items were presented at a 2-second rate. After the students recalled items from the tenth list, Craik sprang a surprise. He asked the students to write down as many items as they could remember from all ten lists.

The probability of recall as a function of the serial position in the 15-item lists is shown in Figure 4-4 for both immediate recall and the "final" recall. As predicted, on the final recall test, when items supposedly must be remembered from secondary memory, the recency items yielded the poorest recall. These items were the best recalled on the immediate test. The relatively poor recall for items from the end of these lists, as revealed in this final recall test, is called the *negative recency effect*. These results are entirely in accord with predictions made from the multistore view. But Craik was to offer a different explanation for these serial position effects. To get to this explanation, we need to introduce an alternative theory.

Craik and Lockhart (1972) argued that memory should not be conceptualized in the manner of Atkinson and Shiffrin and other proponents of a structural view of memory but rather in terms of the kinds of analyses carried out in the process of acquisition. In the levels-of-processing approach, it is assumed that memory strength is directly related to the "depth" to which an item was taken. For the present, you can think of depth of processing, or a deeper level of analysis, as being equivalent to more meaningful or semantic elaboration. For example, remembering the nonsense syllable *FAC* as an important *FACT* to learn would represent semantic elaboration. According to Craik and Lockhart, this would be a deeper level of analysis than merely repeating *FAC* over and over again. We will have much to say about elaboration and the levels-of-processing theory in Chapter 12. Our point here is to examine what this theory has to say about rehearsal.

Craik and Lockhart (1972) distinguished between two kinds of rehearsal. Type I rehearsal, they said, has the sole function of maintaining an item's avail-

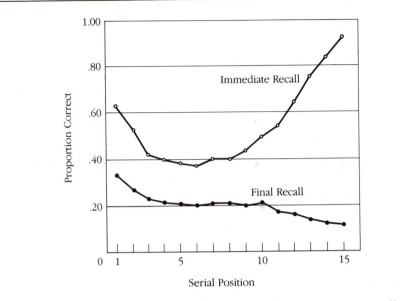

Figure 4-4. Serial position curves for immediate and final free recall. The relatively poor recall for the recency part of the lists on final recall is the *negative recency effect. (From "The Fate of Primary Memory Items in Free Recall," by F. I. M. Craik. In* Journal of Verbal Learning and Verbal Behavior, *1970, 9, 143–148. Copyright 1970 by Academic Press, Inc. Reprinted by permission.)*

ability in memory. It involves the "repetition of analyses which have already been carried out" (p. 676). It can be contrasted with "Type II processing which involves deeper analysis of the stimulus" (p. 676). Only Type II rehearsal is assumed to lead to memory improvement. Type I and Type II rehearsal are more frequently referred to as *maintenance* and *elaborative rehearsal,* respectively (see also Woodward, Bjork, & Jongeward, 1973). We will use these terms in the following discussion. You may see some similarity between maintenance and elaborative rehearsal and simple and active rehearsal, identified by Cooper and Pantle (1967) in their discussion of the total-time hypothesis. However, keep in mind that Craik and Lockhart assumed that maintenance rehearsal does not lead to any increase in memory strength. We must assume that maintenance rehearsal is not the same as simple or rote rehearsal. In other words, under maintenance rehearsal the total-time hypothesis should not be supported.

In a subsequent experimental paper, Craik and Watkins (1973) argued that the negative recency effect found in multitrial free recall was due to maintenance rehearsal. They stated that final recall of recency items was poor, not because rehearsal was simply less for these items (as suggested by the Atkinson and Shiffrin model), but because rehearsal for these items was of a different kind from that for the other items. That is, subjects used maintenance rehearsal for items at the end of the lists. According to the theory, no memory improvement should be expected from this type of rehearsal. Thus a negative recency effect would be expected.

To make their point that it is quality, not quantity, of rehearsal that is important, Craik and Watkins presented undergraduates at the University of Toronto with 12 lists of 12 words under overt rehearsal instructions. Two other characteristics of their procedure were important. First, all the subjects were told that the last four items in each list were particularly important. To emphasize this point, the end items appeared in block letters. Also, subjects were told that recall of each of the lists would be asked for immediately or after a short (20-second) delay. But unlike the delay conditions of Glanzer and Cunitz, the interval was unfilled and subjects were encouraged to rehearse aloud during it. Half of the 12 lists were tested immediately and half were tested after the 20-second delay. Finally, unannounced to the subjects, a final recall test was required for all 144 words when recall of the last list had been completed.

The results of the Craik and Watkins experiment are presented in the three panels of Figure 4-5. In the top panel the mean number of rehearsals is shown for items in both the immediate and 20-second recall lists. Note that the instructions to pay attention to the last four items along with the unfilled interval had the intended effect of dramatically increasing the number of rehearsals given to the last four list items. Rehearsal of these last items was at least as high as for the first items in the list. The left panel shows the recall scores for the immediate and delay groups and shows little difference between the two conditions. In both conditions students took the less-than-subtle hint and recalled nearly perfectly the last four items. In the right panel of the figure are the results for the final recall test with the two conditions (immediate and delay) presented separately. The important result is that, although rehearsals for the last four items were very high, especially in the delay condition (see top panel), there was no effect in the final recall test for these additional rehearsals. Repeating the end items all those times did not appear to affect long-term retention.

Craik and Watkins argued that the results are what would be expected given that the students were rehearsing only to maintain the final items so as to recall them on the immediate test. Under these conditions the levels-of-processing argument expects no lasting effect on memory.

The results of the Craik and Watkins experiment revealed serious deficiencies in both the total-time hypothesis and the multistore view of rehearsal. Substantial increases in rehearsal per se did not lead to an increase in retention, as these views of memory would predict. Further, these results raised a problem of definition. You may recall that the total-time hypothesis predicted a relation-

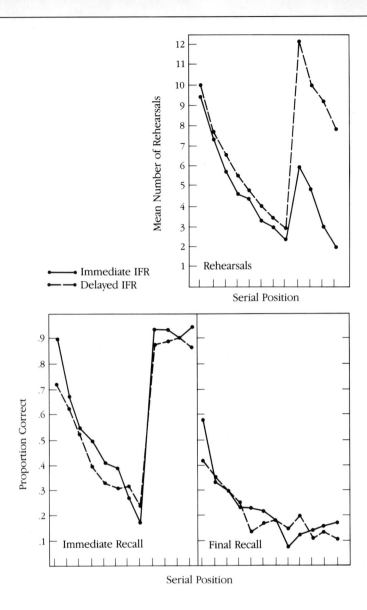

Figure 4-5. Average number of rehearsals (top panel), proportion correct on the immediate free-recall test (left panel), and proportion correct on the final recall test (right panel) as a function of serial position. The two lines in the graph show the results for groups that recalled after no delay or after a 20-second delay in the immediate free-recall test. *(From "The Role of Rehearsal in Short-Term Memory," by F. I. M. Craik and M. J. Watkins. In* Journal of Verbal Learning and Verbal Behavior, *1973, 12, 599–607. Copyright 1973 by Academic Press, Inc. Reprinted by permission.)*

ship between amount of rehearsal and amount remembered for simple rehearsal. This type of rehearsal was defined as the repetition of items in the form in which they were presented. This definition also appears to fit maintenance rehearsal, except that under maintenance rehearsal there is the implication that subjects do not intend to do anything but hold the items temporarily. Clearly what Craik and Lockhart suggest is that there is a form of rehearsal that does not benefit long-term retention. Does maintenance rehearsal really have no effect on long-term retention? Researchers quickly set out to find a satisfactory answer to this question. Results of some of this research are reviewed in the next section.

REHEARSAL: DICHOTOMY OR CONTINUUM?

Not all psychologists accepted at face value the results of the Craik and Watkins (1973) experiment, and other researchers have not always obtained the same null effect on memory when maintenance-type rehearsal has been investigated (for example, Nelson, 1977). Confusion surrounding this issue has been generated to a large degree by differences in methodologies used to identify and control rehearsal activity. For example, researchers have sometimes simultaneously manipulated frequency of rehearsals and actual presentations of an item. This would be the case when subjects rehearse the same item presented on several different occasions. Therefore both number of actual presentations and amount of mental repetition are being varied. As will emerge from our discussion in the next chapter, there is evidence that simply presenting an item on more than one occasion may often, if not always, produce an effect over and above that found with one presentation. This may be entirely different from the effect of repeated "mental" presentations. Further, as long as methods differ widely from experiment to experiment, there is always the possibility that some procedural difference may explain discrepant results.

A clearer picture of the role that sheer mental repetition plays in memory may emerge from a newly created memory paradigm designed to study specifically this aspect of rehearsal. Working independently, Glenberg, Smith, and Green (1977) at the University of Wisconsin and Rundus (1977) at the University of South Florida proposed a variation on the Brown-Peterson technique in order to study maintenance rehearsal. In this new procedure subjects are told they are participating in a short-term memory experiment, the purpose of which is to investigate number retention. On each trial of the experiment, the subject is presented a short series of digits (for example, 8 6 4 1) and then engages in a distractor activity that requires the overt repetition of a word or words. Subjects are asked to repeat the words for various intervals (for example, 4, 6, and 12 seconds), and then they are tested for their recall of the *digits*. You should recognize this procedure as similar to that of the typical Brown-Peterson task but with the words and numbers having reversed roles. Following a lengthy series of trials in which digit recall has been tested, the subjects are asked to try to remember the words they have been repeating. Rundus (1977) called this procedure a *distractor recall task*.

This paradigm has several unique advantages for the study of rehearsal activity. Because repetition of the words is aloud, the actual number of rehearsals can be measured; and, by varying the retention interval, the experimenter can control the number of repetitions of an item. It is also possible to alter slightly the nature of the distractor activity in order to examine additional variables. For example, subjects can be requested to say aloud two words rather than one, or words rehearsed one time can be used again after another digit series, in order to examine the effect of actual repetitions on memory. However, although Rundus and Glenberg and his associates have used nearly identical procedures, they came to different conclusions regarding the effect of maintenance rehearsal. One reason for the difference appears to be related to the type of memory test given for the distractor words. In one case recall was measured, and in the other recognition was tested. Because we have been dealing almost exclusively with recall up to this point, we will examine first the Rundus experiments, which used recall to measure rehearsal effects on memory.

In the first of a series of experiments, Rundus (1977) used the distractor recall task to examine memory for words that subjects had been repeating for 4, 8, or 12 seconds. All subjects received 36 digit-recall trials, with 12 trials at each of the three retention intervals (or rehearsal times). Half of the subjects were told that at the end of the digit-recall task their memory for the words they had been rehearsing would be tested; the other half were not told about a later word test. Presumably, these latter subjects engaged in maintenance rehearsal. The intentional learning group is an important part of this experiment. For example, if for some reason there was no difference in recall as a function of rehearsal time, even when subjects were told that their memory would be tested, we would have to ask whether there was something about the task that was interfering with memory processing. Without this control group we might, in the presence of null results, wrongly conclude that the amount of rehearsal activity did not make a difference, when, in fact, there was something about the task itself that contributed to no memory improvement. For example, Rundus found that probability of recall for the intentional learning group was .15, .23, and .28 for the three increasing intervals of rehearsal (4, 8, and 12 seconds). This increase was statistically significant and indicated that recall in this condition increased with amount of rehearsal.

When recall was examined as a function of increasing rehearsal time for the maintenance rehearsal group, recall probabilities were .12, .15, and .15. No significant increase in recall was found in the incidental group as a function of increasing amounts of rehearsal. Rundus, on the basis of this experiment and others in this series, concluded that there appears to be a type of rehearsal that does not improve memory. This, of course, is what Craik and Lockhart (1972) had predicted in their levels-of-processing view. Needless to say, the total-time hypothesis breaks down under these rehearsal conditions.

Using the same distractor recall task, Glenberg, Smith, and Green (1977) and Glenberg and Adams (1978) have shown that increasing the amount of maintenance rehearsal can lead to increased performance when recognition memory is tested. In other words, although subjects apparently do not show differential recall of distractor words, they do show differential recognition memory as rehearsal times are varied. But the differences are only slight. In one experiment the probability of correctly recognizing a distractor word increased from .65 to .67 to .74 as rehearsal time increased from 2 to 6 to 18 seconds. Apparently, when a more sensitive test of retention is used, some effect on memory is revealed for maintenance-type rehearsal (see also Woodward, Bjork, & Jongeward, 1973).

Glenberg and Adams (1978) argued that a dichotomy does not exist between maintenance and elaborative rehearsal. They suggested instead that rehearsal must be viewed as a continuum—anchored at one end by the minimal processing performed in a situation in which maintenance is clearly the subject's goal and at the other end by the elaborative type of rehearsal that takes place in more complex verbal processing. Theoretical distinctions are often made in absolute terms, and such has been the case for rehearsal types. In light of current research findings, we must begin to look to the middle ground rather than the extremes and acknowledge, as Postman (1975b, p. 303) noted when discussing types of rehearsal, that "dichotomies have a way of becoming points on a continuum."

POSTSCRIPT

We can safely say that memory researchers will continue to ask questions regarding the nature of rehearsal for some time to come. Even if we do accept the conclusion that the most "mindless" repetition has an effect on long-term retention, the effect is clearly small and is apparently revealed only when a recognition test is given. Further, if maintenance rehearsal lies on a continuum with rote rehearsal and elaborative rehearsal, it remains for psychologists to specify the nature of this continuum. As yet there are no satisfactory answers to the question of how these types of rehearsals may be differentiated. It also remains to be seen whether amount of rehearsal can be lawfully related to retention, as psychologists attempted with the total-time hypothesis. Finally, the original assumptions about rehearsal made in the multistore model of Atkinson and Shiffrin (1968) no longer appear valid, although Rundus (1977) has recently suggested that Atkinson and Shiffrin were not really talking about maintenance-type rehearsal when they discussed the transfer of information from one memory store to another.

Given that maintenance rehearsal has practically no effect on long-term retention, what good is it? One answer may be that it is a particularly efficient way to process information that is needed only temporarily. When you think about it, there are many cognitive activities that require such processing. For example, doing math problems often requires that we "carry" a remainder. Looking up a telephone number and rehearsing it until we have finished dialing is another example. However, when long-term retention is the goal, we would be advised to "shift" to a more effective type of rehearsal. (Characteristics of elaborative processing will be discussed more fully in Chapters 12 and 13.)

Shifting to an effective rehearsal activity when long-term retention is required is not necessarily something all learners do. Shaughnessy (1981) used a variation of the Craik and Watkins (1973) task to investigate whether subjects change their rehearsal activities according to task demands. He asked several groups of students to study ten 5-word lists. Some of the subjects were given a recall test 20 seconds after each list was presented. As in the Craik and Watkins experiment, these subjects were encouraged to use maintenance rehearsal to hold the items in memory until recall was requested. Specifically, the subjects were instructed to overtly pronounce the items over and over again during the short retention interval. Other subjects were treated exactly the same except they were not given any particular instructions about how to rehearse. It was assumed that subjects in this "free-rehearsal" group would recognize that only maintenance-type rehearsal was needed for this task and would process the items in the same manner as the maintenance-instructed subjects. A third group of subjects was presented the same 5-word lists for study but was told that a final recall test would be given for all 50 words after the tenth list was presented. These subjects received no immediate tests and were permitted to rehearse in whatever manner they wished. As in the Craik and Watkins experiment, all subjects were given a final recall test, although this was unexpected for only some of the students in the Shaughnessy experiment.

Subjects expecting only immediate tests and allowed to choose their own manner of rehearsal were expected not to differ from the maintenance-instructed groups on the final recall test. And they did not. Therefore it can be assumed that subjects in this free-rehearsal group used maintenance rehearsal to process the list items. However, subjects expecting a final recall test and permitted to rehearse in whatever manner they wished should, in order to improve long-term retention, do something other than use maintenance rehearsal. Shaughnessy found evidence that subjects did that, but the difference in final recall between the free-rehearsal group expecting only immediate tests (and presumably using maintenance rehearsal) and the free-rehearsal group expecting a final recall test was very small (10.05 and 12.50 mean recall, respectively). Further, when subjects in these two groups filled out a postexperimental questionnaire asking about the nature of their rehearsal activities, in both free-rehearsal groups the most frequently reported activity was "constantly repeating the items over and over silently." Apparently, not all subjects, or even most, switched to a more effective rehearsal strategy when a long-term retention test was expected.

A reasonable interpretation of these findings is that most subjects are not aware of the differential effectiveness of various types of rehearsal. Shaughnessy, in fact, presented evidence of this by asking subjects in a subsequent experiment to predict which of two pairs of items would be more likely to be recalled. One pair had been studied under maintenance rehearsal, and the other pair had been studied under elaborative rehearsal (creating mental images). Subjects judged the pairs studied under the different rehearsal conditions to be equally likely to be recalled, even though recall following elaborative rehearsal was 60% greater than following maintenance rehearsal. Therefore we need to understand better those conditions that lead people to rely on maintenance rehearsal when more effective strategies are called for.

Summary

Although mental repetition, or rehearsal, is a common memory strategy for most of us, it is, in fact, something we have learned. Young children, for instance, may not rehearse when asked to remember something. Although rehearsal is generally associated with processing of verbal material, there is evidence for a kind of rehearsal or prolongation of an event when pictures or images are to be remembered. Rehearsal has figured prominently in theoretical accounts of memory processing. The total-time hypothesis predicted a direct relationship between amount remembered and amount of rehearsal. Atkinson and Shiffrin (1968) originally suggested that rehearsal has the effect of moving information from a short- to a long-term memory store. Their multistore theory was often used to explain the typical serial position curve obtained in a free-recall task. Experiments in which recall was delayed following the presentation of a free-recall list, as well as studies using the overt rehearsal technique, have supported the multistore view of rehearsal.

However, both the total-time hypothesis and the multistore view of rehearsal are challenged by theorists who advocate a levels-of-processing approach to memory. In this view, maintenance and elaborative rehearsal are distinguished. Only elaborative rehearsal, which is generally associated with some type of semantic analysis, is assumed to lead to long-term reten-

tion. In fact, the results of several studies show that increases in the amount of maintenance rehearsal do not necessarily lead to increases in recall, although there may be a small effect on recognition memory performance.

What has emerged from this line of research is evidence that we can (and do) make choices in how we rehearse information. Further, there is evidence that these choices may not always be what is best for retention. It is important to recognize the differential effectiveness of various "types" of rehearsal and to investigate the conditions under which they will be used effectively.

Recommendations for further reading

Students of human memory should take time to read Ebbinghaus's famous monograph, *Memory* (1885/1964). With the power of hindsight, we can see the problems an undue emphasis on rote repetition has produced. Nevertheless, this pioneer investigator began work on many of the issues still researched today, including the effect of repetition, the nature of forgetting, and the effect of distributing practice. There are no convenient summaries of the literature on rehearsal, but the story can be pieced together by reading several of the articles mentioned in this chapter. Particularly helpful are discussions found in the articles by Glenberg, Smith, and Green (1977), Glenberg and Adams (1978), and Shaughnessy (1981). Research supporting the original total-time hypothesis is reviewed in an article by Cooper and Pantle (1967). Although beset with problems, this hypothesis accounts for a wide number of experimental findings. Finally, as we will suggest at other points, the article written by Postman (1975b) provides an insightful analysis of many contemporary issues, including rehearsal. (Readings relevant to the levels-of-processing argument are found at the end of Chapter 12.)

5

Memory Consolidation

Introduction/overview

Just how long does it take for a memory to become fixed in our minds? Is something to which we attend immediately deposited in the brain in a form that is capable of lasting the 60, 70, or more years we may have need to recall it? Or does it take time for a memory to become permanently stored in the brain? For many years psychologists have suggested that memory consolidation, *the process by which memory achieves a stable if not permanent form, takes a significant amount of time. However, estimates of the time needed for memory consolidation to be completed have ranged from seconds to hours to even days. In fact, as you will see in this chapter, there is evidence that the processes contributing to a stable memory may continue for years.*

Research into the question of memory consolidation has largely centered on the study of memory deficits that accompany cerebral trauma (for example, concussion), brain disease, or surgical intervention in the brain. In this chapter we will look at what has been learned about memory con-

solidation from the study of two major classes of memory disorders—retro-grade and anterograde amnesia. Both these memory phenomena were at one time thought to provide compelling evidence for a disassociation of primary and secondary memory. Specifically, retrograde and anterograde amnesia were seen as evidence for theories that divide memory into short-term and long-term stores. Today this interpretation no longer appears war-ranted. But we are getting ahead of our story. Exactly what are retrograde and anterograde amnesia, and what do they tell us about memory formation? Answering these questions is our goal in this chapter.

RETROGRADE AMNESIA

A case history

Russell and Nathan (1946, p. 291), in a review of memory problems asso-ciated with injury to the head, described the following case history:

A greenkeeper, aged 22, . . . was thrown from his motor cycle in August, 1933. There was a bruise in the left frontal region and slight bleeding from the left ear, but no fracture was seen on X-ray examination. A week after the accident he was able to converse sensibly, and the nursing staff considered that he had fully recovered consciousness. When questioned, however, he said that the date was in February [1922], and that he was a schoolboy. He had no recol-lection of five years spent in Australia, and two years in this country working on a golf course. Two weeks after the injury he remembered the five years spent in Australia, and remembered returning to this country; the past two years were, however, a complete blank as far as his memory was concerned. Three weeks after the injury he returned to the village where he had been working for two years. Everything looked strange, and he had no recollection of ever having been there before. He lost his way on more than one occasion. Still feeling a stranger to the district he returned to work; he was able to do his work satisfactorily, but had difficulty in remembering what he had actually done during the day. About ten weeks after the accident the events of the past two years were gradually recollected and finally he was able to remember everything up to within a few minutes of the accident.*

After the accident the motorcycle rider was confused and was not able to remember events that had occurred years before the accident, but with the passage of time his memory loss decreased. Memories he recovered during this period were recovered in the order they had been established and not, as might be expected, in the order of their importance. Older memories recovered

*From "Traumatic Amnesia," by W. R. Russell and P. W. Nathan. In *Brain,* 1946, *69,* 280–300. Copyright 1946 by Oxford University Press. Reprinted by permission.

before more recently established memories. But memory recovery was incomplete. He could not remember what happened immediately before the head injury. This type of memory deficit is called *retrograde amnesia* because the memory loss (amnesia) is for events backward in time (retrograde) from the occurrence of the head injury. Retrograde amnesia has been used by many a mystery writer to thicken a plot—for instance, by having a key character forget vital information after being struck on the head—but it has been of considerable interest to memory theorists, too. Let's see why.

Consolidation theory

In 1949, D. O. Hebb proposed a neurophysiological account of an idea that had been around for some time in psychology—that the period of memory consolidation outlasts the event that initiated it. Hebb suggested that, when an event is experienced, it is first represented in the brain in the form of neural activity. This can be thought of as a kind of electrical reverberation. The activity stage, or reverberatory period, of memory processing permits temporary storage of the memory. The memory does not, according to Hebb, achieve a stable or perhaps permanent form until a second stage occurs. At that time, specific physiological changes take place in the brain—for example, an alteration of brain synapses or changes in brain chemistry. This second stage brings about permanent storage of the memory. As you no doubt recognize, the multistore theories of memory, such as those of Broadbent (1958) and Atkinson and Shiffrin (1968) discussed in previous chapters, are consistent with Hebb's theory of memory consolidation. These theories assume information is held only temporarily in a short-term store before being transferred to a long-term store. For many researchers, the brief holding of information in a short-term store is equivalent to the activity, or reverberatory, stage of memory processing hypothesized by Hebb. Transfer of information to a long-term store is considered equivalent to the structural changes suggested to occur during the second stage of memory fixation.

Retrograde amnesia could also be predicted on the basis of Hebb's two-stage theory of memory consolidation. For example, consider how the theory would account for the memory loss seen in the motorcycle rider we just discussed. The rider's memories for the events in the interval immediately prior to the blow on the head would still be in the reverberatory stage of memory processing. The fall from the motorcycle would interrupt this activity; therefore the second stage of processing, when the brain is physically modified to store the event, never took place. Why the initial retrograde amnesia may extend over a rather long period of time and then shrink or why memory for remote events generally recovers before memory for more recent events has never been adequately explained by consolidation theory. These observations have led some researchers to speculate that the longer a memory has been established, the less susceptible it becomes to interference. Research to be reviewed later appears to support this idea.

Retrograde amnesia and electroconvulsive shock

Numerous experimental treatments—including anoxia, hypothermia, and the application of various chemical substances directly to the brain—have been used to induce retrograde amnesia in laboratory animals. However, the most commonly used agent has been electroconvulsive shock (ECS). This treatment is basically the same as that sometimes used in electroconvulsive therapy of severely depressed mental patients. Therefore retrograde amnesia has been studied not only by training animals in a particular task and then assessing retention following ECS but also by asking mental patients to learn material prior to regularly scheduled electroshock therapy and then testing retention after treatment. The ECS treatment consists of passing a strong electrical current through the subject's cerebrum. Because the shock produces physical convulsions, clinical patients undergoing electroshock therapy receive a muscle relaxant before treatment and are physically restrained to guard against injury.

An experiment by Duncan (1949) was an early attempt to test the consolidation theory using ECS with laboratory animals. The question in this study, as it has been in most studies of this kind over the years, was how long after a learning experience ECS could be given and an effect on memory be observed. The time between a learning trial and the application of ECS wherein some effect on memory is seen is called the *retrograde amnesia gradient*. As we have indicated, the length of this gradient has been a matter of considerable debate for some time in psychology. Duncan used an active avoidance procedure that required a rat to move to one side of a two-chambered box in order to avoid an electric footshock in the other chamber. On each trial the rat was placed in the shock side of the apparatus and received footshock after 10 seconds if it had not yet moved to the safe side. Once they experience footshock, the animals would normally be expected to learn to run to the other side when placed in the shock side. The major independent variable in Duncan's experiment was the interval between a learning trial and the administration of ECS. At intervals ranging from 20 seconds to 14 hours following a run to the safe side, the animals were picked up by the experimenter and given ECS by means of electrodes attached to ear clips. A control group did not receive ECS. If ECS erases memory for the footshock, the experimental animals should be slower to learn to leave the shock side than the control animals.

Duncan's results are shown in Figure 5-1. The figure shows the mean number of successful avoidance runs for 18 trials across 18 consecutive test days, for the various experimental groups as well as the control group. When ECS

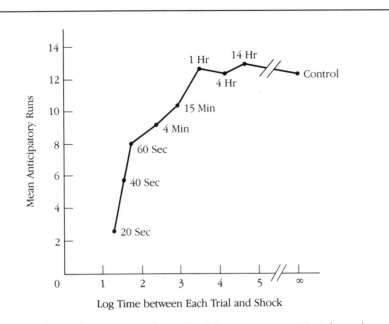

Figure 5-1. The mean number of avoidance runs over 18 trials made by different groups of rats that differed according to the interval between the learning trial and ECS. Intervals are expressed in log units. *(From "The Retroactive Effect of Electroshock on Learning," by C. P. Duncan. In* Journal of Comparative and Physiological Psychology, *1949, 42, 32–44.)*

was given within an hour of the trial, the experimental animals were significantly impaired in their avoidance learning, relative to the animals in the control group. However, when ECS was applied an hour or more after the trial, the experimental animals did not differ from the control animals. The retrograde amnesia gradient apparently extended up to one hour.

Although the results of Duncan's experiment suggested that memory consolidation takes as much as an hour to be completed, critics argued that the results did not necessarily reveal interference with memory processing (for example, Coons and Miller, 1960). The possibility was raised that conditioned fear due to the repeated ECS treatments may have caused the animals to "freeze" in the shock side of the apparatus and therefore not show normal avoidance learning. It was also possible that the animals in Duncan's experiment were, in a manner of speaking, choosing the lesser of two evils. If the animal stayed where it was and received the relatively mild footshock, it could avoid the ECS. The poorer avoidance learning of the experimental animals might therefore reflect a punishment gradient, not an amnesia gradient.

Chorover and Schiller (1965) provided an experimental demonstration of retrograde amnesia that seemed to eliminate many of the interpretive difficulties found in Duncan's and similar experiments. At the same time, they provided evidence of a considerably shorter retrograde amnesia gradient. The task was passive avoidance learning. On the first day the animal was placed on a platform raised several inches from the floor of the apparatus. As soon as it stepped down, it received an aversive footshock. Chorover and Schiller varied the time between the footshock and a single ECS treatment. Retention was measured 24 hours after receiving the footshock. If the animal has learned from its experience, it should tend to stay on the platform at the time of the retention test. Note that explanations of avoidance behavior that involve conditioned fear and freezing by animals or that suggest ECS acts to punish the animal must also predict that the animal would stay on the platform after treatment. The hypothesis that ECS disrupts memory consolidation predicts that the experimental animals will step off the platform during the retention test as if nothing had happened to them.

Chorover and Schiller found that animals receiving footshock followed by ECS did in fact appear to lose their memory for the footshock; but this happened only when the footshock-ECS interval was 10 seconds or less. When ECS was given within 10 seconds after footshock, experimental animals showed significantly shorter step-down latencies than animals given ECS at intervals longer than 10 seconds or than animals receiving only footshock. The retrograde amnesia gradient was drastically shortened. The idea that memory consolidation did not last longer than a few seconds was intuitively more appealing to investigators than the suggestion that minutes or even hours might be involved. Permanent retrograde amnesia exhibited by individuals experiencing head injury is rarely for periods longer than a few minutes before the traumatic event (Russell & Nathan, 1946). Yet, as was the case with previous experiments in this area, things were not as simple as they appeared.

Amnesia and cerebral trauma

Not all investigators using a passive avoidance technique and ECS to investigate retrograde amnesia have come to the same conclusion as Chorover and Schiller regarding the time needed for memory consolidation. Estimates of consolidation time have varied from experiment to experiment, apparently because of slight changes in procedural details and possibly because researchers have not all used the same animal species (Chorover, 1976). The time for memory consolidation for a rat was apparently not the same as for a mouse or a chicken. Estimates of consolidation time even differed depending on the strain of rat used in the experiment. In the face of this incredible diversity of results,

Chorover (1976) reluctantly concluded that finding a single estimate of consolidation time based on ECS studies may be impossible.

The theoretical assumptions underlying the ECS-produced retrograde amnesia gradient also came to be questioned (for example, Lewis, 1969). The initial assumption behind the use of ECS was that the application of cerebral shock served to disrupt the reverberatory period of memory processing and thereby prevented permanent memory fixation of recently experienced events. As we have seen, the phenomenon of retrograde amnesia is compatible with this assumption. However, it is also possible that amnesia arising from cerebral trauma is caused by disturbances in the storage or retrieval phases of memory. For example, suppose a memory becomes fixed in the brain in a relatively brief period of time, perhaps a fraction of a second. The effect of cerebral trauma could be to disrupt memory organization—scramble things, so to speak—so that the memory is not meaningfully ordered with other memories. The act of remembering would be like looking for a paper you had filed in a drawer of papers that just dropped to the floor, scattering the contents. Similarly, it is possible that neither fixation nor storage processes are interfered with by brain trauma; instead, retrieval may be blocked. An analogy would be a drawer that does not open to allow you access to its contents. Interference with any of these phases of memory processing, fixation, storage, or retrieval would produce a "loss" of memory and, hence, retrograde amnesia.

Several important series of experiments provided evidence that ECS does not completely prevent fixation of a memory. One such series produced what is called a "reminder effect." Giving experimental animals a second footshock after the initial footshock-ECS treatment but before the retention test reduces or eliminates the memory impairment seen with ECS (Miller & Springer, 1972). The additional footshock is given outside the original training situation. The interpretation offered for this interesting effect is that the second footshock serves as a "reminder," enabling the animal to retrieve a previously inaccessible memory. Another set of experimental demonstrations showed that memory recovers if repeated test trials are given (Quartermain, McEwen, & Azmitia, 1972; Schneider, Tyler, & Jinich, 1974). In one experiment (see Quartermain et al., 1972), animals given footshock followed by ECS did not show retention of the experience 24 or 48 hours later. However, on a third retention test 72 hours after training, the memory had recovered. It was also found that a reminder footshock accelerated the memory recovery observed with repeated test trials. Another series of experiments demonstrated that memory consolidation could take place in less than half a second *if* the animals were well familiarized with the experimental apparatus before the footshock-ECS treatment (Lewis, Miller, & Misanin, 1968, 1969). Familiarization apparently has the effect of making the learning situation a relatively simple one, wherein the footshock experience is more easily integrated with the animal's existing knowledge of its environment (Lewis, 1969).

The results of these various experiments indicate that ECS-induced retrograde amnesia is not necessarily due to memory fixation being interrupted or a newly formed memory being erased. Rather, the evidence shows that a memory can be established fairly quickly but that ECS can interfere with its subsequent expression. Moreover, the problem appears to be with retrieval rather than with storage. For example, it would not seem reasonable to expect a reminder effect unless the original memory was somehow meaningfully stored.

Evidence for retrieval rather than storage deficit is further demonstrated by the finding that ECS can interfere with old but "reactivated" memories just as it does with newly formed ones (Mactutus, Riccio, & Ferek, 1979; Misanin, Miller, & Lewis, 1968). To demonstrate this interesting phenomenon, Misanin, Miller, and Lewis (1968) first trained thirsty rats to approach and drink from a water tube in the side of an experimental chamber. Then they gave all the animals a fear-conditioning trial. They presented a noise stimulus simultaneously with footshock. All this took place in the experimental chamber. One group of animals was given ECS immediately following the fear-conditioning trial and then removed to their home cages. The remaining animals were returned to their home cages after the fear-conditioning trial and were not given ECS at this time. Twenty-four hours later, some of the animals that had received only a conditioning trial were taken to a different apparatus and the noise stimulus was presented, followed immediately by ECS. It was assumed that the presentation of the conditioned stimulus would "reactivate" the memory of the footshock. The question was whether forgetting of the fear stimulus would occur in this reactivation condition and be similar to the forgetting observed when ECS immediately followed the conditioning trial. Animals were tested for retention of the fear conditioning on the next day.

Memory for the fear conditioning was tested by presenting the noise stimulus when the animals were given the opportunity to drink. Conditioned fear will normally cause animals to slow down or interrupt an ongoing behavior. The investigators found that animals given an ECS immediately after the fear-conditioning trial *and* those given an ECS immediately following the "reactivation" of the memory established on the previous day showed memory loss for the conditioned fear. Animals not receiving the reactivation treatment or ECS still remembered the fear-conditioning experience, as evidenced by depressed drinking rates when the noise stimulus was presented.

A memory, once it has been stored, is apparently susceptible to retrograde amnesia if it is activated at the time ECS is delivered. This implies a certain similarity between newly formed memories, which are still in an active state, and older memories, which have been reactivated (see Lewis, 1979). This is certainly an important area for future research and is consistent with recent theories that view primary memory as an active subset of secondary or inactive memory (see Shiffrin, 1976, and Chapter 3). For the present, ECS-induced retrograde amnesia is probably best viewed as being due to retrieval failure rather than to any interruption of memory consolidation (Lewis, 1979; Miller & Marlin, 1979).

The effect of a single presentation

In the original formulation of Hebb's consolidation theory the first, or activity, stage of memory processing was assumed to leave no permanent mark. As we have just seen, the phenomenon of retrograde amnesia was once thought to be consistent with this view of memory formation. Hebb (1961) later did a simple experiment that led him to change his mind regarding this assumption. Each of 40 subjects was given a series of trials that tested his or her memory span for strings of nine digits. There were 24 strings, and the experimenter read each nine-digit string to the subject at the rate of one digit per second. Immediately after hearing the ninth digit, subjects attempted to repeat back the nine digits in the order in which they had been read. Another trial began as soon as recall was completed. Each string contained all the digits 1 through 9; so there were no repetitions of digits in the string. What was unusual about this otherwise simple test of memory span was that the same nine-digit string was repeated on the 3rd, 6th, 9th, . . . and 24th trials. The other 16 strings were different, and none of these was repeated.

Hebb predicted that subjects would not show improvement in their ability to recall the repeated strings because they would not have had time to rehearse these strings. The activity trace set up for the string would be interrupted by the next trial, and the second stage of memory consolidation would not occur. However, the results of this simple experiment were not what a strict version of Hebb's consolidation theory predicted. As seen in Figure 5-2, there was obvious improvement for the repeated strings. Melton (1963) repeated this experiment and showed that an effect of the repetitions was evident even when as many as eight different strings separated the repeated strings. You might be thinking that subjects in this experiment simply "caught on" to the fact that strings are repeated and that this knowledge somehow contributed to the effect. Surprisingly, most subjects did not report noticing the repetitions. Furthermore, when the results were dropped from consideration for those subjects who acknowledged that they knew the strings were repeated, the effect of repetition was still present.

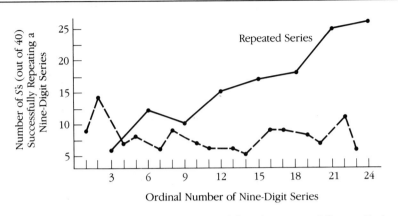

Figure 5-2. Number of subjects, out of 40, who successfully recalled a nine-digit series on an immediate recall test as a function of the position of the nine-digit series in the 24 trials. The "repeated series" refers to the same nine-digit series that occurred in positions 3, 6, 9, 12, . . . , and 24. *(From "Distinctive Features of Learning in the Higher Animal," by D. O. Hebb. In J. F. Delafresnaye (Ed.),* Brain Mechanisms and Learning: A Symposium. *Copyright 1961 by Blackwell Scientific Publications Limited. Reprinted by permission.)*

Memory consolidation

Purpose

To determine whether an event experienced only one time and not rehearsed leaves a "permanent mark" in memory.

Materials

Nineteen different series of nine digits are needed. The digits 1 through 9 are used, each digit appearing only once in each series. Similarity between series of digits is minimized by imposing the restriction that no two digits occur more than three times in the same order across series and that no two consecutive series contain these repetitions. There are actually 24 digit series presented to subjects, but one digit series is repeated on 6 of the 24 presentations.

Procedure

The task is one of measuring a person's memory span. A series of digits is read to a subject at the rate of one digit per second. The subject's task is to repeat the series exactly as it was presented. Recall is begun immediately after the last digit is read. Immediately following attempted recall of a series, another series is presented, and this continues until all series have been tested. Unannounced to the subjects is the fact that the same series of digits is presented on the 4th, 8th, 12th, 16th, 20th, and 24th trials. For each subject a different nine-digit series should be randomly selected to be repeated. The remaining 18 strings should then be randomly ordered for every subject. All subjects should be questioned after the 24th trial as to whether they noticed "anything unusual" about the presentation of the digit series. The purpose of this interrogation is to determine whether a subject realized that a digit string was repeated.

Instructions to Subjects

This is an experiment to see whether your memory span improves with practice. I am going to read to you a series of numbers. You are to listen carefully and then repeat the numbers in the exact order I gave them to you. Don't worry that you can't do this task perfectly every time. Simply do the best you can on each trial. We will do this 24 times. After I read a series of digits and you recall, I will immediately begin another trial. Are there any questions? Ready? (The experimenter must, of course, be prepared to record the subject's responses on each trial.)

Summary and Analysis

The number of subjects correctly recalling a 9-digit series on each of the 24 trials is determined. A string is scored correct only if all digits are recalled in the proper order. A graph can be made showing the percentage of subjects correctly recalling the nonrepeated and repeated series on each trial. It is of interest whether the repeated series shows improvement as a function of number of repetitions (trials). If sufficient subjects have been tested, separate graphs can be constructed based on the performance of subjects who reported that they noticed the repetitions and of those who did not.

Recommended Minimum Number of Subjects

Total of 24.

Based on an experiment by Hebb (1961).

Experiments reviewed in the previous chapter using the distractor recall task developed by Rundus and Glenberg also appear to support the idea that a single repetition leaves some mark on memory. The distractor recall technique asks subjects to rehearse words during a retention interval as part of a memory test for digits. Unexpectedly, subjects at the end of several trials of rehearsing are asked to recall or to recognize the words that have been rehearsed as part of the distractor task. Rundus (1977) found that increasing the time spent in overt maintenance rehearsal did not lead to increases in recall. However, he also found that, when a word was presented on more than one occasion—for example, by using it twice or three times as a distractor item—recall was inevitably enhanced relative to a once-presented item. This was true even when total rehearsal time was held constant. For example, Rundus compared recall of items that had been presented once for 12 seconds of rehearsal with recall of items presented three times, each time for 4 seconds. For this particular comparison, probability of recall was .21 for the 12-second, once-presented item and .40 for the 12-second, thrice-presented item. In other words, recall improved as a function of rehearsal time only when an item was presented on different occasions and not when subjects merely engaged in maintenance rehearsal.

Both the Hebb experiment and the findings from the distractor recall task suggest that it is difficult, if not impossible, to prevent the physical presentation of an item from leaving a mark on memory. This is true whether subjects' processing activity is quickly interrupted (Hebb experiment) or whether subjects are obviously not intending to encode an item (distractor recall task). It would appear, as Melton (1963, p. 19) concluded on the basis of the Hebb data, that "a consolidation process extending over more than a few seconds is not a necessary condition for the fixation of a structural trace." None of the evidence reviewed would appear to contradict this conclusion. Indeed, the evidence can be viewed as saying that memory consolidation is nearly "instantaneous" and that Hebb's original two-stage hypothesis cannot be right (see Lewis, 1979; Miller & Marlin, 1979).

Although apparently quickly formed, not all memories are equally resistant to interference. In an interesting study of mental patients who received electroshock therapy, Squire, Slater, and Chace (1975) found that, following therapy, retrograde amnesia extended for several years prior to the treatment, but memories formed before that time were undisturbed. The memory test required the patients to recognize the names of television shows that had been broadcast for only a single season between 1957 and 1972. Patients were tested both before and after the electroshock therapy. The series of treatments reduced the patient's memory for the shows that appeared one to three years before the treatment, but their memory for shows seen earlier than three years prior to treatment was the same as it had been before therapy. These results suggest that memories become more resistant to disruption with the passage of time. Further, the retrograde amnesia was temporary, indicating, as did the animal studies reviewed earlier, that memories were not erased but for a while could not be retrieved.

ANTEROGRADE AMNESIA

A case history

On September 1, 1953, a young man underwent brain surgery in an attempt to save him from a life of nearly complete incapacitation due to uncontrollable epilepsy. The surgical technique was clearly experimental and the results uncertain. However, the man's epileptic seizures had reached a point that even the heaviest medication did not lessen their severity. Having obtained permission of the patient and his family, the surgeon performed a bilateral resection of areas in the brain known to be involved in epileptogenic activity. Sites within the temporal lobes and, in particular, part of a subcortical structure called the *hippocampus* were destroyed. Psychological analysis following surgery showed that his seizures were reduced and his personality was undisturbed, but his ability to remember was not the same. This famous case history follows.

> **Case 1, H. M.** This 29-year-old motor winder, a high school graduate, had had minor seizures since the age of 10 and major seizures since the age of 16. The small attacks lasted about 40 seconds, during which he would be unresponsive, opening his mouth, closing his eyes, and crossing both arms and legs; but he believed that he could "half hear what was going on." The major seizures occurred without warning and with no lateralizing sign. They were generalized convulsions, with tongue-biting, urinary incontinence, and loss of consciousness followed by prolonged somnolence. Despite heavy and varied anticonvulsant medication the major attacks had increased in frequency and severity through the years until the patient was quite unable to work.
>
> The aetiology of this patient's attacks is not clear. He was knocked down by a bicycle at the age of 9 and was unconscious for five minutes afterwards, sustaining a laceration of the left supra-orbital region. Later radiological studies, however, including two pneumoencephalograms, have been completely normal, and the physical examination has always been negative.
>
> Electro-encephalographic studies have consistently failed to show any localized epileptogenic area. In the examination of August 17, 1953, Dr. T. W. Liberson described diffuse slow activity with a dominant frequency of 6 to 8 per second. A short clinical attack was said to be accompanied by generalized 2 to 3 per second spike-and-wave discharge with a slight asymmetry in the central leads (flattening on the left).
>
> Despite the absence of any localizing sign, operation was considered justifiable for the reasons given above. On September 1, 1953, bilateral medial temporal-lobe resection was carried out, extending posteriorly for a distance of 8 cm. from the midpoints of the tips of the temporal lobes, with the temporal horns constituting the lateral edges of resection.
>
> After operation the patient was drowsy for a few days, but his subsequent recovery was uneventful apart from the grave memory loss already described. There has been no neurological deficit. An electro-encephalogram taken one year after operation showed increased spike-and-wave activity which was maximal over the frontal areas and bilaterally synchronous. He continues to have seizures, but these are less incapacitating than before.
>
> *Psychological Examination.* This was performed on April 26, 1955. The memory defect was immediately apparent. The patient gave the date as March, 1953, and his age as 27. Just before coming into the examining room he had been talking to Dr. Karl Pribram, yet he had no recollection of this at all and

denied that anyone had spoken to him. In conversation, he reverted constantly to boyhood events and seemed scarcely to realize that he had had an operation.

On formal testing the contrast between his good general intelligence and his defective memory was most striking. On the Wechsler-Bellevue Intelligence Scale he achieved a full-scale I.Q. rating of 112, which compares favourably with the pre-operative rating of 104 reported by Dr. Liselotte Fischer in August, 1953, the improvement in arithmetic being particularly striking. An extensive test battery failed to reveal any deficits in perception, abstract thinking, or reasoning ability, and his motivation remained excellent throughout.

On the Wechsler Memory Scale (Wechsler, 1945) his immediate recall of stories and drawings fell far below the average level and on the "associate learning" subtest of this scale he obtained zero scores for the hard word associations, low scores for the easy associations, and failed to improve with repeated practice. These findings are reflected in the low memory quotient of 67. Moreover, on all tests we found that once he had turned to a new task the nature of the preceding one could no longer be recalled, nor the test recognized if repeated.

In summary, this patient appears to have a complete loss of memory for events subsequent to bilateral medial temporal-lobe resection 19 months before, together with a partial retrograde amnesia for the three years leading up to his operation; but early memories are seemingly normal and there is no impairment of personality or general intelligence [Scoville & Milner, 1957, pp. 16–17].*

Although H. M. showed some retrograde amnesia for events occurring before the operation, his most serious problem was of a different kind, something that psychologists call *anterograde amnesia.* H. M. could not remember those things he had experienced since the operation (*antero* literally means "in front of"). He seemed to "recall nothing of the day to day events" (Scoville & Milner, 1957, p. 14). Thirty minutes after eating lunch, he had no recollection of what he had eaten or even that he had eaten. His mother reported that she had to tell him where the lawnmower was kept even though he had used it the previous day. H. M. would read the same magazine over and over again without finding it familiar. Yet, as Scoville and Milner reported, to a casual observer he seemed to be a relatively normal individual because his understanding and reasoning were not diminished by the operation. Observations of patients with case histories similar to that of H. M. indicate a direct relationship between the amount of destruction of the hippocampal complex and degree of memory impairment (Scoville & Milner, 1957).

*From "Loss of Recent Memory After Bilateral Hippocampal Lesions," by W. B. Scoville and B. Milner. In *Journal of Neurology, Neurosurgery and Psychiatry,* 1957, *20,* 11–19. Copyright 1957 by the British Medical Journal. Reprinted by permission.

The anterograde amnesia seen in H. M. following bilateral excision of the hippocampus and surrounding area is similar to that seen in patients suffering from Korsakoff's syndrome, a disorder that strikes chronic alcoholics. In this case the memory deficit apparently arises from a deficiency of vitamin B-1 (thiamine). Alcohol not only does not contain B-1, but the high level of carbohydrates in alcohol increases the body's need for it. Structures within the limbic system of the brain (including the hippocampus) apparently are particularly sensitive to thiamine deficiency (see Rozin, 1976).

Although numerous studies have been done with H. M. to understand more fully the nature of his memory problem, perhaps the most revealing was that by Drachman and Arbit (1966). They compared the memory performance of students from an introductory psychology class with that of H. M. and several patients with similar bilateral hippocampal lesions. Retention was assessed on an immediate memory span task as well as on an extended digit span test. To measure memory span, the subjects were read digit strings of increasing lengths at the rate of one digit per second. After each string was read, the subjects attempted to repeat the digits in the order in which they had been presented. Memory span was defined as one less than the length of the digit string that subjects could not repeat correctly after three attempts. The psychology students had an immediate memory span of 8.30 digits. H. M. and the other hippocampal patients recalled an average of 7.00. Although the students were slightly better than the patients, the difference was not significant statistically. Immediate memory capacity was judged to be approximately the same for patients and students.

In the extended digit span task, subjects were first presented with a digit string of the length they had failed to repeat on the immediate memory test. They were given repeated trials until they remembered that string. A new string of digits, one digit longer than the last, was then presented. The number of trials required to learn consecutively longer strings of digits was recorded. Results of this test are shown in Figure 5-3. The patients required many more learning trials than the student controls in order to remember digit strings at each length. Testing was discontinued if a subject could not remember a particular length of digits after 25 trials. Figure 5-3 shows that the patients were not able to recall a string of 12 digits even after 25 trials; the student controls were able to remember digit strings of 20 after only about 10 trials. Drachman and Arbit concluded that, although the short-term memory ability of these patients was normal, their ability to consolidate new information was severely impaired.

Memory theorists quickly pointed out the relevance of H. M.'s memory deficit to the question of the possible dual nature of memory. For example, it was suggested that here was an individual who, while having an intact short-term store, was not able to get information into a long-term store. In presenting

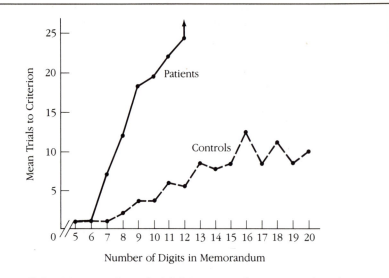

Figure 5-3. Mean number of trials hippocampal patients and student controls took to learn digit series of increasing lengths. *(From "Memory and the Hippocampal Complex," by D. A. Drachman and J. Arbit. In* Archives of Neurology, *1966, 15, 52–61. Copyright 1966 by the American Medical Association. Reprinted by permission.)*

their information-processing approach to memory, Atkinson and Shiffrin (1968, p. 97) stated that the effects of hippocampal lesions on memory were "perhaps the most convincing demonstration of a dichotomy in the memory system." As you will see, over the years this demonstration has become less than convincing.

Interference with fixation, storage, or retrieval

Whether anterograde amnesia results from interference with fixation, storage, or retrieval phases of memory processing is a question just as it was with retrograde amnesia. Drachman and Arbit (1966) and others initially looked at this problem as one of interference with fixation; that is, nothing got registered in secondary memory. However, there is other evidence indicating that anterograde amnesia is due to problems arising in the storage or retrieval stages (for example, Kinsbourne & Wood, 1975; Warrington & Weiskrantz, 1970).

Baddeley and Warrington (1970) tested a patient with symptoms similar to those of H. M., as well as several alcoholic Korsakoff patients, using a variety of standard memory tasks. In most of these tasks the patients behaved as one would expect if there was trouble getting information into secondary memory but if primary memory was undisturbed. For example, in a free-recall task the patients showed a typical recency effect but, relative to a control group, the

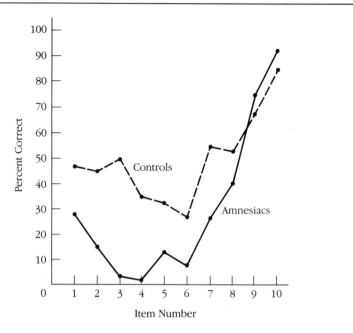

Figure 5-4. Mean percentage correct in immediate free recall as a function of serial position for amnesiacs and controls. *(From "Amnesia and the Distinction between Long- and Short-Term Memory," by A. D. Baddeley and E. K. Warrington. In Journal of Verbal Learning and Verbal Behavior, 1970, 9, 176–189. Copyright 1970 by Academic Press, Inc. Reprinted by permission.)*

primacy effect was impaired (see also Brooks & Baddeley, 1976). These results are shown in Figure 5-4. In a Brown-Peterson type task the patients did not differ from controls in their ability to remember information over the short intervals used in this task. Yet in one task the results were not as expected. Using Hebb's repeated digit task, discussed earlier in this chapter, *both* patients and controls showed an increase with repetitions. Improvement in this task has been interpreted as reflecting increasing strength in secondary memory, so these results are clearly not what would be expected if anterograde amnesia is due to a failure of memory consolidation. Something, in other words, apparently "got in."

Warrington and Weiskrantz (1970) employed a unique form of memory test to provide evidence that the problem was not at the fixation stage but rather during storage or retrieval. The subjects, eight controls and four amnesiacs, were tested for their memory of eight common words read aloud at the rate of one word every 2 seconds. Four types of retention tests were given following

Figure 5-5. Example of fragmented-word stimuli used to test reten-
tion of patients with anterograde amnesia. *(From "Amnesic Syndrome:
Consolidation or Retrieval?" by E. K. Warrington and L. Weiskrantz. In*
Nature, *1970, 228, 628–630. Copyright © 1970 by Macmillan Journals
Limited. Reprinted by permission.)*

a 1-minute period of backward number counting. Two tests were recall and
recognition. The other two retention tests used partial information to cue the
target words. In one test, fragments of the words were presented. In the other,
the first three letters of each word were provided as cues. An example of the
fragmented-word stimuli is shown in Figure 5-5. Subjects were given the most
incomplete form of the word first, then the less incomplete version, and finally
the whole word. The dependent variable was the number of times subjects
needed more than the most fragmented cue to identify the words. Although the
controls were far superior to the patients on the standard recall and recognition
tests, there was no difference between the groups when retention was tested
by the partial-information method. As the authors conclude, "the fact that information in long-term memory is available even after learning by conventional
methods if a particular retrieval method is used is further evidence that it is
inappropriate to characterize the amnesic syndrome as being a failure of registration or consolidation" (Warrington & Weiskrantz, 1970, p. 629).

   You may be thinking that these results are not totally in agreement with
the last conclusion. After all, the patients did poorer than the controls on a
recognition memory test. Recognition, it would seem, would offer the best cue
because the complete word is presented and the subject need only accept or
reject it as a word previously heard. However, Warrington and Weiskrantz argued

that it is just this problem—namely, one of sorting out wrong information—that is at the basis of the amnesiac's memory deficit. They suggested that amnesiacs suffer from a kind of permanent proactive inhibition; that is, previously stored information cannot be inhibited in a normal fashion, and therefore interference arises. Partial information (word fragments or initial letters) works to reveal a memory because the patients know that the information in front of them is part of the target word (unlike a recognition memory test, where there is no sign that the stimulus presented is actually the target word). Presenting parts of the target item apparently allowed the amnesiacs to reject wrong alternatives that did not match the partial information.

Winocur and Weiskrantz (1976) found additional evidence for the unusual level of interference suffered by these amnesiacs. Several Korsakoff patients as well as two other individuals diagnosed as amnesiacs were each asked to learn two lists of 12 pairs of words. The pairs in each list were semantically related, and the same first word appeared in each list (for example, List 1: army–soldier; List 2: army–battle). Of interest is that, after presentation of the first list, recall was the same for the patients and the controls. However, the patients were severely impaired in their learning of List 2. When the nature of errors was examined, it was clear that the patients continued to give appropriate List 1 responses throughout presentation of List 2. They apparently could not inhibit the first-list responses, and therefore interference was produced. In another experiment in this series, the amnesiacs were found to be unable to learn pairs of words that were not semantically related (for example, silent–yellow), confirming the previous evidence that they cannot seem to acquire "new" information. Winocur and Weiskrantz (1976) argued that List 1 learning of the semantically related items was possible only because the responses were limited due to the meaningful relations between the items. Therefore, as in the partial information test used by Warrington and Weiskrantz (1970), the amnesiacs could restrict their responses to the correct answers.

The peculiar nature of the amnesic syndrome

We haven't been altogether fair with you up to this point. There is an important characteristic of anterograde amnesia that we have not yet discussed. Namely, amnesiacs are not impaired in their ability to remember everything. In fact, they sometimes do as well as normals on perceptual-motor tasks (Brooks & Baddeley, 1976; Corkin, 1968). For example, Corkin (1968) tested H. M. on several motor skill tasks, including rotary pursuit and bimanual tracking tasks. In a rotary pursuit task the subject must learn to keep a metal stylus in contact with a target that rotates on a disk. Both time on target and number of contacts are recorded. Bimanual tracking required H. M. to maintain contact with a moving track using a stylus in each hand. Although H. M.'s overall performance level was inferior to that of the controls, he nevertheless showed steady improvement across practice sessions in both the pursuit and tracking tasks. In fact, H. M. showed nearly perfect retention of the pursuit skill one week after the last training trial. These results are particularly dramatic because at any given practice session H. M. would show little if any recollection of how he had done in a previous session.

The ability to learn and remember new musical pieces may also not be lost. Rozin (1976) described an amnesiac with symptoms similar to those of H. M. who was a piano player. He played in the hospital band and one afternoon was asked to learn a new song. He learned the song quickly but the next day did not remember the name of the song or that he had ever played it. However, when a few bars of the song were hummed for him, he said, "Oh, that piece," and immediately played it correctly.

It appears, therefore, that individuals with anterograde amnesia are mainly deficient in "higher-level" cognitive learning (for example, establishing new verbal associations). They do not appear to be deficient in the acquisition of "lower-level" sensorimotor skills (for example, rotary pursuit learning). Yet we saw that amnesiacs showed evidence of higher-level learning when partial information from target words was used to cue retention as well as when the to-be-remembered words were semantically related. Further, amnesiacs show profound effects of associative interference. Is there a way to make sense of all this? Wickelgren (1979) recently proposed a theory that attempts to do just that.

Wickelgren (1979) argued that individuals with hippocampal damage are not able to form new cognitive associations but are capable of strengthening existing associations. Perceptual-motor learning would be an example of learning that requires the use of habits acquired prior to the onset of amnesia. The learning of associations between semantically related words and using fragments of highly familiar words also would be examples of situations where amnesiacs can use existing associations. Because amnesiacs cannot form new cognitive associations, Wickelgren argues that they are particularly vulnerable to associative interference. Several of the studies we have reviewed appear to provide evidence of this assertion (for example, Warrington & Weiskrantz, 1970; Winocur & Weiskrantz, 1976). The theory proposes that hippocampal lesions are likely to prevent new cognitive learning but are less likely to block simple stimulus-response learning or the strengthening of existing associations of any kind. The theory is complex, as is the myriad of data from animal and human studies investigating hippocampal involvement in learning and memory (see, for example, Thompson, 1976). There will no doubt be opponents of any theory that once again places the amnesic deficit in the registration stage rather than in the storage or retrieval stage of memory processing. Yet the theory is a truly impressive effort to tie together the complex findings in this area and will be a necessary complement to future discussions of memory consolidation.

Summary

Hebb (1949) proposed a two-stage theory of memory consolidation: a brief activity, or reverberatory, stage, followed by a stage in which structural changes take place in the brain. Retrograde amnesia, which often results from cerebral trauma, was explained by this theory. It was assumed that cerebral trauma interrupted the activity stage, thereby preventing the second stage, when memory was permanently fixed, from occurring. Hebb's theory was also seen as compatible with multistore theories of memory that suggested that information is held briefly first in a short-term store before being transferred to a long-term memory store. Early laboratory studies of retrograde amnesia using animal subjects indicated that memory consolidation required at least an hour, if not more time. Later studies reduced this estimate considerably, and even more recently studies have provided evidence that retrieval failure, rather than interruption of memory fixation, is the cause of retrograde amnesia. Hebb, too, on the basis of studies showing improvement in retention for briefly repeated strings of digits, altered his original view. Memory consolidation apparently takes place very rapidly, although there is evidence that resistance to interference can continue to grow for some time, perhaps years.

Anterograde amnesia is a memory deficit that results in an apparent inability to learn new information. This type of amnesia was also originally viewed as evidence for a disassociation between primary and secondary memory. However, understanding of this interesting memory problem, which usually involves damage to a brain structure called the hippocampus, is complicated by the fact that not all new learning is prevented. Deficits are seen mainly in the acquisition of new cognitive associations, and acquisition of new motor skills or other simple habits is apparently unaffected.

The history of research on retrograde and anterograde amnesia provides an important example of how our understanding of human memory can be advanced through the clinical analysis of memory disorders as well as through the use of animal subjects. Few can possibly provide a theoretical synthesis of these areas on the scale, for instance, attempted by Wickelgren (1979); but further steps, even small ones, in this direction are needed.

Recommendations for further reading

The book *Short-Term Memory*, edited by Deutsch and Deutsch (1975), contains several important articles describing contemporary research and theory on memory consolidation. An impressive collection of papers describing the physiological bases of learning and memory is found in Rosenzweig and Bennett's (1976) *Neural Mechanisms of Learning and Memory*. The ECS literature and various theoretical arguments are discussed in "Amnesia following Electroconvulsive Shock," an informative chapter by Miller and Marlin (1979) in the book *Functional Disorders of Memory*, and in a recently published article by Lewis (1979). Lewis's article and Wickelgren's (1979) theoretical synthesis of the amnesic literature are necessary reading in order to understand the complexities of this fascinating yet problematic area of research. These articles also make significant headway in bringing together the often disassociated work with animal subjects and contemporary models of human memory. Memory problems and other neuropsychological consequences of long-term alcoholism are discussed in a journal article by Oscar-Berman (1980).

6

Principles of Forgetting: Interference and Altered Stimulus Conditions

Ebbinghaus's Classic Forgetting Curve
Interference Theory
Paradigms
Mechanisms of Retroactive Inhibition
Mechanisms of Proactive Inhibition
Interference in the "Real World"
Altered Stimulus Conditions
Types of Stimulus Contexts
State-Dependent Retrieval

Introduction/overview

Why do we forget so much? Many times after learning something, we find we have forgotten more than we remember. And our memory for day-to-day events often seems to disappear like chalk under the eraser. What did you do this morning? What did you eat for breakfast? You can probably fill in a significant number of details about this morning's activities. But what about the morning exactly one week ago? A month ago? What did you do on those mornings? What did you have for breakfast? Like most of us, your memory for routine activities is likely to be vague, sketchy, and without detail, if you can remember anything at all.

Philosophers and psychologists who have speculated about why we forget no doubt looked at their own memories, as you just did. Early explanations for forgetting were probably not much different from those you might offer. For example, Ebbinghaus (1885/1964), in reporting the results of his systematic study of memory, discussed what were then the popular views of forgetting. Some philosophers, he pointed out, argued that memories are actually permanent but are buried or overlaid by the more intense impressions of the most recent past. Others said that the "tendency" to recreate a memory was suppressed with time, causing it to lose intensity, to fade, so to speak. Yet another idea was that over time a memory broke into its components, leaving only fragments of the original memory. These ideas about the forgetting process have not lost their appeal. The idea that with time a memory fades or becomes fragmented is a part of some contemporary thinking about failures to remember (for example, see Brown & McNeill, 1966).

In this chapter we will discuss two major principles psychologists have offered as explanations for forgetting: interference and altered stimulus conditions. Both were outlined in an article written in 1932 by the famous experimental psychologist John A. McGeoch (pronounced "McGeu"). Since that time, the study of forgetting has been largely identified with the study of interference. McGeoch's account of altered stimulus conditions as an explanation for forgetting had less of an impact on memory researchers, but that is now changing. Forgetting due to changes in the stimulus context present at learning and at a retention test, such as when study and test take place in different rooms, has been found to have sizable effects on retention. This topic of altered stimulus conditions, introduced here, will be discussed further in Chapter 10 when we consider the dynamics of recall and recognition. At this point let us provide some background to McGeoch's classic article. Then we will discuss traditional studies of interference, chiefly those that have used lists of words or nonsense syllables. Later in this chapter we will show how principles of forgetting derived from these investigations are applied to "real world" material such as sentences and prose passages.

EBBINGHAUS'S CLASSIC FORGETTING CURVE

Ebbinghaus (1885/1964) provided the first systematic demonstration of the nature of forgetting. On 163 different occasions between 1879 and 1880, this tireless investigator learned a series of nonsense syllables to a criterion of two errorless recitations (the method used was serial learning). Then, after intervals varying from 20 minutes to 31 days, he relearned the syllable series to the same criterion as the original learning. He measured retention (or its opposite, forgetting) by the *method of savings*. To calculate a savings score, he subtracted the time it took to relearn the syllable list from the original learning time and expressed the difference as a percentage of the original learning time. For example, if learning initially took 1071 seconds and relearning took just 382 seconds, then the savings amounted to 689 seconds, a savings score of 64.3%. Modern memory researchers have not often used the method of savings, or relearning, although it may be the most sensitive measure of retention. In Chapter 10 we will review results of several recent experiments using the method of relearning and will contrast relearning with the more typical measures of retention: recall and recognition. Although Ebbinghaus frequently calculated savings in terms of *time* to learn, savings scores are more often based on the number of trials necessary to learn and then relearn a verbal series. (Because Ebbinghaus was his own subject, it was difficult for him to count the number of repetitions it took him to learn while he was also trying to learn the items. Therefore he relied on a time measure to avoid the distraction associated with keeping track of repetitions. When Ebbinghaus did count repetitions directly, he relied on a string with wooden buttons that he held in his hand during learning. After each successful repetition, he moved a button to the right. A quick glance gave him his results for a particular syllable series.)

Ebbinghaus's forgetting curve is shown in Figure 6-1, which demonstrates the percent savings at retention intervals of up to 2 days. Most forgetting took place soon after learning. In fact, after one hour Ebbinghaus found he had to spend nearly half the original time to relearn the nonsense syllable list. However, as time passed, forgetting was more gradual. Although not shown in Figure

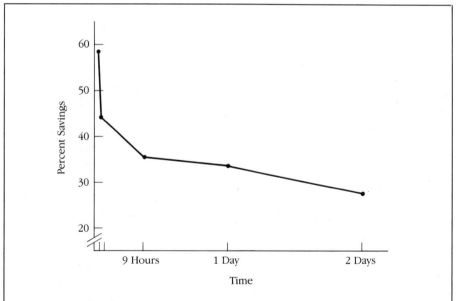

Figure 6-1. Retention of nonsense syllable lists learned by Ebbinghaus as measured by the method of "savings." *(From* Memory: A Contribution to Experimental Psychology, *by H. Ebbinghaus. Copyright 1964 by Dover Publications, Inc. [Originally published, 1885.] Reprinted by permission.)*

6-1, amount of savings dropped only about 12% between 1 and 31 days. For reasons that will soon become apparent, Ebbinghaus's classic forgetting function overestimates the amount of forgetting generally seen when retention is tested soon after learning. However, in accord with Ebbinghaus's findings, rate of forgetting is initially very fast and then slows down as the retention interval increases.

For several decades following the publication of Ebbinghaus's forgetting curve, the most widely accepted explanation for forgetting was *disuse theory,* which assumed that unattended and unpracticed memories fade with time. Another name for this is *decay theory*. We mentioned in previous chapters that loss of information from a visual sensory memory is likely due to decay (Chapter 2), and decay is possibly involved in forgetting from primary memory (Chapter 3). Investigators also harbor the idea that decay can explain some forgetting in secondary memory (for example, Atkinson & Shriffin, 1968), but most forgetting over long retention intervals is thought to involve other mechanisms.

INTERFERENCE THEORY

At about the time many individuals began to look on Ebbinghaus's forgetting curve as reflecting memory decay over time, the seeds of an alternative theory were being planted. Hugo Munsterberg (1889), a student of one of the founders of experimental psychology, Wilhelm Wundt, and a contemporary of William James, is said to have foreseen the major principles of an *interference theory* with informal experiments based on his own simple motor habits (cited in McGeoch, 1942). Having been accustomed to carrying his watch in one pocket, Munsterberg shifted it to another pocket and then observed his fumbling and delay when subsequently asked for the time. You have likely experienced similar hesitations or perhaps have initially gone in the wrong direction when an item was changed from a familiar location to an unfamiliar one. The basic principle of interference theory is that new habits conflict with old ones.

Experimental evidence accumulated only gradually in favor of an interference theory of forgetting, and the theory was not considered officially launched until 1932. In that year McGeoch published an article entitled "Forgetting and the Law of Disuse," in which he forcefully rejected the idea that time per se accounts for anything in nature. For example, although we might speak of rust forming on metal as a function of "time," McGeoch pointed out that what we really mean is there are chemical reactions and other events occurring *in time* that bring on the rust. Similarly, if we think of a memory as disappearing with "time," we must mean there is something going on in time that produces memory loss. And although there may be yet undiscovered brain processes creating the rust of the mind that is forgetting, McGeoch argued that more readily observable processes were the major cause of forgetting. Specifically, he suggested that interference from things experienced after the acquisition of to-be-remembered information was the major cause of forgetting.

One of the more famous early experiments to support the interference theory of forgetting was that of Jenkins and Dallenbach (1924). It was based on an apparent anomaly in Ebbinghaus's otherwise systematic forgetting curve. Close inspection of the curve (see Figure 6-1) reveals that forgetting appears to "slow down" during the 15 hours between the retention intervals of 9 and 24 hours. The 15-hour period contained an 8-hour sleep period, so Jenkins and Dallenbach suggested that sleep might slow forgetting. They argued that Ebbinghaus's activities while he was awake contributed more to the rate of forgetting than did sleep.

To test their hypothesis, they asked two Cornell University students to live in the memory laboratory from April to June and to learn lists of ten nonsense syllables either early in the day or just before going to bed. Retention was tested after 1, 2, 4, or 8 hours of either sleep or normal daily routine. When learning was at night, before the subjects went to sleep, testing retention meant subjects had to be awakened at various times during the night. To test retention of material learned in the morning, subjects were simply told to report back to the memory lab at a particular time. The results of this classic study are shown in Figure 6-2. Clearly, more forgetting was observed when the subjects were awake during the retention interval than when they were asleep. Because time was held constant, only the nature of the activity during the retention interval differed. A decay theory did not appear to explain these results. Forgetting was attributed to interference with original learning produced by the subjects' activities while they were awake.

Researchers continue to be interested in retention differences shown by awake and sleeping subjects. Intriguing hypotheses are that different stages of sleep, such as dream and nondream periods, or different hours of the sleep period (early versus late) affect memory differently (see Ekstrand, 1972). Results have been equivocal as to the possibility that retention depends on whether subjects have been dreaming, but there is some positive evidence that subjects remember more following the first 4 hours of a night's sleep than following the second 4. This latter result was obtained by comparing retention of subjects who learned before going to sleep and then were tested halfway through the 8-hour sleep period with retention of subjects who learned after being awakened in the middle of the night and were tested following the second half of the sleep period. Forgetting was significantly less following the first half-night's sleep than the second half. In fact, forgetting during the second half of the sleep

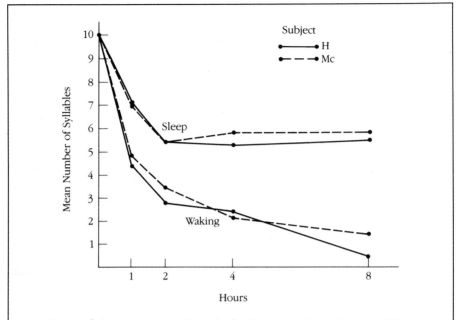

Figure 6-2. Average number of syllables remembered by two subjects after varying time intervals of waking or sleep. *(From "Obliviscence during Sleep and Waking," by J. G. Jenkins and K. M. Dallenbach. In* American Journal of Psychology, *1924, 35, 605–612.)*

period was not much different from that shown by subjects who were awake for 4 hours (Ekstrand, 1972).

Perhaps the sleep researchers' most interesting result is that retention is better when sleep comes immediately after learning than when it is delayed. In an experiment described by Ekstrand (1972), the subjects learned a list of paired associates and were then tested for retention after 24 hours. One group of subjects went immediately to bed for 8 hours after learning and then spent the remaining 16 hours of the retention interval going about their usual daily activities. The other group of subjects stayed awake for 16 hours and then slept the last 8 hours of the retention interval. Recall of the paired associates was better for the immediate-sleep group than for the delayed-sleep group. Because sleep during a retention interval is apparently best for memory if it occurs immediately after learning, this is something to think about the next time you are up late preparing for an exam. We must also point out that these results do not appear to be explained by a simple interference theory. Amount of sleep and activity within the retention interval was the same for the two groups, but retention still differed.

Paradigms

In Chapter 3 we provided a brief introduction to the interference theory of forgetting and introduced the major paradigms used to investigate interference-produced forgetting. We strongly suggest you reread that material now. (Don't worry. The savings will be appreciable.)

According to interference theory, when something is learned and then retention is tested, forgetting of original learning is produced either by learning that occurred prior to original learning *(proactive inhibition)* or by learning that occurred after original learning but before a retention test *(retroactive inhibition)*. Both proactive and retroactive inhibition are defined by the difference in retention between an experimental group and a comparison group. These major paradigms are described in Table 6-1 in a slightly different form than we showed you in Chapter 3. Let us briefly explain Table 6-1.

Interference theory has traditionally been stated in terms of the conflict between associations of stimuli and responses—for example, between the stimulus "What time is it?" and the response of reaching for your watch. Remember that in Munsterberg's little experiment he changed only the response. An interference task in which the stimulus remains the same (request for time) but the response changes (new pocket) is called A-B, A-C. Interference of this kind can be measured using either a proactive or retroactive inhibition paradigm. Subjects in the comparison group do not learn the potentially interfering associations, either A-C in a retroactive inhibition paradigm or A-B when proactive inhibition is assessed. Rather, these subjects usually perform some unrelated activity during this time.

TABLE 6-1. Major Verbal Learning Paradigms Used to Investigate Forgetting

	Learn	*Learn*	*Test*
Retroactive Inhibition			
Group E	A-B	A-C	A-B
Group C	A-B	———	A-B
Group E	A-B	A-B$_r$	A-B
Group C	A-B	———	A-B
Proactive Inhibition			
Group E	A-B	A-C	A-C
Group C	———	A-C	A-C
Group E	A-B	A-B$_r$	A-B$_r$
Group C	———	A-B$_r$	A-B$_r$

Another major paradigm that has played an important role in understanding interference processes is that described as A-B, A-B$_r$. In this case stimuli and responses are the same between two occasions of learning but are "repaired." For example, assume Munsterberg was used to reaching for his watch when asked the time and to tipping his hat at the sight of a lady. An A-B, A-B$_r$ task could be created by requiring him to reach for his watch when a lady walked by and to tip his hat when someone asked for the time of day. The A-B, A-B$_r$ task, as you might expect, does not generally involve such outlandish associations. As with the A-B, A-C task, it has been most frequently used in the investigation of verbal habits. For example, an association recently learned between two words, such as car-knife (A-B), is likely to interfere with retention of another association, such as car-house (A-C).

Mechanisms of retroactive inhibition

When McGeoch (1932) presented his now classic arguments against decay theory, he left no doubt as to what he considered to be a major cause of forgetting—namely, retroactive inhibition or the interference due to a subject's activities between original learning and retention test. The specific mechanism operating to produce retroactive inhibition was identified as *response competition* (McGeoch, 1942). Response competition can be nicely illustrated by thinking once again about poor old Munsterberg trying to get his hand in the right pocket. Munsterberg's errors and fumbling when pockets were switched represented to McGeoch the competition between the two responses vying for the same stimulus. In terms of A-B, A-C associations, forgetting was assumed to occur when a new response (C) blocked or somehow inhibited the response of the old association (B). However, response competition was soon shown to be an insufficient explanation for all the forgetting observed in a retroactive inhibition paradigm.

Just as evidence for response competition in Munsterberg's simple experiment was errors made in reaching, researchers have long documented response competition in learning and memory experiments by the number of errors subjects make after learning two lists of items. For example, when a list of A-B associations is learned followed by acquisition of A-C associations, subjects sometimes mistakenly respond with C responses when tested for retention of the A-B associations. Researchers initially assumed that the greater the number of second-list intrusions during first-list recall, the greater was response competition and therefore the greater should be forgetting. Melton and Irwin (1940) showed, however, that the relationship between interlist intrusions (response competition) and forgetting was not this simple.

These investigators required subjects to learn two lists of nonsense syllables by the method of serial learning. The first list was learned for 5 trials and the second list, the interpolated list, was learned for 5, 10, 20, or 40 trials. Another group "rested" for 30 minutes, which was the time needed by the 40-trial group to learn the second list. When subjects in the 5-, 10-, and 20-trial groups finished their interpolated learning, they also rested until 30 minutes were up. This was done to keep time constant for all groups between first-list acquisition and recall. Recall of the first list was then tested. Retroactive inhibition was defined as the difference in retention between the 30-minute rest group and those groups having interpolated learning. Response competition was measured by the number of interpolated list intrusions observed during recall of original learning. Both degree of retroactive inhibition and amount of response competition as a function of number of trials on the second list are shown in Figure 6-3.

Melton and Irwin discovered that response competition as measured by second-list intrusions increased only up to a point and then decreased as a function of the number of trials on the second list. But as you can see in Figure 6-3, forgetting continued to increase with increasing amounts of interpolated learning. Because response competition did not appear to keep pace with the total amount of retroactive inhibition, it could not be the only mechanism responsible for forgetting. An additional factor was involved. Initially labeled

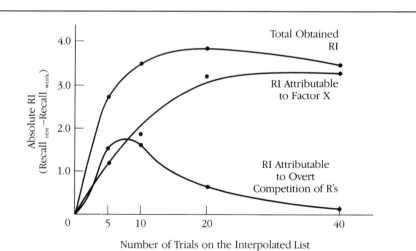

Figure 6-3. Total retroactive inhibition (RI) and amount of RI estimated to be produced by response competition and "factor X," or unlearning, as a function of number of trials on an interpolated list. *(From "The Influence of Degree of Interpolated Learning on Retroactive Inhibition and the Overt Transfer of Specific Responses," by A. W. Melton and J. M. Irwin. In* American Journal of Psychology, *1940, 53, 173–203.)*

"factor X," this second factor was assumed to be the "unlearning" of first-list associations due to interpolated learning. Once unlearned, a response was assumed to be no longer available.

The interference theory of retroactive inhibition was now a two-factor theory: response competition and unlearning. Although many researchers accepted the two-factor theory, unambiguous evidence for the working of an unlearning mechanism was some time in coming. For instance, it was not clear that because subjects could not remember a response, it was no longer available. Conceivably, competition between responses could cause a response to be blocked or inhibited without it actually being unlearned.

Barnes and Underwood (1959) were the first to offer evidence for unlearning when response competition was thought to be minimized. They employed a paired-associate learning task that required subjects to learn two lists conforming to an A-B, A-C relationship. Stimuli were nonsense syllables and were identical for the two lists, but different adjective responses were used in list 1 and list 2 (for example, CAH-crazy; CAH-spoken). The major innovation of the Barnes and Underwood experiment was the introduction of a new method of testing retention, *modified-modified-free-recall* (MMFR). (In an earlier chapter we introduced a free-recall task in which there is no constraint on the way subjects recall responses. A modified free-recall test, MFR, originally referred to a situation in which subjects gave only one response from either of two lists they had learned. As you can see, the MMFR is a "modification" of the MFR test. See Keppel, 1968, n. 3.) After subjects learned the first list of eight paired associates to a criterion of 1 perfect trial, different groups of subjects received 1, 5, 10, or 20 trials on the second list. Then subjects were asked to recall *both* list-1 and list-2 responses. Each of the eight nonsense-syllable stimuli was listed and two spaces provided for the adjectives that had been paired with each stimulus in list 1 and list 2. Given that the recall test was unpaced (subjects could take their own time filling in the responses) and that both responses were required, response competition was not considered a major factor in the MMFR test. (However, see Postman, Stark, & Fraser, 1968.) The question was how many of the list-1 responses would subjects be able to remember after list-2 learning.

The results of the Barnes and Underwood experiment are seen in Figure 6-4. With increasing degrees of list-2 learning, subjects became less able to recall list-1 responses. An association just learned apparently became unlearned, so to speak. But note that unlearning was not complete. There was substantial recall of list-1 responses even after 20 trials on the interpolated list. In fact, unlearning rarely exceeds 50% in retroactive inhibition designs of this sort, a result not necessarily explained by traditional interference theory (although see Petrich, 1975, for an interesting analysis of this problem).

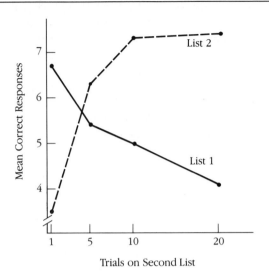

Figure 6-4. Mean number of list-1 and list-2 responses correctly re-called following A-B, A-C learning as a function of the number of trials on the second (A-C) list. *(From " 'Fate' of First-List Associations in Trans-fer Theory," by J. M. Barnes and B. J. Underwood. In* Journal of Exper-imental Psychology, *1959, 58, 97–105. Copyright 1959 by the American Psychological Association. Reprinted by permission.)*

Unlearning of associations

Purpose
To investigate the "fate" of list-1 associations (A-B) after learning list-2 asso-ciations (A-C).

Materials
Eight nonsense syllables (CVCs) with association values between 60% and 73% (Glaze, 1928) are used as stimulus terms (see Table D in the Appendix). Response terms are 16 two-syllable adjectives (see Table E in the Appendix). Adjectives should be selected so as to minimize preexisting associations that might be present between them. Syllables are chosen so that no consonants are used more than twice and four vowels are each used twice.

Two lists of paired associates are constructed (A-B, A-C) by randomly pair-ing each of the 8 syllables with two different adjectives. One set of 8 syllable-adjective pairs is arbitrarily designated as list 1 (A-B) and the other set as list 2 (A-C). (If an experimenter tests more than one subject in each condition, the sets should serve equally often as list 1 and list 2.) Each of the 16 different syllable-adjective pairs is printed on an individual 3 × 5-inch card for presentation to the subjects. Test cards are made by printing each of the 8 syllables on two separate cards, making 16 syllable-only cards. For each list the cards are arranged so the 8 syllable-adjective cards form one set and 8 syllable-only cards make up another set. An additional card with an "X" on it should be inserted between the sets of syllable-adjective cards (study) and syllable-only cards (test) for each list. On the back of each syllable-only card the response term paired with that syllable should be noted.

Procedure

The experiment is best performed with the experimenter sitting at a table across from the subject. The 8 syllable-adjective cards of list 1 are shown to each subject followed by the 8 syllable-only cards. The experimenter should practice presenting the cards so that each card is presented for approximately 2 seconds. Subjects are instructed to study the pairs when both items are present and to say aloud the adjective when only the syllable is presented. After presentation of each study and test sequence (one trial), the cards are shuffled. Therefore each study-test sequence contains a new order of the study and test items. The procedure continues until the subject is able to say correctly all 8 responses in a test series. The number of trials to reach a criterion of one perfect recitation is recorded.

When all eight associations are learned, the experimenter introduces the second list of paired associates. Subjects are told that the procedure for the second list will be the same as that for the first and that although the syllables will remain the same for this list, there will be new response terms. The second list is presented like the first. However, half the subjects are randomly designated to receive only 2 study-test sequences on the second list and the other half receives 12 sequences on the second list. After subjects in the 2-trial condition are finished with list 2 learning, the experimenter should engage them in some form of nonverbal distractor activity (for example, math problems) for about 8–9 minutes, which is the approximate time it takes the subjects in the 12-trial condition to complete list-2 learning (including time for the experimenter to shuffle study and test items). At the end of either 2 trials plus distractor activity or after 12 trials, subjects are presented with a sheet of paper that lists the eight syllables and includes two spaces to write the response terms from each list (for example, CVC, L1 _____ , L2 _____). Subjects are given 4 minutes to try to recall the adjectives that were paired with the syllables in each of the two lists.

Instructions to Subjects

LIST 1

In this experiment you are asked to learn an association between two items, a nonsense syllable and an adjective. The syllable and adjective are printed on cards. A number of cards with these syllable-adjective pairs will be shown to you at a rather rapid rate. Please study the pairs so that if you were to see only the syllable, you could remember the adjective that was paired with it. After all the pairs are presented, a card with an "X" on it will be shown to you. This signals that cards containing only the syllables are about to appear and you should get ready to tell me the adjective that goes with each syllable. I will then shuffle the cards and we will repeat this procedure. We will do this until you are able to remember each adjective when only the syllable is presented. Are there any questions? (No mention is made that a second list will follow.)

LIST 2

Now we will do the same thing with a slightly new list of pairs. The syllables are the same in this list but the adjectives are different. Please try to learn this list as you did the previous one. (No mention is made as to the number of trials to be given.)

RECALL

Now I want you to write down the adjectives that were paired with each of these syllables in the two lists you just studied. You will have 4 minutes to do this. Do not worry if you cannot remember all the adjectives, but try your best and guess whenever possible. Spaces are provided for both list-1 and list-2 adjectives; so when you write down an adjective, try to make sure you identify it with the correct list.

Summary and Analysis

The number of trials each subject takes to learn the first list should be recorded. The 2- and 12-trial groups can be considered equivalent in terms of learning ability if the average number of trials to learn list 1 is approximately the same for the two groups. The main data of concern are the number of responses correctly recalled (and identified with the appropriate list) for the two lists in both the 2- and 12-trial conditions. Therefore each subject provides two scores (number recalled from list 1 and number recalled from list 2). Results may be graphed by plotting the mean number of list-1 and list-2 responses correctly recalled by subjects in the two conditions. Statistical treatment requires a 2×2 analysis of variance, treating locus of recall (list 1 versus list 2) as a within-subjects factor and number of trials on list 2 (2 versus 12) as a between-subjects factor.

Recommended Minimum Number of Subjects

Total of 32; 16 in each of two conditions.

Based on an experiment by Barnes and Underwood (1959). In the original study recall was tested immediately after list-2 learning in all conditions. This means that the time between the end of list-1 learning and the retention test increases with the number of list-2 trials. It could be argued that there are factors other than those associated with list-2 learning operating in this time interval to produce forgetting of the first list. Anticipating this criticism, Barnes and Underwood tested another group of subjects who did not learn list 2 but instead, following list-1 learning, performed a distractor activity for a period of time equivalent to that taken by subjects having the greatest number of list-2 trials. Retention of list-1 responses in this control condition was essentially perfect. These original procedures have been combined here.

As we have noted before, interference theorists have always shown a strong affinity for stimulus-response (S-R) language and for explanations of learning and forgetting in terms of processes similar to those thought to govern conditioning of responses in the animal laboratory. It was only natural, therefore, for researchers in this tradition to view unlearning as a process analogous to, if not the same as, *extinction* (for example, see McGovern, 1964). Most students of learning are aware of Pavlov's (1927/1960) original demonstration of this phenomenon. He first established a conditioned response in his laboratory animal by pairing a neutral stimulus (for example, the sound of a metronome) with a stimulus known reliably to elicit a salivation response (for example, meat powder placed on the tongue of a hungry dog). After sufficient pairings of the sound and meat powder, the sound alone came to elicit a salivation response, the *conditioned response*. Pavlov then sounded the metronome many times without presenting the meat powder. Soon the animal ceased to salivate when the metronome was heard. The cessation of responding brought about by unreinforced presentations of the *conditioned stimulus* (sound) is called *extinction*. Then Pavlov waited for a few minutes and once again started the metronome. The conditioned response of salivation reappeared, a phenomenon called *spontaneous recovery*.

Interference theory maintains that nonreinforced elicitation of B responses during A-C learning leads to extinction of the A-B associations (Postman & Underwood, 1973). Further, it is assumed that verbal associations, once extinguished, will recover with time. That is, verbal associations, like the conditioned associations of Pavlov's dogs, should show spontaneous recovery.

Nevertheless, the idea that extinctionlike processes operate to produce a loss of first-list associations in an A-B, A-C paradigm was challenged by the important finding that specific associations are not actually lost (Postman & Stark, 1969; Postman, Stark, & Fraser, 1968). This is shown when an *associative matching task* is substituted for the MMFR task used by Barnes and Underwood (1959). In an associative matching task, subjects are given stimuli and responses and asked to match them as they appeared during learning. Although subjects cannot recall B responses after A-C learning, they can "recognize" the associations if shown the stimulus (A) and response (B and C) items. However, for retroactive inhibition observed following A-B, A-B$_r$ learning, associative matching does reveal significant amounts of associative loss (Postman, Stark, & Fraser, 1968). Why associations are lost after A-B$_r$ learning but not after A-C learning is one of the unresolved issues of interference theory.

If individual associations are not lost after A-C learning, what produces the response loss Barnes and Underwood (1959) demonstrated? One answer is that unlearning in an A-B, A-C retroactive inhibition paradigm is due to suppression of the entire *set* of list-1 responses. Unlearning, in other words, is due to competition during second-list learning between list-1 and list-2 response sets, resulting in the inhibition or suppression of all list-1 responses. Response set inhibition apparently dissipates significantly over a short interval, as revealed by the spontaneous recovery of responses over relatively short intervals (Postman, Stark, & Fraser, 1968), and can be reduced by allowing subjects to perform a task that "reinstates" the first-list responses before a retention test is given (Postman & Gray, 1978).

An example of response suppression without loss of individual associations is sometimes seen when two foreign languages are learned. Suppose you learn German first and then Swedish. The mechanism of response suppression suggests that while you're learning Swedish, your response repertoire in German may be suppressed. You might find it difficult to readily come up with the German equivalents for English words soon after learning Swedish. However, it is likely that, given a matching task, you could demonstrate that you can still recognize the German-English translations. In order to prevent unlearning due to response set interference, the response repertoires of both tasks must be maintained throughout the acquisition of the second task. For example, if you continued to review your German while studying Swedish, you could prevent unlearning of German. Interestingly, this procedure leads to little interference in learning the second task, at least with pairs of unrelated items (Postman & Parker, 1970).

Mechanisms of proactive inhibition

For many years following McGeoch's formulation of the interference theory of forgetting, memory failures were generally attributed to mechanisms operating in retroactive inhibition—namely, response competition and unlearning. From the point of view of one major researcher in the field, this put an undue burden on interpolated activity as a cause of forgetting. Underwood (1957) reviewed the then-available literature dealing with forgetting of a single list of verbal items over a 24-hour period. The somewhat surprising finding was that subjects could be counted on to forget about 75% of what they had learned. For example, if a list of 12 paired associates was learned, the next day subjects were able to remember only about 3 or 4 of these associations. For Underwood this was just too much forgetting to be explained by an interference theory that relied exclusively on processes operating in retroactive inhibition. He commented on this predicament for the interference theory as follows:

> Most of the materials involved in the investigations cited above were nonsense syllables, and the subjects were college students. While realizing that I am

viewing these results in light of data which McGeoch and others did not have available, it seems to me to be an incredible stretch of an interference hypothesis to hold that this 75 percent forgetting was caused by something which the subjects learned outside the laboratory during the 24-hour interval. Even if we agree with some educators that much of what we teach our students in college is nonsense, it does not seem to be the kind of learning that would interfere with nonsense syllables [Underwood, 1957, pp. 50–51].

Underwood argued that researchers had overlooked perhaps the most significant contribution to forgetting—namely, proactive inhibition. But where did proactive inhibition come from?

Underwood suggested that an important source of proactive inhibition was to be found right in the laboratory. A common practice of early investigators was to provide subjects with practice lists as well as to require them to participate in all conditions of the memory experiment, often serving in a particular experimental condition many times. In other words, although memory for a single list of words might be measured after a 24-hour interval, it was unlikely that this was the only list of verbal items subjects had been required to remember during the experiment. For example, the two subjects in the Jenkins and Dallenbach (1924) study lived in the laboratory for 2 months, being tested and retested in all conditions of this famous sleep investigation. And of course Ebbinghaus, being both experimenter and subject, studied and then tested himself on hundreds of nonsense-syllable lists.

To show that previous laboratory experience affected subjects' retention of a single list, Underwood (1957) went about organizing the memory literature in terms of the number of previous lists a subject had learned while in a particular experiment. The summary of Underwood's findings are shown in Figure 6-5. Most forgetting could be attributed to what the subject had learned previously in the laboratory. Retention of "naive" subjects (those with no previous history of laboratory learning) was not 25%, as previous estimates had suggested, but rather 75–80%.

In order to "explain away" the remaining 20–25% memory loss seen over 24 hours in naive subjects, Underwood and Postman (1960) turned their attention to possible *extraexperimental sources* of proactive inhibition. Given that the typical subject in a memory experiment is approximately 19 to 20 years old, it seemed to these investigators that there were more potent sources of interference in the subjects' prior 20-year learning history than in the 24 hours between study and test of a list of verbal items. Underwood and Postman identified two likely sources of extraexperimental interference. But before we examine these possible sources of interference, let us review briefly the mechanisms believed responsible for proactive inhibition.

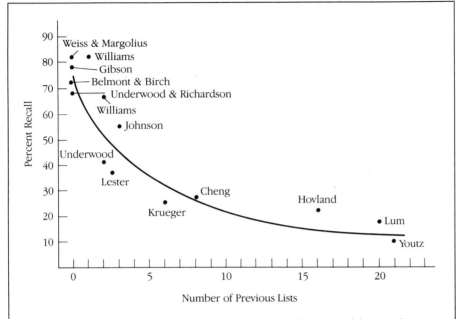

Figure 6-5. Percent recall of a single list as a function of the number of previous lists learned in the experiment. *(From "Interference and Forgetting," by B. J. Underwood. In* Psychological Review, *1957, 64, 49–60. Copyright 1957 by the American Psychological Association. Reprinted by permission.)*

Traditionally, only one mechanism is assumed to operate in proactive inhibition—namely, response competition. Interference theory holds that habits acquired prior to learning intrude or conflict with the acquisition of new learning. These old habits are extinguished, or should we say unlearned, then recover and compete with the newly acquired associations at the time of the retention test. Our friend Munsterberg, in other words, might acquire a new reaching response by suppressing his old habits, but at some later time he is likely to find his old habit once again intrudes. You might have had a similar experience when the combination of a school locker was changed. You soon "unlearn" the old combination when acquiring the new set of numbers. But if you are like most of us, you will occasionally find yourself hesitating in front of your locker, bothered once again by that memory of the original set of numbers. According to interference theory, the intrusion, extinction, and finally spontaneous recovery of old habits accounts for these memory problems.

Underwood and Postman (1960) identified two likely "old habits" that may yield proactive interference with laboratory learned associations. The first was *letter-sequence interference.* Through a long verbal learning history many patterns of letters are very familiar to us. Because laboratory learning will involve numerous new letter sequences—for example, those found in nonsense sylla-bles—our old habits might get in the way of this new learning. It is possible that while learning the nonsense syllable *HET,* such previously established hab-its as *THE* and *HIT* will intrude. The second possible conflict between previous learning and laboratory learning was what Underwood and Postman called *unit-sequence interference.* While subjects acquire an association between two ar-bitrarily chosen words, as *OVER-PRETTY,* previous associations between words (units) might intrude—for example, *OVER-THERE, OVER-HILL.* These old habits would be unlearned and therefore, according to the theory, will later recover and compete with new habits at the time of test. However, Underwood and Postman (1960) could find little evidence for the extraexperimental interference hypothesis, and experimental studies in general have failed to support this idea (see Keppel, 1968). Nevertheless, the rationale behind the extraexperimental theory of interference seemed right even if the data did not. Underwood and Ekstrand (1966) suggested there might be something about the way extraex-perimental habits are acquired that keeps them from interfering with laboratory learning. They argued that associations learned outside the laboratory are dis-tinguished from laboratory associations in terms of their high degree of learning and by the fact that acquisition of these habits has been distributed over long intervals of time. Either degree of learning or distributed practice might keep extraexperimental habits from interfering as these researchers felt they logically should.

Underwood and Ekstrand (1966) attempted to mimic these characteristics of extraexperimental habits by requiring subjects to learn the first of two lists of 12 paired associates for 12, 32, 48, or 80 trials. Learning was either at one sitting (massed practice) or took place over several days (distributed practice). Subjects in the distributed learning condition came to the laboratory on 4 successive days and practiced the paired-associate lists for one-quarter of their required number of trials. Immediately following the four installments in dis-tributed learning or after the required total number of trials in the massed condition, subjects learned a new paired-associate list to one perfect criterion. The relationship between pairs in list 1 and list 2 was A-B, A-C. After 24 hours, recall and relearning of A-C was required (proactive inhibition), and then sub-jects were tested using the MMFR technique for their memory of both list-1 and list-2 responses.

Recall of the A-C associations under the conditions of the Underwood and Ekstrand experiment is shown in Figure 6-6. When learning was distributed over several days, there was no effect of degree of prior list learning on A-C retention. However, when prior learning was massed, proactive inhibition in-creased with increasing amounts of first-list learning. It was as if distributing

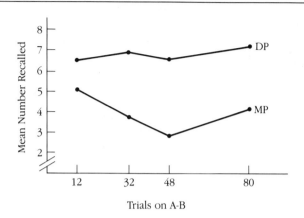

Figure 6-6. Recall of the second list (A-C) as a function of degree of first-list (A-B) learning for both massed and distributed practice on A-B. *(From "An Analysis of Some Shortcomings in the Interference Theory of Forgetting," by B. J. Underwood and B. R. Ekstrand. In* Psychological Review, 1966, 73, 540–549. *Copyright 1966 by the American Psychological Association. Reprinted by permission.)*

learning on the first list (A-B) "protected" later learning from possible interference. Retroactive inhibition measured by recall of list 1 on the MMFR test was also drastically reduced when first-list learning was distributed. It would appear that in order to protect learning from interference of any kind, learning should be under conditions of distributed practice.

Assuming that extraexperimental habits do not interfere, there remain two unresolved problems. First, how does an interference theory explain the forgetting that occurs over 24 hours in the naive subject? Second, how does the theory account for the cumulative proactive inhibition found as number of previous laboratory learned lists increases—for example, as Underwood (1957) described (see Figure 6-5 and Greenberg & Underwood, 1950)? The latter question was investigated by Postman and Keppel (1977), who found only marginal support for an explanation of cumulative proactive inhibition based on an extension of the response set competition hypothesis considered earlier as an explanation for retroactive inhibition. In the following chapter we will discuss more fully the issue surrounding cumulative proactive inhibition, particularly as it is found in the Brown-Peterson paradigm.

Despite the fact that nearly 50 years have elapsed since McGeoch officially proposed the interference theory, the theory has not yet identified the specific mechanisms operating in the simplest situation in which long-term retention is measured. A naive subject comes into the laboratory and learns a list of words.

After 24 hours, the subject returns and takes a retention test. The retention loss, now known not to be particularly substantial, does not seem to be adequately explained by interference theory as presently formulated. With the failure of the extraexperimental interference hypothesis, Keppel (1968) suggested we look again at retroactive inhibition as a cause of forgetting. Because it is nearly impossible to identify specific sources of interference arising in a 24-hour retention interval, Keppel suggested that forgetting might be caused by the sheer amount of activity during the time between original learning and a retention test. However, this nonspecific interference theory has received little experimental validation (Keppel, 1972). It seems that a complete explanation of forgetting will necessarily include factors other than those traditionally associated with the operation of retroactive and proactive inhibition (for example, unlearning and response competition). Another potential source of forgetting is that due to changes in the stimulus context between study and a retention test. Evidence for forgetting due to altered stimulus conditions will be reviewed at the end of this chapter (and in Chapter 10). There may be yet other causes of forgetting as well. Some of these will be discussed in Chapter 14. However, before leaving the story of interference theory, let's examine evidence for interference in the "real world." Although the particular mechanisms governing interference may not be completely clear at this time, the effects of interference on everyday kinds of learning are clear.

Interference in the "real world"

Up to this point the story of interference theory has been about experiments performed in psychology laboratories. To-be-remembered materials have usually been nonsense syllables or individual words arranged into lists with such insipid names as A-C or A-B$_r$. There is no doubt that interference effects found with these kinds of materials and tasks are real. One need only replicate the well-known Barnes and Underwood (1959) experiment to show how easily a set of responses is forgotten after interpolated learning. But what about interference outside the laboratory, with "real" kinds of materials, for instance, sentences and prose passages? The memory psychologists' preoccupation with experimental lists has until recently provided few examples of interference effects in nonlaboratory settings or with prose material. Yet when these experiments have been done, they have provided firm evidence of the reality of interference. We will cite just a few examples of this research to make our point.

Kalbaugh and Walls (1973) examined both retroactive and proactive inhibition for students' memory of school-related material. The subjects were eighth graders enrolled in a public school in West Virginia. The to-be-remembered material was either a short, fictional biography or a science passage describing common minerals. Students in the proactive interference condition learned 0, 2, or 4 passages *prior* to reading the critical passage; students in the retroactive inhibition conditions studied the same number of passages *after* studying the critical passage. The passages were similar in structure but the factual information was different. For example, two selections from different biographical passages were

1. Payton was born in Hampstead, at the end of October, 1795. When he was only 8 years old, his father, who kept a livery stable, was killed by a fall from a horse.
2. Fowler was born in Liverpool, at the end of October, 1810. When he was only 5 years of age, his father, who was a servant, was killed by a robber.

Retention of the critical passage was tested after 6 minutes and after 48 hours. Both retroactive and proactive inhibition increased as the number of passages increased. For example, when the biographical material was learned and proactive inhibition measured, at the time of learning the critical material children answered approximately ten questions correctly when either 0 or 4 previous passages had been learned. After 48 hours, students with no previous learning were still able to answer about nine questions concerning the passage, but those students who learned four previous passages answered only about three questions.

Bower (1974) revealed that interference may operate at one level of prose material while facilitation is operating at another level. He differentiated between the *conceptual macrostructure* of a passage and its *detailed microstructure*. Conceptual macrostructure refers to the main idea or "gist" of a passage. For example, in the first biographical selection of the Kalbaugh and Walls experiments, the major idea is that the main character's father, who had some occupation, was killed somehow when the character was some years old. The microstructure of the passage would include the particular events, facts, names, and other details. Note that in these examples the macrostructure is basically the same between the first and second selection but the microstructure differs. Using a retroactive inhibition design and materials similar to those of Kalbaugh and Walls, but with college students as subjects, Bower (1974) tested retention of a passage following interpolated learning of conceptually related or conceptually unrelated passages. Specific details of the interpolated passages also differed from those in the original passage. He measured retention in terms of the number of "idea units" (macrostructure) as well as the number of specific details (microstructure) subjects recalled. Results demonstrated retroactive facilitation for the macrostructure but retroactive inhibition for the microstructure.

Bower (1978) used sentences to construct paired-associate lists of to-be-remembered items comparable to the more typical A-C and A-B$_r$ lists using syllables or single words. A sentence-subject was paired with a verb phrase of the sentence. For example, some of these sentences appeared as follows:

A-B	*A-C*
The fireman watered his plants.	The fireman gave to charity.
The teacher sold his house.	

A-B$_r$

The fireman sold his house.

Subjects learned three lists, of which the latter two either were interference lists of the type previously described or were unrelated to the original list. An additional group "rested" by rating Peanuts cartoons for "funniness" during the time the experimental groups took for interpolated learning. Retention of the original list of sentences (A-B) was measured in several ways, including paced recall of the verb phrases from the first list, an unpaced test requiring recall of everything paired with a particular sentence-subject (MMFR), and a recognition test. The retention results and the pattern of list intrusions seen during learning were the same for these sentence materials as many laboratory experiments had demonstrated for nonsense syllables or single words. For example, after A-C learning, subjects exhibited significant response loss for A-B items on the MMFR test; however, a recognition test revealed that first-list associations (A-B) between sentence-subject and verb phrases were still intact. Further, the A-B$_r$ task revealed the most interference and also produced associative loss on the recognition test. The results, according to Bower, were not merely because subjects somehow treated this as a "rote-learning" task. On the contrary, subjects, he pointed out, were encouraged to learn the sentences as if they were learning about characters in a small town—that is, as they might when reading a story. He concluded,

> Interference theory can be used to predict transfer and retention of meaningful sentences, of the conceptual knowledge that such sentences express. Although ideas from psycholinguistics are needed to understand relationships among sentences and the knowledge they express, when we turn to questions concerning transfer and retention of propositional learning, it seems, we must fall back upon interference theory and look for some interpretation of the linguistic materials that permits clear application of interference concepts. In the present case, the part of the sentence used to cue its recall (the grammatical subject) was construed to be the "stimulus" or "A term" of an A-B association, and the verb phrase of the sentence was construed

to be the "response" term. With those identifications, the interference theory was easily applied and the experimental paradigms were simply constructed. The results, it must be conceded, were a resounding success for the theory [Bower, 1978, p. 584].

ALTERED STIMULUS CONDITIONS

It is frequently overlooked that in McGeoch's (1932) classic argument against decay theory *two* likely sources of forgetting were mentioned. One was retroactive inhibition. The second was *altered stimulus conditions*. Forgetting, in this view, is due to lack of a proper eliciting stimulus, or cue, for recall caused by changes in the learner's environment. McGeoch (1932, pp. 365–366) stated,

> The absence of the necessary stimulus will occur as a result of change in the stimulating context of the individual. At least until learning has been carried far beyond the threshold, the learner is forming associations, not only intrinsic to the material which is being learned, but also between the parts of this material and the manifold features of the context or environment in which the learning is taking place. Two contexts must inevitably be present. One includes all of the stimulating conditions of the external environment; the other includes all intra-organic conditions. During time these contexts alter and it is at least highly probable that such alteration may remove the necessary eliciting stimulus.
>
> Large numbers of practical cases of forgetting seem to illustrate this. The missionary, after being for some time in this country, loses his command of Chinese, but regains it, with almost no relearning, upon return to the stimulating environment in which he had learned and habitually used the language. One forgets the name of a person who appears unexpectedly, until some trick of speech, mannerism, or other aspect of the individual stimulates recall. The student fails to answer an examination question because it is phrased in a manner to which he is unaccustomed; perhaps the difference is only that synonyms for the familiar words have been used. In these and in many similar cases the material has not been lost from the subject's repertoire, but it cannot be reinstated when wanted; it has been lost functionally for a certain period.*

Memory failure due to the absence of an appropriate retrieval stimulus has been termed *cue-dependent forgetting* (Tulving & Madigan, 1970). As McGeoch indicated, forgetting in this case does not mean a memory is lost, that it is unavailable; rather, the memory is inaccessible for a period. Given the appropriate cues, the memory can be retrieved. This type of forgetting differs from

*From "Forgetting and the Law of Disuse," by J. A. McGeoch. In *Psychological Review*, 1932, *39*, 352–370. Copyright 1932 by the American Psychological Association.

trace-dependent forgetting, which refers to the actual loss of a memory trace from storage. If a memory is no longer recorded (is unavailable), then no amount of retrieval scheming can produce it. Just how much of forgetting is cue-dependent and how much is trace-dependent is an unanswerable question at this time (and maybe at any time). For reasons McGeoch outlined, no psychologist would ever claim that all forgetting is trace-dependent. However, some psychologists have taken the opposite view—namely, that all forgetting is due to the lack of an appropriate retrieval cue. This interesting proposition, which implies that all memories are permanently available but not always accessible, will be discussed further in Chapter 14. For now, let us look at some of the evidence supporting the conclusion that forgetting occurs due to altered stimulus conditions.

Types of stimulus contexts

McGeoch (1932) differentiated between two stimulus contexts: the external environment in which learning takes place and the learner's internal environment. The latter context necessarily includes the learner's thoughts and feelings present at the time of learning as well as the learner's psychophysiological state, such as condition of arousal or mood. Changes in the stimulus conditions of both these contexts have been found to affect retention. However, perhaps because of problems defining internal context, early studies designed to test the effect of altered stimulus conditions generally manipulated the learner's external environment at the time of learning. Specifically, several experiments showed that retroactive inhibition is reduced if original and interpolated learning take place in different environments (Bilodeau & Schlosberg, 1951; Greenspoon & Ranyard, 1957). For instance, a typical procedure was to have subjects in one condition learn list 1 in room A and then learn list 2 in room B. Retention of list 1 was then tested in the same room as original learning (room A). Retroactive inhibition was generally less in this condition than in a condition where learning of list 1 and list 2, as well as the test for recall of list 1, took place in the same room.

An experiment by Strand (1970) added an interesting twist to the results of these early experiments and to their possible explanation. She took subjects for a walk between the learning of the first and second lists. The subjects returned to the same or a different room to learn the second list. When list learning was interrupted in this way, a similar reduction in interference was found regardless of which room the subjects returned to for list-2 learning. Moving about between list-1 and list-2 learning apparently provided a cue by which the two lists could be differentiated. Increases in list differentiation are known to reduce interference (Abra, 1972). Whatever its source, the disruption effect that Strand obtained represents a potential confounding variable when environment is manipulated. Are the results due to a change in context per se or to the disruption caused by changing contexts? Several recent experiments have helped resolve this question by showing relatively large effects on retention due to altered stimulus conditions that do not appear to be explained by the disruption caused by taking subjects from one context to another.

A rather unusual experiment carried out by Godden and Baddeley (1975) tested subjects for free recall of words either on land or underwater. The subjects, members of a university diving club, were asked to learn the words either on land or underwater and were subsequently tested for recall on land or underwater. Therefore the four conditions were learn land-recall land, learn land-recall underwater, learn underwater-recall underwater, learn underwater-recall land. For underwater learning and recall, subjects were outfitted with a special underwater communication device that allowed them to hear the to-be-remembered words as well as listen to the experimental instructions. Subjects recorded their responses on weighted formica boards that were sealed in such a way as to permit them to record responses with pencils in either the water or land environment. When learning or tested on land, the subjects sat next to the water in their diving apparatus. When learning or tested underwater, the subjects sat submerged in about 20 feet of water. There was a 4-minute interval between study and test. This was enough time for subjects in the altered stimulus conditions to change environments between study and test. If memory is context-dependent, then better retention should be seen when learning and recall take place in the same environment than when learning and recall take place in different environments. This is exactly what Godden and Baddeley found. Their results are shown in Figure 6-7. To see whether the results were due to the disruption caused by subjects changing environments, they performed a second experiment that compared retention of subjects who learned and were tested on land. However, half the subjects were required to enter the water between study and test, to swim a short distance, to dive to about 20 feet, and then to return to land. The remaining subjects did not experience this disruption. No difference in retention was found between the subjects who took the swim and those who did not. Apparently, the disruption between study and test does not account for the lower recall of subjects in the altered stimulus conditions of the first experiment.

The context-dependent nature of memory has been revealed when changes in environment have been far less dramatic than moving from land to underwater. Several experiments have replicated the basic finding of Godden and Baddeley (1975) when the context manipulation entailed only a change in rooms (Smith, 1979; Smith, Glenberg, & Bjork, 1978). Perhaps the most interesting of these experiments was by Smith (1979). On the first day all subjects were presented a list of 80 common words for study. Learning took place in a

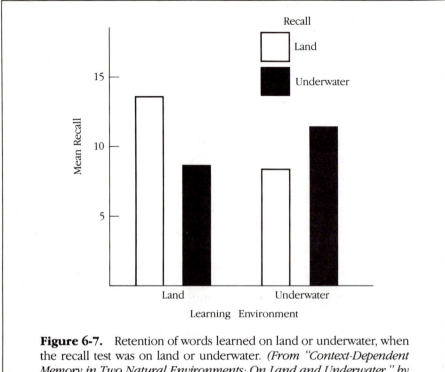

Figure 6-7. Retention of words learned on land or underwater, when the recall test was on land or underwater. *(From "Context-Dependent Memory in Two Natural Environments: On Land and Underwater," by D. R. Godden and A. D. Baddeley. In British Journal of Psychology, 1975, 66, 325–331. Copyright 1975 by the British Psychological Society. Reprinted by permission.)*

distinctive room in the basement of the psychology building. The room had carpeting, orange drapery hanging from the ceiling, posters and pictures on the walls, a table and chairs. Immediately after list learning the subjects were given a recognition memory test for some of the words from the list. Subjects were then invited back for more of the experiment on the following day. The purpose of the partial recognition test was to lead the subjects to think the experimenter was no longer interested in the word list. Therefore subjects would not likely rehearse the words before returning. On the second day all subjects were given an unannounced test of free recall for the words learned the previous day. One group of subjects was tested for recall in the same room as original learning (same-context group). Another group was tested in a different room (different-context group). The second room was on the fifth floor of the psychology building, was filled with computer equipment, and contained a soundproof chamber in which subjects sat for the recall test.

Average recall of subjects in the same-context group was 18. Average recall of subjects in the different-context group was 12. Therefore forgetting was significantly greater under altered stimulus conditions than when learning and recall were in the same environment. However, the most intriguing aspect of Smith's experiment was the average recall of a third group of subjects. These subjects, too, learned and were tested in different rooms. But they were given special instructions to try to reinstate their memory for the first room before attempting recall. Subjects were asked to try to list as many as ten things they could remember seeing in the first room, to take a couple of minutes to think about the other room, and to try to use their memory for the first room to help them recall the words learned there. Recall for this group of subjects averaged 17.2, essentially the same as that found in the same-context group. Apparently, the context of the original learning environment was reinstated by requesting the subjects to think about the first room. Contextual associations can therefore be reinstated by either placing subjects in the appropriate physical context or by instructing them to remember the original learning environment at the time of recall. You might find a practical application of these findings the next time retention is tested in a different environment from that of original learning— for example, when material you learned in a dormitory room is tested in a classroom. Retention may be facilitated by mentally constructing the environment in which learning took place. On the other hand, only a test of recall is likely to be affected. The effects of context change on recognition memory have been harder to demonstrate. Neither a change in rooms nor a change from land to underwater affected retention when a recognition memory test was given (Godden & Baddeley, 1980; Smith, Glenberg, & Bjork, 1978).

State-dependent retrieval

Context changes in an internal environment are also likely to affect retention. That retention is greater when the subject's mood or "state" is the same between occasions of learning and test than when it is different is called *state-dependent retrieval* (Eich, 1980). For example, intoxicated subjects cannot always remember what happened to them while they were under the influence. But, if they're asked the same questions when inebriated once again, their memory is better (see Weingartner, Adefris, Eich, & Murphy, 1976).

Bower, Monteiro, and Gilligan (1978) investigated whether subjects' emotional mood would provide a distinctive context for encoding and retrieving word lists. The subjects were chosen because of their high susceptibility to hypnosis, being "able to enter trance easily" (p. 576). In one experiment subjects were hypnotized and asked to create a happy or sad mood while they learned two different lists of words. They were later tested for retention of both lists in the same or different mood as one of the original lists. For example, a subject in one condition of this experiment learned list 1 while "happy," list 2 while "sad," and then while "sad" was tested first for recall of list 1 and then for list 2. Retention of a particular list was best when recall was tested in the same mood as the list being recalled and worst when recall was in a different mood from that of the target list.

Much of the research investigating memory loss as a function of altered stimulus conditions is relatively recent. This area of investigation has lagged behind investigations of forgetting that emphasize traditional mechanisms of forgetting such as unlearning and response competition. However, this emphasis is changing. For example, although many theorists have steadfastly pursued traditional interference explanations of retroactive inhibition, others have aligned themselves with an explanation of retroactive inhibition based on altered stimulus conditions (Tulving & Psotka, 1971). In general, these memory theorists suggest that conditions giving rise to retroactive inhibition—for example, as seen in A-B, A-C learning—might be better understood through an analysis of stimulus and response encoding during original and interpolated learning than by traditional interference mechanisms (Greeno, James, & DaPolito, 1971; Martin, 1971; Martin & Greeno, 1972). The issues are complex and the outcome of this important dispute among memory theorists is far from clear; however, it appears that changes in stimulus encoding as an explanation for forgetting will supplement rather than replace the traditional framework of interference theory (Postman & Underwood, 1973). One important addition to our understanding of forgetting is the principle of encoding specificity, which will be discussed in Chapter 10.

Summary

Ebbinghaus (1885/1964) was the first person to study forgetting systematically. He showed that most forgetting occurs soon after initial learning. Many early investigators thought that memory simply decayed. However, McGeoch (1932) forcefully argued that the major cause of forgetting was interference produced by activities occurring between original learning and a retention test, or retroactive inhibition. Jenkins and Dallenbach's famous sleep experiment supported an interference theory. In McGeoch's original theory, response competition was assumed to be the major mechanism of retroactive inhibition. Later experiments indicated that response competition was insufficient to explain all retroactive inhibition, and another factor, unlearning, was identified. Barnes and Underwood (1959) provided evidence for an unlearning mechanism. Using an MMFR test and an A-B, A-C paradigm, they found that subjects were unable to recall first-list (B) responses following second-list learning. However, forgetting in the A-B, A-C paradigm may not reflect unlearning of specific A-B associations but rather the suppression *of first-list responses. Only in the A-B, A-B$_r$ paradigm is clear evidence obtained for loss of specific A-B associations.*

Forgetting may also be due to proactive inhibition, the interference produced by learning prior to acquiring the to-be-remembered material. The traditional view of proactive inhibition is that old associations are unlearned during acquisition of the target information and then recover over time to compete at the time of the retention test.

Traditional interference theory has amazing predictive accuracy, as illustrated by Bower's (1978) experiments testing memory for sentences. However, the particular mechanisms responsible for interference are not clear, particularly in the case of proactive inhibition.

Another explanation of forgetting offered by McGeoch was that due to changes in the learner's environment, either internal or external. Altered stimulus conditions presumably reduce or remove stimuli capable of eliciting the to-be-remembered material. Experiments have supported this explanation of forgetting by showing dramatic losses in retention due to changes in the physical environment (for example, the room) between learning and a retention test. The phenomenon of state-dependent retrieval also supports this view of forgetting.

To explain forgetting, we need to pay attention to traditional interference concepts and to understand more fully the role of altered stimulus conditions. Future theories of forgetting will undoubtedly represent a combination of these views of forgetting.

Recommendations for further reading

McGeoch's (1932) classic article on forgetting is still worth reading. An excellent review by Keppel (1968) will bring you nearly up to date on the changes in interference theory since McGeoch's article. More recent reviews are found in the Postman and Underwood (1973) article, as well as a chapter written by Postman (1976). These latter two sources also summarize the recent stimulus-encoding theories of retroactive and proactive inhibition. Original introductions to these particular views of forgetting are found in articles written by Greeno, James, and DaPolito (1971) and Martin (1971). Glenberg (1979) has given a theoretical analysis of the influence of contextual changes on memory. For those readers wishing to learn more about state-dependent retrieval, a good starting point is a critique by Eich (1980).

7

Evidence for Encoding on Multiple Dimensions

Feature Encoding
Identification
How Many and How Fast?
Release from PI
An Attention-Getting Device?
Overestimation of Feature Encoding?
Release from What?
Retrieval Mechanisms
Applications

Introduction/overview

What's in a word? Take the word house. *What are some of its physical characteristics? You probably noticed that it has five letters, that it is typed in lower case and in black ink, and that it has one syllable. What about its semantic features? A dictionary will tell you it is a building in which people live. It belongs, in other words, to the semantic category type of building. Can you think of a synonym? How about* residence? *What else does the word* house *lead you to think of? What associations do you have to this word? What are its syntactic features—that is, is* house *a noun or verb, singular or plural? Words obviously have many different attributes or features. A complete list of a word's features would be quite long. We could also mention modality (was the word spoken or written), imaginal (does the word elicit a visual image), and several others.*

   A number of psychologists have taken the position that when we hear or see a word, we encode it along a number of different dimensions (Anisfeld & Knapp, 1968; Bower, 1967; Underwood, 1969; Wickens, 1970, 1972). They assume that our memory for a word is multidimensional, including physical, semantic, and syntactic features. There are several important issues surrounding the investigation of memory features, not the least of which is just how many features we encode when a to-be-remembered item is presented. Another important question involves the "automaticity" of feature encoding. For example, do features of a word get encoded without our being aware? Yet another topic to be discussed in this chapter is the question of what produces cumulative proactive inhibition. We began this discussion in the preceding chapter. We will now look at how psychologists have attempted to use the cumulative proactive inhibition observed in the Brown-Peterson task to investigate feature encoding.

FEATURE ENCODING

Identification

   There are many different techniques used to identify the features encoded with a word. Tulving and Bower (1974) provided an informative review of eleven different methods used to investigate memory encoding. One method is to examine the kinds of errors subjects make in memory experiments. In Chapter 3 we discussed an experiment by Conrad (1964) that identified an acoustic code for items in primary memory. Subjects were asked to recall a series of letters that had been presented either visually or auditorily. Conrad found that even when subjects *saw* the to-be-remembered items, their recall errors tended to be letters that *sounded* like the target letters. This indicated the letters had been encoded acoustically. Another experiment discussed in Chapter 3 used a probe recognition task to investigate feature encoding. Shulman (1972) first presented subjects a short list of to-be-remembered words. He then revealed another word (the probe), asking subjects quickly to decide whether or not it had been in the list. When the probe was a synonym of a word from the list, subjects made more errors than when it was an unrelated word. On the basis of this finding Shulman concluded that semantic features are also encoded in primary memory.

   Sometimes psychologists simply ask subjects what they can remember about items that have been presented. Hintzman, Block, and Inskeep (1972) found that subjects could remember whether a word was printed in upper or lower case or whether it was spoken in a male or female voice. Zechmeister and McKillip (1972) required subjects first to read a lengthy prose passage and then asked them where on the page particular sentences had appeared (see also Rothkopf, 1971). The fact that subjects remembered where on a page they had read the sentences provides evidence for a spatial attribute of memory. You might have encountered this type of attribute when, as part of a class examination, you found yourself unable to recall a specific answer to a question but were able to recall exactly where in the textbook and in what position on the page the answer was.

A related and equally frustrating memory phenomenon sometimes occurs when we fail to recall a specific fact but feel that our retrieval effort is on the verge of being successful. Brown and McNeill (1966) investigated this "tip-of-the-tongue" experience in a classic experiment. In order to induce a tip-of-the-tongue feeling under laboratory conditions, Brown and McNeill read subjects the definitions of various uncommon words. For example, what word means "favoritism shown or patronage granted by persons in high office to relatives or close friends?" If subjects knew the word upon hearing the definition, they immediately wrote it down. However, if they could not identify the word but felt they were close to getting it—that is, it was on the tip of their tongue—then they proceeded to answer a series of questions about the features of the yet-unidentified word. Questions were printed on sheets given to the subjects and included the following: How many syllables does it have? What is the initial letter? What words sound like that word? What words are similar in meaning? If you happened to experience a tip-of-the-tongue feeling on the basis of the above definition, you might try to answer some of these questions before reading further. Subjects' answers when they were in the tip-of-the-tongue state showed they knew a great deal about the features of the word they were trying to recall. Subjects were correct 57% of the time when guessing the initial letter of a word they couldn't recall. By the way, the definition given fits the word *nepotism.*

Sometimes we can generate information about a word's features even though we never experienced the word. This type of knowledge must be separated from the knowledge of a word's features we obtained when a word was encoded. For example, realizing a word is from a particular class of words may allow us to identify some of its features (Koriat & Lieblich, 1974). If you know a word is technical or scientific, you might correctly guess that it has several syllables. Nevertheless, some of the features subjects can identify when in the tip-of-the-tongue state are specific to the to-be-remembered word, attesting to the multiplicity of features present in memory.

There have been several interesting extensions of the Brown and McNeill experiment. Yarmey (1973) used photographs of famous people rather than definitions to precipitate the "feeling-of-knowing" experience. Subjects behaved as you possibly do when seeing "what's his name" in an old movie. When unable to recall a particular name, subjects could still remember such things as where and when they last saw this individual. Eysenck (1979) reversed the Brown and McNeill task by giving subjects rare words and asking for definitions. Even when subjects could not provide an accurate definition of the word, they were able to recognize semantically related words. This finding suggests people have partial access to semantic features of a word that cannot be defined.

How many and how fast?

Just how much information is encoded with a word? Because we can remember that a word begins with a certain letter or that it was spoken in a male rather than a female voice does not necessarily mean that *all* possible features of a word are encoded. How many might we encode? Wickens (1970, p. 1), at Ohio State University, says "a lot."

> I do not think we have, at present, any notion of the richness of the encoded material, but I suspect it is far richer than most of us imagine. Further, I do not think that the identity of the many encoding attributes or dimensions enter very much into the individual's consciousness. Consequently, we are unaware intellectually of the richness of the encoding of a single word. If we were to consciously recognize this richness, then so much time would be required for the perceptual ingestion of a single word that we would find it next to impossible to listen to a series of words and remember any but the first and last of them. We handle the intellectual and conceptual meaningful reactions to common words with the same kind of automatic skill as the veteran big league outfielder who turns his back to a hard-hit fly ball, runs at top speed, and then without stopping and almost without looking, raises his gloved hand at exactly the right instant and in exactly the right location to grasp the ball.

Wickens not only argues that many attributes or dimensions are encoded whenever we experience a single word, but he suggests that much of this encoding goes on unconsciously, without our being aware of the richness of a single word. How many is "many" and to what extent encoding is unconsciously automatic, like snaring that fly ball, has been a major controversy for some years.

The technique Wickens and his associates used to investigate memory encoding, and from which he draws his conclusions regarding the multiplicity and automaticity of feature encoding, is called *release from PI.* The PI means, of course, proactive inhibition. This technique takes advantage of the cumulative proactive inhibition found in the Brown-Peterson task introduced in Chapter 3. Because most of what follows is based on experiments using this technique, your next job is to understand fully the release from PI procedure.

RELEASE FROM PI

Interference theorists explain forgetting in the Brown-Peterson task on the basis of proactive inhibition. In the original Peterson and Peterson (1959) experiment, a single consonant trigram was first presented, followed by a brief interval of backward number counting, and, finally, recall of the consonants was requested. Substantial forgetting of the letters was seen over an 18-second retention interval (see Figure 3-1). Similar forgetting occurs when three words rather than three letters are studied and tested in this task. Although some researchers have argued that forgetting over such short intervals is evidence for memory decay, Keppel and Underwood (1962) argued that interference from previously learned items was responsible for the memory loss. As evidence for an interference interpretation, they showed that forgetting of the first to-be-remembered item in the Brown-Peterson task was negligible but that retention worsened with successive items. In other words, proactive inhibition from previous trials was present in the Brown-Peterson task (see Figure 3-3). As we saw in Chapter 3, the fact that interference "works" in a similar fashion in short-term memory tasks as in long-term memory tasks is sometimes used to argue against the notion that different memory processes are involved in primary and secondary memory.

In an experimental demonstration that gave rise to the release from PI technique, Wickens, Born, and Allen (1963) tested an important assumption of the interference explanation of forgetting in the Brown-Peterson task. Because similarity among to-be-remembered materials is known to be a critical factor in producing interference in long-term memory, these investigators argued that interference in the Brown-Peterson task should also depend upon the degree of similarity between successive to-be-remembered items. They predicted that proactive inhibition would increase when the to-be-remembered items were all from the same class of items—for example, letter trigrams—and that changing the class of to-be-remembered materials, such as to number trigrams, would reduce the effect of interference.

Wickens, Born, and Allen asked students to learn a series of either consonant trigrams (CCCs) or number trigrams (NNNs) in a Brown-Peterson experiment. The procedure was as follows. To begin a trial, the experimenter read a to-be-remembered trigram to a subject. Then a green light went on, signaling the subject to begin naming colors that appeared on a revolving drum. Color naming continued (usually for 10 seconds) until a red light came on, signaling the subject to attempt recall of the trigram. Color naming rather than the more typical backward number counting was employed to prevent rehearsal in order to eliminate potential interference between number counting and memory for number trigrams.

Some subjects in the experiment studied and were tested on the same class of trigrams on each trial of the experiment. Other subjects first learned one type of trigrams and then shifted to a different class of trigrams. For example, one group of subjects received letter trigrams (CCCs) on the first three Brown-Peterson trials and then got number trigrams (NNNs) on the fourth trial. Recall performance in this shift group was compared to performance in a group that did not experience a shift in the class of to-be-remembered items. Wickens, Born, and Allen showed that recall performance on the first several trials progressively declined for all groups of subjects but that the shift to a new class of items led to a marked increase in recall. It was as if subjects were "released" from the effects of cumulative interference.

Figure 7-1 illustrates the general nature of the PI release obtained in the Wickens, Born, and Allen experiment. As you will see, similar results have been obtained in many other experiments using this technique. The results of the Wickens, Born, and Allen experiment supported the interference interpretation of forgetting seen in the Brown-Peterson task. More important, the results revealed a new and novel way to investigate memory encoding. Wickens (1970, p. 3) described it this way:

> In the STM situation, triads or trigrams, all elements of which are homogeneous with respect to a psychological class, seem to be encoded not only as unique items but also as members of the same psychological class. If the next item is drawn from a different class, then interference no longer exists—or

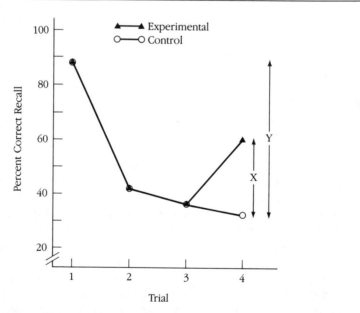

Figure 7-1. Idealized presentation of results from PI experiment. Percentage release is given by the formula X/Y times 100. *(From "Characteristics of Word Encoding," by D. D. Wickens. In A. W. Melton and E. Martin (Eds.), Coding Processes in Human Memory. Copyright 1972 by Hemisphere Publishing Corporation. Reprinted by permission.)*

is minimized—and performance is raised. Further reasoning and speculating suggested the possibility that the shift procedure could be used as something of a projective technique of cognitive organization; a way of asking the subject what classes are being employed without requiring him to identify and label them—or even, as we shall see later, of being aware of them.

Release from PI

Purpose

To demonstrate that cumulative proactive inhibition in the Brown-Peterson task can be lessened by shifting to a new class of to-be-remembered items.

Materials

Four low-association consonant trigrams (CCCs) (see Table B in the Appendix) and four number trigrams (NNNs) are needed. The trigram stimuli should be carefully selected so that the set of four CCCs includes nine different consonants (three consonants appear twice). No consonants are to be repeated within a particular CCC. Using only digits 1–9, select four NNNs from a table of random numbers (see Table A in the Appendix). Six digits are used once and three digits are used twice in the set of four NNNs. No digits, however, are to be repeated within a particular trigram and familiar number sequences should be avoided (for example, 345). Each of the eight trigrams can be typed or printed on individual 3 × 5-inch cards. A list of category names is needed for the distractor task. Approximately eight to nine names will be required. Categories such as "fruits," "trees," "movie stars," and "TV shows" may be used.

Procedure

There are four conditions in the experiment, which is based on the Brown-Peterson task. In each condition a subject is presented four different trigrams for study and test. The experimenter reads aloud the trigram and then immediately says the name of a category. The subject then begins to identify instances of the category. When a subject "runs out" of instances or pauses noticeably, the experimenter says a new category name aloud. After 20 seconds of this distractor activity, the experimenter says "recall" and the subject attempts to recall the trigrams. Six seconds are allowed for recall and then another trigram is presented for study and test. The experimenter should record the subject's responses on the cards with the to-be-remembered items. The conditions of the experiment are determined by the selection of to-be-remembered trigrams. Subjects are randomly assigned to one of four conditions. Two groups of subjects are presented a letter trigram or a number trigram on each of the four study trials (CCC, CCC, CCC, CCC or NNN, NNN,

NNN, NNN). Two other groups of subjects receive either CCCs or NNNs for the first three trials and then are shifted to a different class of trigrams on the fourth trial (CCC, CCC, CCC, NNN or NNN, NNN, NNN, CCC). Each trial should take approximately 30 seconds. The experimenter should take 3–4 seconds to read the trigram and to present a category name. As many category names are presented as are needed to keep the subject occupied for the 20-second retention interval and then 6 seconds are given for recall of the trigrams.

When all subjects have been tested, the four letter and four number trigrams should have been used an equal number of times on each of the four trials of the experiment. This will mean that each of the to-be-remembered items is tested an equal number of times on the fourth or critical trial in all groups. Also, every experimenter should test at least one subject in each condition of the experiment. If an experimenter tests more than one subject in a condition, an equal number of subjects should be tested in all four conditions.

Instructions to Subjects

This is an experiment involving a test of your memory for short sequences of letters or numbers. When we begin, I will read aloud three items—either three letters or three numbers. Immediately after this I will say the name of a category, such as "four-legged animals." You are immediately to begin naming as many instances of the category as you can. Please say the instances as fast as possible. I may give you more than one category during the short retention interval. When I say "recall," please stop naming members of the category and try to recall the three items I read to you before the category task. Guess if you are not sure. After about 6 seconds I will say "next" and then read another three items for you to remember. (Subjects in the shift groups are *not* informed that the class of items will change.) We will do this a number of times. It is important that, once we start, you give me your complete attention. Do you have any questions? OK, let's begin.

Summary and Analysis

An item is recalled correctly only if all three letters or numbers are recalled in their original order. For each subject it is determined whether the trigram was recalled correctly on each of the four trials. The total number of trigrams correct on each trial (across subjects) is divided by the number of subjects in a group and multiplied by 100 to give the percentage correct on each trial. Results for the two groups not shifting to a new class of items can be combined, as well as the results for the two groups having a shift. This will provide two groups for comparison: shift and no-shift.

Data can be summarized by graphing recall performance for the shift and no-shift groups as a function of trials on the Brown-Peterson task. Percentage release from PI can be calculated by the formula: release = X/Y times 100, where X equals the percent correct recall for the shift group on the fourth trial minus the percent correct recall for the no-shift group on the same trial, and Y equals the percent correct recall for the no-shift group on trial 1 minus the percent correct recall for the same group on trial 4. (Y, in other words, is the total decline in performance over four trials for the no-shift group.) To test for statistical significance, a chi-square test can be used to compare recall and nonrecall of trigrams on the fourth or critical trial for the shift and no-shift groups.

Recommended Minimum Number of Subjects

Total of 48; 12 in each of the four experimental conditions.

Based on an experiment by Wickens, Born, and Allen (1963). Of the many experimental procedures outlined in this text, we must admit to having the most reservations about the results of this experiment. A release from PI experiment often requires a large number of subjects for an effect to be seen. Wickens (1972) reports that the "usual" number of subjects for this experiment is about 200.

According to Wickens, memory psychologists now had a projective technique, like those used by clinical psychologists, that would enable them to tap the unconscious encodings of memory.

Wickens and his associates, and many other investigators, have used the release from PI technique to investigate possible memory encoding along many different dimensions. Besides shifting from numbers to digits or vice versa, other experiments have explored shifts from adjectives to verbs, abstract to concrete words, masculine to feminine words, one- to two-syllable words, as well as shifts on a variety of other attribute dimensions. Figure 7-2 shows the percentage release from PI found in many of these experiments. (Wickens, 1970, 1972, describes these dimensions more fully.) To calculate percentage release from PI, the difference in recall between the experimental (shift) and control (no-shift) groups is obtained for the shift trial ("X" in Figure 7-1). This difference is then divided by the difference in recall performance shown by the control group from trial 1 to trial 4 ("Y" in Figure 7-1). The result is multiplied by 100 to yield a percentage. A typical release from PI experiment actually involves four different groups of subjects. For a particular dimension a shift in the class of to-be-remembered items is always carried out in both directions (for example, from letters to numbers and numbers to letters). This requires two control groups that learn items from only one class (either all numbers or all letters). Interestingly, the shift along various dimensions is generally symmetrical, and therefore results are usually summarized by averaging performance of the two shift groups as well as that of the two control groups.

Figure 7-2 indicates that amount of PI release is generally greatest for semantic features, substantially less for physical features, and practically nonexistent for marking-syntactic features. An apparent exception is the modality

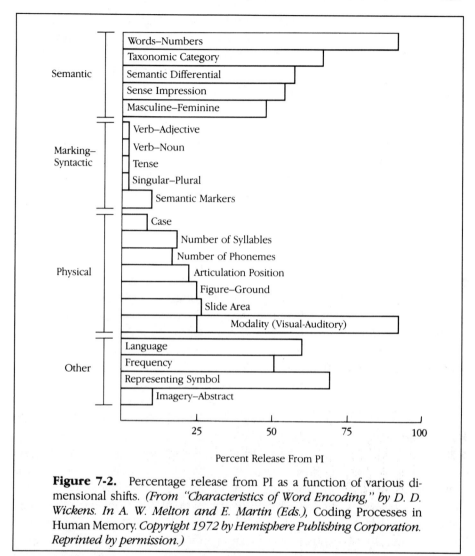

Figure 7-2. Percentage release from PI as a function of various dimensional shifts. *(From "Characteristics of Word Encoding," by D. D. Wickens. In A. W. Melton and E. Martin (Eds.),* Coding Processes in Human Memory. *Copyright 1972 by Hemisphere Publishing Corporation. Reprinted by permission.)*

attribute that is a physical feature and shows a large amount of PI release. Shifts of the modality of to-be-remembered items (for example, from auditory to visual presentation) are apparently affected by the modality of the distractor activity (Hopkins, Edwards, & Cook, 1973). The PI technique has also been used with short verbal passages as the to-be-remembered materials (Blumenthal & Robbins, 1977; Gunter, Clifford, & Berry, 1980). We will have more to say about that later. In another interesting extension of the original Wickens procedure, Russ-Eft (1979) showed that release from PI may occur for individual items within a set of to-be-remembered items. When only one word in a to-be-remembered triad was changed from one semantic category to another, release was obtained for the shifted word but not for the remaining two words. This finding has implications for interpretations of the release from PI effect, which we will now discuss. There is significant disagreement as to the memory mechanisms thought to be involved in this effect.

An attention-getting device?

After several trials with the same kind of material, subjects in a release experiment are shifted to a new kind of material. It is conceivable that the shift "alerts" the subject, leading to increased attention to the material on the shift trial. Consider the subject who has just been presented three consonants and then out of the blue is asked to remember three numbers. If the shift in the class of materials increases the subject's attention to the items, improved performance on the shift trial may be due to increased attention rather than to differential encoding.

Although the attention hypothesis as an explanation for release from PI appears quite reasonable, there are several arguments against it. Shifting the class of material, as from letters to numbers, represents quite a noticeable change, but other dimensions have shown release from PI when the shift has been much less obvious. Consider shifts along dimensions of the Osgood semantic differential (Osgood, Suci, & Tannenbaum, 1957). This instrument describes the connotative meanings of words along three dimensions: evaluation, potency, and activity. Several release from PI experiments have been carried out for words differing on the extremes of these dimensions (Wickens, 1970; Wickens & Clark, 1968). For example, words having a high positive evaluation are *religious, success, nice, knowledge, true,* and *enjoy.* Words that connote a negative evaluation are *kill, danger, worry, lose, disease,* and *debt.* When subjects were presented triads of words from one end of the evaluative dimension for several trials and were then shifted to triads of words from the other end, performance first declined and then improved on the shift trial, indicating they had encoded this semantic aspect of the words. Differences in the nuances of these words are certainly less obvious than changes on other dimensions—for example, letters to numbers. In fact, when subjects experience these more subtle changes in a release from PI task, many do not report noticing anything different about the to-be-remembered items even though release from PI was obtained (Wickens, 1970).

MacLeod (1975) directly tested the attention explanation of release from PI by alerting subjects to an upcoming trial. The to-be-remembered items were shifted from one taxonomic category to another (names of animals to names of vegetables) or there was no shift. Besides the usual groups of subjects in the shift or no-shift condition, two other groups (shift and no-shift) saw a "bright red warning light" before the critical trial. However, MacLeod obtained improved recall on the critical trial only if the taxonomic category was also shifted. The bright red light did not improve memory for the to-be-remembered items. You may recall that Russ-Eft (1979) obtained release from PI for only one word of a triad. Her results are also evidence against the attention hypothesis if it is assumed that any change would increase attention to all the items. Changes in attention are apparently insufficient to explain release from PI.

Overestimation of feature encoding?

Experiments using the release technique to investigate feature encoding have identified an impressive array of features that produce release from PI (see Figure 7-2). However, in the vast majority of cases only one feature has been varied at a time. That is, any one subject in a release experiment experiences a shift on only a single feature dimension (although see Wickens, 1972, for some exceptions to this statement). Is it valid to assume from these studies that a single word is encoded on *all* of these dimensions every time it is presented? Although Wickens seems to say yes, other researchers clearly say no.

Underwood (1972) argued that the release from PI technique overestimates the number of features likely to be encoded with a single word. He also suggested that encoding may not be as "automatic" as Wickens and others claim it to be. Underwood's major criticism of the technique involves the possible *priming* of subjects. Priming occurs whenever experimental procedures serve to "instruct" the subjects what to do. For example, consider possible strategies for subjects in a Brown-Peterson procedure when several words are presented for a memory test. Subjects will likely look for some way to group the words together in order to facilitate later retention. If all the words come from the same class of items (for example, all are members of the taxonomic class "vegetables"), it is possible for subjects to discover this feature and encode words according to this feature. The experimental requirements therefore serve to control subjects' behavior. Under different circumstances, we cannot necessarily conclude subjects will encode a word on this particular dimension. Experimental support for the priming hypothesis comes from the fact that PI release increases with increased numbers of pre-release trials despite the fact that amount of PI tends to level off after a few trials (Bennett & Bennett, 1974). The more trials that precede a shift, the greater is the likelihood subjects will "discover" the dimension the experimenter has selected and encode items on that basis.

Postman and Burns (1973) made a related argument against the multiplicity of encoding. They pointed out that if a word is actually encoded on many different dimensions, a change in only 1 dimension would not be particularly salient. In other words, if a word is normally encoded on 20 different dimensions, why should release occur when only 1 of these dimensions is changed? A shift in only 1 dimension should be comparatively unnoticed. A plausible answer is that only a relatively few features are encoded, thus producing a large effect on performance when one is changed.

Additional evidence that the release from PI technique overestimates feature encoding is found in an interesting set of experiments by Gardiner, Klee, Redman, and Ball (1976). They investigated possible release from PI due to changes in the physical characteristics of the to-be-remembered items. In two experiments, they presented subjects with items printed in one color for three trials and on the fourth trial shifted to items printed in another color. The only difference between the two experiments was the nature of the to-be-remembered items. In the first experiment subjects attempted recall of three common two-syllable words on each trial. In the second experiment recall was tested for three consonants (CCC). These researchers found release from PI due to color change when consonants were used, but color change did not produce release from PI when common words were used.

Given that release from PI was found in this experiment to depend on the nature of the to-be-remembered items, it becomes difficult to generalize about possible feature encoding on the basis of any single experiment. To conclude that a particular feature is important in producing release may be overestimating a feature's potency given that this same feature may or may not produce release when different items are used. As Gardiner and his associates point out, their findings suggest that previous experiments have underestimated the effect of changes in physical characteristics of to-be-remembered items. Physical changes have generally not yielded significant amounts of PI release (see Figure 7-2). However, most of these experiments have used words. As we just saw, when consonant trigrams were used, a physical change in the item yielded significant PI release.

Release from what?

From an interference-theory point of view, proactive inhibition in short-term memory experiments, like those using the Brown-Peterson task, works exactly the same way as it does in long-term memory tasks. It is assumed that subsequent learning suppresses or in some manner causes unlearning of previously learned material. With the passage of time, the suppressed material recovers and intrudes at the time of the retention test, producing response competition. As we discussed in Chapter 6, experimental findings have not strongly supported this traditional view of proactive inhibition.

The response-competition explanation of proactive inhibition has also not fared well in explaining cumulative proactive inhibition in the Brown-Peterson task. For example, Dillon (1973) attempted to remove previously learned items as a source of recall interference by identifying them for the subjects at recall. Subjects were tested for retention of CCCs in a typical Brown-Peterson procedure. However, when the cue was given for recall, some subjects were provided the CCC from the previous trial and told this was *not* the correct to-be-remembered item. It is difficult to imagine that response competition occurs when a major "competitor" has been eliminated. However, Dillon reported that recall was not aided by this manipulation, suggesting that response competition is not a major factor in explaining cumulative proactive inhibition.

Yet one need only look at recall performance over the first few trials of the Brown-Peterson task to see that it quickly worsens with increasing numbers of trials. Why? One explanation suggests the problem is with the quality of encoding on subsequent trials of the experiment (Dillon, 1973). Postman, Stark, and Burns (1974) indicated that proactive inhibition in traditional list-learning tasks (as when A-C follows A-B) may be due to subjects using less-effective encoding strategies on the second list than on the first. This would presumably make the second list more susceptible to interference.

Hasher and Johnson (1975) tested the deficiency-of-encoding explanation of proactive inhibition in an interesting way. They asked college students to learn two lists of 12 paired associates conforming to an A-B, A-C relationship (same stimuli, different responses). All subjects were instructed that when learning the paired associates, they were to use one-word elaborators that either "modified or added to the meaning of the stimulus and/or formed a link with the response" (p. 568). They were also informed that after learning each list they would be asked to identify the elaborators they had used. Following this procedure, the experimenters gave these subjects' elaborators to another group of subjects to use in learning a single list of paired associates.

There were four experimental conditions in the second and critical phase of this experiment. As mentioned, all subjects in this part of the study learned a single paired-associate list. (It makes no difference in a single-list experiment whether the list was originally an A-B or an A-C list.) Subjects were told they could increase their learning rate by using elaborators the experimenter provided. During the course of acquisition, the elaborators obtained from the previous subjects were displayed next to the appropriate study items for the new subjects to use. As you have probably guessed, half of the new subjects were given elaborators generated by subjects when learning the previous *first* list and half received elaborators produced by the subjects when learning the *second* list. The encoding-deficiency explanation of proactive inhibition predicts that the second-list elaborators will not be as "good" for learning and retention as are the first-list elaborators. Hasher and Johnson tested this hypothesis by examining learning rates for the single paired-associate list as a function of list-1 and list-2 elaborators as well as by testing retention either immediately or after 1 week, yielding four experimental conditions.

Interestingly, rate of acquisition of the single paired-associate list did not differ as a consequence of using either list-1 or list-2 elaborators. There were also no significant differences between the experimental groups on the immediate retention test. However, when retention was measured after 1 week, subjects who had learned with the list-1 elaborators remembered more than those subjects who had initially encoded the items using elaborators based on list-2 learning. List-2 elaborators were apparently not as good for long-term retention as those produced during list-1 learning. For list-learning experiments when long-term retention is assessed, there appears to be support for the encoding deficiency hypothesis of cumulative PI.

To use the encoding deficiency hypothesis as an explanation for cumulative PI and release in the Brown-Peterson task, it must be assumed that encoding of successive to-be-remembered items deteriorates with trials in the task. That is, the quality of subjects' encoding strategies must somehow decline with successive "lists" of to-be-remembered items. Items less well encoded may be more easily forgotten over the brief retention interval. Changing the nature of the to-be-remembered items on a shift trial would presumably affect the quality of encoding so that items would now either be better "fixed" in memory or be encoded in such a way as to provide a new and better retrieval cue than was present on the pre-release trials. As we will see, evidence has been collected to implicate retrieval mechanisms in the release from PI phenomenon.

Retrieval mechanisms

A particular memory phenomenon may arise due to events occurring at any of the various stages of memory processing: encoding (registration), storage, and retrieval. To this point we have emphasized the possible role of encoding differences in producing release from PI. Results of several experiments have shown the role of retrieval mechanisms in explaining release from PI. Some investigators have even concluded that release is due entirely to things happening at time of retrieval (Watkins & Watkins, 1975).

One of the more interesting experiments to demonstrate the importance of retrieval processes in release from PI was that of Gardiner, Craik, and Birtwistle (1972). Their experiment differed from the typical release experiment in two important ways. First, all subjects were presented items from the same general category on all trials. The category was either flowers or games. The shift involved a change in a subcategory of the general class of to-be-remembered items. For example, the category flowers can be split into the subcategories wild flowers and garden flowers. The category games can be split into subcategories of indoor and outdoor games. After subjects learned items from one subcategory on three Brown-Peterson trials, they were switched, on the fourth trial, to items from another subcategory of the same general class. All subjects in the experiment were shifted in this manner.

The second major change from the typical release procedure involved use of retrieval cues. There were three conditions in the experiment. All subjects were shown the name of the *general* class of items on the first Brown-Peterson trial. For example, the word *flowers* was presented for those subjects learning names of flowers. On the second and third trials no cues were given and subjects were tested for their memory of three words from a particular subcategory of the class revealed on the first trial. It was on trial 4 that things happened to yield three experimental conditions. One group of subjects on trial 4 received a cue identifying the nature of the subcategory of to-be-remembered items *before* the items were presented. For example, when changing from wild flowers to garden flowers, subjects were shown the cue "garden flowers" before seeing the to-be-remembered items on the fourth trial (CP group). A second group of subjects received the same cue at recall time on trial 4—that is, *after* the presentation of the to-be-remembered items and following the 15-second distractor-filled retention interval (CR group). The third group of subjects did not receive any cues at all on the fourth trial (control group). Remember, all subjects experienced a shift between subcategories of items on trial 4.

Results of the experiment are shown in Figure 7-3. *Both* groups receiving subcategory cues (CP and CR) showed release from PI, but the group with no cues (control) did not. The amount of PI release was essentially the same whether the cue was given at presentation of the to-be-remembered items or at retrieval time. These results implicate retrieval processes in producing the release from PI phenomenon because until the time of retrieval, the group receiving no cue (control) and the cued-at-retrieval group (CR) were treated in exactly the same way. The CR group showed release when the control group did not.

Exactly how a retrieval cue operates to produce release from PI is a matter of some debate (see Dillon & Bittner, 1975). However, an experiment and subsequent discussion by O'Neill, Sutcliffe, and Tulving (1976) sheds some light on the issue. These investigators replicated the basic findings of the Gardiner, Craik, and Birtwistle experiment by showing that cues at either presentation or recall were effective in producing release from PI when a subcategory was shifted. In addition, these investigators included two groups of subjects who were not shifted but received appropriate subcategory cues at either presentation or retrieval. They were concerned that presenting the cues might produce an increase in performance even when the subcategory was not changed. If they did, this would mean cues were simply alerting the subjects to the critical trial, perhaps causing them to try harder on these items. Their experiment therefore was a test of the attention hypothesis of release from PI. The results were negative. Only when a shift in subcategories occurred and only when subjects were cued (either at presentation or recall) was there release from PI.

The results of this experiment, combined with the previous demonstration by Gardiner, Craik, and Birtwistle, led O'Neill, Sutcliffe, and Tulving to the

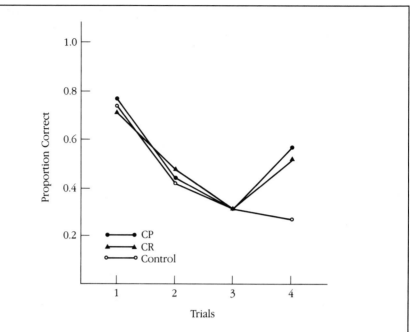

Figure 7-3. Proportion of words recalled when a subcategory cue was given on trial 4 at time of presentation (CP) or at the time of recall (CR) of the to-be-remembered words, and when no cue was given (control). *(From "Retrieval Cues and Release from Proactive Inhibition," by J. M. Gardiner, F. I. M. Craik, and J. Birtwistle. In Journal of Verbal Learning and Verbal Behavior, 1972, 11, 778–783. Copyright 1972 by Academic Press, Inc. Reprinted by permission.)*

following conclusions. They argued that finding PI release when a cue is presented at recall means that subjects actually encoded information about the nature of the subcategory at presentation but that this information was helpful only when a retrieval cue was presented. The cue, in other words, provided access to information that otherwise would be inaccessible (however, see Dillon & Bittner, 1975). The release from PI phenomenon in this view is a joint effect of what is happening at encoding and at retrieval. (This theme will be expanded upon in Chapter 10 when encoding specificity is discussed.) Interestingly, this view led them also to suggest that the release procedure may be underestimating the number of features encoded with a to-be-remembered item. If one examined only the results of the control group in the Gardiner, Craik, and Birtwistle experiment, one would conclude that information about subcategories was not encoded. However, as we have seen, release was obtained when a cue was given at retrieval. Therefore we can assume that important information about the subcategory was encoded but was not accessible until the proper retrieval cue was presented. The absence of a release from PI effect in the control group may not, in this view, be signaling the absence of feature encoding but merely the absence of an appropriate retrieval cue.

We now have what appears to be rather a paradoxical set of conclusions: the release from PI technique may on some occasions *over*estimate the number of features encoded because of priming (Underwood, 1972) but in some cases actually *under*estimate the number of features encoded due to the inaccessibility of critical information at retrieval. This latter conclusion contains the assumption that feature encoding is automatic. Subjects in the subcategory shift experiments reported no conscious awareness of the change in to-be-remembered information. Therefore in order to assume that the retrieval cue is effective because subjects actually encoded the critical information, we must assume further that the information is encoded automatically, without subjects' awareness. According to O'Neill, Sutcliffe, and Tulving, this does not necessarily contradict the idea that release overestimates encoding if it is assumed that priming reflects unconscious encoding as well. Subjects may be led to encode in a certain way due to the experimental requirements (priming), but according to these researchers, the encoding can be unconsciously automatic. Therefore the release experiment possibly overestimates feature encoding due to priming but may also underestimate feature encoding whenever important retrieval cues are not present at recall.

The issue of automatic versus nonautomatic encoding of memory attributes will be discussed further in the next chapter, when we review encoding of frequency information. Before we launch that discussion, however, let us leave you with a thought about possible applications of knowledge derived from the study of cumulative proactive inhibition and the release phenomenon.

Applications

In this chapter we have led you into the middle of a dispute regarding possible memory mechanisms in the release from PI phenomenon. Although no one completely understands this interesting phenomenon yet, a study by Gunter, Clifford, and Berry (1980) alerts us to its possible significance when arranging a sequence of to-be-remembered materials. Before we discuss their experiment, let us consider the extent of cumulative proactive inhibition. In one experiment, Keppel, Postman, and Zavortink (1968) showed that subjects who were able to recall about 70% of an initial list of ten common word pairs, following repeated study and test cycles with the same type of lists, were soon found to remember less than 30%. After additional lists, their recall approached zero! Cumulative proactive inhibition in the Brown-Peterson task may be no less severe. Recall that averages above 80% on the first trial of this short-term memory task may drop to less than half that after only four study-test trials.

Therefore, in both short-term and long-term memory tasks, forgetting due to cumulative proactive inhibition can be quite substantial.

To what extent is more everyday material affected in the same way? Gunter, Clifford, and Berry (1980) investigated the buildup and release from proactive inhibition using television news items. Subjects in this experiment viewed and listened to televised newscasts of actual news items. Items were videotaped and edited for presentation to the subjects. All the subjects received four Brown-Peterson type study and test trials using the news items. Each to-be-remembered set of items consisted of three news items of about 15- to 30-second duration. Total duration of the three items was between 60 and 80 seconds on any one trial. Two news categories were used in this experiment: sports and politics. An example of a political news item is "The Rhodesian government offers a safe return to guerillas who are exiled in neighboring African countries." The subjects studied the news items and then worked on a distractor task for 1 minute. At that time, recall was requested for the three news items. Half the subjects received four study-test trials using news items from the same taxonomic category, either politics or sports, and half were switched on the fourth trial to a different category. Cumulative proactive inhibition was observed. Recall, which averaged approximately 87% on the first trial, dropped to 43% on trial 4 in the no-shift group. Similar cumulative proactive inhibition was seen in the shift group on the first three trials, but on the shift trial recall jumped up to about 74%. The amount of overall PI release was 70%. These results suggest that cumulative proactive inhibition and the release from PI phenomenon should be given consideration in the planning of sequences of to-be-remembered materials. Someone planning a conference or symposium at which many different people will deliver lectures might consider the possible effect on retention of listening to and trying to remember many successive presentations on similar topics.

Summary

Much evidence suggests that we encode material on many different dimensions. It has been argued that this encoding is both automatic and unconscious. This chapter focused on the release from PI technique as a tool for studying memory encoding. This technique is based on the cumulative PI observed in the Brown-Peterson paradigm. If a shift in the dimension of the to-be-remembered items results in improved recall performance over that seen on previous trials, it is assumed that subjects encoded this dimension as part of their memory for the to-be-remembered items. Generally, the strongest release effects are found for shifts in semantic features, less for physical features, and almost no effect is found for marking-syntactic features. Explanations for PI release based on subjects' increased attention on the shift trial do not appear adequate.

Some researchers have argued that the release from PI technique over-estimates the number of features normally encoded because presentation of successive sets of items may prime subjects to encode a particular dimension. Paradoxically, others have suggested that the technique underestimates the number of features encoded. This controversy warns us to be careful in generalizing about memory encoding based on the results obtained using one method of feature detection.

Research using the release from PI technique may offer an insight into the mechanisms responsible for cumulative PI. The buildup of PI is usually very rapid and retention suffers dramatically. One possible explanation for the retention loss, and perhaps the improvement in retention when material is altered, is that the quality of encoding deteriorates with trials.

There appears to be a consensus that some feature encoding is automatic and that encoding is multidimensional. This aspect of our memory processing will be understood only by combining the results obtained with the release from PI technique with results produced by other methods used to investigate coding. Recent research has examined the significance of cumulative PI, and release, in natural settings. We hope this line of research will continue because the extent of forgetting due to cumulative PI makes it important that we understand this type of forgetting and evaluate its significance in our everyday activities.

Recommendations for further reading

Tulving and Bower (1974) provide an informative review of methods used in feature analysis. Underwood's (1969) often-cited article, "Attributes of Memory," is an excellent introduction to thinking about memory in terms of features or attributes. A somewhat different brand of attribute theory is presented by Wickens (1970, 1972); these articles also contain important reviews of the release from PI phenomenon and its use in feature identification.

8

Memory for
Frequency of Events

Introduction/overview

Are there more Volkswagens or Toyotas on the highways? How many days did it rain last month? Is the letter a found more often in English words than the letter u? Are there more divorces than suicides? What is the probability of being struck by lightning?

Perhaps you learned the correct answer to one or more of these questions by hearing a weather report or by reading a newspaper. However, it is likely that to answer these questions, you must depend on your memory for the frequency of past events. Considering all the cars you have seen while driving, were there more VWs than Toyotas? Of all the English words you have seen or heard, were there more with the letter a or more with the letter u?

In this chapter we look at some of the characteristics of our memory for frequency of events. There is evidence that we are quite sensitive to the frequency of an event's occurrences, leading some researchers to argue that memory for frequency is a very basic, even "automatic," memory process. Our memory for the number of times we've experienced an event is related to a wide variety of decisions, including those that are part of verbal discrimination tasks, like a multiple-choice examination, as well as those about various societal risks, like those depending on our memory for the occurrences of lethal events. And although we are demonstrably sensitive to event frequency, we are not without certain biases when judging frequency. We will discuss just what these biases are and what role they play in frequency judgment tasks. An interesting aspect of our ability to remember frequency is that sometimes fact and fantasy get confused. We shall present evidence to show that frequency of "real" occurrences and occurrences that are only imagined can affect each other. Finally, we will review several theoretical models of frequency presentation. That is, what are the memory mechanisms used to make a frequency judgment?

Many learning and memory studies, beginning with those of Ebbinghaus (1885/1964; see Chapter 4), have been directed toward understanding the effect of frequency of repetitions on the acquisition of new information. In these experiments frequency of an event is controlled (is the independent variable), and its effect on retention is assessed. The dependent variable may be counting the number of correct responses in a paired-associate task or determining the number of words recalled in a free-recall task. In this chapter we are mainly concerned with frequency when it is both the independent and the dependent variable. That is, we are interested in understanding the relationship between the number of times an event is presented (the independent variable) and our estimate of its frequency (the dependent variable).

SENSITIVITY TO EVENT FREQUENCY

When studying frequency judgments, psychologists distinguish between judgments of *background frequency* and judgments of *situational frequency*. Background frequency refers to the accumulated frequency of a lifetime of experiences. Some of these experiences are unique to an individual. The number of times you visited Uncle Fred's farm is something that only you, or those who shared your visits, could reasonably estimate. Other repeated events are common to other individuals with similar histories. The frequency with which you have experienced certain English words will be similar to that of other people of your age and educational background. Situational frequency refers to the number of times an event has been experienced in a particular situation. In many laboratory studies investigating memory for frequency, people are first presented a list of items of varying frequencies and then asked to judge how often each item appeared in the list. They are asked, in other words, to judge situational frequency.

Table 8-1 shows some representative studies of frequency judgments using various kinds of stimulus material. All these studies found people make relatively accurate judgments as to the actual frequency of occurrence of events. That is, estimated frequency increased as true frequency increased. This is the case whether background or situational frequency was judged and whether the events to be judged were letters, syllables, combinations of letters, words, names, sentences, or pictures. For instance, Attneave (1953) reported that subjects' knowledge of the frequency with which different letters of the alphabet occurred in English correlated .88 with actual frequency, a very high degree of correspondence. Howes (1954) presented Harvard undergraduates with the words shown in Table 8-2 and asked them to rank them according to how often they thought college students used them. The correlation between the students' average ranks and actual frequency obtained through word counts was .87, again showing impressive agreement. (Two major sources of information regarding the actual frequency of word usage in written English are the Thorndike and Lorge [1944] and the Kucera and Francis [1967] word counts. Using samples of printed material, they computed the number of times an individual word appears—for example, in every million words of text. The Kucera and Francis count is relatively recent and therefore reflects important changes in word usage

TABLE 8-1. Representative Studies Investigating Memory for Frequency of Events

Stimulus material	Type of frequency judgment	Reference
Individual Letters	Background	Attneave (1953)
Letters and Numbers	Situational	Erlick (1963a, 1963b)
Letter Combinations	Background	Underwood (1971); Underwood and Schulz (1960)
Syllables	Background	Rubin (1974)
Individual Words	Background	Howes (1954); Shapiro (1969)
Individual Words	Situational	Hasher and Chromiak (1977); Hintzman (1969)
Surnames	Background	Zechmeister, King, Gude, and Opera-Nadi (1975)
Words Within Sentences	Situational	Jacoby (1972)
Sentences	Situational	Gude and Zechmeister (1975); Jacoby (1972)
Pictures	Situational	Hintzman and Rogers (1973)

TABLE 8-2. Words Used by Howes (1954) to Investigate Students'
Knowledge of Word Frequency and the Average Ranks
Assigned by Students

Word	Rank	Word	Rank
country	1.5	testify	7
promise	5	surmise	11
example	1.5	dwindle	9
balance	3	irksome	12
welfare	6	vulture	13
venture	8	machete	15
deserve	4	titular	14
		figment	10

Note: Words are listed in order of their normative frequency of occurrence.

From "On the Interpretation of Word Frequency as a Variable Affecting Speed of Recognition," by D. Howes. In *Journal of Experimental Psychology,* 1954, *48,* 106–112. Copyright 1954 by the American Psychological Association. Reprinted by permission.

over the past few decades, but it is based on a smaller overall sample of words and fewer different types of word sources than the older Thorndike and Lorge count.)

An event need not be overtly presented to have its frequency recorded. Our sensitivity to event frequency apparently extends to certain "internal" events such as ideas or images. Gude and Zechmeister (1975) asked college students to make situational frequency judgments of the number of times a particular sentence appeared in a lengthy series of sentences *or* to judge the frequency with which the "gist" of the sentence was repeated. The gist of a sentence referred to its meaning. To separate the gist from the specific wording of a sentence, they used paraphrased sentences such as the following:

The huge policeman halted the expensive automobile.
The large cop stopped the high-priced car.

The researchers assumed that although the wording was different, the gist was essentially the same for these sentences.

They asked college students to read a long list of sentences. Some of the sentences appeared once and some appeared more than once. Of particular importance were the sentences that appeared twice. Their second occurrence either was worded exactly the same or was a paraphrased version of the first occurrence. After reading the sentences, half the students were given the second occurrence of a sentence and asked to judge the number of times this particular sentence—that is, the exact wording—had appeared in the list. The other half were asked to judge the number of times the sentence's meaning was presented. In order to judge accurately the frequency of a sentence's exact wording, the second occurrence of a paraphrased sentence must be judged as occurring once. However, under instructions to judge the frequency of its gist, the same paraphrased sentence should be judged as having occurred twice. The students, by the way, were not forewarned that a frequency judgment task would be required. Nevertheless, the students accurately judged the relative frequency of both the identical repetitions and the repetition of a sentence's meaning. These results show that we are able to keep track of the number of times an "idea" has appeared. This type of memory is no doubt the basis for such everyday statements as "I've heard that one before!" and "How many times have I heard that!"

We must conclude that for a wide range of stimulus events, and for judgments of either situational or background frequency, the human organism exhibits a remarkable sensitivity to the repetitiveness of events.

Automaticity of frequency information processing

Processing of frequency information may be something we do "automatically." Consider the results of an experiment by Hasher and Chromiak (1977). They presented a list of 48 words to students in grades two, four, and six and to college students. The critical words were presented one, two, three, or four times. After viewing the list, the students were shown the list items and asked to write down next to each word their estimates of the number of times it had appeared in the list. Among the items on the test list were ten additional words that had never appeared in the list and would appropriately be assigned a zero frequency. Half the students at each grade level had been told before viewing the study list that a frequency judgment test would be required; the other half had not been told that memory for frequency would be tested.

Figure 8-1 shows the results of this study. The students' estimates of presented frequency corresponded very well to the actual frequency with which the words were presented, attesting again to our sensitivity to event frequency. What is most interesting about these results is that the ability to judge frequency was no greater for college students than for second graders; and although instructions to remember frequency led to overall higher frequency judgments (not shown in the figure), there was no real advantage in making frequency judgments as a function of knowing a frequency test was upcoming. In a second experiment Hasher and Chromiak demonstrated that frequency judgments did not improve with practice even when students were given feedback as to how accurate they had been on a previous test.

Think for a minute what Hasher and Chromiak demonstrated. The ability to judge frequency did not vary between about 8 years of age and the age when we enter college; it is not affected by knowledge that memory for frequency will be tested; and frequency judgments do not become more accurate with

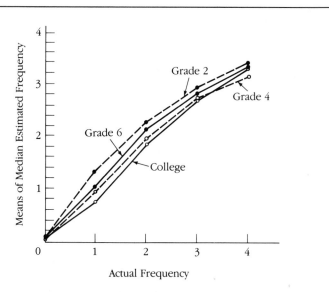

Figure 8-1. Estimated frequency of occurrence as a function of actual frequency of occurrence for subjects in grades two, four, and six and for college students. *From "The Processing of Frequency Information: An Automatic Mechanism?" by L. Hasher and W. Chromiak. In* Journal of Verbal Learning and Verbal Behavior, *1977, 16, 173–184. Copyright 1977 by Academic Press, Inc. Reprinted by permission.)*

practice. In fact, Hasher and Zacks (1979) showed that the ability to discriminate between items of varying frequency is present to generally the same degree among kindergartners and elderly people and that frequency judgments are not affected by mood states (for example, between depressed and nondepressed individuals). It appears, as we suggested earlier, that frequency information is processed automatically (see Hasher & Chromiak, 1977; Hasher & Zacks, 1979). It may even be that the processing of frequency information is something we are biologically "prepared" to do—that is, we are simply built that way.

Automatic information processing can be contrasted with processing that requires considerably more effort and shows definite developmental changes. For example, you saw in Chapter 4 that rehearsal is a very important encoding activity; yet young children do not naturally rehearse information presented to them for a later memory test. It is an activity we must learn and therefore is not done automatically. Also, unlike in processing frequency information, children can benefit from practice at rehearsing (Hagen, Hargrave, & Ross, 1973). As a way of describing memory processes, Hasher and Zacks (1979) argue that encoding activities should be classified as either "automatic" or "nonautomatic."

Besides rehearsal, nonautomatic activities would include organizing to-be-learned information and using mnemonics (see Chapter 13). As a general rule, nonautomatic activities require effort, show developmental changes, are affected by instructions, and can be improved with practice. Automatic processing exhibits an absence of these characteristics. Automatic activities might also include the processing of spatial and temporal information, as well as frequency information. For example, there is evidence that neither spatial nor temporal memory is affected by subjects' knowledge of a forthcoming test (Mandler, Seegmiller, & Day, 1977; Zechmeister, McKillip, Pasko, & Bespalec, 1975; Zimmerman & Underwood, 1968).

Frequency theory of verbal discrimination learning

In a major review of the progress made in understanding the processes involved in human learning and memory, Tulving and Madigan (1970, p. 456) stated that the frequency theory of verbal discrimination learning "must be counted among the few genuine theories that we have. . . . It does explain data from a number of experiments, it does make specific predictions about outcomes of as yet undone experiments, it does deal with important fundamental processes in learning and memory, and it is specific enough so that it is capable of being proven wrong."* These reviewers predicted that the theory would generate considerable attention over the years, and indeed it has.

What is this theory that treats so soundly the basic issues of information acquisition and retention? We can begin our discussion by looking at several experiments based on the learning paradigm that gave rise to this theory, a paradigm called *verbal discrimination learning*.

Among the tasks included in the arsenal of the researcher who sets out to investigate learning and memory, few are as simple as the verbal discrimination task. Typically, subjects are first shown a list of word pairs. Words in the pairs are usually unrelated, and the experimenter arbitrarily designates one member as the "right" item, often by underlining or placing an asterisk next to it. Subjects are instructed to study the word pairs so they will remember which word in each pair is correct. On a subsequent test trial, subjects are shown the same list of word pairs, but this time the right item is not identified and they must attempt to choose the correct word in each pair. After a test trial, another study trial is given, and then a test trial, and so forth, until the subject learns to identify the right item in each pair. The same word is always correct within a pair, although its position (top or bottom, left or right) and the position of the pair in the list are varied during learning so that subjects cannot use spatial or temporal cues

*From "Memory and Verbal Learning," by E. Tulving and S. A. Madigan. In *Annual Review of Psychology*, 1970, *21*, 437–484. © 1970 by Annual Reviews Inc. This and all other quotations from this source are reprinted by permission.

to help them discriminate. The task is relatively simple and learning is often quite rapid, even when the list of word pairs is very long (see Shaughnessy, 1973). Therefore it is particularly interesting to look at those situations in which subjects have difficulty in acquiring a verbal discrimination. Such a situation provided Ekstrand, Wallace, and Underwood (1966) with the basis for the frequency theory of verbal discrimination learning.

The frequency theory was initially developed to explain the results of a verbal discrimination transfer experiment carried out by Underwood, Jesse, and Ekstrand (1964). In a transfer experiment the investigator is interested in the effect learning one task has on learning another. You would be doing a transfer experiment if you sought to investigate the effect of learning to play tennis on learning to play racquetball. In this case the researchers were interested in the effect of learning one verbal discrimination list on learning a second.

There were three groups of subjects in the experiment and each learned two verbal discrimination lists. The first group (control group) learned two different verbal discrimination lists. The two lists were made up of two entirely different sets of word pairs; for example, a list-1 pair might be *glut*-wren and a list-2 pair might be malt-*junk* (italics indicate the correct word in the pair). For another group of subjects (group R), the second list contained word pairs in which the right word in the first list was again the right word, and there was a new wrong word (for example, *glut*-wren and rave-*glut*). Finally, the third group (group W) learned two lists in which the wrong word from the first list was also the wrong word in the second list, but a new right word was present (for example, *glut*-wren and wren-*rave*). All the subjects learned the initial 16-pair list until they could discriminate perfectly on three successive trials. Of interest, of course, is what happened during the learning of the second list.

Figure 8-2 shows the results of this transfer study for the control group and for group W. Group R, with the same right items in both lists, made so few errors on the second list that this learning is not included in the graph. On the initial trial of the second list, group W made many fewer errors than the control group. But note what happened on the subsequent trials. Group W showed little improvement over the remaining transfer trials, and in fact group W's advantage on the first trial had disappeared by the fifth transfer trial. At the end of the tenth trial, group W still did not perform perfectly.

To explain these counterintuitive results, Ekstrand, Wallace, and Underwood (1966) suggested that learning a verbal discrimination depends on the situational frequency of pair members. They proposed that frequency might be "built up" to an item through representational responses (perceptually processing an item, as when we see or hear it), by pronouncing responses (saying an item aloud), by rehearsal responses (silently repeating an item), or through what are called *implicit associative responses*. This latter kind of response may

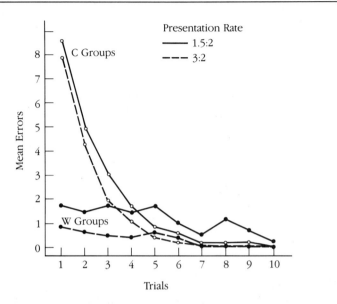

Figure 8-2. Verbal discrimination learning of the transfer list for subjects in groups C and W. The experiment was replicated for two different presentation rates, which is why there are four lines in the graph. *(From "Knowledge of Rights and Wrongs in Verbal-Discrimination Learning," by B. J. Underwood, F. Jesse, and B. R. Ekstrand. In* Journal of Verbal Learning and Verbal Behavior, *1964, 3, 183–186. Copyright 1964 by Academic Press, Inc. Reprinted by permission.)*

occur when an item is capable of eliciting another item because the two items are associatively related. For example, seeing the word *table* may lead you to think of the word *chair*. When this happens, it is assumed that both words gain in situational frequency, *table* through a representational response and *chair* due to an implicit associative response. That thinking of a word affects its situational frequency was demonstrated in a classic experiment by Underwood (1965, discussed in Chapter 10) and by an interesting experiment by Johnson, Taylor, and Raye (1977), which we will review later in this chapter.

Having considered the ways in which frequency might accrue to an item, now consider the interpretation of the results seen in Figure 8-2. We have already documented in this chapter the high degree of sensitivity people have to differences in situational frequency. The frequency theory assumes that items receive differential frequencies due to their role in the list and that subjects learn a verbal discrimination by detecting differences between the situational frequencies of the right and wrong items. For example, if on a study trial subjects say aloud or rehearse the right item more than the wrong item, at test time the right item will have a higher situational frequency than the wrong item. Because subjects are usually required to say aloud the correct item on the test trial, this response also adds to the frequency differential favoring the correct item. Frequency, in other words, is a cue subjects can use to identify the right item on the test trial. The theory doesn't say that subjects realize a frequency differential is the basis for a response. If you ask subjects how they learn a verbal discrimination list, they are likely to give such answers as "the correct item stood out" or "I just know it's right." Frequency is a way of providing operational meaning to the notion of familiarity. We could say that subjects recognize the right item because it is more familiar than the wrong item in this particular situation; however, that would tell us nothing about the mechanisms that produce differences in familiarity.

Perhaps you can begin to anticipate how the frequency theory accounts for the results in the Underwood, Jesse, and Ekstrand experiment. First consider group R. Remember, this group's performance on the transfer list was nearly perfect. Frequency theory predicts this because the same right items are present in the second list. These items would have gained substantial situational frequency because of their role in the first list. Therefore when asked to discriminate between items during second-list learning, subjects can readily detect a difference in frequency between the old right item and the new wrong item. According to the frequency theory, group W should also do very well on the first trial of the transfer list because this group, too, would experience a sizable frequency difference between members of the second-list pairs. For group W the frequency differential on the second list would favor the wrong item because it was included in the previous list whereas the right item had not been. It is suggested that subjects learn to respond correctly by selecting those pair items with lower frequency (sometimes called rule-2 learning, see Ekstrand, Wallace, & Underwood, 1966). That is, we can imagine that the wrong item initially "stands out" as the one *not* to choose. But think now what happens as a subject in group W learns the second list. The right item will quickly gain in frequency because it will be rehearsed and then pronounced on the test trial. As frequency increases to the right item, the theory predicts that discrimination between the right and wrong item will become more difficult. No longer does one item stand out. As you saw in Figure 8-2, group W subjects had considerable difficulty learning the second list. This is exactly what the theory predicts.

Well, the results in Figure 8-2 are not exactly what the theory predicts. If when group W subjects learn the second list and frequency builds up to the right item in such a way that situational frequency between the pair members "evens out," can you predict what performance should be like when the frequency of rights is equal to the frequency of wrongs? There should be a point when discrimination based on a frequency differential is impossible and sub-

jects' performance goes to chance (which would be 50:50 in a two-choice situation). Although some investigators have found an initial deterioration of performance in such transfer tasks (Pasko & Zechmeister, 1974; Raskin, Boise,
Rubel, & Clark, 1968), results have not been what a strict interpretation of the
theory would predict (see also Wallace & Sawyer, 1974). At some point during
second-list learning, subjects apparently use information other than frequency
to discriminate (Hintzman & Block, 1971; Underwood & Freund, 1970b). This
result should not detract from the fact that frequency theory predicts discrimination performance in many experimental situations (see Ekstrand, Wallace,
& Underwood, 1966; Underwood & Freund, 1968b; Underwood & Freund,
1970a; Zechmeister, McKillip, & Pasko, 1973).

The rationale behind the many tests of the frequency theory is straightfor-
ward. An experimental manipulation that increases the frequency of the right
items relative to the wrong items should enhance discrimination learning. Manipulations that result in similar situational frequencies for right and wrong
items should impair discrimination learning. For example, Underwood and
Freund (1968b) asked subjects to learn a verbal discrimination list under one
of three conditions: pronounce the correct item four times on each study trial;
pronounce both the correct *and* incorrect words two times; or they were given
no particular strategy. The list learning for subjects in these three groups is
shown in Figure 8-3. As the theory predicts, the group told to pronounce the
correct item aloud did the best, performing nearly perfectly from the initial
trial. Subjects who were required to pronounce each pair member aloud (and
hence increase situational frequency to both right and wrong items) had difficulty learning the list and, unlike the control group, had not learned the 14-
pair list even after ten trials.

The frequency theory helps to explain performance in nonlaboratory situations—for example, on multiple-choice examinations (Underwood, Patterson, & Freund, 1972)—as well as in recognition memory tasks (Underwood,
1971). Frequency cues may aid you in discriminating among answers on a
multiple-choice exam if situational frequency is higher for the right alternative
(because you studied that item more times) than for the wrong alternatives.
However, Underwood, Patterson, and Freund (1972, p. 7) described a possible
dilemma that may confront you when taking a multiple-choice exam:

> Consider a case in which the frequency of the correct alternative is marginally
> distinguishable from one or more incorrect alternatives. The subject may, at
> this point, "study" the various alternatives carefully in order to get additional
> information to help reach a decision. However, the act of gathering this in-
> formation may increase the frequency of the alternatives to the point that they
> are no longer distinguishable from the correct alternative. Therefore, unless

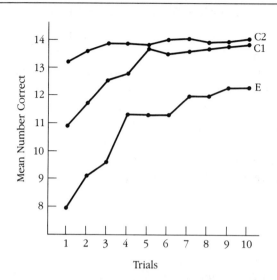

Figure 8-3. Acquisition of a verbal discrimination list by subjects required to pronounce both the correct and incorrect words two times on the study trial (E), to pronounce the correct word four times on each study trial (C2), or given no particular strategy (C1). *(From "Two Tests of a Theory of Verbal-Discrimination Learning," by B. J. Underwood and J. S. Freund. In* Canadian Journal of Psychology, *1968, 22, 96–104. Copyright 1968 by the Canadian Psychological Association Reprinted by permission.*

the additional information clearly leads to a correct decision, the decision can no longer be based upon a frequency differential. In short, poorer performance may result if too much time is spent in trying to arrive at a decision.

The frequency theory is not without its shortcomings. For example, background frequency for an event must necessarily arise from the fact that we have experienced this event in many situations. The theory doesn't explain how situational frequency is assimilated into background frequency (see Underwood & Freund, 1970b). Also, it is now clear that when subjects are instructed to use various strategies in learning discriminations—for example, to imagine the correct item or to consider an item's meaning—learning is *not* based primarily on frequency information (Ghatala, Levin, & Subkoviak, 1975; Zechmeister & Gude, 1974). Nevertheless, tests of the frequency theory have strongly supported the idea that in the absence of other information, memory for frequency of an event's occurrence is a dominant cue used in making verbal discriminations. The relationship between memory for frequency and recognition memory will be discussed in Chapter 10 and briefly again in Chapter 15.

FREQUENCY JUDGMENTS: BIASES

Up to this point we have shown how faithful a recorder of frequency information the human organism is and how our sensitivity to event frequency may permit us to discriminate correctly among verbal events that differ in situational frequency. Nevertheless, there are some situations where we are prone to make systematic errors when judging frequency. An analysis of these situations and the kinds of errors made will tell us more about how we judge frequency. Knowledge of the biases present when we judge frequency should also help us make better decisions when those decisions depend upon knowledge of the repetitiveness of past events.

Nature of stimulus material

Biases in frequency judgments can arise due to the nature of the stimulus material to be judged. For example, abstract words (words that do not denote specific objects, such as *democracy* or *time*) are generally judged to have higher background frequency than concrete words (words denoting objects, such as *house* and *tree*), even when the actual frequency is the same (see Galbraith & Underwood, 1973). Judgments of situational frequency are also affected by the "context" in which items are repeated (Malmi, 1977; Rowe & Rose, 1977). Malmi (1977) found that frequency judgments for words were different when the to-be-judged items were preceded by a high-frequency context (5 words presented 6 times each) than when preceded by a low-frequency context (30 words presented 1 time each). Also, as we will see later in this chapter, there is evidence that frequency judgments of real and imagined events are sometimes confused.

Availability heuristic

A serious error made when judging frequency of events arises from a deceptive frequency-judging strategy that relies on remembered availability of instances. Tversky and Kahneman (1973) refer to this strategy as an *availability heuristic*. You can think of a heuristic as a helpful strategy or learning aid. We use an availability heuristic, or strategy, whenever we estimate frequency by the ease with which we can bring to mind instances of a category. Tversky and Kahneman asked subjects to estimate the number of instances they could name from each of several categories. For example, how many Russian novelists can you name? How many flowers? They compared subjects' estimates with the number of instances they could actually produce. The correlation was very high, .93. They argued that to answer such questions, a person first determines the ease with which names of a category come to mind—that is, how "available" the names are. If we can easily and quickly think of several names of flowers, we are likely to give an estimate that is higher than if we have trouble thinking of any names or can think of only one or two.

Tversky and Kahneman provided the following illustrations of the potential bias in frequency estimation arising from using an availability heuristic. In one task they presented subjects with five letters: *R, K, L, V,* and *N.* Subjects were to judge whether each letter appeared more frequently in the first or third position in all English words (excluding words of fewer than three letters). Subjects also estimated the ratio of the most frequent letter to the least frequent. For example, if subjects judged that the letter *R* appeared more often in English words in the third position than in the first, they then had to say how much more frequent *R* was in the third than the first position. Of 152 subjects tested, 105 (69%) judged that the majority of the five letters was more likely to occur in the first position than the third. The average ratio was 2:1, meaning that overall the letters were thought to appear twice as frequently in the first than the third position in English words. In fact, all these letters occur more frequently in the third position in English words. Tversky and Kahneman argued that subjects err in their frequency estimates because they use an availability heuristic. That is, they apparently try to think of as many words as they can that either begin with a particular letter or have that letter in the third position. Because it is easier to think of words that begin with a letter than those that have a letter in a certain position, there will be more first-letter words available to subjects. Hence they misjudge this category as most frequent.

Another task these researchers used provided more convincing evidence of an availability heuristic because it involved a measure of availability as well as estimates of frequency. A large group of subjects listened to a list of 39 names, including names of both well-known and not-so-well-known personalities. Among the well-known names were Richard Nixon and Elizabeth Taylor. Names from the not-so-well-known group were William Fulbright and Lana Turner. The list always included 19 well-known names and 20 less-well-known names. For half the subjects the well-known names were all female names and the not-so-well-known names were male names. For the other half the reverse was true. Remember, the better-known names were always the less frequent. After listening to the list, subjects estimated whether it contained more female than male names. Of 99 subjects tested, 80 mistakenly judged that the sex represented by the well-known names was the more frequent. When another group of subjects was asked to recall the names from the list, average recall was about 12 for the well-known names and 8 for the less-well-known names. The well-known names were more available and evidently led subjects to make the wrong decision regarding actual frequency of occurrence.

Availability as a heuristic for judging frequency

Purpose

To demonstrate how an availability heuristic is used to judge frequency of an event's occurrence.

Materials

The experiment requires two lists of 39 names of known personalities of both sexes. Names of movie stars may be used (see Table F in the Appendix). One list contains 20 names of not-too-well-known female personalities and 19 names of well-known male personalities. In the other list the sex associated with the famous and less-famous class of names is reversed: 20 names of not-too-well-known male personalities and 19 names of well-known female personalities. First names are always included so the personality's sex is unambiguous. The 39 names are randomly ordered within a list with the restriction that no more than three names of a given sex appear consecutively.

Procedure

Any one subject is presented only one list, the two lists being used equally across all subjects in order to balance the sex of the famous and less-famous names. The list is read aloud at the rate of one name every 3 seconds. Subjects are asked to listen attentively to the list because their memory for information in the list will be tested. After listening to the 39 names, subjects judge whether the list contained more names of men or more names of women. (The experiment can be expanded by having additional groups of subjects attempt recall of the names rather than give frequency judgments. Number of names recalled from the famous and less-famous classes can be used to define availability.)

Instructions to Subjects

In this experiment I am going to read you a long list of names of movie stars. You should easily recognize the names in the list. When I am finished, I will test your memory for what you just heard. I cannot tell you the nature of the memory test at this time. Please listen carefully to all the names in the list. Ready? (After presenting the list, ask all subjects whether there were more names of *male* movie stars or more names of *female* movie stars.)

Summary and Analysis

Data of interest are the number of people erroneously judging the less-frequent sex (that is, the more-famous names) as the more frequent. It can first be determined whether errors differ for the two lists. For example, are errors greater when male or female names represent the more-famous class? Then sum the number of people making errors across both lists and express this as a proportion of the total number of people tested. A chi-square test may be used to determine statistical significance.

Recommended Minimum Number of Subjects

Total of 40; approximately 20 subjects tested with each list.

Based on an experiment by Tversky and Kahneman (1973).

Over-underestimation

Results of several studies at the Decision Research Institute in Eugene, Oregon, reveal another bias that appears in many frequency judgment tasks, one called *over-underestimation*. In one interesting experiment, researchers asked students at the University of Oregon to estimate the frequency of various "lethal events" (see Lichtenstein, Slovic, Fischhoff, Layman, & Combs, 1978). First, the students were given a "standard" to help them make their judgments. One group was told the frequency of deaths due to motor vehicle accidents in the United States was 50,000. The standard was based on true frequency information and was meant to provide subjects with a number from which their estimates could vary. The students were then presented many different causes of death (smallpox, measles, electrocution, poisoning, diabetes, and so forth) and asked to judge the frequencies of these events relative to the standard. The results of this experiment are shown in Figure 8-4.

The students' average estimates for the various lethal events tended to overestimate the frequency of events with relatively small true frequencies and to underestimate the frequency of events with large true frequencies. This bias toward over-underestimation appears regularly when many frequency judgments are required over a wide range of frequencies, even in laboratory studies of situational frequency (see Hintzman, 1969). In fact, if you will refer back to Figure 8-1, which contains the results of the Hasher and Chromiak (1977) study, you will see a tendency toward over-underestimation in those data. The reason for this frequency judgment bias is not clear, but it may be an "anchoring" effect. In general, anchoring is the tendency to adopt a certain reference (the anchor) and then to make judgments around the number. The number might be something like the average frequency in the list or a number subjects know. As mentioned, the standard or known frequency for the frequency judgments summarized in Figure 8-4 was 50,000, the frequency of motor vehicle fatalities. If estimates are not "extended" far enough above or below the standard, judged frequencies would tend to show a flatter curve than is appropriate—that is,

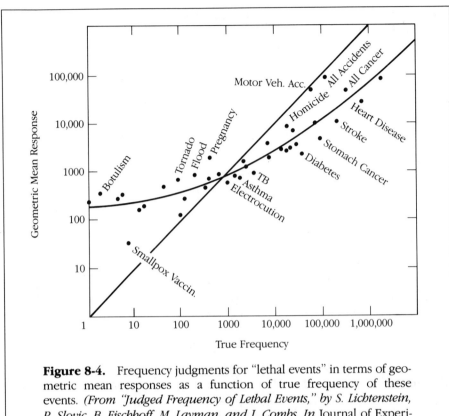

Figure 8-4. Frequency judgments for "lethal events" in terms of geometric mean responses as a function of true frequency of these events. *(From "Judged Frequency of Lethal Events," by S. Lichtenstein, P. Slovic, B. Fischhoff, M. Layman, and J. Combs. In* Journal of Experimental Psychology: Human Learning and Memory, *1978, 4, 551–578. Copyright 1978 by the American Psychological Association. Reprinted by permission.)*

judgments would reveal over-underestimation. When the Oregon researchers gave a different standard to another group of subjects, one that was much smaller (the number of deaths in a year by electrocutions, 1000), the overall frequency judgments for the same lethal events were lower, indicating that subjects were influenced by the known value. (Tversky and Kahneman, 1974, provide an interesting discussion of anchoring problems in judgments of subjective frequency.)

You may have spotted another bias in these results, one that appears to be most appropriately assigned to an availability heuristic. Careful examination of Figure 8-4 reveals that certain lethal events were greatly overestimated. For example, students judged cancer to be as frequent as heart disease. They also estimated deaths from floods to be about the same as deaths from asthma, but deaths from asthma are nine times more frequent than deaths from floods.

Tornado deaths were judged to be about ten times more frequent than they actually are. A possible explanation for these errors is the differential availability of instances of these events. Certain sensational events, such as deaths from floods and tornadoes, attract a lot of media attention and hence likely increase the availability of instances from these categories. When is the last time you heard a death from asthma reported in the headlines of a newspaper?

To test the notion that frequency estimates are biased by differential media coverage, leading to differential availability of instances of a category, Lichtenstein, Slovic, Fischhoff, Layman, and Combs counted the number of inches in the local newspaper devoted to the reporting of various deaths over a year. They found that 153.5 inches were devoted to coverage of tornadoes and 1.9 inches to deaths due to asthma, 5042.9 inches to homicides and 356.7 inches to suicides (there are actually more suicides than homicides). The correlation between amount of newspaper coverage and frequency judgments was higher for estimated frequency than for true frequency, supporting the idea that disproportionate reporting of lethal events in the media results in biased frequency estimates.

Given these results for frequency estimates of "real-life" events, researchers at the Decision Research Institute (Lichtenstein et al., 1978) are more pessimistic about our ability to judge frequency than are researchers who have investigated frequency for laboratory events and who have found generally accurate frequency reporting. Because estimating frequency is often the basis for assessing social risks, these researchers are quite concerned about the average citizen's ability to judge these risks accurately:

> People do not have accurate knowledge of the risks they face. As our society puts more and more effort into the regulation and control of these risks (banning cyclamates in food, lowering highway speed limits, paying for emergency coronary-care equipment, etc.), it becomes increasingly important that these biases be recognized and, if possible, corrected. Improved public education is needed before we can expect the citizenry to make reasonable public-policy decisions about societal risks. . . . The experts who guide and influence these policies should be aware that when they rely on their own experience, memory, and common sense, they, too, may be susceptible to bias [p. 577].

Can we reconcile these demonstrations of frequency judgment biases with the results of laboratory studies showing that frequency encoding is a relatively basic process that yields generally accurate judgments? We can if you consider several important differences between laboratory studies of frequency and investigations of frequency estimation for real-life events. First, biases are revealed most dramatically when the frequency information provided the subject is ambiguous or incomplete. Tversky and Kahneman (1973) found that subjects misjudged the names of famous personalities in a manner predicted by the availability heuristic. Yet the frequency difference in this situation was 20 versus 19. That we are very sensitive to frequency does not mean we are perfect. When information is unclear, it makes sense that we consider a strategy like availability to help us make decisions. After all, availability is a perfectly reasonable strategy in many situations. You should also note that Tversky and Kahneman asked subjects to judge how frequently a particular category of items appeared, not how frequently a specific item from the category was presented. Availability biases are more likely to be seen for category judgments than for item judgments.

Another major difference between studies investigating memory for frequency of laboratory events and those investigating memory of real-life events is that many real-life events are rarely, or only infrequently, experienced directly. In other words, subjects may have little direct knowledge of the events to be judged. How many electrocutions have you witnessed? In laboratory studies of situational frequency, subjects' experience of the number of events is controlled; or when judgments of background frequency are required, subjects are assumed to have had similar personal histories. Without direct experience, subjects must guess. These guesses are no doubt influenced by factors contributing to differential availability. To what extent subjects use an availability heuristic in more traditional laboratory tasks is not clear at this time.

FREQUENCY AND CREDIBILITY

Do you believe everything you hear? Of course not. But when you hear the same thing repeated on several different occasions, does it become more believable, even in the absence of any externally validating evidence? There is interesting empirical evidence for the somewhat cynical proposition that if people are told something enough times, they tend to believe it.

Hasher, Goldstein, and Toppino (1977) asked college students to help them construct "a new test of the general knowledge of college students." To do this, students listened to a lengthy list of statements, some of which were true and some of which were false. All the statements were plausible assertions but were relatively unknown bits of information, so students would not likely know whether a particular statement was true. For example, several questions from the categories of "History" and "Government and Politics" were the following:

1. Kentucky was the first state west of the Alleghenies to be settled by pioneers.
2. The People's Republic of China was founded in 1947.
3. French horn players get cash bonuses to stay in the U.S. Army.
4. Zachary Taylor was the first president to die in office.

The second and fourth are false and the first and third are true. On three different occasions, separated by 2-week intervals, students listened to a list of 60 sentences and rated each sentence on a 7-point scale as to how sure they were that it was true or false (1 = definitely false, 4 = uncertain, 7 = definitely true).

The experiment was not designed to create a new knowledge test but was planned to investigate the effect of repetition on judgments of a statement's veracity. A critical manipulation was that some of the sentences were repeated from one occasion to the next. When this happened, their average rating increased across the three test sessions; the average rating for nonrepeated sentences did not change. In other words, repeating a sentence led to its being rated as more true on the second and third occasions. And this occurred whether the sentence was really true or false.

A group of Canadian researchers (see Bacon, 1979) replicated these findings and offered evidence that the increase in credibility for repeated sentences may be mediated by subjects' recognition that a sentence was actually experienced previously. They asked students in their experiment first to identify whether a sentence was repeated from an earlier test or whether it was new (one not repeated) before they rated the sentence as true or false. The data from this experiment indicated that increases in credibility occurred only when a sentence was recognized as one repeated. In fact, even new sentences were rated as more true if students mistakenly thought they had heard them previously.

The tendency to believe something is true because it was repeated could lead us to distort reality should fact and fantasy get mixed together. Suppose we were to demonstrate that experiencing repetitions of a purely imaginary event serves to increase our estimates of the frequency of occurrence of the real event. Would we then find ourselves in the position of tending to believe certain things (because they were repeated) even though previous repetitions of that event had been imagined? We can only speculate as to whether frequency of imagined events increases the credibility of a real event (see, however, Johnson and Raye, 1981), but we can offer evidence that imagined occurrences affect our memory for the frequency of real events.

FREQUENCY JUDGMENTS OF IMAGINED EVENTS

When we are asked to make frequency judgments, sometimes we confuse fact and fantasy. Johnson, Taylor, and Raye (1977) showed that when people are called upon to judge the frequency of certain internally generated events (for example, thinking of a word) and to judge the frequency of similar externally generated events (for example, actually viewing a word), there was a tendency for the frequency of one to influence the other, and vice versa. This intriguing finding is clearly seen in an experiment that also provided evidence that certain individuals may be more susceptible to confusing imaginations with actual perceptual experiences than are others (Johnson, Raye, Wang, & Taylor, 1979).

In this experiment both pictures and words were presented to introductory psychology students as part of a test of imagery. The students studied the pictures and were then shown words corresponding to the names of the pictures. Upon seeing a word, they were to generate an image of the picture and then rate how similar their image was to the actual picture. There were 36 different pictures and all subjects saw each picture either two, five, or eight times. Students also generated images for each picture two, five, or eight times. Therefore the frequency of pictures and words (images) was combined factorially to yield nine different combinations (for example, a picture presented twice was imagined two, five, and eight times, similarly for pictures appearing five and eight times). Unannounced to the subjects, a frequency judgment test was administered immediately after they viewed and imagined the pictures. For the frequency judgment test the names of the pictures were read to the students and they wrote the number of times they had actually seen them projected on the screen in front of them. Finally, the students were given standard tests of visual imagery and divided into "good" and "poor" imagers on the basis of their scores on these tests.

Figure 8-5 shows the average judged frequency of the pictures as a function of the number of times the subjects had also imaged a picture. For example, consider the line in the graph marked "2" for the good imagers. Points along this line represent the average frequency judgments for items shown twice and imaged either two, five, or eight times. If imaging the pictures had no effect on frequency judgments of actual occurrences, then the line would be flat. Clearly it is not. A picture that was presented two times was judged to have been more frequently presented the more times it was imaged. Note that the effect of imaginary repetitions on judged frequency of actual presentations is present for all frequency levels and for both good and poor imagers. However, the effect is more dramatic (the lines are steeper) for the good than for the bad imagers. This suggests that the quality of the imaginary representation may have something to do with the influence that imagined frequency has on judged frequency of real events. As Johnson, Raye, Wang, and Taylor (1979, pp. 238–239) stated,

> These results indicate that one factor in producing confusion between memory representations of perceptions and the memory representations of imaginations may be the faithfulness with which an imagination matches the memory of original perceptual experience. We may fairly often confuse thoughts with imagination of relatively simple events, such as whether we imagined a particular statement during a conversation or actually heard it. One thing that may protect us from more debilitating confusion is the generally schematic

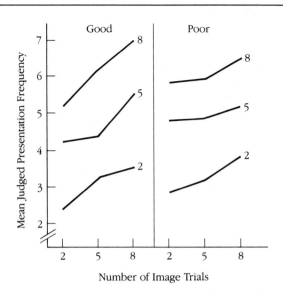

Figure 8-5. Mean judged frequency as a function of the number of times an item was imaged. Each line represents a different presentation frequency. Results for good imagers are shown on the left and results for poor imagers are on the right. *(From "Fact and Fantasy: The Roles of Accuracy and Variability in Confusing Imaginations with Perceptual Experiences," by M. K. Johnson, C. L. Raye, A. Y. Wang, and T. H. Taylor. In* Journal of Experimental Psychology: Human Learning and Memory, *1979, 5, 229–240. Copyright 1979 by the American Psychological Association. Reprinted by permission.)*

and nondetailed character of our imaginations. Perhaps we normally do not confuse fact and fantasy too much because we generally do not or cannot generate faithfully the complexity of many experiences.

In Chapter 13 we discuss an individual who, through the use of a highly developed visual memory, was able to remember nearly everything he ever heard or saw. Yet on many occasions he was unable to separate reality from what he had imagined (see Luria, 1968). Finally, in an interesting follow-up to their experiment, Raye, Johnson, and Taylor (1980) showed that judgments of the frequency of generated events were less affected by actual frequency of occurrence than the reverse. In some situations, therefore, we may be more sensitive to frequency of internally generated events than to frequency of externally generated ones. In most cases, however, research has shown that judgments of an event's frequency are still closer to the actual frequency of its occurrence than to its imagined frequency of occurrence. Therefore for most of us, at least, reality is distinguishable from fantasy.

THEORIES OF FREQUENCY REPRESENTATION

That we can judge the relative frequency of an event does not necessarily tell us how we do it, although, as we saw, an availability heuristic may sometimes come into play. Several theories of the nature of the information used to make frequency judgments have been proposed, but like many other issues you will encounter in this book, no one theory has yet won out over the others. Let's look at some of the alternatives.

Strength theory

One possible consequence of repeating an event is to increase its *memory strength*. Although a somewhat vague concept, memory strength has been traditionally defined by measures of performance on both immediate and delayed memory tests. It is assumed that "stronger" items are more likely to be remembered and to show the least forgetting over time. The *strength theory of frequency representation* says that frequency estimates are a matter of "reading" the strength of a memory. A major problem with this theory, however, is that even assuming we have access to some internal representation of memory strength, the strength theory fails to explain how the strength dimension yields frequency information. How do we know that a "strong" memory represents an event that appeared five times rather than four times? Another problem with the strength theory is that our own introspection tells us that many memories are very strong (for example, those associated with certain traumatic or emotional events in our lives); yet we do not necessarily judge these events as having occurred many times. Another problem is that laboratory studies have shown that experimental variables that presumably affect memory strength (for example, the duration of an item's presentation) do not affect frequency judgments in a similar fashion (Hintzman, 1970). Because of these difficulties, few researchers today accept a strength theory of frequency (see also Wells, 1974).

Attribute theory

One way to make frequency independent of strength is to assume that frequency information is part of the memory (Underwood, 1969). We might postulate an internal "counter" that adjusts frequency each time we experience an event. Because frequency would be an attribute of the memory, it need not be decoded from some other index such as strength. The internal counter would provide the necessary information and we, like the gas man, would only have to read the meter. An *attribute theory of frequency* is the basis for the frequency theory of verbal discrimination learning as well as for a theory of recognition memory we will discuss in Chapter 10 (see Underwood & Freund, 1970c). One major problem with the attribute theory is that it must explain how frequency judgments can be accurately made for fractions of larger units—for example, for letters we experience in words or for words that are parts of sentences (see Table 8-1). Do we have frequency counters for every conceivable stimulus fragment? One suggestion is that frequency information is processed for whatever is a "natural" element of the stimulus configuration (Underwood & Zimmerman, 1973).

Propositional encoding

Yet another way to conceive of frequency representation is to assume we provide our own verbal description of an event's history. When the movie *Star Wars* was released in 1977, it became a national craze, especially among pre-teens. (Well, some of us older people also went.) A neighborhood child reported to us he had seen the movie seven times. We do not doubt his estimate was accurate, yet how did he remember frequency? It is likely that he simply updated his memory for frequency of viewing each time he went to the theater. We can imagine that as he left the theater on each occasion, he would say something like "Now, I've seen it five times." This manner of representing frequency is referred to as *propositional encoding*. Hintzman (1976, p. 51) described how a subject might encode frequency information using propositions in a laboratory study in which words are repeated. He suggested that if we could get inside a subject's head, we might hear something like this as the word *cat* is repeated:

1st presentation: "Hmm ... *cat*. Try to remember *cat*."
2nd presentation: "*Cat*. I remember seeing that one before."
3rd presentation: "*Cat*. That must be three or four times *cat* has occurred."
4th presentation: There's *cat* again. I've seen *cat* several times already."

Of course, the subject would have to remember only the proposition encoded on the last occurrence in order to provide an accurate judgment of the item's frequency. You might remember that when we discussed memory for the gist of sentences, we suggested that we sometimes hear ourselves saying "I've heard that before." This would be another example of propositional encoding.

Although propositional encoding likely plays some role in memory for an event's repetition, it cannot be the complete answer. Remember the results of the Hasher and Chromiak (1977) experiment we reviewed earlier. They found no difference in frequency estimates between groups of subjects forewarned that a frequency test was to be given and those not forewarned or between young children and adults. Knowing that a frequency test is coming and the fact that as we get older we are more verbally adept should affect both the quality and number of propositions. Therefore a propositional theory would predict that frequency estimates should differ in these situations. The "automatic" nature of frequency encoding is more compatible with an attribute theory of frequency than with a propositional theory.

Multiple-trace theory

None of the theories mentioned thus far adequately explains a very important aspect of our frequency judging ability—namely, that we are capable of partitioning the frequency of an item according to different contexts in which we have experienced it. Hintzman and Block (1971) demonstrated that not only could subjects identify an item's frequency within a list of words but they could also accurately identify where in the list an item was repeated. Additionally, when presented with two lists of words in which the same item was repeated in both lists but with varying frequencies, subjects accurately judged the frequency of a list-1 item relatively independently of the same item's frequency of occurrence in list 2 (see also Macey & Zechmeister, 1975). Whitlow and Estes (1979) also showed that subjects are sensitive to shifts in the relative frequency of occurrence of items even when there are no distinctive breaks in item presentation, as would be the case when two different lists are used. A complete theory of frequency representation must take into account this ability to discriminate between the different contexts of an item's repetitions. To do this, Hintzman and Block proposed a *multiple-trace* hypothesis. The assumptions of this theory are that each presentation of an item produces its own memory trace, that the traces of an event's occurrences coexist (that is, they are all represented in memory), and that the traces of different presentations of the same item can be discriminated on the basis of other information encoded with them (see Hintzman, 1976). The context-dependent nature of frequency information may be particularly important in some situations, for instance, multiple-choice testing. On a multiple-choice exam the student is looking not for the most familiar (frequent) alternative in general. Rather, the stem of the question helps define the context within which frequency is assessed.

The multiple-trace theory must be considered the leading candidate for a theory of frequency representation. To explain how we are able to keep frequencies separate for different contexts or lists, strength theory or attribute theory would have to suggest that an item has different "strengths" for different contexts or that the frequency counter assumed in the attribute theory is able to "subtotal" frequencies for various contexts. Similarly, the propositional theory would necessarily have to postulate different verbal descriptions for the various situations in which an item is repeated (parts of a list, different lists, and so forth). A subject would be lost in a mass of verbal descriptions. The multiple-trace theory suggests that, in order to make frequency judgments, a person either retrieves the relevant traces of an item and then counts them or estimates how many traces there are on the basis of retrieved information. These estimates may somehow be based on the "availability" of item traces in a particular context. Nevertheless, our ability to make accurate and relatively quick judgments of frequency in what seems to be an automatic fashion argues against our always using mechanisms that rely on counting traces or assessing availability. A combination of the multiple-trace theory and one or more of the other theories we reviewed will probably be needed for a complete account of frequency representation.

Summary

One of the remarkable aspects of our memory is its ability to keep track of the repetitiveness of events. We are often very accurate in our estimates of both situational and background frequency. This ability has even been called "automatic," which means that memory for frequency does not require significant cognitive effort, the ability to judge frequency does not change appreciably as we grow older, and it doesn't vary with practice or as a function of being informed of the nature of the memory test. Our sensitivity to event frequency has played a major role in the frequency theory of verbal discrimination learning. The theory assumes that differences in situational frequency aid performance in a variety of situations, including multiple-choice examinations and recognition memory tests. Although frequency is often a dominant cue in making verbal discriminations, research has revealed when it becomes a secondary or less-dominant cue.

There are systematic biases present in our judgments of an event's frequency, two of which are over-underestimation and overreliance on an availability heuristic. The number of times information has been repeated also appears to affect our judgments regarding a statement's truthfulness. In addition, an interesting series of experiments discussed in this chapter alerts us to the fact that frequency judgments of "real" events can be affected by the frequency of imagined events.

Researchers do not yet agree on how frequency information is registered in memory. Possible explanations include strength theory, attribute theory, propositional theory, and the leading candidate, a multiple-trace theory. Several lines of research that will no doubt occupy researchers for some time to come are those investigating the automaticity of frequency (and other attribute) encoding, identifying the relationship between internally and externally experienced events, and the continuing theoretical inquiry into how frequency is represented in memory.

Recommendations for further reading

Reviews of verbal discrimination learning are found in Eckert and Kanak (1974) and Wallace (1972). The frequency theory of verbal discrimination learning is outlined in Ekstrand, Wallace, and Underwood (1966). Possible extensions and modifications of the original frequency theory have been described by Kausler (1974). A discussion of experiments that indicate sensitivity to event frequency and the relationship of frequency sensitivity to recognition memory (a topic to be more fully discussed in Chapter 10) is found in Underwood (1971). Howell (1973) and Hintzman (1976) review theories of frequency representation. A more complete understanding of the availability heuristic can be gotten by reading the interesting articles by Tversky and Kahneman (1973, 1974). We particularly recommend the highly readable and informative paper by Hasher and Zachs (1979), which contrasts automatic and effortful processes in memory. Finally, Johnson and Raye (1981) describe a model of "reality monitoring," or the ability to distinguish whether a memory has an external or internal source.

9

Distribution of Practice

Introduction/overview

We would like to ask you a question about the following situation:

Student A and Student B are enrolled in the same class. An assignment is given to the class and it is announced that an examination (test of retention) will be given on the assignment later. Student A and Student B spend an identical amount of time preparing for the exam; however, Student A "distributes" her study time among several practice periods while Student B "masses" his study in one concentrated effort. Both students finish their preparation at the same time.

The question, of course, is who will do better on the examination, Student A or Student B. Which is better, distributed practice or massed practice of to-be-remembered material?

The problem is one of the oldest to be investigated by psychologists in the field of learning and memory (see McGeoch & Irion, 1952). As you can readily see, there are numerous areas in which an understanding of practice effects may have application. Yet many questions regarding the most effective distribution of study time are still unanswered and recommendations given by educators and psychologists regarding most efficient practice are some-times in error or made without full knowledge of the limitations of practice effects. Perhaps we can indicate something of the complexity of this issue by looking at your answer to the question just presented.

Most people are likely to say Student A will do better on the exami-nation. After all, what student hasn't heard about the "evils" of cramming? Consider one such indictment against massed study, given by the eminent 19th-century psychologist William James (1890, p. 663), who had much to say about memory processes that still rings true today.

> The reason why cramming is such a bad mode of study is now made clear. I mean by cramming that way of preparing for exam-inations by committing "points" to memory during a few hours or days of intense application immediately preceding the final ordeal, little or no work having been performed during the previous course of the term. Things learned thus in a few hours, on one occasion, for one purpose, cannot possibly have formed many associations with other things in the mind. Their brain-processes are led into by few paths, and are relatively little liable to be awak-ened again. Speedy oblivion is the almost inevitable fate of all that is committed to memory in this simple way. Whereas, on the con-trary, the same materials taken in gradually, day after day, recurring in different contexts, considered in various relations, associated with other external incidents, and repeatedly reflected on, grow into such a system, form such connections with the rest of the mind's fabric, lie open to so many paths of approach, that they remain permanent possessions.

Apparently Student B doesn't have a chance. His memory for the assignment is destined to "speedy oblivion." But before we rush to that conclusion, let's take a second opinion, one reached by a well-known experimental psy-chologist who spent many years studying distribution of practice. (To make things simpler, we will occasionally refer to this issue as the MP-DP problem, meaning that massed practice, MP, and distributed practice, DP, of to-be-remembered material have been compared.) In fact, Underwood and his students at Northwestern University conducted research on the MP-DP issue for so many years that he published an important article in 1961 under the title, "Ten Years of Massed Practice on Distributed Practice." After all that practice, Underwood (1961, p. 230) reached the following conclusion:

If one wishes to use an efficiency measure for learning, it would be very inefficient to learn by DP; the subject would be much further ahead to learn by MP if total time to learn (including the rest intervals in DP) is the criterion. Even under the most favorable conditions for facilitation by DP, one could not recommend its use in an applied setting where verbal materials are to be mastered.

Can this be right? Is there really no difference to speak of when massed and distributed practice are compared? What about cramming? Was William James wrong? Would Student B do as well as Student A?

These two psychologists' conclusions are not really at odds. Whether massed or distributed practice is a superior mode of study depends on certain critical factors, which by the way were not identified in the situation described for you. The best response to our question would have been to ask for more information. What was the nature of the assignment? How long was the interval between the end of practice and the retention test or between periods of practice?

In this chapter we will first examine how psychologists investigated the MP-DP issue using traditional verbal learning tasks such as serial learning and paired-associate learning. These studies were overshadowed in the early 1960s by the discovery of MP-DP differences of another sort. Whereas the MP-DP differences found in paired-associate learning resulted from manipulating the interval between presentations of lists of to-be-remembered items, more recent MP-DP phenomena have resulted from controlling the interval between presentations of single items. The nature and extent of MP-DP differences found when retention of individual items is investigated has led to a theoretical controversy that is far from settled. We will review briefly this research and the controversy surrounding it. Finally, we will introduce you to another MP-DP phenomenon where the distribution of test trials, not study trials, is of interest. Through it all you will gain important information about how to organize practice to produce optimal learning and retention.

THE TRADITIONAL CASE FOR DP SUPERIORITY

The idea that distributed practice is better than massed practice has been around for some time. Based on his study of nonsense syllable lists, Ebbinghaus (1885/1964, p. 89) suggested that *"with any considerable number of repetitions* a suitable distribution of them over a space of time is decidedly more advantageous than the massing of them at a single time." In his influential textbook, McGeoch (1942, p. 119) stated, "The generalization that some form of positive distribution yields faster learning than does massed practice holds over so wide a range of conditions that it stands as one of our most general conclusions." Although the results of many experiments, ranging from maze learning with rats to inverted alphabet writing with humans, appeared to support this statement, the magnitude of MP-DP differences frequently varied from experiment to experiment. In fact, some experiments showed no facilitation for distributed practice, and in some cases massed practice was found to be superior in task acquisition. In the midst of these discordant findings it was not surprising that researchers found it impossible to agree on a single explanation for MP-DP differences. In a later edition of his textbook, McGeoch and Irion (1952) proposed no fewer than eight theories to account for differences in learning and retention as a function of distribution of practice.

Task acquisition

Whether distributed practice is superior to massed practice in the acquisition of a task is now known to depend chiefly on the nature of the task. Learning of a perceptual-motor skill is generally more efficient when practice is distributed than when it is massed. An early experiment by Lorge (1930, reviewed by McGeoch & Irion, 1952) illustrated the dramatic differences observed in the rate of skill learning when practice schedules were contrasted. Subjects were given 20 practice trials on a *mirror drawing task*. Mirror drawing requires that subjects draw a picture or geometric form by observing their progress in the reversed image of the mirror. Not an easy task until you get the hang of it. When practice was massed, one practice trial immediately followed another. For distributed practice the trials were spaced at either 1-minute or 24-hour intervals. Figure 9-1 shows learning as a function of practice conditions. Performance was clearly superior under conditions of distributed practice, and, interestingly enough, there was little difference between a 1-minute or a 24-hour interval. Similar practice effects are commonly found when a perceptual-motor skill is learned, and experiments similar to Lorge's have become standard laboratory demonstrations in experimental psychology courses. The recommended mode of practice for perceptual-motor learning, whether it be mirror drawing, bicycle riding, or gymnastics, is distributed practice.

When the task to be learned involves verbal material, there is often little if any advantage found for distributed practice when compared with massed practice. As we just saw, this was Underwood's (1961) conclusion after he reviewed many MP-DP studies that were performed using such traditional tasks as paired-associate learning. In the majority of these studies learning was considered to be massed when the interval between presentations of a list of items was relatively short—for example, less than 8 seconds. Learning was defined as distributed when the interval between list presentations was greater than 15 seconds but usually no longer than a couple of minutes. With practice defined in this way distributed practice yielded superior learning of paired associates only under a limited set of conditions, and even then the differences between

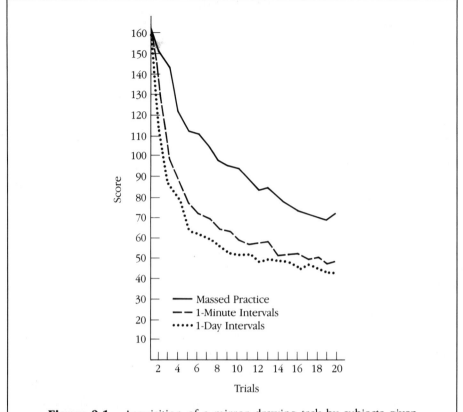

Figure 9-1. Acquisition of a mirror drawing task by subjects given massed practice or distributed practice (either 1 minute or 1 day between practice periods). *(From* The Psychology of Human Learning, Second Edition, *by John A. McGeoch and Arthur L. Irion. Copyright 1952 by Longmans, Green & Co., Inc.; renewed © 1980 by Arthur L. Irion. Reprinted by permission of Longman Inc., New York.)*

practice schedules were small. For example, DP schedules produced faster learning than MP schedules only when the response terms in the paired-associate list were likely to interfere with learning, as when a high degree of physical similarity was present among nonsense-syllable responses (CAQ, CAK, KAQ). The explanation for DP superiority in these cases was that an interval between trials allowed for more effective extinction of error tendencies than was possible under massed practice. With this information you may be questioning the value of distributed practice when verbal materials, for instance, psychology facts, are to be mastered. However, up to this point we have been discussing the *acquisition* of a task. Retention is another story.

Task retention

Retention is generally greater after distributed practice than massed practice if the intervals between practice periods are relatively long—for example, 24 hours (Cain & Willey, 1939; Keppel, 1964, 1967). When distributed practice intervals are relatively short, no more than a few minutes, the magnitude of retention effects as a function of practice schedule is generally small and, as we saw for verbal learning, occur only under a limited set of circumstances (see Underwood & Schulz, 1961).

Keppel (1964, 1967) designed two experiments to assess the effect of distributed practice on long-term retention of a list of paired associates when the interval between practice was relatively long. In both experiments the critical list consisted of paired nonsense syllables and adjectives. Subjects were asked to learn a relationship between the items so that when presented with the syllable, they could provide the adjective. Subjects studied the critical list for eight trials. However, some subjects studied the list with the eight trials each separated by only 4 seconds (MP); others had every two trials separated by 24-hour intervals (DP).

The two experiments differed according to what was learned *prior to* the critical list. In the first experiment (Keppel, 1964), the critical list was actually the fourth list subjects learned, the previous three lists having been learned under MP schedules and all having had the same syllables but different adjectives as the critical list. As you may recall from Chapter 6, this situation can be described as A-B, A-C, A-D, A-E. Significant proactive inhibition should be present when retention of the critical list (A-E) is tested. In the second experiment (Keppel, 1967), subjects learned only the critical list. Retention of the eight-pair list was tested in both experiments after 1 day or after 8 days.

Results of the multiple-list experiment and the single-list experiment are shown in Figure 9-2. Memory for the adjective terms of the critical list was greater at both 1-day and 8-day retention intervals when learning was distributed. The findings are particularly impressive in the multiple-list experiment, where substantial proactive inhibition due to learning the previous three lists was expected. After 1 day, in this case, there was massive retention loss for those subjects who learned under massed conditions. When retention followed distributed practice, subjects experienced no such retention loss.

Keppel's (1967) explanation for the dramatic differences in retention seen as a function of practice conditions turns out to be different from that provided by William James. James argued that distributed practice allows more different associations to be developed between the material and what we already know. Increasing the number of associations to an item produced, in James's words, more "paths of approach," or as we would say today, more retrieval cues. Modern theorists refer to this type of explanation as a *variable encoding hypothesis*

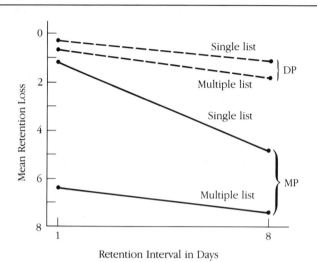

Figure 9-2. Mean retention loss over 1 day and 8 days as a function of massed (MP) and distributed (DP) learning when a single list was learned or when the critical list was the last learned in a multiple-list experiment. *(From "A Reconsideration of the Extinction-Recovery Theory," by G. A. Keppel. In* Journal of Verbal Learning and Verbal Behavior, *1967, 6, 476–486. Copyright 1967 by Academic Press, Inc. Reprinted by permission.)*

(Martin, 1968; Melton, 1970). An encoding variability hypothesis assumes that a to-be-remembered item is encoded differently from one presentation to another. It is generally assumed that the degree of variable encoding is positively related to the interval between presentations: the greater the interval, the more likely an item is to be encoded differently on each of its presentations.

Keppel's explanation for superior retention following distributed practice emphasized the quality, not the quantity, of associations that might develop during distributed learning. He suggested that during acquisition a subject tries to find some way to link the verbal items of a pair together, perhaps using some word or idea to "hook up" the two items. That is, some associations that are formed between members of a pair during learning will be better than others. The better the associative link, the better the chance the item will be remembered at some later time. (For example, see Hasher & Johnson, 1975, and Chapter 7.) Now consider what possibly happens when learning is distributed and intervals between practice sessions are quite long. As subjects return for additional practice, they discover that some of their associations formed during the previous practice session have been forgotten and that they must now find new ways to hook up the verbal items. Therefore under distributed learning the subjects have the opportunity to "test" their associations and continually to replace weak associations with newer and more stable ones. At the end of acquisition, it is assumed that the associations subjects developed under distributed practice will be qualitatively better than those developed under massed study; hence, retention should be greater after distributed learning. Interestingly, there have been few attempts to distinguish between Keppel's explanation for DP superiority and that based on a variable encoding hypothesis (although see Maki & Hasher, 1975).

DP superiority in the long run

By now you should have sufficient information to answer the question we presented at the beginning of this chapter. Assuming that verbal material (for example, information from a textbook on psychology) is to be learned, then we cannot expect large differences in the *acquisition* rate of the material as a function of practice conditions. Student A and Student B could very well know the same amount of material at the end of their respective study periods. In fact if the retention test was given immediately after study, there might be little difference in their performance. This is something students probably discover for themselves and no doubt creates the dangerous impression that massed study is as "good" as distributed study.

However, if there was a significant length of time between the end of study and the retention test and if the intervals between periods of distributed study were relatively long (24 hours, say), then we can be fairly confident that Student A will succeed and Student B will not. Further, because significant amounts of proactive inhibition will be present for most students (from all those previous courses and tests), when long-term retention is the goal, the use of distributed practice is particularly crucial. In short, a premedical student might perform adequately on a series of tests in various courses by massing study right up to the time of the examination. But should a comprehensive exam be required at some later time (for instance, the MCAT), this student will undoubtedly need to spend more time on review than a student who consistently organized study in a distributed fashion.

DP AND SINGLE-ITEM RETENTION

On several occasions we have referred to an important experimental procedure known as the Brown-Peterson paradigm. In Chapter 3 we saw that the introduction of this paradigm in the late 1950s began a controversy that has lasted for more than two decades. Is forgetting from primary memory due to decay, interference, or displacement? In Chapter 7 we saw that the same paradigm has been used to investigate multiple encoding in the context of release from proactive inhibition (PI). The introduction of the Brown-Peterson task signaled an important change in how psychologists investigated memory. This technique, wherein an individual item is first presented and then retention is tested after a distractor-filled interval, was an important break from more traditional methodologies, such as paired-associate learning and serial learning, wherein *lists* of items are presented for study before retention is tested. The Brown-Peterson task helped to focus attention on the conditions surrounding encoding and retention of individual items.

Continuous paired-associate learning

Interest in the retention of single items led to yet another paradigm to investigate memory processes, one called *continuous paired-associate learning* (Peterson, Saltzman, Hillner, & Land, 1962). In this task subjects are given single pairs of items to study. As is the case for more traditional paired-associate learning, they are instructed to learn an association between the first and second members of the pair so they can produce the second member when the first is presented. Unlike more traditional association tasks, however, retention of a single pair is tested after a short interval filled with the presentation and test of other paired associates. The continuous paired-associate learning task affords investigators an opportunity to examine the retention of individual associations over very brief intervals, as is done in the Brown-Peterson task. It also has the advantage of allowing data to be quickly collected on many pairs at several different retention intervals because study and test trials are intertwined continually. Table 9-1 shows a typical study and test series when distribution of practice is investigated in this type of task.

In several experiments Peterson and his associates (Peterson et al., 1962; Peterson, Wampler, Kirkpatrick, & Saltzman, 1963) used the continuous paired-associate task to investigate retention differences as a function of the spacing of two repetitions of a single paired associate. (Rather than talk about MP-DP differences when retention of single items is tested, researchers prefer to describe study conditions in terms of the spacing between individual items. A zero spacing—that is, no intervening items—is equivalent to massed study; intervals of spacing greater than zero are considered distributed study. Superior retention following distributed study of single items relative to massed study is frequently called a *spacing effect*.) In one such experiment (Peterson et al., 1963, Experiment III) the pairs to be remembered were familiar single-syllable words. They were presented once or twice before being tested. Half the twice-presented pairs were presented at zero spacing; for the other half there were four items intervening between repetitions. Both the massed and distributed items were tested for retention after 4 and 16 seconds. At the long interval (16 seconds), retention of single pairs was greater following spaced than massed pre-

TABLE 9-1. Example of a Continuous Paired-Associate Learning Procedure

Trial number	Study (S) or test (T) trial	Type of item: single, MP, or DP	Item
1	S	DP (1)	dog–car
2	S	Single	cup–desk
3	S	MP (1)	pen–wood
4	S	MP (2)	pen–wood
5	S	Single	rat–book
6	S	DP (2)	dog–car
7	T	Single	cup–?
8	S	DP (1)	brick–tree
9	T	MP	pen–?
10	T	Single	rat–?
11	T	DP	dog–?
12	S	Single	floor–card
13	S	DP (2)	brick–tree
•	•	•	•
•	•	•	•
•	•	•	•

Note: To-be-remembered items are presented one time or two times in a massed or distributed fashion. The number of items intervening between study and test trials determines the retention interval. For example, if each item is presented for 4 seconds, then four intervening items produce a retention interval of 16 seconds.

sentations. The finding is something of a paradox because greater forgetting of the first presentation would be expected with spaced than with massed repetitions. However, two spaced presentations produced better retention than two massed presentations.

Although continuous paired-associate learning sounds somewhat esoteric, it is actually similar to a task you have likely employed in your attempts to learn a list of facts. Students at all grade levels use flash cards to help their study. The to-be-remembered item is put on one or more cards and then a query card is constructed to permit a test of memory without revealing the complete answer. Many different study and query cards are assembled in a deck, and practice involves continuously presenting and testing the to-be-remembered items. The results of the Peterson experiments make it clear that when two study cards are used, their presentations should be spaced in the list. Later in this chapter we will have something to say about how to position a query card for optimal retention.

The spacing effect

Researchers quickly found that the spacing effect obtained with continuous paired-associate learning was a remarkably robust phenomenon. It is produced easily in many different memory tasks and with many different kinds of materials, from nonsense syllables to words to sentences and pictures. An experiment by Underwood (1970) reveals the magnitude of the spacing effect when the free-recall method is used. He tested children between the ages of 9 and 14 years for their memory of 42 nouns. He presented words on a tape recorder at the rate of one per second. Some of the words appeared only one time; others appeared two, three, or four times. Half the repeated items were presented in a massed fashion and the others were presented in a distributed fashion. The spacing between repetitions of distributed words was nonsystematic—that is, there was no set interval between item repetitions. Children's recall of the words was measured immediately after the last word was presented. The results of this experiment are summarized in Figure 9-3.

Words presented in a spaced fashion were recalled better than massed items at each frequency level. The size of the spacing effect (the difference in retention following zero and spaced study) increased with the frequency of repetitions. In fact, recall of a word presented two times under distributed study was superior to that of a word presented four times under massed study. Results similar to these are found with adult subjects when free recall is tested.

The spacing of repetitions in free recall

Purpose
To observe the differential effect on retention of repeating items in either a massed or distributed fashion in a list presented for free recall.

Materials
The free-recall list contains 28 common, two-syllable nouns (see Table C in the Appendix). Four of the nouns are randomly selected to serve as a primacy "buffer" and the remaining 24 are critical items.

The independent variables are the number of presentations of an item (1 or 2) and the spacing between presentations (zero or 3–5 intervening items) in the list. The procedure for constructing the list can best be explained by considering the 24 items as representing four blocks of 6 items. In each block, 2 of the 6 items are presented only one time (1P), 2 are presented twice in a massed fashion (MP, or zero spacing), and 2 are presented twice in a distributed manner (DP). Therefore each block requires 10 list positions. Spacing of the DP items is nonsystematic, with either 3, 4, or 5 items intervening between the two presentations of an item. Two items of the same type (either 1P, MP, or DP) should not appear consecutively in a block. The four buffer items are presented first. Two of these buffer items are presented once and 2 are presented twice, 1 MP and 1 DP. The final list therefore has 46 positions.

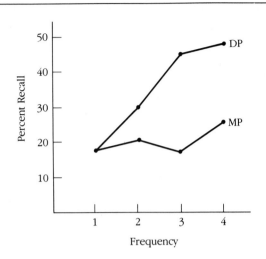

Figure 9-3. Percentage of free recall of words by children ages 9–14 years as a function of frequency of repetitions and massed or distributed presentations. *(From "A Breakdown of the Total Time Law in Free-Recall Learning," by B. J. Underwood. In* Journal of Verbal Learning and Verbal Behavior, *1970, 9, 573-580. Copyright 1970 by Academic Press, Inc. Reprinted by permission.)*

Procedure

Free-recall instructions are first read to the subjects. Items are then presented at the rate of one every 3 seconds. After hearing the last item, subjects are asked to count backward by threes for 30 seconds. (If subjects are tested in a group, the backward number counting should be performed silently.) Three minutes are then given for free recall.

Instructions to Subjects

This is a free-recall experiment. I am going to read a list of words for you to remember. Please listen to each word carefully because after I finish reading them, I want you to write down as many as you can remember. You may remember the words in any order you wish. Some of the words will be repeated in the list. Do not let this disturb you. Simply try to remember as many of the words in the list as possible. Are there any questions? (After the last word is read, subjects are asked to count backward by threes starting from a three-digit number the experimenter provides. Following 30 seconds of backward number counting, 3 minutes are given for free recall.)

Summary and Analysis

The number of 1P, MP, and DP items each subject recalls is recorded. There are eight of these three item types in the critical set. Buffer items are not scored. The effect of spacing can be tested statistically by using a repeated-measures (within-subjects) *t* test to compare the difference in mean recall between MP and DP items. It will also be of interest to see how different recall of MP items is relative to recall of 1P items.

Recommended Minimum Number of Subjects
Total of 16.

The procedure for this experiment is similar to that of several published experiments that have investigated spacing effects.

For those who enjoy empirical puzzles, the spacing effect has turned out to be a real delight. We will briefly consider one major approach to solving this puzzle.

Attenuation of attention hypothesis

Of the many theories offered to account for the spacing effect, the one receiving the most empirical support has been the *attenuation of attention hypothesis* (see Hintzman, 1974, 1976). This explanation was apparently first proposed by Peterson and his colleagues to explain the spacing effect in continuous paired-associate learning (Peterson et al., 1963). The attenuation of attention hypothesis makes the seemingly plausible assertion that the learner pays less attention to subsequent presentations of an item when repetitions occur close to its initial presentation (zero spacing) than when repetitions are spaced. If attention is attenuated, there is less processing. Therefore massed and spaced items will not be processed to the same degree. As reasonable as this hypothesis seems, not all the evidence has been favorable toward it.

Major support for the attention hypothesis has been provided by experiments designed to measure subjects' degree of attention for repeated occurrences of the same item. Shaughnessy, Zimmerman, and Underwood (1972), for example, tested subjects for free recall of a list of words containing both massed and spaced presentations of repeated items. What made this spacing experiment different from others was that subjects were allowed to pace their own study of the to-be-remembered words. By pressing a button that activated a slide projector, each subject could control the amount of time spent viewing individual words in the list. The study times were automatically recorded for all items in the list. A typical spacing effect was obtained for retention of the words. Also, the results based on study times for individual items showed that when left on their own, subjects spent less time studying massed repetitions of an item than distributed repetitions.

Another experiment supporting the attention hypothesis (Johnson & Uhl, 1976) required subjects to perform a simple reaction time task at the same time they were attempting to learn words from a list containing both massed and spaced repetitions. A weak auditory signal was presented to subjects in their left ear while to-be-remembered words were presented in their right ear. The subjects were instructed to press a button whenever they heard the tone but otherwise to study the items for a memory test. This unique experimental arrangement was based on the logic that the more processing a subject gave to committing an item to memory, the less processing capacity would be "left over" to process the auditory signal. In other words, the faster the reaction time, the less effort the subject was presumably spending to memorize the list items. The important comparison, of course, involved reaction times to the auditory signal when it occurred during massed and spaced repetition. Figure 9-4 shows the reaction time results for once-presented items as well as for twice-presented items under the two conditions of spacing. Reaction times were clearly faster, and processing of list items presumably less, when the signal was heard during a massed presentation than when the signal was heard during a spaced presentation of an item.

Although these studies have provided results in line with the attention hypothesis, critics have argued that demonstrations of this sort are based on

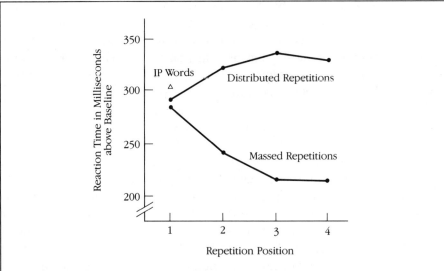

Figure 9-4. Mean reaction time scores for words appearing one time (1P) and for words repeated four times in either a massed or distributed fashion. Reaction times were obtained for each repetition position in the massed or distributed series. *(From "The Contributions of Encoding Effort and Variability to the Spacing Effect on Free Recall," by W. A. Johnston and C. N. Uhl. In* Journal of Experimental Psychology: Human Learning and Memory, *1976, 2, 153–160. Copyright 1976 by the American Psychological Association. Reprinted by permission.)*

"obtrusive" measures that may cause the subjects to behave in a way not typical of their behavior in standard learning conditions (Hintzman & Stern, 1977). Another criticism of the attention hypothesis arises from the fact that attempts to control subjects' processing of massed repetitions have not been particularly successful in altering the spacing effect (for example, Hintzman, Summers, Eki, & Moore, 1975; Shaughnessy, 1976). A further argument against the attenuation of attention hypothesis is that it does not explain "why" a subject turns off processing under massed repetitions (Hintzman, 1974). Some of these criticisms are considered in the next few paragraphs.

Although several different approaches have been taken in an attempt to alter subjects' attention to massed presentations of an item, perhaps the most direct route was taken by Hintzman and his co-workers at the University of Oregon (Hintzman et al., 1975). These researchers used something that tends to get our attention very quickly—namely, money. Subjects viewed a lengthy list of pictures, which were presented at a 3-second rate. They were told that some of the pictures would be accompanied by a tone and that they should make a special effort to remember these pictures. They were also told that they would be paid for every picture they remembered and that they would receive four times as much for remembering pictures with the tone as for remembering pictures without tones ($.04 versus $.01). The tone, as you probably have guessed by now, appeared during the second presentation of a massed or spaced item repetition. Actually, half the repeated items were presented with the tone and half were not. The attention hypothesis predicts the tone would lessen the spacing effect. That is, the difference in retention for massed and spaced items should be less when subjects are paid to attend to the second presentation of repeated items. This did not happen. The overall retention level as measured by frequency judgments for repeated items was greater for pictures with tones than for pictures without tones, but the spacing effect was exactly the same for both types of presentations. Assuming that subjects increased their attention to the items when the tone was sounded, this increased attention did not seem to change the spacing effect. Of course, if subjects increased their attention equally to *both* massed and distributed items when they heard the tone, a spacing effect might still be expected because attention to massed presentations was perhaps not yet equivalent to that for spaced items.

In defense of the attention hypothesis, there are several reasons subjects might turn off processing when an item is presented in a massed fashion. One is that a subject, having just worked on an item, may treat its repeated occurrence as time better spent on processing other items in the list (see Waugh, 1970). Another possibility is that having just seen an item, subjects are mistakenly led to think they already know it well enough to remember it and hence do not need to devote further processing to it (Shaughnessy, 1976; Zechmeister &

Shaughnessy, 1980). Motivational inducements to pay attention to massed repetitions (for instance, offering extra money) might not be expected to work if
subjects perceive they already have the job done. A recent experiment reported
results bearing on this explanation of attenuated processing of MP items.

Zechmeister and Shaughnessy (1980) asked subjects to study a list of words
in preparation for a free-recall test. For some of the words, which appeared
once or twice in either a massed or spaced fashion, the subjects were asked to
"predict" how well they thought they knew the item they had just studied.
Subjects were given a rating scale on which to estimate their confidence that
they would remember a particular item on the upcoming memory test. Ratings
were made immediately following a once-presented item or after the second
occurrence of a twice-presented item. (People's ability to judge what they know
and don't know is an interesting topic in itself and will be treated in Chapter
11.) These investigators found that subjects accurately predicted that items appearing twice in the list would be remembered better than those appearing
once. However, subjects misjudged their ability to remember massed and distributed items. Although recall was significantly higher for distributed than for
massed items (the spacing effect was found), average predictions of recall for
these two kinds of items did not differ significantly and in fact were slightly
higher for massed than distributed items. It is possible that subjects' confidence
in an item's memory strength is somehow inflated by the massing of repetitions
or, conversely, that repetition of an item after an interval teaches subjects that
the item has dropped in strength. For example, when a to-be-remembered item
is presented and then immediately repeated (zero spacing), subjects may turn
off processing because they feel they have successfully solved the problems of
getting the item into memory.

Jacoby (1978) at the University of Toronto showed that there is a problem-
solving aspect to memory encoding in an interesting series of studies. He suggested that we look at the task of memorizing a list of words as being similar
to that of solving a series of problems. The problem from the learner's point of
view is to find a way to put each of the items into memory. You will recall from
our earlier discussion of MP-DP differences associated with list learning that
Keppel's explanation of the MP-DP effect was based on the idea that subjects
are continually trying to solve the problem of hooking up pairs of items. Solving
the problem when a single item is studied may involve forming an image,
relating the word to other words in the list, taking advantage of some unusual
association suggested by an item, or using whatever seems to make the item
memorable. We shall review the results of one of Jacoby's interesting experiments in order to examine this problem-solving analysis of memory processing.

The task Jacoby gave his subjects was similar to solving a crossword puzzle.
He presented two words simultaneously to the subject, one word serving as a
cue for the other, which had some letters missing (for example, *foot, s— —e*). The

subject's task was to identify the partially spelled word (shoe, in this example). He presented a number of such problems to subjects in a long list. For some of the problems the solution appeared in the list *prior* to the problem itself. That is, for our previous example the subjects would be presented with *foot shoe* some time before seeing the problem *foot s– –e*. Of interest to Jacoby was the spacing between the solution and the problem. For some items the problem was made particularly easy in that the solution appeared immediately (no intervening items) before the problem. For other items there were 20 intervening items between the solution and the problem. The list also contained repetitions of solutions (no problem), which were either massed or spaced.

Jacoby told his subjects he was interested in how long it took them to solve problems similar to those of a crossword puzzle. He informed subjects that their reaction times to solve the problems would be recorded. As soon as they knew the answer to a problem, they were to push a button and say aloud the word that fit the solution. Because some of the word pairs contained two intact words (that is, the solution was presented), subjects were also told that their reaction time to "read" the intact pairs *(foot shoe)* would be used to evaluate their times for problem pairs *(foot s– –e)*. Therefore when both words were intact, the subjects were to push a button and read the words aloud. Reaction times were not actually recorded and, unannounced to the subjects, a memory test followed the presentation of the list. For the memory test the left-hand member of each pair was presented and subjects were asked to provide the right-hand member. This type of test is called *cued recall*.

The results of Jacoby's rather unusual memory experiment are shown in Figure 9-5. These results demonstrate that constructing a solution to a problem produces greater retention than merely "reading" it (see also Slamecka & Graf, 1978). Further, the advantage for constructing an answer depends on the spacing between the solution and the problem. When the problem immediately followed the solution, the results were approximately the same as if two solutions had been presented—that is, as if subjects had simply read the solution twice. When 20 items intervened between a problem and its solution, there was a sizable effect due to spacing. This spacing effect was much greater than when the second occurrence of an item was a solution repeated. Note that retention of a once-presented problem is greater than twice-presented solutions whether the solutions were massed or spaced. These results tell us that constructing an answer enhances retention, whereas mere repetition of a solution does not. In the next section we draw a parallel between construction of a solution and performance on a test trial. For the present let us consider the application of these results to the spacing effects as found in more standard memory tasks.

Attenuation of attention may result from subjects being more likely to assume that the problem of getting an item into memory has been solved when it is immediately repeated than when a repetition is delayed. The consequence

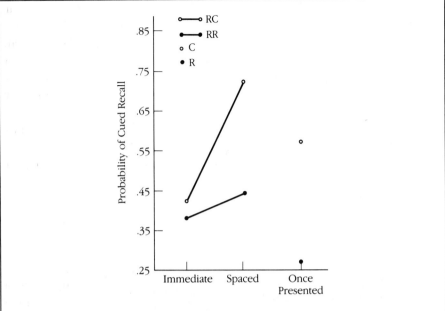

Figure 9-5. Probability of cued recall as a function of whether a problem was merely read (R) or an answer was constructed (C) and when a
problem was read twice (RR) or first read and then an answer constructed (RC) as a function of spacing. *(From "On Interpreting the Effects of
Repetition: Solving a Problem versus Remembering a Solution," by L. L.
Jacoby. In* Journal of Verbal Learning and Verbal Behavior, *1978, 17,
649–667. Copyright 1978 by Academic Press, Inc. Reprinted by permission.)*

would be making less of a response to a massed repetition of an item than to
a spaced repetition. As Jacoby (1978, p. 661) commented,

> Presentation of an event whose solution or encoding can be easily remem-
> bered does not give rise to an orienting response or heavily involve con-
> sciousness; presentation of such an event will also have little impact on later
> retention. The necessity of construction, in contrast, gives rise to an orienting
> response, involves consciousness to a greater degree, and produces a sub-
> stantial effect on later retention performance. The spacing of repetitions has
> its effect by determining whether a solution or encoding can be remembered
> or must be constructed.

The attenuation of attention hypothesis is by no means the only explanation offered to account for the effect of spacing on an item's retention. Another
major hypothesis is the variable encoding hypothesis, which William James
invoked to explain the effect of distributed practice on long-term retention of

verbal material (see also Melton, 1970). Encoding variability might occur within a list of items if it is assumed that relative to massed presentations, distributed presentations of an item lead it to be rehearsed within different groups of items (contexts) or encoded with different associations. However, tests of this hypothesis as it applies to the retention of single items have not been particularly supportive (Hintzman, 1974; Jacoby, 1978; Maki & Hasher, 1975). Yet more than one explanation of the spacing effect may be required. That is, although some researchers have assumed the reason for the spacing effect is the same in the many different situations in which it has been observed (for example, Hintzman, 1974), others have questioned whether all spacing effects appear for the same reason (Underwood, Kapelak, & Malmi, 1976). For example, it seems likely that some form of attenuation of attention can account for part of the spacing effect but not all (Zimmerman, 1975).

The mapping out of the various contributions of the available theories to the spacing effect will no doubt occupy researchers for some time. (You have to enjoy puzzles to be in this business.) At the same time, we must not lose sight of the fact that research on the spacing effect has revealed powerful effects on retention that can provide practical suggestions in many areas in which memory is tested.

The spacing effect is not limited to tasks employing item-by-item presentation of to-be-remembered words. Hall, Smith, Wegener, and Underwood (in press) presented college students with words for free recall, either item by item or in a complete list. In the complete-list condition, words were typed in a single column, double spaced, in the middle of a sheet of paper. In the item-by-item condition, a slide projector was used to present the words. In both conditions some of the words appeared more than once, and their occurrences were either massed or spaced. In the complete-list condition, the repeated items occurred either next to one another or with other items intervening in the column.

Retention was better for spaced than for massed items in both presentation methods, although the difference was smaller following complete-list presentation. Further, even though total study time was the same for the two presentation conditions, recall was significantly greater after complete-list presentation than after the usual laboratory procedure of presenting items one at a time. To explain these findings, the researchers suggested that during complete-list presentation, subjects may go through the list more than one time. Recycling study would have the effect of giving spaced presentation to all items in the list and would therefore raise the overall level of recall. Also, items that were massed would now be "spaced," which would reduce the overall spacing effect of complete-list presentation. As we saw, this is just what happened. Therefore, not only is the spacing effect found across a wide variety of tasks and procedures, but this interesting phenomenon may be the basis for improved retention whenever learners study in a manner that produces the functional equivalent of spaced presentation.

Spacing of test trials

Sometime in your psychology career you likely discussed the shaping of behavior according to principles of operant conditioning. Perhaps you have even seen a "live" demonstration of shaping that involved teaching a rat to press a bar for food reinforcement. Shaping is the reinforcement of successive approximations to a desired response. For example, to shape a rat to press a bar, you might first give reinforcement when the animal is standing next to the bar. You might give subsequent reinforcement only when the animal moves closer to the desired response—for example, raising a paw near the bar. You continue this process until the animal is performing the desired behavior. Shaping is a powerful learning technique, which, although often illustrated with a rat learning to press a bar, nevertheless has numerous applications in situations where a new behavior is to be acquired.

What behavior do we wish to acquire in a memory task? Most likely it is the ability to recall something after a long interval. Perhaps "shaping" could be accomplished by gradually lengthening the interval between study and test until it approaches a long interval. By using spaced repetitions of test trials rather than study trials, Landauer and Bjork (1978) revealed how memory behavior just might be shaped in this manner. There has been little research on the effect of spacing of test trials when single items are presented for a memory test (although see Whitten & Bjork, 1977). Therefore the results of this experiment present a new look at spacing effects.

These researchers presented large groups of subjects the task of learning people's names. Each subject was given a deck of cards on which the names of fictitious individuals were written. Study cards combined both the first and last names of the individual; test cards contained only the first name. As in traditional paired-associate learning, subjects were to provide the appropriate second name when only the first name was given. After both names were presented once for study, the first name only was presented for three successive test trials. The major variable was the nature of the spacing between the three test cards. The various patterns of spacing that Landauer and Bjork (1978) used are shown in Figure 9-6. As you can see, several "uniform" spacings were contrasted with both "expanding" and "contracting" spacings. Expanding spacing would be most similar to shaping. If the desired behavior is long-term retention, an expanding series first gives the subject an opportunity to remember after a short interval, then after a little longer interval, and then after an even longer interval. This

Spacing of Tests

Uniform Short

0, 0, 0   and   1, 1, 1

Uniform Moderate

4, 4, 4   and   5, 5, 5

Uniform Long

$9 \leq (x, y, z) \leq 11$; average 9.3 to 10.3

Expanding

0, 3, 10   and   1, 4, 10

Contracting

10, 3, 0   and   10, 4, 1

Figure 9-6. Types of spacing patterns used by Landauer and Bjork (1978). An item was presented once for study and then followed by three test trials. Therefore there were three intervals between tests. Numbers in the figure represent the number of intervening items between successive test trials for a particular item type. *(From "Optimum Rehearsal Patterns and Name Learning," by T. K. Landauer and R. A. Bjork. In M. M. Gruneberg, P. E. Morris, and R. N. Sykes (Eds.),* Practical Aspects of Memory. *Copyright 1978 by Academic Press, Inc. (London) Ltd. Used by permission.)*

presumably approaches the desired response of long-term retention. In one expanding pattern of test trials, the first test appeared after one intervening item, then was repeated after four more intervening items, and finally was presented for the third time following ten additional items (pattern: 1, 4, 10).

A cued-recall test of the fictitious names was given 30 minutes after presentation of the list. These results are shown in Figure 9-7 in terms of the *average* spacing of the tests. For example, the two moderate uniform intervals, 4, 4, 4 and 5, 5, 5, were combined for an average spacing of 4.50. Performance was measured both in terms of proportion recall (left ordinate) and percentage improvement over retention of a name presented one time for study with no subsequent test trials (*P* only; right ordinate). As you can see from Figure 9-7, memory performance was best for the expanding test series. We can assume that "shaping" worked by guaranteeing a high probability of correct response at each retention interval. A subject is more likely to respond correctly after an initial retention interval of one item (expanding) than a retention interval of five items (uniform).

Further research on "programmed testing" may have important conse-

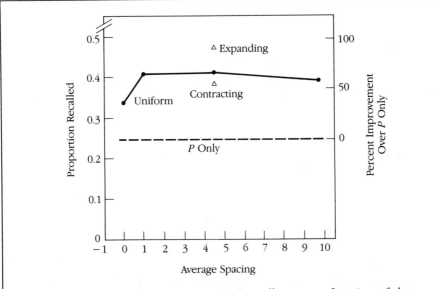

Figure 9-7. Performance on a final recall test as a function of the spacing pattern of test trials. "*P* only" refers to items presented only one time during study and not tested. See Figure 9-6 for an explanation of the test patterns. *(From "Optimum Rehearsal Patterns and Name Learning," by T. K. Landauer and R. A. Bjork. In M. M. Gruneberg, P. E. Morris, and R. N. Sykes (Eds.),* Practical Aspects of Memory. *Copyright 1978 by Academic Press, Inc. (London) Ltd. Reprinted by permission.)*

quences for the way material is presented for optimal retention. The next time you make a deck of flash cards for study, you might try testing yourself according to an expanding series. We hope your memory will be appropriately shaped.

Summary

In this chapter we have focused on a problem of both theoretical and practical significance. How does repetition of to-be-remembered information affect its retention? The question has often been investigated by comparing the effects of massed (MP) and distributed practice (DP). Results of early studies revealed that although acquisition of a verbal task (such as paired-associate learning) was not necessarily affected by practice conditions, retention of verbal material was. Specifically, retention is generally better following DP than MP when the interval between practice periods is relatively long. Explanations for this effect include those that emphasize differences in number of encodings (the encoding variability hypothesis) and differences in the quality of encoding as a function of practice.

When we look at the conditions surrounding the acquisition and retention of a single item, we find that retention is substantially better when item repetitions are spaced rather than massed. A major explanation of this "spacing effect" is the attenuation of attention hypothesis, which suggests that subjects "turn off" processing of massed but not distributed repetitions of an item. There is support for this hypothesis, but it appears that other factors are involved. Encoding variability has also been offered as an explanation of this effect. Spacing effects are also obtained when retention is observed following different distributions of test trials rather than study trials. Although the effects are new and additional research is needed, there is some evidence that an expanding spacing of test trials leads to optimal retention.

The theoretical controversy surrounding explanations of practice effects should not detract from the many possible practical applications offered by our knowledge of these phenomena. Laboratory research will no doubt continue on this problem for some time, but an equally important task is to test the application of these powerful effects in "real-life" situations.

Recommendations for further reading

Melton (1970) has provided an interesting historical review of the research on massed and distributed practice. This review appears in the same issue of the *Journal of Verbal Learning and Verbal Behavior* as do several other important articles dealing with this problem. More recent reviews and a discussion of the theoretical controversy surrounding the spacing effect are found in articles by Hintzman (1974, 1976). Selected aspects of the spacing problem are also reviewed and a new theoretical analysis of the encoding variability hypothesis of the spacing effect is presented in a recent article by Glenberg (1979). For those interested in learning more about perceptual-motor tasks, we recommend chapters by Bilodeau (1969) and Noble (1978).

10

Recall, Recognition, and Relearning

Introduction/overview

Could you imagine yourself saying, "I can recall the name, but I wouldn't be able to recognize it?" Of course not. We would all agree that recognition is generally "easier" than recall. In fact, when people cannot recall something, they can often accurately predict whether or not they will recognize it (Hart, 1965, and Chapter 11). But why? What are the memory mechanisms governing recognition? Do they differ from those processes used in recall? Is recognition the most sensitive test of what is in memory? Psychologists have tried to answer such questions for some time in order to understand our memory more completely. This investigation has revealed important and often surprising facts about the nature of recall and recognition. For example, under some circumstances we may actually be able to recall something we cannot recognize. Also, we may relearn things we can neither recall nor recognize faster than we learn new things.

There are two major reasons for investigating retention differences as a function of the type of memory test given. The first we have alluded to already: comparing performance on different types of retention tests yields evidence as to the nature of memory processes in different tasks. A major question we consider in this chapter is whether recognition involves retrieval of information from memory. On the theoretical side, this investigation contributes to a better understanding of memory in general. On the practical side, such an investigation serves to identify those conditions that will lead to optimal retention. For example, should you prepare differently for a recall test than for a recognition test? What kinds of stimulus material are you most likely to recall or recognize?

A second reason to investigate retention under different testing conditions is related to the definition of memory itself. In the very first chapter we alerted you to the fact that memory is inferred from behavior. Evidence for memory is sought in a subject's performance on a memory test. But what can be inferred about memory depends on how it is tested. For example, students are often asked "How much can you remember?" Such a question can be answered only in the context of a particular type of memory test. It will probably not surprise you to learn that the answer depends on how memory is tested.

SHEPARD'S (1967) EXPERIMENT

Several important issues to be discussed in this chapter are highlighted in a study conducted by Shepard (1967) while he was at Harvard University. He asked Harvard undergraduates to inspect a lengthy series of items in preparation for a memory test. Students studied the items at their own pace and then viewed a series of test pairs. One member of each pair was an item from the study list; the other member was not. The students' task was to select the item in each pair that had appeared in the study list. In other words, recognition memory for items presented in the study list was tested.

Students actually studied one of three types of items: words, sentences, or pictures. The word list presented for study contained 540 words, half of which were words that appear very frequently in written English (for example, *child, office*); the other half were words appearing only rarely in print (for example, *ferule, wattled*). Sixty words were randomly selected from the lengthy study list for the recognition test. There were four different types of test pairs. Both frequent and rare words from the study list were paired with frequent and rare words not from the list. Therefore of the 60 test pairs, 15 pairs included a frequent word from the list and a frequent word not from the list; 15 pairs consisted of a frequent study word and a rare word not from the list; and so forth. Another group of students viewed 612 sentences (for example, *The colt reared and threw the sick rider*) before seeing 68 test pairs. Two additional students were asked to look at 1224 sentences before being tested in the same manner. Finally, other students studied a list of 612 colored pictures (usually objects cut out of magazine advertisements) and were tested after several retention intervals, including one interval of 120 days. The results of Shepard's experiment, based on percentage correct recognition of the various types of items, are shown in Table 10-1. There are three important findings we wish to call to your attention.

The first is the extraordinary level of performance when recognition memory is tested. After viewing more than 500 different words, subjects correctly identified the study item in 88% of the test pairs. When free recall is tested, recall following a single study trial is seldom greater than 50% even with com-

TABLE 10-1. Results of Shepard's (1967) Classic Experiment Investigating Recognition Memory for Words, Sentences, and Pictures

		Percent Correct
Words		
After viewing 540 words		
Test Pairs		
(Old)	*(New)*	
Frequent	Frequent	82.1
Frequent	Rare	86.7
Rare	Frequent	93.0
Rare	Rare	92.0
Sentences		
After viewing 612 sentences		89.0
After viewing 1224 sentences		88.2
Pictures		
After viewing 612 pictures		
and tested after delay of:		
2 hours		99.7
3 days		92.0
7 days		87.0
120 days		57.7

From "Recognition Memory for Words, Sentences, and Pictures," by R. N. Shepard. In *Journal of Verbal Learning and Verbal Behavior,* 1967, 6, 156–163. Copyright 1967 by Academic Press, Inc. Reprinted by permission.

paratively short lists (for example, see Murdock, 1962). Recognition memory was as good for sentences and even better for pictures. After inspecting 612 pictures, the students correctly recognized 87% of them after 7 days. A second important finding by Shepard was that recognition memory is better for pictures than words. Other experimenters have found similar results (Paivio, 1971), and later in this chapter we will examine possible explanations for the fact that pictures are easier to recognize than words.

A third major result of Shepard's experiment was that rare words were recognized better than frequent ones. This is the opposite of what happens in recall, where more-frequent words are generally remembered better than less-frequent words (Gregg, 1976; Hall, 1954). This result is called the *word-frequency effect,* and it too has been found by many other experimenters (see Crowder, 1976; Murdock, 1974). The word-frequency effect has been at the very center of the debate concerning processes thought to be responsible for recall and recognition. Before we get to this controversy, however, let's examine more closely the methodologies associated with tests of recognition memory.

RECOGNITION MEMORY PARADIGMS AND MEASURES

There are three major methodologies used to investigate recognition memory: *forced choice, absolute judgment* (or *yes-no*), and *continuous recognition memory* tasks.

Forced choice

In Shepard's (1967) experiment subjects were first presented a list of to-be-remembered items and then asked to inspect a series of pairs of items, each pair consisting of one item from the study list and one item not from the study list. Subjects attempted to identify which item in the test pair had appeared in the study list. This kind of recognition memory task is a *two-alternative forced-choice* procedure. Items from the study list are called "old" items (they have appeared earlier in the experimental situation). Test items are called "new" items or often *distractors* or *lures* because they have not appeared previously in the study list. A forced-choice procedure may, of course, involve more than two alternatives. For example, classroom examinations often involve four-alternative forced-choice procedures. A forced-choice procedure, in other words, is essentially a multiple-choice test.

Using a forced-choice procedure, an investigator can vary the *type* of distractor, as Shepard did when he compared recognition memory for high-frequency old items paired with high- and low-frequency new items. The *number* of distractors can also be varied using this procedure. As you might expect, recognition memory is generally poorer the more similar the new items are to the old items and the more distractors that are present (Postman, 1950, 1951). With adult subjects, the most common recognition memory error is to select a new item that is associatively related to the old item (Underwood & Freund, 1968a). But children—for example, third graders—usually err in a forced-choice recognition memory task by selecting words that sound like the old item (are acoustically related; see Bach & Underwood, 1970). Analyzing the kinds of errors subjects make in a forced-choice recognition task provides important information about the representation of an item in memory. The fact that acoustic errors are more common than associative errors in children's recognition memory performance suggests that the "sound" of a word is more likely to be incorporated into a child's memory for a word than is its meaning.

Absolute judgment

A second major recognition memory paradigm is the *absolute judgment* task. Following study, subjects are presented a series of test items, one at a time. Some of the test items (usually half) are old items and others are new. Because instructions often require subjects to say yes when an old item is presented and no when a new item is presented, the absolute judgment task is also called a *yes-no recognition task*.

The yes-no recognition task raises an important methodological problem that is not present in the forced-choice procedure. In a forced-choice task subjects are operating under only one rule: choose the old item. Because subjects must make a choice (forced), only one kind of error is possible: saying a new item is an old item. We assume subjects are "biased" toward identifying the old item on the basis of whatever information is present in memory. But when a yes-no procedure is used, subjects must operate under two rules: (1) choose an old item and (2) reject a new item. Therefore not only are two kinds of correct decisions possible, but two kinds of errors are possible as well. Figure 10-1 shows the possible outcomes in a yes-no recognition task and the common labels for these responses.

Probabilities associated with each of the four responses shown in Figure 10-1 are not independent. Consider what would happen if a subject said yes to every test item. Correct identification of old items would be 100%, or the probability of a hit would be 1.00. However, the probability of a miss would be 0.00. In other words, the subject would never make the mistake of saying no to an old item. Further, by saying yes all the time, our hypothetical subject would be mistakenly saying yes to all new items. Therefore the probability of a false alarm would be 1.00. Similarly, in this extreme case the probability of a correct rejection (responding no to a new item) would be 0.00. Fortunately, subjects don't usually respond this way. Rather, on the basis of the information in memory, they generally try to decide whether an item is old or new and then respond accordingly.

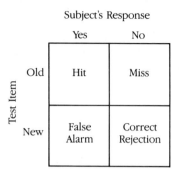

Figure 10-1. Possible outcomes in a yes-no (absolute judgment) recognition memory task. These outcomes are not independent. The probability of a hit plus the probability of a miss always equals 1.00. Likewise, the probability of a false alarm plus the probability of a correct rejection must equal 1.00.

Yet people are likely to differ in the way they use information in memory to make a decision. Consider a hypothetical case wherein an old item is weakly but equally well registered in two subjects' memories. When this particular item is presented for a recognition decision, the two subjects could come to different decisions on the basis of the same information. Perhaps one subject is rather "conservative" and considers the information in memory insufficient to warrant a decision that the item is old. Not wanting to say it is old when it is not (false alarm), this subject may decide to say the item is new, making a miss. The other subject might be more easily swayed by the information in memory to say the item is old. Not wanting to incur a miss, this subject may say it is old, producing a hit. Exactly how a subject will respond on the basis of the information in memory is determined by the subject's *response bias* or *response criterion*. Let's face it, it takes more information to convince some of us than it does to convince others. Some people are just more likely to say no (or yes) than are others given the very same information.

Response bias or criterion is also affected by the experimental conditions surrounding a decision. The tendency to say an item is old (or new) is influenced by such variables as instructions, previous experience in the situation, and the costs/payoffs (rewards) associated with incorrect/correct responding. As an extreme example, knowing there is a $10,000 reward for correctly identifying a person who committed a crime may bias a witness to say yes when shown a picture of any suspect. The problem raised by the yes-no recognition procedure is to control for differences in subjects' biases or guessing strategies. Unlike in a forced-choice task, which is generally judged to be "criterion-free," the experimenter using an absolute judgment or yes-no task *must* take into account possible response biases.

Signal detection theory

A traditional formula used to correct for guessing in a yes-no recognition test is Prob HIT − Prob FA (Woodworth & Schlosberg, 1954). This formula indicates that a subject's recognition memory score must reflect not only the ability to identify what is an old item (HIT) but also the ability to reject a new item. In effect the formula penalizes the subject for saying an item is old when it is new (false alarm). Another measure of recognition memory performance in the yes-no task has been Prob HIT − Prob FA/(1 − Prob FA) see Kintsch, 1977, for a discussion of the assumptions behind these formulas). Another method for measuring recognition memory performance uses the *theory of signal detection* (Egan, 1958). Applying signal detection theory to the analysis of recognition memory is not without its problems (see Lockhart & Murdock, 1970), but it is one of the most popular methods for scoring recognition in a yes-no task and appears to be more "criterion-free" than the more traditional corrections for guessing (see Healy & Kubovy, 1978).

Signal detection theory was developed in the context of experiments on sensory perception. Consider a typical signal detection task involving auditory stimuli. The subject's task is to detect the presence of a signal (a tone or beep) when it is presented against the background of noise (for example, a hissing sound like escaping air). On any one trial the signal is present or it is absent from the noise and the subject must decide which it is. You can see that the subject's decisions in this kind of task are similar to those identified in Figure 10-1. A trial on which the signal is present is analogous to the presentation of an old item in a recognition memory task; a trial on which only noise is present is analogous to presentation of a new item. As in a recognition memory task, subjects attempting to detect the presence of an auditory signal in the midst of noise are also capable of misses and false alarms. The theory of signal detection was developed to provide a measure of the subject's ability to detect a signal when it was really there, referred to as *sensitivity,* which was independent of the subject's response criterion.

To measure sensitivity and response criterion in a recognition memory task, the theory assumes that old and new items lie along a single continuum or dimension, presumably something like response strength or familiarity. It is further assumed that because the old items were presented previously in the experiment, their average memory "strength" or familiarity is greater than the average familiarity of the new items. To put it another way, old items on the average will appear more familiar than new items. The theory also assumes that the familiarity distributions of old and new items are normal in form. Figure 10-2 illustrates these assumptions and shows what is likely to occur in most detection experiments—namely, that there will be some overlap of the two

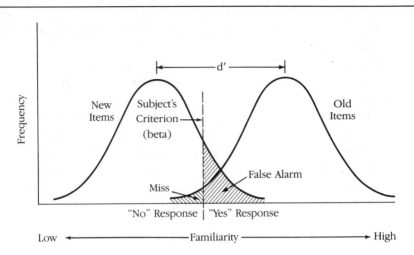

Figure 10-2. The major assumptions of the theory of signal detection, on which measures of sensitivity *(d')* and criterion *(beta)* are based. The probability of a miss corresponds to the relative frequency of mistakenly responding no to an old item. Similarly, the probability of a false alarm is the relative frequency of saying yes to a new item. The probability of a hit corresponds to the area within the distribution of old items, which is above (to the right of, in the figure) the subject's criterion. The probability of a correct rejection is defined by the area within the distribution of new items, which is below (to left of) the subject's criterion.

theoretical distributions. There will be instances in a recognition memory task when a new item looks more familiar than other new items. Therefore it is likely to fall within the familiarity distribution of old items. Similarly, there will be old items whose response strength or familiarity is relatively low, and they will appear more like new items.

In a recognition memory experiment the subject's problem is where to establish a "cutoff" on the familiarity dimension, the point at which an item will be judged old and not new, and vice versa. Where the subjects set this cutoff or criterion for their decisions will determine the relative number of false alarms and misses and the relative number of hits and correct rejections. According to the signal detection theory, the probability of these responses corresponds to areas under the theoretical normal curve. Knowledge of the probabilities associated with a hit and false alarm therefore can be used to calculate the difference between the means of the old and new distributions. This difference is calculated as *d'* and is a measure of *sensitivity,* which is independent of the subject's cutoff value or criterion. Having calculated the probabilities of a hit and false alarm, an experimenter can consult a table showing the *d'* values for various combinations of these values (for example, Elliot, 1964). The measure of criterion is called *beta* in signal detection terminology and can be determined using the values obtained from this analysis.

Because it is not always known whether the assumptions of the signal detection model are supported in a particular recognition memory situation, and given that the theory is not theoretically neutral as to the conceptualization of recognition memory (for example, it assumes a single underlying response dimension; see Murdock, 1974), researchers have continued to look for other ways to measure performance in the yes-no recognition task (see Underwood, 1974). Also, it is not uncommon for researchers to report more than one measure of performance—for example, using the more traditional corrections for guessing described earlier. Whatever measure is chosen, information as to specific hit and false alarm rates should always be provided when the results of a yes-no procedure are reported. To those who find this measurement problem somewhat unsettling, there is always the forced-choice task.

Continuous recognition

A third recognition memory paradigm is the *continuous* or *running recognition memory task*. It was first introduced by Shepard and Teghtsoonian (1961), who investigated recognition memory for three-digit numbers. We will describe this task by referring to an experiment by Underwood (1965) because it not only illustrates the continuous recognition memory task but also tells us something about processes contributing to recognition errors. In this task, study and test items are intermixed in much the same fashion as in a continuous paired-associate learning task (see Chapter 9). For example, Underwood's subjects listened to a list of 200 words presented at the rate of 1 word every 10 seconds. As each word was read, subjects decided whether it had been presented earlier in the list (yes/no). Decisions regarding the first few words in the list are necessarily quite easy, but as you can imagine, the task must get more difficult as more words are presented. In this particular case the task was made even more difficult by the kinds of items Underwood inserted in the list.

There were four types of items in the experimental list. One type consisted of critical stimulus words. These words would presumably elicit in the subject a particular *implicit associative response* (IAR). The appearance of a critical stimulus word was assumed to lead the subject to think of another word. For example, what word do you think of when you hear the words *warm, chill, freeze, frigid, hot,* and *ice?* You would be rather unusual if these words did not remind you of the word *cold. Cold* is an IAR. In this case the critical stimulus words all "converge" on the IAR, *cold.* Converging associations were one type

TABLE 10-2. Examples of Items Underwood (1965) Used to Investigate the Effect of Implicit Associative Responses (IARs) on Recognition Memory

Word type	Critical stimulus words	Experimental words (IARs)	Control words
Antonym appearing 1 time	bottom	top	down
Antonym appearing 3 times	rough, rough, rough	smooth	weak
Converging associations	sugar, bitter, candy	sweet	salt
Superordinates	maple, oak, elm, birch	tree	fish
Sense impressions	barrel, doughnut, dome, globe, spool	round	sharp

of critical stimulus words Underwood used. Others included sense impressions, superordinates (instances of categories), and antonyms, which appeared either once or three times. Examples of the five kinds of critical stimuli are shown in Table 10-2.

The IARs were the experimental words in this task. Following the presentation of one or more critical stimulus words, but not too soon after, the subject heard an experimental word. The experimental word always appeared close to a third type of word, a control word that was not related to the critical stimulus word. Finally, the fourth type of list items were fillers, and these appeared either one, two, or three times in the list so that some words in the list actually were repeated.

The purpose of the experiment is probably clear to you. Underwood was testing whether the presence of the critical stimulus words would lead subjects to make recognition memory errors for the experimental words. The subject's task, you will remember, was to listen to the list and to decide whether each item had been presented previously. Underwood hypothesized that IARs are an important source of recognition memory errors. Thus if the word *cold* is elicited by a critical stimulus word during study of the list, when the word *cold* is actually presented, the subject may mistakenly say it had appeared previously when it had not. In other words, the IARs should be a source of false alarms. The control words were used to measure the subject's "normal" false alarm rate for positions in the list that contained the experimental words. For three classes of critical stimulus words, antonyms appearing three times, converging associations, and superordinates, the false alarm rate for experimental words was greater than that for the control words. These results reveal that judgments of a word's familiarity can be influenced by a word's implicit appearance on a previous occasion.

TRADITIONAL DISTINCTIONS BETWEEN RECALL AND RECOGNITION

Single-process versus two-process theories

A traditional view of recall and recognition is *strength* or *threshold theory* (Kintsch, 1970). According to this theory, performance on a recognition test generally exceeds that seen when recall is tested because recognition is more sensitive than recall to memory strength. A memory that is not sufficiently strong to allow it to be recalled could nevertheless sometimes be recognized. Strength theory suggests that both recall and recognition are tapping the same thing, memory strength. This is often referred to as *single-process* view of recall and recognition. Today few memory theorists accept the idea that the relationship between recall and recognition can be so simply stated (Murdock, 1974; Tulving, 1976).

Alternatives to a strength theory of recall and recognition are the so-called *two-process* or *two-stage theories.* Although there are several versions of these theories (for example, Anderson & Bower, 1972, 1973; Bahrick, 1970; Kintsch, 1970), they are often looked upon as basically the same (see Tulving, 1976). A two-stage theory assumes that recall involves the *retrieval* of available information followed by the *discrimination* or checking of retrieved information for the target material. This is sometimes called a *generate-and-edit theory of recall.* Recognition is viewed as eliminating the need for retrieval because the target items are present at test. Thus recognition involves only the discrimination or editing stage. Two-stage theories therefore suggest that recall and recognition involve qualitatively different memory mechanisms. This view has a considerable number of proponents (McCormack, 1972; Murdock, 1974; Underwood, 1972). As we will see, the unraveling of the processes involved in recall and recognition has not proved to be an easy task.

The word-frequency effect

If recall and recognition involve the same rather than qualitatively different memory processes, then logically each should be affected in the same way by a particular experimental variable. For instance, if differences in performance associated with recall and recognition arise simply because the two tasks show a differential sensitivity to memory strength, then a variable that increases memory strength should lead to increases in both recall and recognition. However, it turns out that there are several variables that have different, even opposite, effects on recall and recognition (see Kintsch, 1970). The most obvious of these is word frequency. As Shepard (1967) showed, low-frequency words are generally recognized better than high-frequency words; the reverse is usually true when recall is tested. The *word-frequency effect* or *frequency paradox,* as it is sometimes called, has been a major piece of evidence against a single-process theory of recall and recognition (Murdock, 1974).

The word-frequency effect

Purpose

To compare recognition memory for high-frequency (HF) and low-frequency (LF) words.

Materials

A total of 300 words of four to nine letters in length are randomly selected from the Thorndike and Lorge (1944) word count. (See Tables G and H in the Appendix.) Half the words are selected from those appearing only 1–4 times per million words of text (LF words), and half are chosen from words with frequencies of at least 50 per million words of text (HF words). The experiment requires two different study lists, one consisting of 100 LF words and the other consisting of 100 HF words. These lists can be formed by randomly sampling 100 items from each of the 150-word sets originally chosen from the Thorndike and Lorge word count. The order in which the 100 items are sampled determines the presentation order of the items in the two study lists.

Recognition memory is tested using a two-alternative, forced-choice procedure. Test lists for both the HF and LF study lists are constructed in the same way and should proceed as follows. Randomly choose 50 words from each study list, 25 words from the first half of the list (1–50) and 25 words from the second half (51–100). These words will serve as "old" items on the recognition test. The 50 old words are randomly paired with the 50 words remaining in the original 150-word sets. The LF old items are paired with LF new items and HF old items are paired with HF new items, yielding two different 50-pair test lists. Presentation order of the test pairs should be randomly determined, and within each 50-pair list old items should appear an equal number of times (25) as the left and right (or top and bottom) members of the test pair. Both study and test items can be printed on individual 3 × 5-inch cards for presentation to subjects. Recognition can be conveniently scored if you prepare an answer sheet numbered 1 to 50 with the letters L (left) R (right) next to each number.

Procedure

Subjects are seen individually. Half are randomly assigned to the HF list and half to the LF list. Study items are presented singly, one word about every 3 seconds. Test pairs are each shown for 5 seconds. The experiment is easily performed with the experimenter sitting opposite each subject and holding the study or test cards in front of the subject. The experimenter should practice presenting the cards at the proper rate. (Tones or other auditory signals may be recorded on tape to cue the experimenter when to turn the cards.)

Instructions to Subjects

STUDY

This is a test of your recognition memory for words. I am going to show you a long list of words, one word at a time. Please study each word carefully; later I will ask you to recognize words from the list when they are paired with words not from the list. Are there any questions?

TEST

I will now give you the recognition test. I will show you a series of word pairs. One word in each pair is from the list you just studied; one word is not from the list. When each pair is shown, please circle a letter on your answer sheet to indicate which word in the pair, the one on the left (L) or the one on the right (R), you think was in the list. You will have to work efficiently, and you are to select a word in every test pair even if you have to guess. Are there any questions?

Summary and Analysis

Recognition memory for HF and LF words is compared by examining the average number of words subjects correctly identified in the two conditions of the experiment. A t test for independent groups (between subjects) can be employed to determine whether the difference between the means is statistically significant.

Recommended Minimum Number of Subjects

Total of 32; 16 in each of the two conditions.

This particular procedure is based on several published experiments that have used a between-subjects design. The word-frequency effect for recognition memory is revealed by showing that low-frequency words are recognized better than high-frequency words. As mentioned in the text, the "reverse" effect is generally found when recall is tested. By presenting somewhat shorter study lists than described here and testing free recall rather than recognition, the word-frequency effect for recall may also be demonstrated.

A word is defined as either high or low frequency on the basis of the number of times it appears in the printed language (often referred to as background frequency, see Chapter 8). For example, when a count was made of the frequency with which different words appeared in various books, newspapers, and magazines, the word *dollar* was found to appear more than 100 times per million words of text; the word *doily* appeared only 1 time in every million printed words (Thorndike & Lorge, 1944). Even when there are wide differences in persons' backgrounds, we can assume they have experienced high-frequency words more times than low-frequency words.

Frequency of exposure is different, but high- and low-frequency words differ on other characteristics as well (see Gregg, 1976). Words that differ in frequency of occurrence also differ structurally and semantically. Low-frequency words, relative to high-frequency words, are generally longer (Zipf, 1945), differ in phonemic and graphemic composition (Landauer & Streeter, 1973), are learned at a later age (Carroll & White, 1973), and elicit fewer associative responses or IARs (Deese, 1960). In short, not only is a low-frequency word experienced less often than a high-frequency word, but it is likely to look and sound different from a high-frequency word and will likely lead to differences in semantic processing. The problem has been to identify those characteristics that are critically involved in the word-frequency effect.

It is usually assumed that the high-frequency words' recall advantage is due to the fact that they are more easily grouped or organized than low-frequency words because they have more interitem associations. Interitem associations may be thought of as ways items might "go together" or be meaningfully related. You can readily see that the interitem associations are greater among words like *child, office,* and *supply* than *ferule, julep,* and *wattled.* Given that recall emphasizes retrieval of information that is not actually present, it is facilitated by interitem associations, either those the learner imposes or those the experimenter builds in. For example, many studies have demonstrated that recall is enhanced if to-be-remembered words within a list represent members of one or more different conceptual categories (names of trees, animals, or colors) (Tulving & Donaldson, 1972). However, although organization facilitates recall, it has less of an effect on recognition (Kintsch, 1977).

If recall emphasizes retrieval, recognition emphasizes discrimination among available items. To say that recognition memory is better for rare than common words is in a sense to say that low-frequency words are more discriminable than high-frequency words. Consistent with this view, Shepard (1967) proposed that rare words are more likely to be recognized than common words because low-frequency words are somehow "stranger" than high-frequency words. Therefore, he suggested, they may stand out in the study list and be processed differently than high-frequency words. As evidence for the role that "strangeness" might play, there is evidence that orthographic (spelling) distinctiveness can influence recognition memory. Distinctive orthography is defined as those structural features of a word that make it physically unusual or interesting (Zechmeister, 1969). For example, uncommon words subjects rated as highly distinctive are *xylem, sylph,* and *phlox;* words of the same frequency rated as less distinctive are *parse, scone,* and *poser.* Zechmeister (1972) found recognition memory to be greater for high than low orthographically distinctive words. Structural unusualness may lead somehow to memory traces that are more discriminable (see also Landauer & Streeter, 1973).

Although structural features, such as orthography, likely contribute to differential recognition memory for high- and low-frequency words, other factors undoubtedly play a role. Evidence for this comes from the fact that the word-frequency effect is a very robust phenomenon, occurring in a wide variety of experimental situations. Shepard (1967) showed subjects a list of words containing both high- and low-frequency words. It is reasonable to assume that mixing the frequency classes within a list may cause low-frequency words to stand out because they can be contrasted with high-frequency words in the same list. However, an effect of word frequency on recognition memory is found when study lists contain only high- or low-frequency words and recognition memory is compared between groups of subjects (Kinsbourne & George, 1974; Underwood & Freund, 1970c), when words are presented auditorily rather than visually (Schulman, 1967), and when modality (auditory or visual) is varied between study and test (Lee, Tzeng, Garro, & Hung, 1978). It is unlikely that structural differences can account for all these findings. More direct evidence for the role of additional factors, particularly semantic ones, in the word-frequency effect is found in several experiments that have examined recognition memory as a function of the subject's familiarity with a word's meaning. These experiments also demonstrate that the relationship between word frequency and probability of correct recognition is not as simple as once thought.

To say that low-frequency words are recognized better than high-frequency words does not mean that the lower the word frequency the better is recognition memory, although some researchers once assumed this to be the case (see Murdock, 1974). Probability of correct recognition is most appropriately described as a curvilinear function of word frequency (Gregg, 1976; Schulman, 1976). That is, as word frequency decreases, recognition memory gets better and then gets worse. Consider the results of an experiment by Schulman (1976), who investigated recognition memory for "extremely rare" nouns as well as uncommon surnames. In several experiments subjects first rated their familiarity with the low-frequency items and then were tested for recognition memory of the rated items. In each experiment, probability of correct recognition increased as rated familiarity increased. Among uncommon items, words rated as definitely unfamiliar were recognized least well. Because he had used only *very* low-frequency words, Schulman reasonably predicted that probability of correct recognition memory in general is a curvilinear function of word frequency, first increasing and then decreasing as word frequency increases.

Zechmeister, Curt, and Sebastian (1978) provided an actual test of this proposal. They presented college students with a long list of items, including nonwords, very low-frequency words (appearing less than 1 time per million words of text), low-frequency words (appearing 1 to 10 times per million), and high-frequency words (frequencies greater than 40 per million) (Thorndike & Lorge, 1944). The students rated their knowledge of an item's meaning, as it might be found in a dictionary, or their familiarity, referring to the frequency with which they had seen this item. No mention was made that a memory test would be given. Following the rating task, students were given a forced-choice recognition test for their memory of the four classes of verbal items. As seen in Figure 10-3, following meaningfulness or familiarity ratings, recognition memory was a curvilinear function of word frequency. In fact, very rare words were recognized no better than high-frequency words. Meaningless nonwords were recognized least well.

It is likely that differences in semantic processing account for the curvilinear relationship between frequency and probability of recognition. Put yourself in the place of a subject called upon to decide whether you know the meaning of a word. Presumably, you could easily and quickly decide you do not know the meaning of a very low frequency word. You may just as easily and quickly

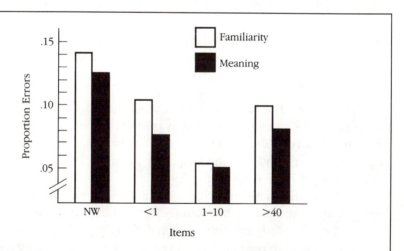

Figure 10-3.   Proportion of recognition errors made by two groups of college students after rating verbal items for either familiarity or meaning. The items were nonwords (NW) and words appearing less than 1 time, 1 through 10 times, and more than 40 times per million in the Thorndike-Lorge count. *(From "Errors in a Recognition Memory Task are a U-Shaped Function of Word Frequency," by E. B. Zechmeister, C. Curt, and J. A. Sebastian. In* Bulletin of the Psychonomic Society, *1978, 11, 371–373. Copyright 1978 by The Psychonomic Society, Inc. Reprinted by permission.)*

judge you do know the meaning of a very high frequency word. But words "in between" these two frequency extremes likely require greater processing in order to determine whether you know the meaning. There is evidence for these assumptions from an experiment by Kolers and Palef (1976). They measured college students' reaction times when asked to decide whether they knew a word well enough to use it in a sentence. The reaction time scores revealed a U-shaped function between response time and occurrence frequency of the item in the language. Response was fastest for very low and very high frequency words, but not as fast for moderately frequent words. Assuming that greater semantic effort or elaboration leads to better memory (and evidence to be reported in Chapter 12 suggests it does), then differences in the amount or kind of semantic processing of words of different frequencies may help to explain the word-frequency effect. Yet once again we must suggest that other factors are likely also involved.

As we have noted, high-frequency words are more likely than low-frequency words to elicit implicit associative responses (IARs), and there are more interitem associations among high-frequency than low-frequency words. The frequency theory of recognition memory (Underwood, 1971), which is based on the frequency theory of verbal discrimination described in Chapter 8, accounts for the word-frequency effect on the basis of IARs (see Underwood & Freund, 1970c). This important theory assumes that subjects in a recognition memory task are using frequency cues in order to recognize old and new items. Old items, because they have been presented previously, have a situational frequency of at least one, whereas new items will generally have a situational frequency of zero. The theory assumes that subjects' decisions as to whether an item appeared before will be guided by this difference in situational frequency between old and new items. As we saw in Chapter 8, our sensitivity to situational frequency is very good, and the frequency theory of recognition memory has received considerable empirical support.

Frequency theory assumes that high-frequency new items are likely to have their frequency, and hence their familiarity, augmented because they appeared as IARs when the study list was presented. Simply put, when subjects study a lengthy list of high-frequency words in preparation for a memory test, they are likely to "think of" many high-frequency items not actually on the list. Sometimes these IARs will appear as high-frequency new items on the recognition test. As Underwood (1965) showed in the study described earlier, a word elicited as an IAR is often judged to have appeared before when in fact it did not, at least not in the list of to-be-remembered items. Given that low-frequency words elicit fewer IARs than high-frequency words, subjects will make more recognition errors (false alarms) when high-frequency words are presented and tested than when low-frequency words are used. Therefore in addition to the possible differences in memory processing produced by structural and semantic characteristics of words of high and low frequency, memory researchers must incorporate into their theories of the word-frequency effect the differential elicitation of IARs by words of varying frequency (see also Glanzer & Bowles, 1976).

We mentioned when introducing the word-frequency effect that it is used as evidence against the view that recall and recognition are qualitatively the same. After all, the effect of word frequency is obviously different in these two kinds of tasks. However, some researchers have begun to hedge on accepting the word-frequency effect as sufficient evidence for differences in recall and recognition. For one reason, the whole issue tends to involve a bit of circular reasoning (see Tulving, 1976). For example, the generate-and-edit view of recall and recognition differences can explain word-frequency effects in these two tasks by assuming that high-frequency words are easier to generate (recall) but harder to discriminate than low-frequency words. What is the evidence for this? Well, there is the word-frequency effect. Do you see the circular logic?

Another reason the word-frequency effect cannot be sufficient evidence for qualitative differences in recall and recognition is that such an effect might reasonably be expected because recall and recognition *emphasize* different kinds of memory information. Recall clearly depends on information in memory that aids retrieval (such as interitem associations); recognition relies heavily on information that aids discrimination (such as situational frequency). This does not necessarily mean that recognition never involves memory retrieval, as the generate-and-edit view suggests. As we will see in the next section, there appear to be situations where we must retrieve information in order to recognize an item. Nevertheless, evidence obtained from an examination of the word-frequency effect clearly argues against any simplistic view of memory dynamics—for instance, that suggested by a traditional strength theory. One influential theory in this area of memory research has recently provided evidence against both the traditional one-process and popular two-process theories of recall and recognition. We will now look at this approach.

ENCODING SPECIFICITY

Many of us have been embarrassed by our failure to recognize friends or acquaintances when we meet them "out of context." We may not recognize a person we see every day at school or work when we see her in a restaurant or at the theater. When she says "you stared right past me," we find ourselves apologizing with some excuse like "I didn't recognize you when you were all dressed up." As we will see, these awkward memory failures can be explained by the principle of *encoding specificity*. This important memory principle also tells us something of the memory processes involved in recall and recognition.

Tulving and Osler (1968) conducted an experiment that set the stage for the encoding specificity principle. The experiment was complex, involving 19 different experimental conditions and a total of 674 schoolchildren from ten different schools in the greater Toronto, Ontario, area. Fortunately, the more critical findings are based on only 4 of these experimental conditions (see Tulving, 1979). The procedure in these conditions was similar to a paired-associate task in that the children were presented 24 pairs of words to study. The first word in each pair was called the cue word and was typed in lowercase letters. The second word was the to-be-remembered word, or target word, and it was typed in capital letters. Cue words were *weak associates* of the target words. A weak associate is a word given relatively infrequently by a large group of people when asked to free-associate to a word (see Palermo & Jenkins, 1964). Although a weak associate is not the most likely word you would come up with when associating to the target word, it is usually not hard to discover a meaningful relationship between the two. Examples of weak associates and their targets are *fat,* MUTTON and *body,* HEALTH.

All the children were presented the same 24 target words. However, there were two sets of cue words consisting of different, but associatively equivalent, cue words—for example, *fat,* MUTTON and *leg,* MUTTON. Half the subjects were presented target words with one set of cue words (set A) and the other half studied the list with the different set of cue words (set B). All subjects were carefully instructed that, although they would have to recall only the target word, they should nevertheless look for a relationship between the cue word and the target word because this would help them to recall the target word later.

Following study of the 24 word pairs, the children were asked to recall the target words when the cue words were presented *(cued recall).* However, half the subjects were given the same cue word as had appeared during study (Study: *fat,* MUTTON; Test: *fat, _____*). The other half received the different but associatively equivalent cue words (Study: *fat,* MUTTON; Test: *leg, _____*). Subjects were told to try to use the cue words to help them recall the target words. Because there were two sets of cue words (A and B) and subjects received either the same or different cue words in the test, there were four different experimental conditions. Results obtained in these conditions are shown in Figure 10-4.

Tulving and Osler (1968) found an interaction between study and test conditions. Recall was greater when the cue word on the test matched the cue word presented during study than when the cues were "mismatched," despite the fact that the cues were associatively equivalent. The researchers concluded that a cue's effectiveness in aiding target item retrieval is determined by what

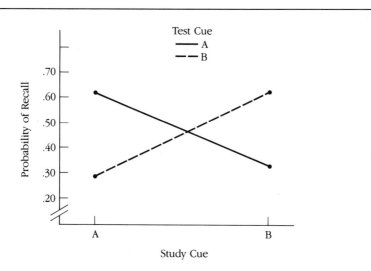

Figure 10-4. Probability of recall as a function of encoding and re-trieval conditions in the Tulving and Osler (1968) experiment. *(Based on data from "Effectiveness of Retrieval Cues in Memory for Words," by E. Tulving and S. Osler. In* Journal of Experimental Psychology, *1968, 77, 593–601. Used by permission.)*

happens during acquisition. In a later experiment in this series Thomson and Tulving (1970, p. 255) explained the results seen in Figure 10-4 this way:

> A retrieval cue is effective if, and only if, the information about its relation to the to-be-remembered (TBR) item is stored at the same time as the TBR item itself. Thus, a specific encoding format of the TBR item seems to constitute a prerequisite for the effectiveness of any particular retrieval cue. The point of view reflected in this inference from the data can be referred to as the encoding specificity hypothesis.

In a nutshell, the encoding specificity principle claims that if a learner does not encode the relationship between *leg* and MUTTON when MUTTON is studied, then presenting *leg* as a cue at recall time will not help in retrieving MUTTON.

Tulving and Osler pointed out that their results appeared to contradict the findings of some earlier experiments. Other investigators had shown that an associative cue presented *only* at recall did facilitate recall (for example, Bilodeau & Blick, 1965). According to the encoding specificity principle, this could happen only if the retrieval cue was present during study. Therefore Tulving and Osler (1968, p. 600) argued that the learners in these experiments must have thought about a particular retrieval cue at the time of study:

> If the TBR word is *bulb* … at least some Ss are quite likely to think of it as something to do with light. If "light" is then presented by E as a retrieval cue, it is effective for those Ss in the same way as it would have been if it had been presented together with *bulb* at input.

You should recognize that Tulving and Osler are talking about implicit associative responses, or IARs, which, as we saw earlier, also play a role in false recognitions (Underwood, 1965). We now see that IARs have a role in recall. The encoding specificity principle says that for a retrieval cue to be effective, it must either have been provided by the experimenter or have been elicited implicitly as an associative response at the time of study.

Tulving and Osler (1968) used only weak associates to provide evidence for encoding specificity. Some researchers were skeptical that the principle would be supported when strong associates were used. Yet the encoding specificity principle is clear: "No cue, regardless of how strongly it might be associated with the TBR item in other situations, can facilitate retrieval of the TBR item in absence of appropriate prior encoding of that item" (Thomson & Tulving, 1970, p. 258). Note they do say *no cue*.

Thomson and Tulving (1970) repeated the basic experimental conditions of the Tulving and Osler experiment in order to test this seemingly extreme view of memory dynamics. The subjects studied target words in the presence of *weak* associative cues (as in the Tulving and Osler experiment) but at the time of test were presented (1) no cues, (2) the same weak cues, or (3) different cues that were *strong* associates of the target items. Examples of target words and both weak and strong cues are *train, white,* BLACK; *knife, meat,* STEAK; *lamb, dumb,* STUPID. Presenting the same weak associates at study and at test led to significantly better recall than when no cues were present at test. In addition, recall in the presence of strong associates was no better than uncued recall. Thomson and Tulving (1970, p. 261) gave a rather colorful analysis of their results:

> The cue "white" cannot provide access to stored information about the occurrence of BLACK as a TBR word, if BLACK has been encoded as part of the "train-BLACK" complex, or as part of a unique event in a series of unique events. The two lexical units, BLACK and BLACK, are identical, but the encoded engram of the unique event BLACK, in the context of "train" and in the context of a specific set of TBR events, may be as different from the pattern of neural excitation corresponding to the generalized concept of BLACK as a beautiful and talented actress receiving an Oscar is different from any one of millions of stars twinkling in the endless night.

Recognition failure of recallable words

As you might expect, given that scientists are a skeptical bunch, the results of these experiments and their interpretation in terms of the encoding specificity principle have not been without critics (for example, see Postman, 1975a). Yet the principle of encoding specificity received an important boost by the discovery of a related phenomenon, one referred to as *recognition failure of recallable words* (Tulving & Thomson, 1973). It is no doubt one of the more significant discoveries in the recent history of memory research.

There are many variations on the experimental procedures used to demonstrate recognition failure of recallable words. However, the general methodology consists of three stages. Subjects first study a list of paired associates, as in the Tulving and Osler experiment, which consists of a series of cue words and their targets. Then recognition is tested for the target words in the presence of cues different from those used in the original list. Finally, a cued recall test is given in which the cues are those from the original list. As you can guess from this phenomenon's name, subjects fail to recognize words in the second stage that they later recall in the third or cued-recall stage.

In practice the specific procedures used to investigate this phenomenon are somewhat more involved. As an example, consider the procedure used by Watkins and Tulving (1975) as outlined in Table 10-3. In this case the experiment had six steps. In the first two steps subjects were presented two different paired-associate lists to learn, and recall of each list was tested with cues that had been present during study (steps 1a, 1b, 2a, and 2b in Table 10-3). This part of the experiment served to establish in the learner a set to encode the target words in relation to the particular cue words.

With this accomplished, the third and critical list was presented (step 3). This list, too, consisted of pairs of cue words (weak associates) and their targets. However, before recall was tested, subjects were asked to free-associate to words that were *strong* associates to the target words in the list. For example, if the target word was CHAIR, then the word used in the free-association task would be *table*. Of course, subjects frequently wrote down among their responses in the free-association task the word that was the target word in the critical list (see steps 4a and 4b in Table 10-3). Following the free-association task, recognition memory for the target words was tested. In some experiments—for example, Tulving and Thomson (1973)—subjects try to identify the target words among words they wrote down in the free-association task. Another variation, illustrated in Table 10-3, is to give subjects a forced-choice recognition test. The distractors in the forced-choice test are usually associatively related to the target word, but this may not be necessary in order to observe the phenomenon (see Watkins

TABLE 10-3. The Basic Methodology (Schematized Sequence of Procedures) Used by Watkins and Tulving (1975) to Demonstrate Recognition Failure of Recallable Words

Step	Procedure	Example
1a	List 1 presented	*badge*–BUTTON
1b	Cued recall of list 1	*badge*–button
2a	List 2 presented	*preach*–RANT
2b	Cued recall of list 2	*preach*–rant
3	List 3 presented	*glue*–CHAIR
4a	Free-association stimuli presented	table ___ ___ ___ ___
4b	Free-association responses made	table chair cloth desk dinner
5a	Recognition test sheets presented	DESK　　TOP　　CHAIR
5b	Recognized items circled	DESK　(TOP)　CHAIR
5c	Recognition confidence of circled items rated	DESK　(TOP₁)　CHAIR
5d	Recall of list cues of circled items attempted	DESK　(TOP₁)　CHAIR
6	Cued recall of list 3	*glue*–CHAIR

From "Episodic Memory: When Recognition Fails," by M. J. Watkins and E. Tulving. In *Journal of Experimental Psychology: General,* 1975, *104,* 5–29. Copyright 1975 by the American Psychological Association. Reprinted by permission.

& Tulving, 1975). Additional variations may require subjects to mark confidence in their choices on the recognition test and in some cases to attempt recall of the cues paired with the target words (steps 5c and 5d in Table 10-3). The last step required that subjects attempt recall of the target words in the presence of the original, weak-associate, cue words. As we mentioned, it turns out that, in the last step of the experiment, subjects recall words they had earlier failed to recognize. Recall, in other words, is successful when recognition is not. The magnitude of the effect varies, depending on slight changes in experimental procedure, and, interestingly, seems to be related in an orderly way to the overall level of recognition performance (Flexser & Tulving, 1978; Tulving & Wiseman, 1975).

　　Recognition failure of recallable words is consistent with the encoding specificity principle, which applies to remembering in general and makes no distinction between processes governing recall and those controlling recognition. According to the theory, both recall and recognition require that the retrieval environment contains information that overlaps with information originally encoded with the to-be-remembered event. For example, in many circumstances when recognition memory is tested, we are likely to process a word in a way similar to when we initially encountered it. Recognition will in this case likely be successful. However, as Thomson and Tulving (1970) have reminded us, lexical units, although nominally identical, may be encoded in very different ways (see also Light & Carter-Sobell, 1970). A (movie) STAR is not a (twinkling) STAR is not a (sheriff's) STAR is not a (Christmas) STAR. If at the time of recognition our processing of a target item is different enough from our processing of the original input, recognition can fail. As is the case for recall failure, recognition failure is due to inadequate or inappropriate retrieval cues. Therefore, according to the encoding specificity principle, recognition can fail when recall is successful. All that is needed is that retrieval cues, which were absent during the recognition test, be reinstated in the recall test.

It is not apparent under what conditions recognition failure of recallable words will be found to occur, nor is this aspect of the encoding specificity issue above criticism (see Light, Kimble, & Pellegrino, 1975; Martin, 1975; Salzberg, 1976; Tulving & Watkins, 1977). For example, Underwood and Humphreys (1979) have questioned whether recognition need always depend on the retrieval of a meaningful context, as when twinkling STAR is substituted for sheriff's STAR in a recognition memory test. Although not denying that recognition can involve retrieval of information, these researchers, and others (Mandler, 1980) argue that recognition is based on the detection of familiarity, which is independent of a meaningful context. As we saw earlier in this chapter, familiarity may be defined in terms of frequency of experience, and some consider frequency to be the fundamental basis for a recognition memory decision (see Underwood & Humphreys, 1979).

Whatever the theoretical outcome of these discussions, encoding specificity and the phenomenon of recognition failure of recallable words will have to be dealt with by any complete theory of memory dynamics. You can be sure that acquaintance of ours (you know, the one we didn't recognize) will be sure to get as part of our apology a lecture on the principle of encoding specificity.

PICTURE MEMORY SUPERIORITY

In a wide variety of memory tasks pictures are often remembered better than words (Paivio, 1976). Shepard (1967) found recognition memory for pictures to be better than that for either words or sentences. Standing, Conezio, and Haber (1970) found that recognition memory for pictures on an immediate retention test averaged better than 90% even when subjects viewed 2560 pictures. (It took these investigators more than 7 hours distributed over 4 days to present the pictures to the subjects.) When these results are compared to Shepard's (see Table 10-1), we see that even when the number of pictures was four times that used by Shepard, the overall level of recognition memory performance dropped very little.

Dual-code theory

A major explanation for picture superiority is the *dual-code theory* (Paivio, 1971, 1976, 1978). This theory assumes that encoding, storage, and retrieval of information involve two (dual) independent but related memory systems. These systems are associated with imaginal or verbal coding of to-be-remembered information and very likely with processing that occurs in different hemispheres of the brain (Bower, 1970; Seamon & Gazzaniga, 1973). According to the theory, processing by the imaginal and verbal systems has additive effects in a memory task. In other words, arousal of *both* verbal and imaginal codes will generally lead to better retention than the arousal of a single code.

The theory assumes that probability of dual coding is highest for pictures, next highest for concrete words (words denoting things that can be perceived by the senses—for example, *house*), and lowest for abstract words (words symbolizing concepts or ideas—for example, *democracy*). Probability of dual coding is greatest for picture stimuli because most people will add a label or description to a picture's imaginal representation in memory. Consider the following:

You undoubtedly found, when looking at these pictures, that you implicitly labeled them or in some manner responded to them verbally. In other words, you constructed two codes for these stimuli. Dual coding is also possible with concrete words *(house, car, tree),* but imagining an object denoted by a word is assumed to be less probable than verbally labeling a picture. Abstract words, of course, are difficult to visualize and would not typically be susceptible to dual coding. We will return to a discussion of dual-code theory and imagery in general when we discuss visual mnemonics in Chapter 13.

Sensory-semantic model

Another approach to explaining word-picture differences in memory tasks has been proposed by D. Nelson and his associates at the University of South Florida (Nelson, Reed, & McEvoy, 1977). They suggest that pictures not only produce qualitatively better sensory codes than words, but differ from words in the way meaning is accessed. Their *sensory-semantic model* assumes that in order to name a picture verbally, as you likely did when processing the simple line drawings shown to you earlier, you must process the meaning of the picture.

You have to know if it is a picture of a car before you can label it a car. But you can obtain the "name" of a word directly by processing the phonemic features of the stimulus, as when you look at the word *car* and think "car." According to the theory, differences in the sensory codes and in the relative access to meaning of words and pictures contribute to differential memory for these kinds of stimuli. The sensory-semantic model is an important alternative to the dual-code theory, but experiments have not produced outcomes totally favorable to either theory (for example, Durso & Johnson, 1979; Postman & Gray, 1979). Memory researchers have a long way to go before they completely understand picture superiority in memory tasks.

RECOGNITION VERSUS RELEARNING

When his son, Benjamin, was 15 months old, Burtt (1941) began to read Greek poetry to him (selections from Sophocles' *Oedipus Tyrannus*). The poetry was in the original Greek, and it was, as Burtt pointed out, tantamount to reading nonsense material to the child. Nevertheless, every day for more than a year and a half, until the boy was 3 years old, Burtt continued to read him three 20-line selections of poetry. He read each 20-line selection for 3 months (90 repetitions). When the child was 8½, 14, and 18 years of age, Burtt compared the boy's learning of the Greek heard in infancy with learning of selections not presented previously. At age 8½, the child required about 27% fewer trials to learn the passages heard as an infant than to learn the new passages. At age 14, learning was 14% faster for old than new selections; but at age 18, there was no difference between the number of trials needed to master the earlier passages and the new selections.

The method Burtt used to measure retention was relearning, a technique developed by Ebbinghaus (1885/1964) that was the basis for the classic forgetting curve discussed in Chapter 6. A relearning score is typically expressed in terms of the "savings" seen when relearning is compared to either original learning or, more appropriately, the learning of control materials (see Nelson, 1971). As we noted, Burtt showed that savings amounted to 27% when Benjamin was 8½, but zero savings were seen when he was 18. Relearning is not used often to assess retention, and on the basis of some early experimental findings (Luh, 1922; Postman & Rau, 1957), it was considered to be less sensitive than recognition in tapping the contents of memory. T. Nelson, working at the University of Washington, challenged this traditional view and not only provided evidence that relearning may be the most sensitive technique for assessing memory but also demonstrated that relearning can be used to investigate specific features of the target memory (Nelson, 1971, 1978; Nelson, Fehling, & Moore-Glascock, 1979; Nelson & Rothbart, 1972). He proposed that recognition and relearning be compared only for items subjects couldn't recall. Specifically, Nelson (1978) asked subjects first to learn a list of number-word pairs. Four weeks later he measured recall of the words when the numbers were presented as cues. Then subjects were given a forced-choice recognition test followed by relearning of the items they had neither recalled nor recognized. Items *not* recalled and *not* recognized were relearned faster than control items. Relearning, it seems, is the most sensitive test of what is in memory.

STUDYING FOR RECALL AND RECOGNITION

Educators have been aware for some time that students report use of different study techniques in anticipation of multiple-choice or essay type tests (Kinney & Eurich, 1932; Meyer, 1935) and that performance on one kind of examination may suffer when students are led to expect another kind of test (Meyer, 1934). Students are usually very interested to learn "what kind of test" will be given to evaluate their memory for course material. It can be assumed that students use this information to prepare differently for different kinds of class examinations.

Results of laboratory experiments investigating performance on recall or recognition tests when either a recall or recognition test was expected have tended to confirm the idea that people develop test-appropriate strategies (Carey & Lockhart, 1973; Connor, 1977; Jacoby, 1973; Tversky, 1973). In other words, the way laboratory subjects encode some information is influenced by the type of information they expect to need at time of test. Because organization of the to-be-remembered material affects recall more than it does recognition, it can be expected that factors contributing to organization (for example, instructions to develop interitem associations and categorized versus noncategorized lists) are more important when recall is anticipated than when recognition is anticipated. More important perhaps, results of these experiments varying test expectancy point to the need to consider a learner's beliefs about what is "good" for memory in a particular task in order to understand what will be remembered. Such a consideration is found in the topic of "metamemory," which is discussed in the next chapter.

Summary

Recognition is generally a more sensitive test of memory than is recall. We first reviewed the major paradigms by which recognition memory is investigated: forced choice, absolute judgment, and continuous recognition. The absolute judgment task raises an important methodological problem related to possible differences in subjects' response biases or criteria. One approach to this problem is based on signal detection theory. We next looked at several theories offered to explain the fact that recognition memory is usually better than recall. Strength or threshold theory assumes that recall and recognition involve the same processes but that recognition is simply more sensitive. So-called two-stage theories suggest that recall and recognition involve qualitatively different processes. Evidence against the traditional strength theory is provided by word-frequency effects, which show that retention of high- and low-frequency words differ as a function of the type of test given. An important theoretical analysis of recall and recognition is provided by the encoding specificity principle. This principle makes no distinction between the processes in recall and recognition and explains retention in terms of the extent to which the cognitive environment at time of test overlaps or "matches" the environment present at time of study. This important theory provides an explanation for the interesting fact that recall can sometimes be successful when recognition is not.

Memory for pictures is often extraordinarily good and better than that seen for individual words or sentences. Two major theories have been suggested to explain picture superiority in memory tasks. The dual-code theory claims that pictures are more likely than words to be represented in memory by both verbal and visual codes, thus leading to better retention. The sensory-semantic theory assumes that pictures require more meaningful analysis than do words and for this reason are better remembered.

In this chapter we also discussed relearning as a measure of retention. Results of recent experiments suggest that relearning may be the most sensitive measure of what is in memory. We are likely to see more research in the future that makes use of this often neglected measure of retention.

It is clear that "what is remembered" depends on the way memory is tested. A knowledge of the processes underlying recall, recognition, and relearning gives us not only a better understanding of memory in general, but also provides information that is important in constructing tests of memory and in explaining why memory "fails" on a test. As we saw in this chapter, students apparently study differently for recall and recognition tests. Knowledge gained from an investigation of these processes can also be used in the preparation of test-appropriate strategies.

Recommendations for further reading

Any complete theory of memory must provide a description of the processes underlying recall and recognition. There is no scarcity of ideas about these processes and numerous sources are available that provide reviews of research in this area. More comprehensive textbooks than this, such as those by Crowder (1976), Kintsch (1977), and Murdock (1974) are good in this regard. On a more theoretical level, we particularly recommend a recent article by Mandler (1980) because it provides both a review and a theoretical integration of much of the research discussed in this chapter. Research on the word-frequency effect is reviewed by Gregg (1976). Paivio

(1976, 1978) outlines the dual-code theory of picture versus word differences in recall and recognition. D. Nelson (1979) presents evidence for the alternative sensory-semantic theory. Interesting experiments based on the measure of relearning, which we discussed only briefly, are found in reports by T. Nelson (Nelson, 1978; Nelson, Fehling, & Moore-Glascock, 1979). Tulving (1976, 1979) discusses the encoding specificity principle. Finally, a lengthy experimental report by Underwood and Humphreys (1979) provides interesting data and important theoretical comments on many of the issues discussed in this chapter.

11

Metamemory:
Knowing about Knowing

Introduction/overview

Consider the following scenario from a science fiction story. The setting is a classroom and it is the last day of the semester. The instructor is about to assign grades based on how much the students know of the information presented in the course. She picks up her class roll and begins calling the names of students in the class: Abbott, Banks, Bradley . . . . As their names are called, the students call out percentages, 80%, 91%, and so forth. The in-structor records the percentages to indicate the amount each student in the course knows. There is no final exam. No long list of multiple-choice questions. No seemingly impossible essay questions to answer. Grades are awarded solely on the basis of each student's judgment about how much he or she knows of the class content.

Our knowledge about what we know is not, of course, as good as that of the students in this story. We would be hard pressed at the end of a course to say exactly how much got into our memory, and most instructors are not likely to give out grades based only on a student's judgment about what he or she knows. But just what do we know about what we know? And how does this knowledge influence our study of what we do not yet know? These are questions about metamemory, which refers to our knowledge and awareness of memory or of those things that are important to information storage and retrieval (Flavell & Wellman, 1977).

More than a decade ago Tulving and Madigan (1970) concluded their important review of research on human memory with the suggestion that investigators should pay more attention to questions of metamemory. Indeed, according to these reviewers, research on metamemory offered the possibility of dramatic new insights into the working of human memory. As they stated,

> Why not start looking for ways of experimentally studying, and incorporating into theories and models of memory, one of the truly unique characteristics of human memory: its knowledge of its own knowledge. No extant conceptualization, be it based on S-R associations or on information processing paradigm, makes provisions for the fact that the human memory system cannot only produce a learned response to an appropriate stimulus or retrieve a stored image, but it can also rather accurately estimate the likelihood of its success in doing it. . . .
>
> We cannot help but feel that if there is ever going to be a genuine breakthrough in the psychological study of memory . . . it will, among other things, relate the knowledge stored in an individual's memory to his knowledge of that knowledge [Tulving and Madigan, 1970, p. 477].

It is too soon, not enough research has been done, to say whether Tulving and Madigan were right, that research on metamemory will produce a "genuine breakthrough" in our understanding of human memory. But there is no doubt that what has been learned so far provides important clues to understanding this memory of ours. In this chapter we will briefly review some of the things that memory knows about itself. We begin with a discussion of exactly what metamemory is and how it fits into the scheme of research on memory. Then we will look at the role of metamemory in making decisions about what will be easy or hard to learn and what we already know (both at acquisition and at time of testing) and in our confidence about what we have retrieved from memory. An important point to be made in this chapter is that effective learning and retention depend on well-developed metamemory skills.

RELATIONSHIP BETWEEN METAMEMORY AND MEMORY

Meta is from the Greek, meaning "behind," "beyond," or "after." In coining the word *metamemory,* Flavell (1970) wanted to draw our attention to an aspect of memory not directly related to memory structure or to the specific process of encoding, storage, and retrieval. To gain some perspective on this topic of metamemory, we might think, as Flavell and Wellman (1977) suggested, of memory phenomena as falling into four general and overlapping categories.

One category would include the most basic operations and processes of our memory system. These processes are relatively automatic and we are not generally conscious of them. For example, look at the objects around you. What do you recognize? What is familiar? What are the names of the objects before you? The memory mechanisms that enable us to recognize objects, retrieve their names, or produce a sense of familiarity in us are very basic components of our memory system. These mechanisms are present from a very early age and probably do not change as we grow older. Their activation appears to be automatic. You may recall that some researchers consider information about frequency of events to be processed automatically (see Chapter 8).

A second category of memory-related phenomena is the influence of present knowledge on future knowledge. As we learn new ideas, we are likely to organize information in memory in a way that reflects this new knowledge. For example, experts at chess and bridge often have better memory for aspects of these games than do novices (Chase & Simon, 1973; Engle & Bukstel, 1978). Part of this superior memory is due to the knowledge the experts have acquired while playing thousands of games. As Chase and Simon (1973) suggested, experienced chess players actually "see" the board differently from inexperienced players. Their cognitive structure, in other words, is different from that of novice chess players, and this influences what they remember. Although the basic mechanisms of memory may not change with age, our cognitive structure certainly does. As we grow older, we experience more things; we learn new concepts. Ideas that did not make sense at an earlier age may make sense now. In Chapter 14 we will look at experiments that demonstrate the important role knowledge plays in comprehending and remembering.

A third category of memory-related phenomena includes various voluntary strategies that help us to remember. We are generally conscious of these memory activities and they are presumably "nonautomatic." For example, in order to remember something, we often find ourselves rehearsing events, creating visual images, or trying to associate new ideas with old ones. These are purposeful activities intended to help us remember. They are often identified as "control processes" in many information-processing models of memory, and as we pointed out in Chapter 4, changes in memory strategies likely account for important differences in retention between children and adults. Flavell and

Wellman (1977) suggest that strategic activities are specific to the human memory system. As they noted, "An adult dog has basic memory 'hardware' (first category) and has certainly acquired knowledge of its world that powerfully affects its mnemonic activity (second category). We are loathe to credit it with much development in the third category, however" (p. 4).

A fourth category is metamemory. This is our knowledge (stored in memory, of course) of the nature and processes of the first three categories of memory-related phenomena. Metamemory is a subcategory of *metacognition* (Brown, 1978). Metacognition refers to knowledge about *all* cognitive processes, their products, and anything related to them. We use metacognition when we monitor the activities of our cognitive system and its output. Metacognition includes knowledge that our verbal skills are better than our quantitative skills, that as a check on division we can multiply the divisor and dividend, that an important step in problem solving is to list all the elements of the problem, and so forth. Metamemory is that aspect of metacognition that is related, as Flavell and Wellman stated, to getting information into and out of memory. To clarify this concept further, we'll describe an experiment that investigated what children know about their memory.

One of the better known studies of children's metamemory was carried out by Kreutzer, Leonard, and Flavell (1975). They asked children in grades K, 1, 3, and 5 a series of questions about memory and memory-related phenomena. They asked the questions in a manner that the children could easily understand and that was designed to elicit specific knowledge the children might have about their memory. For example, consider a question about savings, or re-learning, a topic discussed in the last chapter.

> Jim and Bill are in grade _____ [the interviewer filled in the grade of the
> child being interviewed]. The teacher wanted them to learn the names of all
> the kinds of birds they might find in their city. Jim had learned them last year
> and then forgot them. Bill had never learned them before. Do you think one
> of these boys would find it easier to learn the names of all the birds? Which
> one? Why? [Kreutzer, Leonard, & Flavell, 1975, p. 8].*

For this particular question, a majority of even the youngest children (kindergarten) said that Jim (the relearner) would find it easier to learn the names. Nearly all the older children and more than half the youngest suggested the relearner would do better because something was probably left in memory that would lead to savings.

---

*From "An Interview Study of Children's Knowledge about Memory," by M. A. Kreutzer, C. Leonard, and J. H. Flavell. In *Monographs of the Society for Research in Child Development*, 1975, *40*(1, Serial No. 159). Copyright 1975 by The Society for Research in Child Development, Inc. This and all other quotations from this source are reprinted by permission.

As you might expect, the younger children (grades K and 1) did not always do so well on the interviewers' questions. The researchers found that children in grades 3 and 5 are generally more capable of articulating why something might happen and were more knowledgeable about factors affecting their memory than were the younger subjects. For example, both the younger and older children shared a general sense that amount of time between learning and test affects recall, but only the older children were also aware that learning similar material during the retention interval produces interference. Another example of the superior metamemory found in older children was illustrated by answers to another question, one that asked what the children knew about things that are easiest to learn. Because this question has also been asked of adults, with some interesting results, we will use it to introduce the next section.

KNOWING WHAT *WILL BE* KNOWN

Kreutzer, Leonard, and Flavell (1975, p. 14), as part of their interview study of children's metamemory, also asked the following:

> I'm going to show you a new way of learning things. I'll show you words in pairs and I'd like you to learn them so that when I show you one of the words you can tell me the other word that goes with it.
> [All children learned three practice pairs so that they understood the task. Then, the experimenter showed each child two kinds of word pairs.]
> Here are two longer lists of words that you could learn in the same way. These words are opposites: "boy" goes with "girl," "easy" goes with "hard." . . . And these words are people and things they might do. So "Mary" goes with "walk" (etc.). Do you think one of these would be easier for you to learn? Why?

Older children more than the younger children tended to say the list of opposites would be easier to learn than the people-and-things list. In fact, all the fifth graders interviewed said the opposites list would be easier to learn, whereas fewer than a third of the kindergartners thought the opposites list would be easier. The opposites list was, by the way, shown to be much easier for a preschool child to learn than the relatively arbitrary associations in the people-and-things list. When answering why they felt the opposites list would be easier to learn, most of the older children suggested that the alternatives in the opposites list were more restricted than those in the other list. Said one child: "The opposites would be easier, because you know what the opposite is. . . . People do a lot of different activities, and it would be sort of hard to memorize them" (Kreutzer, Leonard, & Flavell, 1975, p. 15). The younger children, even when they chose the opposites list, were usually not able to explain why it was easier. However, the younger children sometimes justified their choice of *either* list by stating that the items in that list were more "familiar." This suggested to the interviewers that even at a very young age children sense a positive relationship between familiarity and ease of learning.

Ease-of-learning judgments

Older learners—for example, college students—can not only identify which class of items will be easiest to learn but are also rather adept at predicting what *particular items* will be easy or hard to learn (Lippman & Kintz, 1968; Underwood, 1966). Ratings of specific items in terms of how hard they will be to learn are referred to as *ease-of-learning judgments*. The adult learner's ability to discriminate between easy and hard items is nicely illustrated in an experiment by Underwood (1966).

Underwood (1966) asked college students to imagine they were participating in a free-recall task. The to-be-remembered items would be 27 trigrams (three-letter combinations), including both words *(BUG, KIT)* and nonsense items *(XFH, VFR)*. Students were to assume that each trigram would be presented for 2 seconds and following their study of all the trigrams, that recall would be tested. They were further to assume that study and test trials would alternate until they could recall all 27 trigrams correctly. Given this hypothetical situation, students were asked to make ease-of-learning judgments for each of the trigrams. They were to judge whether they would learn a trigram after only a few study trials or after relatively many trials. Some students made their judgments by drawing lines of different lengths to reflect the degree of difficulty of the items. The lines were to be drawn proportionate to item difficulty. For instance, an item judged twice as difficult to learn as another item would receive a line twice as long as the other. Following the judgment task, the students actually learned the trigrams in the manner described in the hypothetical experiment. Another group of students did not do the rating task but simply learned the trigrams.

The correlation between average ease-of-learning ratings (based on average line length) and actual learning (based on the number of times a trigram was recalled by the group of students who did not make the rating) was an impressive .92. Two other groups of students in this study rated the 27 trigrams according to how easy each item was to pronounce and "for the relative number of associates they thought each would elicit" (Underwood, 1966, p. 675). The correlations between ease-of-learning ratings and item characteristics of pronounceability and association value, or meaningfulness, were .94 and .91, respectively. Therefore average ease-of-learning ratings correlated very well with actual learning and also with item characteristics known to influence learning.

Clearly, people can detect those item qualities that contribute to ease of learning. Relatively accurate ease-of-learning ratings have been obtained for sets of trigrams considerably more homogeneous than those Underwood used—for example, when no words were in the list (Lippman & Kintz, 1968), for letter-number pairs (Arbuckle & Cuddy, 1969), and for sentences containing specific to-be-remembered facts (Zechmeister, Christensen, & Rajkowski, 1980). It is likely that a learner's awareness of the familiarity-learning relationship, which we saw develops at a very early age, plays a major role in these predictions. Even among sets of relatively "meaningless" trigrams, some items, due to their particular letter sequences or their appearance in common words, will appear more "familiar" than others, and subjects can be presumed to judge them easier to learn than less-familiar items.

Judgments of prose

Yet more than familiarity is involved in judgments of what will be known. Much of what we need to learn is in the form of connected discourse or prose material. To what extent are learners sensitive to what they will remember from prose material? Brown and Smiley (1977) asked children in grades 3, 5, and 7 and college students to rate the structural importance of prose units in Japanese fairy tales. Japanese fairy tales (translated to English, of course) were chosen so that the stimulus material would be both interesting to the youngest age group tested and not previously experienced by students in all grades. Independent groups of adult judges initially analyzed the stories for the number of different idea units each story contained and for the relative importance of each idea unit to story theme. These ratings served as an independent definition of structural importance. The stories were then presented to the experimental subjects, who also rated structural importance but who, in addition, listened to a story and tried to recall the gist. Selections from one of the Japanese fairy tales Brown and Smiley (1977) used and their rated importance are illustrated in Table 11-1. Higher numbers indicate greater rated importance.

When recall was analyzed according to the independent judges' ratings, students at all ages remembered most frequently those ideas rated as most important and remembered least those ideas rated as least important. Mean proportion correct recall was .23 and .69 for units rated the least and most important, respectively. Recall, in other words, was directly related to the rated structural importance. However, it should be noted that older students recalled more ideas at each level of importance than did the younger children. When ratings of structural importance were analyzed, the researchers found the third graders, and to some extent the fifth graders, were not able to distinguish between even the least and most important levels of importance. For example,

TABLE 11-1. Idea Units and Their Rated Importance from a Japanese Fairy Tale Brown and Smiley (1977) Used to Investigate What Students Know about What Will Be Remembered from Text Material

Unit	Rated importance
1. Once upon a time	1.62
2. there was a rich lord	3.56
3. who liked to collect carvings of animals	3.21
4. (those are like little wooden dolls).	1.06
5. He had many kinds,	1.50
6. but he had no carved mouse.	2.94
7. So he called two skilled carvers to him and said:	3.41
8. "I want each of you to carve a mouse for me."	3.97

From "Rating the Importance of Structural Units of Prose Passages: A Problem of Metacognitive Development," by A. L. Brown and S. S. Smiley. In *Child Development,* 1977, *48,* 1–8. Copyright 1977 by The Society for Research in Child Development, Inc. Reprinted by permission.

the average rating of third graders was 2.41 for the least important level (as defined by adult judges) and 2.56 for the most important level. In contrast, average ratings by college students were 1.61 and 3.52 for the least and most important levels, respectively. These results were obtained even though, as we said, the story recall of all students corresponded to the judged level of importance by the independent group of adult judges.

Implications

As Brown and Smiley pointed out, the ability to identify the relative importance of idea units to the theme of a passage has several implications for training study skills and reading comprehension. If learners cannot distinguish the key points of a passage from the lesser points, then they cannot be expected to select the key points for particular attention during study. Children in the early grades may need help in drawing their attention to the critical elements of a prose passage. This may also be true of deficient learners at all grade levels. In a study that compared retention of theme-related ideas of good and poor readers in the seventh grade, good readers' recall corresponded better with rated gradation of theme importance than did poor readers' recall, suggesting that the poor readers were less sensitive to what was important than the good readers (Smiley, Oakley, Worthen, Campione, & Brown, 1977).

There is also evidence that academically successful students are better able to judge the relative difficulty of a verbal passage than are less academically successful students (Owings, Petersen, Bransford, Morris, & Stein, 1980). In one experiment, fifth graders were asked to read short stories that had been constructed so as to be easy or difficult to comprehend and remember. For the difficult stories the subjects and predicates of many of the sentences were inappropriately related. An easy story might contain such sentences as "The tall boy had played basketball" and "The hungry boy had eaten a hamburger." A difficult story would contain sentences like "The hungry boy had played basketball" and "The tall boy had done his homework." An easy and a difficult story were presented together and the children read and then studied each. Children were told to signal when they finished reading and to signal again when they had completed studying for the retention test they had been forewarned would be given. After reading both stories but before taking the retention test, the children were asked to select the story they thought was easier to learn and to explain why.

The researchers found that the more successful students were more likely to select the appropriately written stories as easier to learn. Good students were also better able to say why a story was difficult to learn. Finally, and perhaps most significant, the good students spent more time studying the difficult stories than the easy stories; the poor students studied the easy and hard stories an equal amount of time. Apparently because they were not as sensitive to what constitutes an easy or hard passage, the poor students did not make as efficient use of their study time as did the good students.

Effective learning and remembering apparently depend upon the degree to which a learner can discriminate between the key points of a passage and the less important ones and between those particular items or concepts that will be easy to learn and those that will be hard to learn. How this is accomplished will depend on the learner's metamemory skills.

KNOWING WHAT *IS* KNOWN

Judgments of knowing

When do you know you have had enough? Study, that is. How do you know you have studied something sufficiently so that you will later remember it? Another kind of metamemory task has been used to answer such questions. In this case subjects are asked to make a *judgment of knowing*. This is defined as the rated likelihood of remembering an item that is being studied in preparation for a memory test (King, Zechmeister, & Shaughnessy, 1980). We would like to think that students make this type of judgment when studying for class examinations. At some point during study it would seem advisable to ask whether the to-be-remembered material has been encoded well enough so you can retrieve it at the time of the exam. Although an affirmative answer might bring an end to study, a negative answer should lead to more study. Some students seem to have trouble judging what they know and what they don't know. This is illustrated by the proverbial student who, having done poorly on an exam, approaches an instructor lamenting, "I thought I really knew it."

Laboratory studies of judgments of knowing typically require students to predict later retention of individual items that have been presented for study. The nature of the future memory test is generally explained to subjects before the items are presented for learning. Then some time during study and before a final memory test, subjects are asked to rate the likelihood that they will remember a particular item on the later test. This type of judgment differs from an ease-of-learning judgment in that it is supposed to reflect what *is* known, not what *will be* known. For example, an item rated initially as very difficult to learn (ease-of-learning judgment) could, following several study trials, be rated as definitely known (judgment of knowing).

Despite the apparent relevance of this type of judgment to situations wherein learners must make accurate decisions about the quality of their encoding (as before a class examination), judgments of knowing have been infrequently investigated. One of the first experiments was by Arbuckle and Cuddy (1969). The results of their study not only tell us about our ability to make such judgments but suggest a way such judgments might be made. These investigators asked college students to learn a series of five-pair lists. Two common nouns formed each pair. Students were told that each pair would be presented for 3 seconds and that they should try to learn all five pairs, although recall of only one pair would be tested. The students were not told which pair would be tested. Immediately following the presentation of the fifth pair, the first word of one of the pairs was presented and students attempted to recall the second word of that pair. This method of testing retention is a *probe recall task*. Each student was tested after many different lists and each position in the list was tested an equal number of times. While attempting to learn each item, students were to ask themselves the following question: "How sure are you that you will remember the pair?" They made a judgment of knowing by marking a scale with the words "very likely" and "very unlikely" as endpoints.

Figure 11-1 shows the probability of correctly recalling a pair as a function of the level-of-knowing prediction. The figure shows separately the results for pairs appearing first in the list (serial position 1), in the middle of the list (serial positions 2, 3, and 4), and last in the list (serial position 5). The lower the number on the judgment-of-knowing scale, the more confident the students were that recall would be successful. As you can see, with the exception of pairs appearing in the last serial position (SP5), overall recall was accurately predicted by rated likelihood of remembering. The results for pairs appearing in serial position 5 can be explained by the manner in which retention was tested. Even though the students gave different ratings for pairs in this position, because

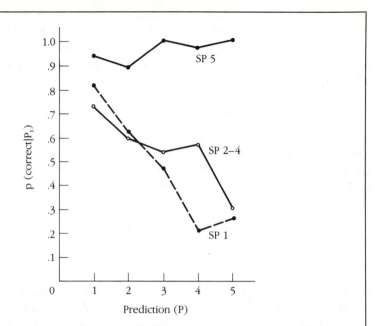

Figure 11-1. Probability of correct response as a function of judgment of knowing. Results are plotted separately for items that appeared in the first serial position (SP1), serial positions 2, 3, and 4 (SP 2–4), and for items appearing last (SP5) in the five-pair lists. *(From "Discrimination of Item Strength at Time of Presentation," by T. Y. Arbuckle and L. L. Cuddy. In* Journal of Experimental Psychology, *1969, 81, 126–131. Copyright 1969 by the American Psychological Association. Reprinted by permission.)*

recall was tested immediately, retention was almost always perfect. Therefore there was no opportunity for differential recall of items in that position.

What do the results of the Arbuckle and Cuddy study tell us about judgments of knowing? Is it that subjects can "look in" and read the strength of a memory and on this basis successfully predict future recall? Arbuckle and Cuddy offered a simpler explanation. They suggested that subjects make judgments of knowing on the basis of the perceived difficulty of the word pairs. In other words, by judging the difficulty of the items (an ease-of-learning judgment), subjects are able to make relatively accurate predictions about the fate of an item on the later recall trial. In another experiment these investigators showed that rated ease of learning was highly correlated with rated predictions of recall. Of course, if subjects can reliably make both ease-of-learning and knowing judgments, then the two kinds of judgments will often be correlated, particularly when there is only a single study trial. After all, both attempt to predict the same thing—

namely, probability of retention. Although we do not know the extent to which perceptions of item difficulty actually influence judgments of knowing, we can presume that characteristics of the to-be-remembered items play a major role in helping learners decide whether retention of presently studied information will be successful.

Memory for remembered events

One kind of information that undoubtedly influences metamemory decisions regarding what is known and not known is memory for previous test outcomes, or what some have called *memory for remembered events* (Gardiner & Klee, 1976; see also King, Zechmeister, & Shaughnessy, 1980). It is very simple. If a learner can remember the outcome of a previous test, then information he or she can use to predict the outcomes of future tests like the previous one is available. Such a strategy is possible, of course, only if test trials are provided and only if the learner can remember the outcomes of previous tests. An experiment by Gardiner and Klee (1976) demonstrated that learners do remember the outcomes of previous tests. They asked college students to attempt recall of ten different 15-word lists. Each list was presented only one time and subjects recalled immediately after each list. Following recall of the last list, all the words from the previous lists were shown to the subjects with the request that they indicate which words they had recalled and which they had not. Although they had not expected this test for remembered events, subjects were generally accurate in distinguishing between previously recalled and nonrecalled words. An exception was words that had appeared (and were recalled) in the last few positions of the list. Apparently, items that are only briefly processed prior to recall are not well remembered as being recalled. Interestingly, memory for remembered events is not that good when recognition memory is tested—that is, subjects have difficulty distinguishing between previously recognized items and nonrecognized items (Klee & Gardiner, 1976).

Memory for whether an item was previously recalled or not is clearly direct and unambiguous evidence for deciding whether it has been sufficiently encoded so as to allow successful retrieval. With this evidence in hand (or is it mind?) an efficient learner could presumably direct encoding efforts more to the unknown than to the known. There is evidence that learners do just that, although once again we find this is a strategy that is not well developed in relatively young children. College students, and to some extent third graders, but not first graders, when given the opportunity, will select for additional study those items they failed to remember on a previous test trial (Masur, McIntyre, & Flavell, 1973; Zacks, 1969). Apparently, it is not that the younger learners do not remember what they had recalled previously, but rather that they do not *use* this information as do the older learners (see Bisanz, Vesonder, & Voss, 1978).

Discrimination-utilization hypothesis

Memory for previous test-trial outcomes is the basis of the *discrimination-utilization* hypothesis of learning presented by Bisanz, Vesonder, and Voss (1978). They argue that, in a multitrial learning task, learners remember whether an item was correct or incorrect on a previous test trial and use this information to distribute their memory processing on subsequent trials. In an interesting test of this hypothesis they asked primary school and college students to learn a paired-associate list with alternating study and test trials. The list of to-be-remembered pairs consisted of pictures of common objects, and all subjects were required to learn the list to a criterion of one errorless trial. A study trial consisted of showing both members of a pair; only the left member of each pair was presented on a test trial. An unusual requirement of this paired-associate learning procedure was that as each pair was presented during a study trial, the subjects were to say yes or no to indicate whether they had gotten that particular pair correct on the immediately preceding test trial. As would be expected, the older subjects were more accurate when remembering what they had previously gotten correct than the younger subjects. However, among the older students (fifth graders and college), those learners who were most accurate at remembering what they had or had not recalled tended to learn the list faster than those who were not as accurate. This result is at least suggestive that those who know what they know and know what they don't know will remember more than those who don't.

The feeling-of-knowing phenomenon

Perhaps the most frequently referenced studies of metamemory are those conducted by Hart (1965, 1966, 1967a) as part of his doctoral dissertation at Stanford University. He systematically investigated a memory phenomenon all of us have experienced at one time or another. It usually occurs when someone asks whether we know a particular fact—for example, the title of a book or the name of a prominent person. We try to retrieve the answer from memory but are unsuccessful. Sometimes, however, we find ourselves with a "feeling of knowing," a sense that what we are looking for *is,* in fact, stored in our memory. Such experiences can be particularly frustrating when they occur during a class examination or in a social gathering when we are asked about something that everyone thinks we should know. A strong feeling of knowing is likely to lead us to predict that we would recognize the correct answer if it was shown to us, if we were given the opportunity to select it from several similar choices. But how accurate are we at monitoring the contents of memory when recall fails? Are our feelings of knowing accurate predictors of what is stored in memory? Are our feelings of *not* knowing as reliable? Until Hart's important series of experiments, memory researchers had little information about these important aspects of metamemory.

In one of his initial experiments, Hart (1965) first asked college students a series of 75 general information questions. Three of these questions were

1. What planet is the largest in our solar system?
2. What sea does West Pakistan border?
3. Who developed the nonsense syllable in studies of learning?

Students were asked to try to answer the questions as the experimenter read them aloud, but they were also advised that the questions had been deliberately chosen so that everyone would fail to answer some of them. When the students were not able to recall the answers, they were to ask themselves this question: "Even though I don't remember the answer now, do I know the answer to the extent that I could pick the correct answer from among several wrong answers?" With this question in mind students rated the items they could not recall on a six-point feeling-of-knowing scale (see Figure 11-2). After the recall and rating part of the experiment, students were given a four-alternative multiple-choice test. For example, the following alternatives were presented for the first two questions:

1. a. Pluto   b. Venus   c. Earth   d. Jupiter
2. a. Arabian Sea   b. Caspian Sea   c. Red Sea   d. Black Sea

We will assume that as a student of memory you had no trouble answering the third question. Answers to the first two are *d* and *a,* respectively.

Hart was interested in the proportion correct recognition that accompanied both feeling-of-knowing and feeling-of-not-knowing responses. Memory mon-

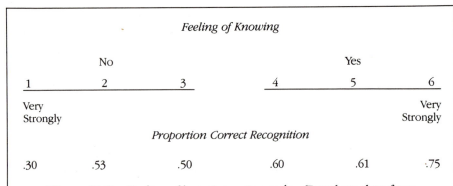

Figure 11-2. Feeling-of-knowing rating scale. *(Based on data from "Memory and the Feeling-of-Knowing Experience," by J. T. Hart. In* Journal of Educational Psychology, *1965, 56, 208–216. Used by permission.)*

itoring accuracy was judged in two ways. First, Hart compared correct recognition for items given a feeling-of-knowing rating (scale points 4, 5, and 6) with recognition of those items students rated as not knowing (scale points 1, 2, and 3). If people can reliably predict recognition memory of unrecallable information, then there should be a significant difference between these two proportions. A second way to evaluate memory-monitoring accuracy was to examine proportion correct recognition as a function of the six scale points used in the rating task. A finely tuned memory-monitoring ability would be reflected by graded recognition performance on the feeling-of-knowing scale. The data in Figure 11-2 indicate that not only did students reliably discriminate between overall feelings of knowing and not knowing, but proportion correct recognition also appeared to reflect different degrees of feeling of knowing. Students expressing a strong feeling of not knowing responded at about chance level on the four-alternative recognition test. However, although strong feelings of knowing (6 on the scale) led to generally high levels of recognition memory performance, recognition based on a very strong feeling of knowing was not 100%. Therefore Hart's experiment established that recognition can be accurately predicted when recall fails but showed that memory monitoring is less than a perfect predictor of what is in storage. Subsequent research has demonstrated that memory monitoring is relatively poor among preschoolers but increases in accuracy over the early school grades (Wellman, 1977).

The "feeling-of-knowing" phenomenon

Purpose
To determine whether a feeling of knowing is a reliable predictor of what is stored in memory.

Materials
Forty general information questions are chosen such that most adults will find the questions meaningful but will not likely be able to recall the answers to all of them. Recall may be tested by reading the questions aloud to the subjects. An answer sheet with spaces for 40 answers should be prepared for each subject. In addition, a four-alternative recognition memory test must be constructed for the 40 questions. (See Table I in the Appendix.) Individual test booklets are needed for each of the subjects. Presentation order of the questions on the recall and recognition tests should be random and different for the two tests.

Procedure
The procedure is simple and is explained in the instructions to the subjects.

Instructions to Subjects

RECALL

In this experiment you will be asked a series of general information questions. The questions cover a variety of topics, including sports, history, and music. This is not an intelligence test. In fact, the questions have been selected so that you will not likely be able to recall the answers to all of them. There are 40 questions, and each will be read aloud at the rate of about one every 10–15 seconds. There are two things you are to do in this first part of the experiment. First, for each question try to recall the answer and write it down on your answer sheet. It is important that you try to write down an answer for every question even if you are not absolutely sure it is right. Next, if you cannot supply an answer to a question, you are to ask yourself the following: "Even though I don't remember the answer now, do I know the answer to the extent that I could pick it from among several alternatives?" In other words, do you think you would recognize the correct answer if it was presented among several wrong answers? Because the questions were chosen so that you will not likely recall the answers to many of them, there should be a number of questions on this test for which you need to ask yourself this question. (Repeat question.) If your answer is yes to the question, please mark a *Y* in the answer space for that question. If your answer is no, then put an *N* in the answer space. After you have tried to answer all 40 questions and have responded yes or no for the answers you could not recall, you will be given a recognition test that will allow you to select the correct answer from among several alternatives. Are there any questions? (Remind subjects to (1) try to recall an answer for each question, including answers they are not perfectly sure are right, and (2) mark the answer sheet with a *Y* or *N* for those questions for which they are not able to recall the answer.)

RECOGNITION

The recognition test contains the same 40 questions just asked. For each question please circle the correct answer among the four alternatives. You may work at your own pace, but you are to circle an answer for *every* question on the test. Are there any questions?

Summary and Analysis

Each subject will provide four scores in the form of proportions. Recognition accuracy is first determined for all questions subjects said they would recognize *(Y)*. The number of correct and incorrect answers on the recognition test for the yes answers are expressed as a proportion of the total number of yes responses. For example, suppose a subject said yes to 12 questions he could not recall, and of those 12, suppose he correctly recognized 8 answers. Therefore the subject's "feeling of knowing" was accurate .67 of the time and wrong .33 of the time. Similar proportions are then obtained for the no responses. For example, suppose a subject responded no to 10 questions. If she later recognized 4 of these questions and did not recognize 6, her "feeling of not knowing" was accurate on .60 occasions and wrong for .40 of the questions. Because subjects will differ in the number of times they respond yes or no to unanswered questions, results can be best summarized by looking at the overall proportions. In other words, for all subjects and for all questions the accuracy of feeling-of-knowing and feeling-of-not-knowing responses can be determined. The greater the difference between the proportion of correct recognition decisions for the yes and no categories, the greater is assumed to be subjects' ability to discriminate between what is and what is not in memory storage. If the feeling of not knowing is a good predictor of what is not in memory storage, then proportion correct recognition for this class of responses should be close to chance, or .25 when a four-alternative recognition test is used. The differences between proportions may be tested statistically using a z test.

Recommended Minimum Number of Subjects
Total of 32.

Based on an experiment by Hart (1965).

Role of partial knowledge

How do we know that recognition will succeed when recall fails? One possible explanation is revealed in the analysis of the "tip-of-the-tongue" state, which we discussed in Chapter 7 in conjunction with features of memory. Brown and McNeill (1966) found that by asking people to recall various uncommon words (for example, *nepotism*) on the basis of hearing the dictionary definition, they could precipitate strong feeling-of-knowing experiences when the target word could not be recalled. These tip-of-the-tongue states often led subjects to identify certain features of the word correctly (for example, the first letter) even though they could not recall the word itself. It is possible that partial knowledge of an item's features is the basis for the feeling-of-knowing experience. Knowing the first letter of a target item may lead you to predict you will recognize the item when it is presented to you.

In a clever set of experiments using the Brown-Peterson task, Blake (1973) examined this possible basis for the feeling-of-knowing phenomenon. In the first experiment he demonstrated that feelings of knowing were accurate predictors of recognition in a short-term memory task just as Hart had shown for a long-term memory task. Subjects in his experiment were first presented a trigram (for example, *KSW*) for 1 second of study. Then they performed a distractor task for 18 seconds before attempting recall. If any part of the trigram was not correctly recalled, subjects were asked to predict whether they would be able to recognize the correct trigram when it appeared with seven alternatives (for example, *KGY, BSW, BSY, KGW, KSY, BGW, BGY*). The probability of correct recognition when subjects said they knew the items was .64 and only .38 when a feeling of not knowing was expressed. The relatively high level of recognition when a feeling of not knowing was indicated (.38) is likely due to the nature of the task. If a subject knew one letter, he might still be led to predict that he would not recognize the whole trigram. However, when the recognition alternatives were presented, a subject's "chance" score would be inflated if he selected only from among those items having the one letter he had remembered.

Although confirming the validity of the feeling-of-knowing phenomenon for short-term memory, Blake's first experiment did not necessarily provide evidence that subjects' feelings of knowing are based on partial knowledge. But his second experiment did. This time he adjusted the recognition alternatives depending on what the subject had recalled. If a subject, when attempting recall of *KSW,* recalled instead *LSV* (the middle letter being correct), then Blake made sure each alternative on the recognition test had *S* as a middle letter. When recognition alternatives were "tailor made" for each subject so that partial knowledge of the target letters could not aid recognition of the correct answer, accuracy of predicting recognition based on feelings of knowing decreased. Blake therefore argued that to some extent the feeling-of-knowing phenomenon is based on knowledge of specific attributes of the target information. However, because Blake found that feelings of knowing still predicted recognition performance when knowing the target letters was no longer an advantage, it is likely that subjects had knowledge of other, as yet unidentifiable, attributes that mediated their feelings of knowing.

Consequences

Knowing that a memory has in fact been established has several important consequences for memory processing (see also Hart, 1967b). First, when we are not able to recall a particular item, a feeling of knowing tells us we should not abandon the search. In other words, realizing that a particular item is stored in memory should lead us to continue looking for effective retrieval cues. A second response to a feeling-of-knowing experience may be to look for a list of alternatives from which we might recognize the correct answer. For example, when we are unable to recall the name of a particular hardware store, a feeling of knowing may cause us to look through all the names in the phone book until we recognize the name we couldn't recall. Unfortunately, Hart's research indicates that a strong feeling of knowing will not always lead to correct recognition. In the next section we will examine some other cases of apparent overconfidence in our memory. Finally, a feeling of not knowing informs us we must make an effort to establish a memory where none exists.

CONFIDENCE JUDGMENT ACCURACY

Who invented the cotton gin? What was the last state to be admitted to the United States? Can you answer these questions? Guess if you must. How confident are you that your answers are right?

An important aspect of metamemory is our awareness of when retrieval from memory has been successful. Can we discriminate between answers that are definitely correct and those that are definitely *not* correct? When we say we are right, are we always right? When we say we are wrong, are we always wrong? The relationship between degree of confidence in an answer and the probability that the answer is correct is a measure of *confidence judgment accuracy*. Consider briefly the results of an interesting experiment that was one of the first systematically to investigate this aspect of metamemory.

Adams and Adams (1961) tested only two subjects in their confidence judgment experiment: a psychologist and an individual diagnosed as schizophrenic. On each of five successive days they presented the two individuals a series of 100 statements dealing with topics in geography, history, and other general information areas. The subjects were to mark each statement as true or false and then assign a probability to their answer indicating their confidence that it was correct. The assigned probabilities could vary between .50 and 1.00 because the guessing rate in the true-false test would be .50. The probability that an answer was correct was calculated for each of six probability categories, .50, .60, .70, .80, .90, and 1.00. The question these investigators asked was how well did the probability ratings "match" the actual probability correct. If a subject, over many responses, said that an answer had a .70 probability of being correct, then to be accurate this degree of confidence should lead to a correct answer about 70% of the time.

The psychologist's and the schizophrenic's confidence judgment accuracies are shown in Figure 11-3. The schizophrenic exhibited marked overconfidence, particularly in the middle range of the probability scale. Answers that he indicated had a .90 probability of being correct were never correct more than about 60% of the time on any of the days he was tested. The psychologist's judgments were much more "realistic"; the probability assigned a particular statement matched fairly well the actual probability values at the upper end of the scale. But of course we would expect most people to be more realistic than a schizophrenic. Yet the results from this particular individual, disturbed as he might be, are perhaps more representative of our confidence judgment accuracy than you might think.

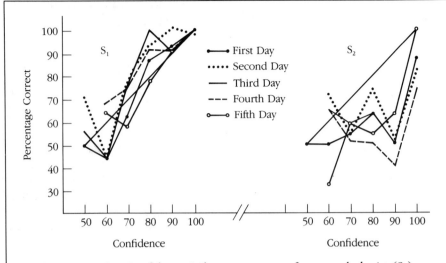

Figure 11-3. Confidence judgment accuracy for a psychologist (S_1) and a schizophrenic patient (S_2) for 100 true-false decisions made on each of 5 days of testing. *(From "Realism of Confidence Judgments," by J. K. Adams and P. A. Adams. In Psychological Review, 1961, 68, 33–45. Copyright 1961 by the American Psychological Association. Reprinted by permission.)*

Calibration curves

How good are "average" people at matching their confidence with actual probability correct? Researchers at the Decision Research Institute in Eugene, Oregon, have examined many different situations in which individuals have attempted to match their degree of confidence in an answer with the actual probability that the answer is correct (see Lichtenstein, Fischhoff, & Phillips, 1977). Because this general area of research is related to social decision making, these researchers are also interested in judgments made by weather forecasters, stock brokers, defense analysts, and others who are called upon to decide whether a particular statement (for example, "stock market prices will go up") is true. Results of these experiments are generally reported in terms of *calibration curves* like those of Adams and Adams (1961) seen in Figure 11-3. A calibration curve shows the degree to which predicted probability matches actual probability. A person who is perfectly calibrated would be able to assign probabilities so that proportion correct is always equal to the probability assigned. This cannot be assessed unless subjects make a large number of responses across a relatively wide range of probabilities. For example, we do not know whether a meteorologist is accurate on a given day when she gives a .70 degree of confidence in rain and it does *not* rain. After all, it could (probability = .30) not rain. However, over the long run we should expect to find that, when an accurate weather forecaster says there is a .70 probability of rain, 70% of the time it rains.

In general, researchers have found that most individuals tend to be over-confident, saying an item has a high probability of being correct when its actual probability is much lower. In one experiment graduate students in psychology and "usual volunteers" (mostly undergraduates at the University of Oregon) were asked a series of general information questions and given two possible answers to choose from (for example, "Bile pigments accumulate as a result of a condition known as: (a) gangrene, (b) jaundice.") (Lichtenstein & Fischhoff, 1977). The calibration curves for the graduate students and the volunteer group are shown in Figure 11-4. Individuals in both groups were markedly overconfident. Their confidence ratings tend to exaggerate what they know as correct.

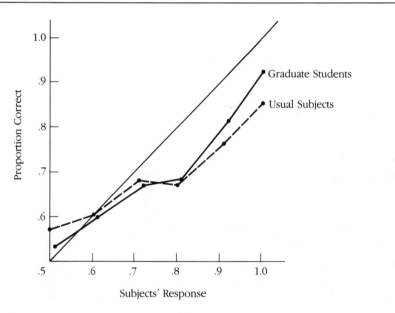

Figure 11-4. Confidence judgment accuracy for graduate students and "usual" volunteers of undergraduate students for two-alternative questions. *(From "Calibration of Probabilities: The State of Art," by S. Lichtenstein, B. Fischhoff, and L. D. Phillips. In H. Jungermann and G. deZeeuw (Eds.),* Decision Making and Change in Human Affairs. *Copyright 1977 by D. Reidel Publishing Company, Dordrecht-Holland. Reprinted by permission.)*

Unwarranted confidence

The tendency for people often to be wrong when they are certain they are right is unaltered even when lengthy instructions are given so that subjects cannot misunderstand the nature of the task or when subjects' motivation is raised by giving them the opportunity to "bet" against the experimenter for real money (Fischhoff, Slovic, & Lichtenstein, 1977). What accounts for this undue confidence in an answer retrieved from memory? It may be that people are generally unaware that memory retrieval involves processes of inference and reconstruction that can introduce error. As Fischhoff, Slovic, and Lichtenstein (1977, p. 563) have suggested,

> People reach conclusions about what they have seen or what they remember by reconstructing their knowledge from fragments of information, much as a paleontologist infers the appearance of a dinosaur from fragments of bone. During reconstruction, a variety of cognitive, social, and motivational factors can introduce error and distortion into the output process.

Given that errors can creep ever so subtly into the process of remembering, we should carefully examine output from memory. However, we do not always ask important questions, and we sometimes ignore relevant information. In the absence of the proper mental cross-examination, we can obtain an unwarranted confidence in the correctness of output from memory. This assumption is supported by the finding that requiring people to list reasons why an answer may be wrong, *before* they rate confidence, improves calibration of confidence judgments (Koriat, Lichtenstein, & Fischhoff, 1980). It is important to underscore the finding that when subjects weighed evidence for and against an answer, listing reasons that contradicted an answer had the most effect on confidence judgment accuracy. As a practical suggestion, therefore, for people who are interested in properly assessing what they know, the researchers point out that it is helpful to retrieve evidence from memory about an answer. But, they continue, such retrieval attempts will be beneficial only if we examine contradictory evidence, something we might normally be biased not to do.

In Chapter 15 we will discuss some of the evidence for the reconstructive nature of remembering that may contribute to our unwarranted certainty that an answer is correct.

Summary

Four general categories of memory-related phenomena have been suggested. They include those related to basic processes and operations of our memory system, to the influence of present knowledge on future knowledge, to voluntary strategies for remembering, and to our knowledge of the first three categories, which is termed metamemory. Investigations of me-

tamemory reveal that at a relatively young age we are aware of many important things about our memory. For instance, young children are aware of savings produced by relearning and of the fact that familiar material will be learned faster than less familiar material. Older children can identify those parts of a story that are more important to the theme and that will most likely be remembered, but younger or less academically successful students cannot. Laboratory studies have shown that college-aged subjects are able to reliably judge which specific items in a group of similar items will be easier to learn and remember than others. There is a strong relationship between these ease-of-learning judgments and judgments of knowing. These latter judgments are estimates of the probability that information presented for study will be remembered later. Such judgments may be particularly critical for efficient learning and remembering because knowing what is or is not yet known would permit effort to be directed to what is not yet known. This assumption is the basis of the discrimination-utilization hypothesis.

Hart (1965) first investigated the feeling-of-knowing phenomenon. He found that when recall is unsuccessful, subjects could predict whether they would correctly recognize information. However, strong feelings of knowing did not always lead to correct recognition, an error in judgment that appears to be similar to errors that are apparent when confidence judgment accuracy is assessed. When asked to give their confidence in the output of their memory, many if not most people are likely to say that an answer is definitely right even though it is not. This unwarranted confidence in our memory appears to be due to a general lack of understanding of the reconstructive nature of remembering and a failure to examine memory output sufficiently.

Much of the research on metamemory has been done with children, so much is still not known about metamemory processes in adult learners. We do know, however, that there are important links between our awareness of memory and its capabilities (or metamemory) and efficient learning and remembering.

Recommendations for further reading

Much of the research on metamemory has been done with children, and excellent reviews of this work are provided by Flavell and Wellman (1977) and Brown (1975, 1978). Individual experimental articles that were referenced in this chapter should be consulted for more background on ease-of-learning and judgment-of-knowing tasks. Lichtenstein, Fischhoff, and Phillips (1977) provide an informative review of studies examining confidence judgment accuracy. The ability to discriminate real from imagined events, or "reality monitoring," is also an aspect of metamemory and was discussed in Chapter 8 (see Johnson & Raye, 1981).

12

Levels of Processing

Introduction/overview

We introduced Chapter 4 with the questions: What kinds of mental activities are good for memory? What should we do, in other words, when we want to "memorize" something? At that time the answer was repetition. Something frequently repeated (or rehearsed) will often be remembered well. (Although, as we showed in Chapter 4, there are also situations where mental repetition does not produce any significant increase in retention.) In this chapter and the next we will answer this question another way. Repetition is not the only mental activity that is important when we wish to memorize something; meaningful elaboration is also important. In fact, by elaborating to-be-remembered information, we can achieve a degree of retention that often surpasses what we obtain by rote repetition. For example, the mental transformation of to-be-remembered items into visual images can increase retention two or three times over that obtained by simple repetition (Bower, 1972; and Chapter 13).

William James (1890, pp. 662–663) considered elaborating a to-be-remembered item the "secret" to forming a good memory:

> The more other facts a fact is associated with in the mind, the better possession of it our memory retains. *Each of its associates becomes a hook to which it hangs, a means to fish it up by when sunk beneath the surface. Together, they form a network of attachments by which it is woven into the entire tissue of our thought. The "secret of a good memory" is thus the secret of forming diverse and multiple associations with every fact we care to retain. But this forming of associations with a fact, what is it but* thinking about *the fact as much as possible? Briefly, then, of two men with the same outward experiences and the same amount of mere native tenacity,* the one who THINKS over his experiences most, and weaves them into systematic relations with each other, will be the one with the best memory. . . . All improvement of the memory lies in the line of ELABORATING THE ASSOCIATES of each of the several things to be remembered.

James's view of mental elaboration was influenced by the dominant view of memory at that time, which was associationism. *In this view memory was conceptualized as a network of ideas whose connections depend on associative principles such as repetition and contiguity. You may recall that Ebbinghaus, in order to isolate the effect that mere repetition had on the formation of associations, not only used material supposedly devoid of previously established associations (nonsense syllables) but sought to study the material by avoiding mental elaboration of any kind (see Chapter 4). Ebbinghaus's study method was* rote *or* simple *rehearsal, and it can be contrasted with* active *or* elaborative *rehearsal. Elaborative rehearsal involves the "thinking about" an item that William James discussed, the "adding to" a to-be-remembered item by mentally elaborating the stimulus. The distinction between these two kinds of rehearsal will be important in our consideration of the levels-of-processing view of memory, which is the major topic of this chapter. This approach to understanding memory provides us with an important example of how contemporary memory researchers have attempted to explain the effect of mental elaboration on retention.*

The levels-of-processing view of memory has not remained static. Since its conception, it has been forced to undergo revisions in the face of experimental findings challenging its major assumptions about memory processing. In this chapter we review the nature of these criticisms of the original theory. As we do this, you will get an insight into the process of theory construction. Once presented, a theory must be defended against its *critics. As modification is demanded, the theory improves, its weaknesses are identified, and, one hopes, it is strengthened in those areas. The process is always ongoing. In this chapter we look at where we have been and where we are headed on perhaps the most significant theoretical path in the last decade of theorizing about human memory.*

A FRAMEWORK FOR MEMORY RESEARCH

A *theory* consists of a set of assumptions or propositions that attempt to explain something. In the simplest case a theory is not much more than a guess, a hypothesis that provides a reason for why something occurs. When we discussed how people remember frequency of events (Chapter 8), we also mentioned strength theory, frequency theory, and propositional theory. In Chapter 10 we distinguished between a dual-code theory and a sensory-semantic theory of picture superiority in studies of retention. A theory can be complex, particularly when it attempts to explain more than a single phenomenon or isolated series of events. A multistore theory of memory, like the one introduced in Chapters 3 and 4, presents a rather complex view of how memory works "in general." A multistore theory makes many assumptions about the way information is held in memory and how it is moved between different memory stores.

A theory, whether it be of memory, nuclear physics, or social events, also provides a way of organizing known facts and serves to guide future research. A theory affects the way people talk about something when they are describing it. For many years memory researchers talked about memory events in terms of associations, as between a stimulus and a response (as James did when discussing mental elaboration). With the introduction of an information-processing approach to studying memory, memory came to be described in terms of memory stores, bits of information, rehearsal loops, and retrieval routines. The information-processing approach, and in particular a multistore theory, provided ways to organize information and to guide memory research. You have seen that a multistore theory provided explanations for the serial position curve found in free recall, limitations on memory span, the effect of rehearsal, and even retrograde and anterograde amnesia. You have also seen that most of these explanations based on the multistore approach have been found lacking and are open to alternative interpretation. In part dissatisfied with a multistore view of memory, researchers sought a different way to conceptualize memory.

In 1972, Craik and Lockhart offered an important theoretical alternative to the multistore view of memory. They called it a *levels-of-processing approach*. Although they modestly referred to it as a "conceptual framework" rather than a formal memory theory, most researchers have treated their ideas as representing an important theory of memory. Levels-of-processing theory has had a tremendous impact on the field of memory research, offering a new way to organize information about memory and providing important assumptions about memory processing that have guided subsequent research (see especially Cermak & Craik, 1979). The levels-of-processing approach has also given us new terminology, a new way to talk about memory phenomena.

Assumptions

As originally proposed in 1972, the levels-of-processing theory made four important major assumptions about memory processing. The first is that memory formation is a product of successive series of analyses carried out on an incoming stimulus. Different analyses correspond to different "levels" of processing. The shallowest level of processing includes the physical analysis of an event and involves processing of such stimulus features as lines, angles, and brightness when information is presented visually and characteristics of pitch and loudness when the information is presented auditorily. Greater depth of processing is associated with semantic "enrichment" or "elaboration" of the stimulus. Therefore the theory views memory as a continuum of processing, from the "transient product of sensory analysis to the highly durable product of semantic-associative operations" (Craik & Lockhart, 1972, p. 676).

The theory's second assumption is that the greater the depth of processing, the more "durable" the memory will be and thus the greater will be retention. When we briefly mentioned levels-of-processing theory in Chapter 4, we offered the following example of "shallow" and "deep" levels of processing. Assuming that the nonsense syllable FAC was presented for study, shallow processing would correspond to the rote repetition of the item in the form in which it was presented—that is, simply repeating the item without any attempt to elaborate it. However, treating the syllable as part of the word FACT and thinking about it as a "fact" to be learned would constitute a deeper level of analysis. Deeper processing corresponds to the mental elaboration involved in weaving an item into a systematic relationship with other items in memory, as William James discussed almost 100 years ago. However, mental elaboration identified with deeper levels of processing is not usually described in terms of associative relationships (see Hyde & Jenkins, 1973). A more commonly invoked description of mental elaboration is "semantic processing."

A third major assumption of levels-of-processing theory is that improvement in memory performance is related only to greater depth of analysis and not to repetition of analyses already carried out. If an item is processed only shallowly, as repeating the syllable FAC to yourself, then presumably the item will not be remembered any better if further processing consists only of repeating analyses at this low level of processing. This assumption is associated with a distinction the theory makes between two different kinds of processing. One type of processing corresponds to the maintenance of information at a particular level of processing. The second type refers to carrying the material to a deeper level of analysis. These two kinds of processing are often called *maintenance* and *elaborative rehearsal,* respectively. Only elaborative rehearsal is assumed to increase retention. This assumption led researchers associated with this point of view to explain the negative recency effect following multitrial free-recall learning by maintenance rehearsal rather than by insufficient rehearsal of recency items in a short-term memory store (Craik, 1970; also see the discussion of these kinds of rehearsal in Chapter 4). The levels-of-processing theory does not distinguish between short- and long-term memory stores. Craik and Lockhart (1972) view *primary memory* as equivalent to the maintaining of information at a particular level of processing and not with a particular memory structure (see Chapter 3 for a discussion of structure versus process views of primary memory).

A fourth assumption of the levels-of-processing theory is tied not to the theory but to a view of how memory should be investigated. Clearly, the emphasis in this theory is on the *nature* of processing and the *kinds* of mental activities associated with information processing. This point of view led Craik and Lockhart (1972, p. 677) to suggest that memory should be studied primarily using an incidental learning paradigm:

> The interesting thing to do is to systematically study retention following different orienting tasks within the incidental condition, rather than to compare incidental with intentional learning. Under incidental conditions, the experimenter has a control over the processing the subject applies to the material that he does not have when the subject is merely instructed to learn and uses an unknown coding strategy.

Under incidental learning conditions a subject is not aware that retention will be tested and presumably processes the critical material in a manner directed by the experimenter. Incidental learning would be tested, for instance, if you were asked to underline all the nouns in a verbal passage and then were tested unexpectedly for your memory of passage content.

Each of these major assumptions of the levels-of-processing theory—that information processing involves a continuum of processing, that greater depth of processing leads to greater retention, that maintaining information at one "level" does not improve retention, and that through an incidental learning paradigm the experimenter can control subjects' encoding activities—has been subjected to important criticisms. Before examining apparent problems with these assumptions, however, we will review some major experimental findings that have provided support for the levels-of-processing theory. Because these experiments have used an incidental learning paradigm, we must first consider what is known about differences in retention following incidental and intentional learning.

Intent to learn

As investigated in the experimental psychology laboratory, *incidental learning* is distinguished from *intentional learning* by the nature of the instructions given to the subjects. When instructions do not prepare the subject for a retention test of the *relevant* material, learning is said to be incidental (see Postman, 1964). In practice, this is done in one of two ways. One method is to expose subjects to the relevant material but not to give them instructions to learn. This generally means that subjects must perform some sort of *orienting task* that leads them to experience the material to be tested but does not lead them to expect a later retention test. In one experiment subjects were asked to inspect a list of words for possible spelling errors (see Jacoby, Craik, & Begg, 1979). No mention was made that retention would be tested. When subjects completed this task, recognition memory for the words was tested. A second way to investigate incidental learning is to ask subjects to learn something, but not the relevant material. In one experiment subjects were asked to memorize a series of geometric shapes filled with different colors. Although the instructions informed subjects that their memory for the shapes would be tested, retention of the colors was tested (Bahrick, 1954).

Which method of testing incidental learning a researcher chooses depends on the theoretical question being asked. Because researchers associated with the levels-of-processing point of view generally seek to examine retention as a function of the type of processing subjects carry out on the relevant material, an orienting task is most often used. Subjects do not expect to be tested, so the experimenter has some control over the nature of the learner's information processing. Retention can be contrasted following different kinds of orienting tasks as well as between incidental and intentional learning conditions.

To compare retention following incidental and intentional learning properly, three experimental groups are required. One group is simply given instructions to try to learn the material in preparation for a memory test (intentional learning). The nature of the learner's mental activities in this group is unknown and can be inferred only on the basis of performance. A second group receives instructions to perform a particular orienting task but is not advised that a retention test will follow (incidental learning). A third group of subjects is asked to learn the material but is also instructed to perform the same orienting task as that performed by subjects in the incidental learning group (intentional learning *plus* orienting task). This third group is necessary in order to assess whether the orienting task interferes with intentional learning. Experiments have generally shown that retention is poorer following intentional learning with an orienting task than following intentional learning without an orienting task. In other words, the orienting task sometimes "gets in the way" of normal memory processing. Therefore estimates of how much "intent" contributes to retention will be less when performance following incidental learning is compared to performance after intentional learning with an orienting task than when it is compared to performance without the task (see Postman, 1964).

As Postman (1964) has pointed out, orienting activities used in the investigation of incidental learning can be viewed as representing a continuum ranging from those activities that are maximally antagonistic to those that are maximally favorable to learning. In fact, differences in retention following incidental and intentional learning shrink as the orienting activities approach those most favorable to retention. As you will soon see, it is not difficult to find *no difference* in retention following incidental and intentional learning. Intent to learn is not the critical variable determining what is learned and what is later remembered. As Postman (1964, p. 190) concluded,

> Analysis of the effects of the orienting task has led us to the conclusion that intent per se is not a significant variable in learning but that the instruction stimulus influences the amount and characteristics of learning by determining the differential cue-producing responses, including deliberate rehearsal, which occur during the period of practice.

Levels-of-processing theorists would discuss the effects of orienting tasks in terms of "processes" rather than "responses," but otherwise they have no quarrel with this conclusion, which was based on traditional laboratory studies of verbal learning (see Craik & Lockhart, 1972). Intent to learn is "good" for memory only indirectly, leading the learner to perform activities that favor retention. By specifying a particular orienting task, an experimenter can "produce" a performance level no different from that achieved by an intentional learning group. This effect was illustrated in an important series of experiments by Hyde and Jenkins.

The Hyde and Jenkins experiments

Substantial support for the levels-of-processing point of view was provided by the results of a series of experiments conducted by Jenkins and his associates at the University of Minnesota (Hyde & Jenkins, 1969, 1973; Till & Jenkins, 1973; Walsh & Jenkins, 1973). Of particular significance was an experiment by Hyde and Jenkins (1973). Their procedure is typical of the many studies that have been interpreted as supporting a levels-of-processing theory. We shall discuss only 11 of the 22 experimental conditions in this study. Hyde and Jenkins sought to examine memory for words as a function of the nature of the subjects' orienting task. Their results, as you will see, were quite interesting.

There were five different kinds of orienting tasks in the Hyde and Jenkins (1973) experiment. On the basis of previous research (Hyde & Jenkins, 1969) and as a result of their analysis of the situation, they chose the orienting tasks to constitute either "semantic" or "nonsemantic" processing. A semantic orienting task is generally considered one in which subjects must consider the meaning of the word in order to perform it. Tasks that can be performed in the absence of any "meaningful" analysis are judged to be nonsemantic. The five different orienting tasks are described in detail in Table 12–1. Two of these tasks were judged to involve semantic processing: rating pleasantness-unpleasantness and rating frequency of usage. According to Hyde and Jenkins, both these tasks required that subjects consider what the word means. For example, to accomplish the frequency rating task, the researchers reasoned that subjects would have to ask the following questions about each word: "What does this mean, and how often do I encounter whatever it means?" (Hyde & Jenkins, 1973, p. 474). On the other hand, the three remaining tasks presumably required little in the way of semantic processing. These tasks asked subjects to analyze ortho-

TABLE 12-1. The Five Orienting Tasks Hyde and Jenkins (1973) Used to Study Incidental Learning

Task	Activity
Pleasantness-unpleasantness rating	Rate the words as to their pleasantness or unpleasantness on a simple five-point scale.
Estimating the frequency of usage	Rate the frequency with which words are used in the English language. Each word was rated on a five-point scale, from very infrequent to very frequent.
E-G checking	Detect the occurrence of the letters E and G in the spelling of the stimulus words. Subjects were instructed to make a check on their rating sheet if either or both of these letters occurred in the word.
Parts of speech	Record whether the words were nouns, verbs, adjectives, or some other part of speech. Subjects were told that if they were not sure about the particular part of speech, they should guess, and in the case where words could be more than one part of speech, to put down whatever they thought of first.
Sentence frames	In this task subjects were presented with two sentence frames and a "does not fit" category. The sentence frames contained no words with semantic reference and were of the form: "It is _____." or "It is the _____." All mass nouns and adjectives fit into the former sentence and all count nouns fit the latter. Subjects were told that, if a word appeared to fit both sentences, they were to choose whatever seemed better.

From "Recall for Words as a Function of Semantic, Graphic, and Syntactic Orienting Tasks," by T. S. Hyde and J. J. Jenkins. In *Journal of Verbal Learning and Verbal Behavior,* 1973, *12,* 471–480. Copyright 1973 by Academic Press, Inc. Reprinted by permission.

graphic or syntactic features. Nonsemantic tasks involved checking a word for the presence of the letters *E* or *G,* identifying the part of speech of a word, and completing a simple sentence frame. In order to do the sentence frame, subjects needed to decide only whether or not it was syntactically correct for a word to be preceded by "the" (see Table 12–1).

Five groups of subjects performed the orienting tasks with no instructions to learn the material (incidental learning). An additional five groups performed the various orienting tasks but were also asked to try to remember the words (intentional learning plus orienting task). As we have noted, requiring a group of subjects to perform an orienting task while under instructions to learn the material is necessary to evaluate to what degree the orienting task interferes with trying to learn the material. Another group of subjects was asked simply to learn the material (intentional learning). Therefore there were 11 experimental conditions.

The critical items were 24 common words. Two additional words were presented at the beginning and at the end of the list in order to minimize primacy and recency effects. These four words were not considered in the analysis of the results. All the words were presented auditorily to the subjects at the rate of 1 word every 3 seconds. Following the presentation of the last list item, all subjects were asked to recall as many of the items as possible in any order (free recall). The results of this experiment are found in Figure 12–1.

There were three important results. First, when considering only the results from the five incidental learning groups, recall performance varied as a function of the kind of orienting task subjects performed. In the researchers' view there was a clear "discontinuity" between the level of recall following the three nonsemantic orienting tasks and that observed following the two semantic orienting tasks. Retention was clearly not as good following nonsemantic processing as following semantic processing. A second major finding was that retention after a semantic orienting task was as good as that seen under standard intentional learning instructions. These results show, as Postman (1964) concluded, that intent to learn is not a critical variable. Whatever processes are involved in the rating of frequency of usage or the pleasantness-unpleasantness of words, these processes are obviously favorable to retention. A third finding should be emphasized. There was little difference in retention between groups that performed each of the five orienting tasks and differed only in terms of "intent." For example, both groups of subjects that identified parts of speech recalled the same amount even though one group knew a memory test was forthcoming and the other did not. This result has been a matter of some concern to critics of the levels-of-processing theory (for example, Postman & Kruesi, 1977).

Although many have taken the results of the Hyde and Jenkins experiments as support for the levels-of-processing approach, Jenkins is not necessarily one

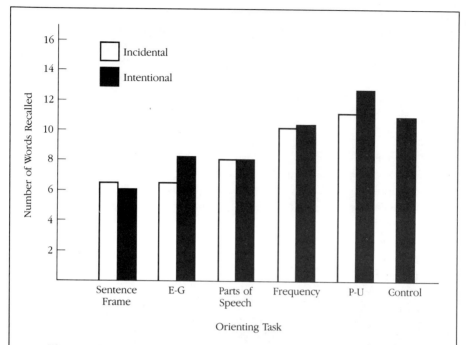

Figure 12-1. Amount recalled as a function of the type of orienting task and whether subjects were told a retention test would be given. One group of subjects (control) received intentional learning instructions and no orienting task. *(From "Recall for Words as a Function of Semantic, Graphic, and Syntactic Orienting Tasks," by T. S. Hyde and J. J. Jenkins. In* Journal of Verbal Learning and Verbal Behavior, *1973, 12, 471–480. Copyright 1973 by Academic Press, Inc. Reprinted by permission.)*

of those people. He is sympathetic to the ideas of those who advocate a levels-of-processing theory, but Jenkins (1974, p. 17) doubted that "things will turn out to be as simple as they postulate." Truer words were never spoken.

Recall as a function of semantic and nonsemantic orienting tasks

Purpose
To investigate differences in recall of unrelated words as a function of semantic and nonsemantic orienting tasks.

Materials

A single study list of 28 common, two-syllable nouns is used. (See Table C in the Appendix.) Items are randomly ordered within the list and the first and last two items are considered primacy and recency buffers, respectively. These four items are not included in the analysis of the results. The orienting tasks require response sheets numbered 1 through 28. Additional sheets will be needed to record recall.

Procedure

The experimental design can be described as a 2 × 2 factorial plus a control group. The first variable is type of orienting task. The two levels of this variable are semantic processing (subjects make judgments about the pleasantness or unpleasantness of a word's meaning) and nonsemantic processing (subjects decide if the word contains the letters *E* and/or *G*). The second variable, intentionality, also has two levels. Subjects are either told that recall will be tested (intentional learning) or are not told that a recall test will follow the processing task (incidental learning). An additional group is not given a particular orienting task to perform and is told to study the words in preparation for a memory test. Therefore there are five experimental conditions differentiated only by the nature of the instructions given to the subjects: control, intentional learning and semantic task, intentional learning and nonsemantic task, incidental learning and semantic task, incidental learning and nonsemantic task.

The 28 words are presented auditorily, either by having the experimenter read the words aloud or by using a tape recorder. Presentation rate is 3 seconds. After the last word is presented, the subjects are provided recall sheets and asked to write down as many words from the list as they can remember. Five minutes are allowed for recall. Subjects should be assigned randomly to the five conditions of the experiment and can be tested individually or in small groups.

Instructions to Subjects

CONTROL

In this experiment your memory for words will be tested. I will read a list of 28 words to you, one at a time. After I read the last word, I will signal you to write down as many words as you can remember. You may recall the words in any order. Simply try to remember as many as you can. Are there any questions?

NONSEMANTIC (INTENTIONAL AND INCIDENTAL)

This is an information-processing experiment. I will read a list of 28 words to you, one at a time. Your task is to decide if the word has an *E*, a *G*, or both in it. If it does, please put a *Y* on your answer sheet next to the word's number. If the word does not have one or both of these letters, put an *N* on the answer sheet for that word. Accuracy is important, so please pay attention to each word. Make a response for every word in the list. (To the intentional group only, add the following: When the processing task is completed, your memory for the words in the list will be tested.) Are there any questions?

SEMANTIC (INTENTIONAL AND INCIDENTAL)

In this experiment I am interested in your judgments of the pleasantness of a word's meaning. I will read a list of 28 words to you, one at a time. As I read each word, I would like you to think of its meaning and decide how pleasant it is for you. If a word has a pleasant meaning for you, put a *P* on your answer sheet next to the number of that word. If the meaning is unpleasant for you, put a *U* next to the word's number. We are interested in how pleasant or unpleasant the word is for you, so please pay attention to each word. Make a response for every word in the list. (To the intentional group only, add the following: When you have finished judging the pleasantness of the words, your memory for the words in the list will be tested.) Are there any questions?

TEST (ALL CONDITIONS)

Now I would like you to try to remember as many words as you can from the list just presented. You may recall the words in any order. Simply try to remember as many as you can. (Note: Do not give subjects recall sheets until this time.)

Summary and Analysis

The number of critical words subjects in each of the five groups recall is recorded and means are obtained. An analysis of variance for a two-variable, between-groups design (2×2) can be used to test the effect of the variables of type of orienting task and intentionality (excluding the control group). Mean recall of subjects in the control group should be compared with that of subjects in each of the other four conditions. Statistical analysis of the differences in mean recall between the control group and each of the other groups can be carried out in several ways, including using a *t* test for independent groups or a multiple-comparison test.

Recommended Minimum Number of Subjects

Total of 60, 12 in each of five conditions.

Based on an experiment by Hyde and Jenkins (1973).

PROBLEMS WITH THE THEORY

In the 1972 version of the levels-of-processing theory, information processing was conceptualized as proceeding from the analysis of physical or sensory features of the stimulus to pattern recognition and abstraction of meaning. This assumption no longer appears to be valid. For example, Baddeley (1978) reviewed results from several experiments demonstrating that semantic processing occurs in the absence of any conscious processing of orthographic or phonological features. Proponents of the theory now acknowledge that structural analysis of a stimulus need not necessarily be completed before semantic processing is begun (see Craik & Tulving, 1975). Were this the only problem with the theory, it would undoubtedly have survived in almost its original form. However, there were more serious problems.

What are "levels" in the levels-of-processing theory?

You will recall that a second major assumption of the theory was that deeper levels of processing led to more durable (more resistant to forgetting) and longer-lasting memory traces than did shallower levels of processing. But what exactly constitutes a "level" of processing and how do we know that one level is "deeper" than another? Levels of processing have been defined chiefly in terms of memory performance. Given two different orienting tasks, the one associated with better performance on a memory test is considered a deeper level of processing. For example, if inspecting a word for the presence of the letters *E* or *G* yielded greater retention on a subsequent test than did deciding what part of speech a word is, then *E-G* checking would by definition be a deeper level of analysis. But clearly there is something wrong here. In order to explain memory phenomena, a theory should first permit predictions regarding memory performance. Then the accuracy of the theory's predictions can be evaluated on the basis of actual performance. However, predictions based on the levels-of-processing theory as originally stated can be neither confirmed nor disconfirmed (see Nelson, 1977). The theory states that retention increases due to a deeper level of analysis, but a deeper level of analysis is defined by an increase in retention. The obvious circularity of this position is not aided by our own intuition or that of memory researchers as to what constitutes a particular level of processing. For example, although Hyde and Jenkins (1973) reasoned that judging a word's frequency involves thinking of its meaning, other researchers do not understand why it should (for example, Postman, 1975b). Without a method of classifying levels of analysis that is independent of memory performance, the theory cannot be disproven.

The fact that the theory fails to provide a scientifically acceptable definition of processing levels has not gone unrecognized by its proponents. Craik and Tulving (1975) conducted a series of experiments, one goal of which was to produce such a definition. They considered the possibility that time to perform a mental operation might be usefully employed as a measure of processing depth and hypothesized that deep processing would take more time than shallow processing. The problem was to design an experiment that permitted retention of individual items to be examined following different kinds of orienting activities but also allowed the time to perform a particular orienting task to be measured. These researchers chose to ask subjects to make different kinds of decisions about words presented in a tachistoscope. (See Chapter 2 for a description of this apparatus.) The subjects were told that the experiment was a test of reaction time and that the experimenter was interested in how fast they could make various decisions about individual words. They were not told, of course, that the experimenter was also interested in their memory for these words.

The kinds of decisions required of subjects in one of the experiments are described in Table 12-2. Subjects were asked to make decisions about structural and phonemic (rhyme) aspects of words and to decide in what semantic category a word belonged and whether it made sense in a particular sentence. On the basis of the experimenters' intuitions, these tasks represented different levels of processing. Subjects were presented a question from one of the four levels of processing. Each question required analysis of a single word, which was also presented. The subjects' task was to decide whether the word was an appropriate answer to the question. Subjects pressed a yes or no button to signify their decision and a timer automatically recorded latency to make the decision. Half the words shown with the target questions were appropriately answered yes and half no. Following a series of reaction time trials using many different items from each of the four categories of questions, subjects were tested for their recognition memory of the words that had appeared as possible answers.

In accord with the researchers' intuitions, recognition memory performance increased systematically as a function of increasing "depth" of processing. Overall proportion correct recognition was about .85 after deciding whether a word fit in a sentence and less than .20 after deciding whether a word

TABLE 12-2. Kinds of Questions and Answers Craik and Tulving (1975) Presented to Subjects

Level of processing	Question	Answer	
		Yes	*No*
Structural	Is the word in capital letters?	TABLE	table
Phonemic	Does the word rhyme with WEIGHT?	crate	MARKET
Category	Is the word a type of fish?	SHARK	heaven
Sentence	Would the word fit the sentence: "He met a ___ in the street"?	FRIEND	cloud

From "Depth of Processing and the Retention of Words in Episodic Memory," by F. I. M. Craik and E. Tulving. In *Journal of Experimental Psychology: General*, 1975, *104*, 268–294. Copyright 1975 by the American Psychological Association. Reprinted by permission.

was printed in capital letters. Further, mean reaction time across the experimental conditions was directly related to recognition memory performance. Therefore in this particular experiment deeper processing (and greater retention) could be said to be predicted by time to perform the task. Had an important definition of processing depth now been identified? The answer was no, for at least three reasons.

Although the results of several other experiments in this series supported the finding that memory performance and time to perform an operation were directly related, there were other results that did not. Processing time differed systematically *between* tasks, as did memory performance, but there was no systematic relationship between time and retention *within* a particular orienting task. For example, the time to decide whether a word belonged to a particular semantic category was not related to word retention within that particular orienting task. If time was to define depth of processing, then longer decision times, whenever they are seen, should reflect deeper processing and, consequently, greater retention. This was not the case. Another problem with using time to define depth of processing was that words accompanying a yes decision were remembered better than words accompanying a no decision, although time to make yes and no decisions was the same. This finding not only argued against the time definition but, as we will see, suggested an important change in the theory. Finally, the futility of using time to define processing levels was further demonstrated because it was not hard for the researchers to find an intuitively "shallow" processing task that was more difficult to perform, and hence would take longer than a supposedly deeper processing task, but that resulted in lower retention. In another experiment Craik and Tulving (1975, Exp. 5) examined retention following two types of decision tasks. In one task the subjects decided whether a word corresponded to a particular vowel and consonant pattern. A subject might see CCVVC (where C = consonant and V = vowel) before seeing the word *brain* and have to decide as quickly as possible whether the word fit that particular order of consonants and vowels. They compared retention following this apparently nonsemantic shallow processing task with retention following decisions about the appropriateness of a word in a sentence (see Table 12-2). The nonsemantic task took longer than the semantic task but resulted in a lower level of recognition memory.

At present, the levels-of-processing theory does not have a definition of processing depth that is independent of memory performance. Some theory proponents have suggested it is too soon to seek such definitions, that "one needs a better understanding of levels of processing before it can be usefully defined" (Jacoby, Bartz, & Evans, 1978, p. 344). Needless to say, postponing this crucial step in theory construction does not sit well with many critics of this view of memory (see Postman, Thompkins, & Gray, 1978).

Maintenance versus elaborative rehearsal

As we saw, Craik and Lockhart (1972) also distinguished between mainte-nance and elaborative rehearsal. Elaborative rehearsal was associated with greater depth of processing and only elaborative rehearsal was assumed to lead to increased retention. In Chapter 4 we reviewed the evidence for this assumption of the levels-of-processing theory. Although some experiments appeared to sup-port this assumption (Rundus, 1977), other studies revealed that retention increased, albeit only slightly, as maintenance rehearsal increased (Glenberg & Adams, 1978). Further, in Chapter 5 we saw that subjects who experienced repetitions of digit strings in the Hebb task showed an increase in retention of these digit strings, although the task emphasizes maintenance rehearsal (see also Nelson, 1977). You may find it helpful to review the discussion of rehearsal types found in Chapter 4 in order to examine more closely the evidence against this assumption of the levels-of-processing theory.

Depth plus elaboration

The results of another experiment reported by Craik and Tulving (1975, Exp. 7) suggested the need for yet another modification in the original levels-of-processing theory. In this experiment the researchers varied the complexity level of the questions asked within a so-called semantic level of analysis. The task was the same as previous ones in that subjects were asked to make decisions about whether a word fit a specific sentence. Both a sentence and a word were presented on each trial. However, in this experiment there were three types of sentences, which the researchers defined as simple, medium, and complex. Examples of each of these types are as follows:

Simple: She cooked the _____ .
Medium: The _____ frightened the children.
Complex: The great bird swooped down and carried off the struggling _____.

Following tachistoscopic presentation of 60 sentences (20 sentences of each complexity level), the usual unexpected retention test was given for the words presented as possible answers for the three sentence types. One memory test was cued recall. Subjects were given a sentence and asked to recall the word that had been presented with it. As found previously, words associated with yes responses were remembered better than words associated with no responses. But retention also increased directly with the complexity of the sentences. Con-sidering only yes response items, the proportion of cued recall for words accom-panying complex sentences was twice that obtained for simple sentences.

That retention should increase with sentence complexity was troublesome for the theory because all three sentences reflected a semantic level of analysis.

Retention could not be explained in this case by simply saying that an item reached a semantic level of processing. Clearly, the theory had to make allowances for elaboration within a semantic level of processing. Therefore the original 1972 theory was amended to take into account meaningful elaboration of the stimulus once a semantic level of processing was reached.

The finding that words associated with yes responses were remembered better than words associated with no responses was seen as compatible with this modification. That is, a response that led to a yes response—namely, one that answered the question correctly—could, in these authors' view, be better integrated with the question and a "more elaborate unit formed" (Craik & Tulving, 1975, p. 291). This effect is also seen as reflecting a principle of integration or *congruity* of encoding (see Schulman, 1974). Depth of processing *plus* meaningful elaboration (or congruity) are apparently good for retention. But are they?

Meaningful processing

Bransford and his associates at Vanderbilt University questioned whether semantic processing and meaningful elaboration of a to-be-remembered item are always "good" for memory (Bransford, Franks, Morris, & Stein, 1979; Morris, Bransford, & Franks, 1977; Stein, 1978). These investigators suggest that researchers have taken too narrow a view of "meaningful" processing. Is it not possible, they argue, that in some situations many so-called "nonsemantic" processing tasks may be very meaningful activities? In other words, to be meaningful, an orienting task need not involve thinking about the meaning of a word. To make their point, they suggest we consider the kind of task that might be used in a speech class (Morris, Bransford, & Franks, 1977, p. 520).

> Assume that one wants to teach principles of speech perception and articulation to students. The present authors' experiences (as well as those of colleagues who have taught speech perception) suggest that an especially helpful teaching technique involves asking students to attend to the position of their lips and tongue while pronouncing words. Students usually find this to be an extremely *meaningful* exercise, despite the fact that they are not prompted to process the *semantic meaning* of the words used in the exercise. Indeed, the semantic meaning of the words presented is not necessarily a meaningful component of such an instructional exercise. Similarly, if one wants to teach students about rhyming, the semantic meaning of the words presented as illustrations is not necessarily a meaningful aspect of the task at hand.

Further, as these researchers note, it would certainly not be a meaningful exercise to test students for their retention of speech principles and articulation by determining whether they knew the meaning of the words used in the speech exercises. In their view, whether a particular orienting activity is "good" for memory depends on how memory will be tested. One kind of processing is not inherently better than another; rather, different kinds of processing allow people to learn different kinds of information about an event. An experiment by Morris, Bransford, and Franks (1977, Exp. 1) illustrates this point.

The experimenter read aloud 32 sentences to the subjects. One word was missing in each sentence. One type of sentence required that subjects judge whether a target word fit a particular sentence frame. For example, subjects might hear "The *blank* had a silver engine," followed a few seconds later by the word *train*. Subjects checked yes or no on their answer sheet to indicate whether they felt the word did or did not fit the sentence. A second type of sentence required subjects to decide whether a particular word rhymed with another. For example, subjects might hear "*Blank* rhymes with legal," followed by the word *eagle*. Half the target words in each condition (sentence frame and rhyming) required yes responses and half required no responses. Subjects were told that the experimenter was collecting normative data on these types of decisions and no mention was made of a later retention test.

Up to this point the methodology Morris, Bransford, and Franks (1977) used was similar to that used in the Craik and Tulving (1975) experiments reviewed earlier. In both cases the nature of the orienting activity was varied by asking subjects to make different kinds of decisions about sentences and target words presented to them. Yet there is a very important difference. Craik and Tulving gave one type of retention test to see whether target word retention varied following the different orienting activities, but Morris, Bransford, and Franks used two kinds of retention tests. One was the standard recognition memory test for the target words—the same as that used by Craik and Tulving. The second was a rhyming recognition memory test. For this test the subjects were asked to recognize rhymes of the target words. For example, if the target word *eagle* was presented during the orienting task, subjects might be asked to recognize *regal*. The to-be-recognized items on the rhyming recognition test had never appeared in the first phase of the experiment. Proportion correct responses on the two types of recognition memory tests as a function of the type of encoding task are shown in Figure 12-2.

There was a clear interaction between the type of orienting task and the nature of the recognition memory test. Although semantic processing was better for retention when the standard retention test was administered, the nonsemantic rhyming task produced better retention when the test was for rhymes of the target words. There was also a significant effect for congruity, as Craik and Tulving had found. Recognition memory was better overall for target words associated with yes responses than words associated with no responses.

Morris, Bransford, and Franks interpreted their findings as supporting a *transfer-appropriate processing* view of memory. This view assumes that what

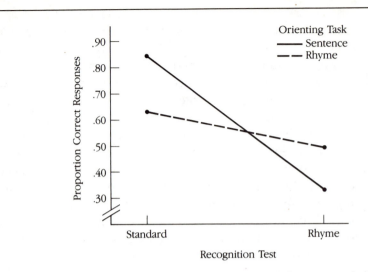

Figure 12-2. Overall proportion correct on a standard or rhyme recognition memory test following either a sentence-frame (semantic) or rhyme (nonsemantic) orienting task. Only the results for yes responses in the orienting task are shown. *(Based on data from "Levels of Processing versus Transfer Appropriate Processing," by C. D. Morris, J. D. Bransford, and J. J. Franks. In Journal of Verbal Learning and Verbal Behavior, 1977, 16, 519–533. Used by permission.)*

is important about an acquisition task is how it "transfers" knowledge to the test situation (see Bransford et al., 1979). The "goodness" of a particular orienting activity must be considered only in relationship to the manner in which memory will be tested. As we have seen from the results displayed in Figure 12-2, it is impossible to say that either nonsemantic or semantic processing is good or bad for retention until we consider how memory will be tested. A transfer-appropriate processing view emphasizes the relationship between the encoding task and the retention task or, in other words, between those mental activities governing acquisition and those activities required at test time. You should see that this particular view of memory processing bears more than just a passing resemblance to the encoding specificity principle discussed in Chapter 10. Both of these principles suggest that we must interpret what is "good" for memory in terms of the relationship between acquisition and test situations (see also Jenkins, 1979).

Controlling memory processing

A major reason for using an incidental learning paradigm to investigate memory processing is the assumption that imposing an orienting task serves to "control" the nature of the learner's encoding activities. Subjects, in other words, encode the to-be-tested items in a way that the experimenter wants. However, an orienting task may not always control subjects' learning activities the way the experimenter believes it does.

Postman and Kruesi (1977) pointed out that an important difference between many of the so-called semantic and nonsemantic tasks is the requirement that subjects rate to-be-tested items on some subjective scale during semantic processing. They suggested that activities associated with performing the rating task may contribute to the superior retention often found following these types of tasks. For example, consider how you might go about rating pleasantness-unpleasantness of words, as Hyde and Jenkins (1973) required their subjects to do. Recall following this orienting task was as good as that of an intentional learning group. You are given a scale, varying from 1 to 5, and asked to rate your impressions of the pleasantness or unpleasantness of the meaning of various words. It is likely that in order to use the rating scale in a consistent fashion, you must continually compare items in the list (see also Shaughnessy, 1976). That is, should you rate the pleasantness-unpleasantness of a word as 2 on the scale, later in the list you will likely find yourself wanting to recall the 2 word so that you can give another word an appropriate rating relative to the previous one. This process of comparing items and their ratings, to the extent that it occurs, may help retention by developing interitem associations and by producing additional rehearsals of the to-be-tested items. In many nonsemantic tasks, such as checking whether a word has an *E* or *G,* there would be no need to make such intralist comparisons; therefore this type of task would not benefit from the additional rehearsals or associations produced when a rating task is used. If this is the case, then retention differences should be found as a function of whether or not a rating task is employed, irrespective of whether a semantic or nonsemantic attribute of the item is to be rated. Investigators have found just such effects (Postman & Kruesi, 1977; Shaughnessy, 1979). It is not the case, therefore, that retention differences following different orienting tasks need to be due to differences in processing level per se.

Postman and Kruesi (1977) considered another, somewhat puzzling aspect of the incidental learning procedure. As we noted previously, Hyde and Jenkins (1973) found little difference in retention between intentional and incidental learning when both intentional and incidental learning groups performed the same orienting task. When the orienting task was checking for the presence of the letters *E* or *G,* recall did not differ between the incidental learning group and the intentional learning group (see Figure 12-1). To Postman and Kruesi this seemed an odd finding; surely subjects in the intentional group would have done something more than just look for *E*s and *G*s. After all, they knew a retention test was coming. Although it was possible that the orienting tasks interfered to the extent that it was simply not possible to do anything extra, Postman and Kruesi (1977) suggested that the problem lay with the instructions given to the subjects. If the instructions served to emphasize the importance of the orienting task more than the requirement to get ready for a recall test, then subjects may have put more effort into the orienting task than into memorizing the words.

Postman and Kruesi (1977) tested this hypothesis by varying the emphasis on the recall requirement among groups that were asked to perform the orienting task. The experiment included a group given pure incidental learning instructions, a group given "weak" intentional instructions, one presented with "strong" intentional instructions, and a pure intentional learning group that did not do the orienting task. Under weak intentional instructions a single sentence stating that recall would also be tested was placed at the end of the instructions for the orienting task. Under strong intentional instructions the subjects were told that the experimenter was interested in whether performing the orienting task would interfere with their ability to remember the words. Recall increased systematically with the increase in emphasis on the recall part of the task. Postman and Kruesi (1977) also found that the strong intentional learning group recalled significantly more words than did the pure incidental learning group. It appears that performance in incidental learning tasks is sensitive to the instructional manipulations regarding intent to learn and, as we have seen, to the nature of the task requirements—for example, rating or not rating. Therefore differences in performance in this paradigm need not be determined exclusively by the type of processing associated with the orienting task.

COGNITIVE EFFORT AND DISTINCTIVENESS

In Chapter 9 we discussed the results of an experiment by Jacoby (1978) that demonstrated that constructing an answer to a word problem was more beneficial for later retention than was merely reading the answer. Jacoby reasonably argued that constructing the solution required greater involvement of consciousness than did merely repeating the answer. One possible consequence of increased consciousness of processing is a greater level of arousal. Perhaps you have to "get up more steam" to find an answer than to repeat one that is given to you. There is, in fact, evidence that heightened arousal—such as that which might accompany a traumatic or highly emotional event—serves to increase retention (see Jacoby, 1978).

Further, greater conscious involvement may reflect greater cognitive effort. That is, it is also reasonable to say that more effort is required to find a solution to a problem than to read a solution. And although increasing cognitive effort may be associated with higher levels of arousal, it is possible that "cognitive effort" in and of itself is good for memory (see Kahneman, 1973). Some researchers have suggested that "cognitive effort" is a reasonable alternative to "depth of processing" as a way to describe memory processing. A construct like "effort" has the advantage of sometimes being definable independent of per-formance by using a divided attention task like the one Johnston and Uhl (1976) used to test a voluntary attention theory of the spacing effect (see Chapter 9; and Tyler, Hertel, McCallum, & Ellis, 1979). However, defining cognitive process-ing in terms of effort does not specify the mental operations involved in a task (see Jacoby, Craik, & Begg, 1979). Advocates of a levels-of-processing view of memory feel they have a better idea. We can follow their reasoning by examining an experiment by Jacoby, Craik, and Begg (1979) that varied the degree of decision difficulty in a semantic orienting task.

College students were asked to make decisions about the relative size of objects represented by common nouns. A list of noun pairs was presented to the subjects with instructions to rate the difference in size of the named objects (1 = no difference and 10 = vast difference). The actual difference in the named objects varied from pair to pair. Among the pairs subjects rated were the following: crumb-tomato, kettle-football, donkey-tiger, frog-kangaroo, and ant-flea. When subjects were given an unexpected test of recall for the words in the pairs, retention was inversely related to the size of the actual difference between the named objects. In other words, the students were more likely to recall a noun from a pair of nouns representing two objects similar in size (donkey-tiger) than they were to recall a noun associated with a pair depicting objects of vastly different sizes (frog-kangaroo). This result confirmed what Craik and Tulving (1975, Exp. 7) had found previously: that variations in process-ing activities within a semantic level of analysis were associated with retention differences.

When Craik and Tulving (1975) found retention differences as a function of different processing activities at a semantic level of analysis, they suggested that the construct of "elaboration" be added to the levels-of-processing view of memory. Retention, in other words, would benefit not only from a greater depth of analysis but would also increase with more meaningful elaboration within a semantic level. However, Jacoby, Craik, and Begg (1979) admitted that the orig-inal levels-of-processing view of memory presented too narrow a view of mean-ing. For example, we have already seen that what constitutes a meaningful analysis depends on the relationship between the encoding activity and how retention is tested (Morris, Bransford, & Franks, 1977). Moreover, it was origi-nally assumed that greater depth of processing reflected greater processing of *the* meaning of a stimulus. Elaboration served only to emphasize that more complex processing of *the* meaning of a stimulus would aid retention. This appears to be an inadequate treatment of meaningful processing. As Jacoby and Craik (1979, pp. 2, 3) commented,

> A concrete object does not have a single name or description. Rather, what
> an object is called or how it is described depends on the other objects from

which it is to be discriminated. For example, a chair is a chair; but it is equally a piece of furniture, a thing, a wooden artifact, and any number of other descriptions, depending on what the chair is to be distinguished from. Similarly, the meaning of a word in a given context depends on distinctions that are to be conveyed by that word in that context. . . . Meaning is a set of contrasts resulting from distinctions required when interpreting the item in the context of some task.

Jacoby and Craik (1979) suggested that more meaningful processing produces greater *distinctiveness* of encoding. This results from making more distinctions between and giving more precise descriptions to events. For example, consider how much more precise your description must be when you analyze the difference in size between an ant and a flea than when you compare the difference between a frog and kangaroo. These two comparisons presumably differ in the cognitive effort required due to the greater and more precise distinctions that must be made, but it is the resulting "distinctiveness" of the memory trace that is considered to be the cause of greater retention according to this recent version of the levels-of-processing theory.

Choosing distinctiveness of encoding over depth or elaboration as an explanatory construct appears to make the levels-of-processing view more compatible with the notion of transfer-appropriate processing as well as with the principle of encoding specificity. All these ideas emphasize the relationship between the encoding and test contexts. What produces distinctiveness of encoding depends on how an item is presented—that is, on its context or encoding—and whether that context is reinstated at retrieval time.

> Distinctiveness is a relative, not absolute term; an object or description is distinctive relative to some particular background. In the present case, also, the distinctiveness of a memory record will always be relative to a given context, and the same context must be reinstated at retrieval if the encoded distinctiveness of the memory trace is to be optimally utilized. Accordingly, distinctiveness cannot be discussed without reference to conditions of study and conditions of testing. It is this relativity of the memory record to its context that distinguished our use of the term "distinctiveness" from "elaboration" (Craik & Tulving, 1975). Elaboration often refers to the addition of further information, so that the trace becomes richer and more detailed. In using "distinctiveness," however, we mean to emphasize the contrastive value of information in the trace [Jacoby, Craik, & Begg, 1979, pp. 596–597].

Distinctiveness of encoding, however, suffers from similar problems of definition as have accompanied the earlier constructs of depth and elaboration (Baddeley, 1978; Postman, Thompkins, & Gray, 1978). Whether this new look to the levels-of-processing theory will remain unscathed from the attacks of its critics only time will tell. But the notion of distinctiveness of encoding provides a much needed beginning to the job of conceptualizing the effects of cognitive effort, a factor that most of us would agree is important for retention. Many of our attempts to encode information—for example, when we prepare for a classroom examination—apparently fail because they lack "involvement of consciousness" or cognitive effort. It requires considerable mental effort to make precise descriptions, subtle comparisons, and meaningful distinctions among events we wish to remember. Too often we do not bother. In Chapter 14 we will see how meaningful distinctions made in the processing of sentences are related to retention of prose material. Before that we will turn our attention in the next chapter to another form of stimulus elaboration, one often part of mnemonic devices.

Summary

The levels-of-processing theory is a contemporary approach to understanding the effect of different kinds of activity on retention. As originally proposed, the theory stated that memory formation is the product of a successive series of analyses carried out on a stimulus, that greater depth of processing leads to a more durable memory, and that improvement in retention is related only to greater depth of processing and not to repetition of analyses already performed. This latter assumption is the basis for the distinction between maintenance and elaborative rehearsal. Tests of this theory have tended to employ an incidental learning paradigm because it is often assumed that this paradigm allows "control" over subjects' encoding activities. As you have seen, this control may be less than complete.

Many studies have shown that "intent to learn" is not a critical variable affecting retention. What is critical is the nature of the learner's mental activities during study. This is illustrated by the results of experiments like that of Hyde and Jenkins (1973). Although their results, and those of many other experiments, have supported the levels-of-processing theory, all the major assumptions of the original theory have been challenged and revised. A particularly serious problem is obtaining a definition of "depth" that is independent of memory performance. It also appears that the original theory offered too narrow a view of "meaningful" processing. Research has revealed the need for such concepts as elaboration and congruity. It can also be shown that meaningful (that is, semantic) processing does not always lead to better retention. Rather, retention is best when the retention test emphasizes the information emphasized at time of study. We also need to consider cognitive effort and distinctiveness of encoding in our memory theories. Distinctiveness of encoding now appears to be a more appropriate explanatory construct than either depth or elaboration.

Research surrounding the levels-of-processing theory provides an important illustration of the way science progresses. By focusing research on

the learner's mental activities, the theory has guided research in an impor-
tant way. New knowledge about the nature of rehearsal, about elaboration
and distinctiveness of encoding, and about what leads to optimal retention
has been obtained from experiments this theory generated. Levels-of-
processing theory has been and will continue to be an important impetus
for research on memory encoding.

Recommendations for further reading

You can follow the evolution of the levels-of-processing theory by reading
(in order) articles by Craik and Lockhart (1972), Craik and Tulving (1975),
and Jacoby and Craik (1979). The latter article is the first chapter in *Levels of*
Processing in Human Memory, a book edited by Cermak and Craik (1979).
The book resulted from a conference of researchers in the field of human
memory that was held to discuss both theoretical and empirical progress
made following the presentation of the original theory in 1972. The book
contains many interesting chapters, not all of them necessarily praising the
levels-of-processing approach. Also not praising this approach are major cri-
tiques presented by Nelson (1977), Baddeley (1978), and Postman, Thompkins, and Gray (1978).

13

Mnemonics

Introduction/overview

What would it be like to have a perfect memory, to remember all that you experienced? Would it be a chance of a lifetime, sending you on your way to fame and fortune? Or would you rue the day that you wished to be able to remember everything? In this chapter we describe an individual who had very near to what might be called a perfect memory. As you will see, such an ability to remember can bring on unforeseen problems. Perhaps if our wish for a perfect memory were granted, we would find ourselves in the position of King Midas, who asked for a golden touch.

For years people have sought ways to improve their memory. Methods for improving memory were described by Greek and Roman teachers more than 20 centuries ago (Yates, 1966). Today there are few bookstores that do not do a regular business in marketing books with such titles as How to

Improve Your Memory. *In this chapter we examine some methods for improving retention, including those recommended by professional "memory trainers" who write books with titles like the one we just mentioned. A technique for improving memory, or a memory aid in general, is called a* mnemonic. *Many mnemonics, as you will see, rely on the use of visual imagery, as when you create a mental picture of an object or event. The study of mental imagery has had a long and stormy history in psychology. After reviewing some of the more popular imagery mnemonics, we will look briefly at this history and examine the current status of research on mental imagery. You will see that at one time the concept of mental imagery was "banished" from psychology. However, today there is a vigorous and exciting research effort directed toward understanding mental imagery. What exactly is a mental image? How does mental imagery aid memory? A good place to begin is with the story we promised, a true story of an individual with an exceptional memory. Mental imagery played an important role in his ability to remember.*

A PERFECT MEMORY

The famous Russian psychologist Alexander Romanovich Luria (1968) recounts how one day a man, who at the time was a newspaper reporter, came to his laboratory and asked that his memory be tested. The man, called S. to preserve his anonymity, was soon found to have a memory that appeared to have no limits, and he became Luria's experimental subject and friend for more than 30 years. As Luria (1968, pp. 11–12) commented,

> Experiments indicated that he had no difficulty reproducing any lengthy series of words whatever, even though these had originally been presented to him a week, a month, a year, or even many years earlier. In fact, some of these experiments designed to test his retention were performed (without his being given any warning) fifteen or sixteen years after the session in which he had originally recalled the words. Yet, invariably, they were successful.*

These facts are even more amazing when one considers that S. became a professional entertainer, using his memory to dazzle audiences, who shouted out long lists of words, nonsense syllables, numbers, or whatever for him to remember. Yet these thousands of lists apparently produced little interference with the lists Luria gave him.

Luria's subject apparently could remember things that happened when he was very young. This is unusual in that the average person generally shows a substantial memory loss for events experienced before the age of 5 or 6, a

*From *The Mind of a Mnemonist,* by A. R. Luria. Copyright 1968 by Basic Books, Inc., Publishers, New York. This and all other quotations from this source are reprinted by permission.

phenomenon referred to as *infantile amnesia* (see Spear, 1979; White & Pillemer, 1979, for excellent reviews of this phenomenon). Consider, for example, what S. related to Luria (1968, pp. 76–77) in August of 1934:

> I was very young then ... not even a year old perhaps.... What comes to mind most clearly is the furniture in the room, not all of it, I can't remember that, but the corner of the room where my mother's bed and my cradle were. A cradle is a small bed with bars on both sides, has curved wickerwork on the under part, and it rocks.... I remember that the wallpaper in the room was brown and the bed white.... I can see my mother taking me in her arms, then she puts me down again.... I sense movement ... a feeling of warmth, then an unpleasant sensation of cold.

Luria had no way to verify whether these events actually occurred. They were possibly only the product of S.'s rich imagination. Yet given his proven ability to remember events in general, we must at least entertain the possibility that S. remembered events that occurred in the first few years of his life.

How did he do it? Luria's record is quite clear as to S.'s method of remembering. The primary mechanisms S. used were visual ones, either continuing to see something that had been presented or converting to-be-remembered information into visual images. The ability to convert material into visual images was the fundamental basis for his remarkable memory. Everything he experienced was at once turned into a visual impression that S. was capable of "seeing." As he explained,

> When I hear the word *green,* a green flowerpot appears; with the word *red* I see a man in a red shirt coming toward me; as for *blue,* this means an image of someone waving a small blue flag from a window.... Even numbers remind me of images. Take the number 1. This is a proud, well-built man; 2 is a high-spirited woman; 3 a gloomy person (why, I don't know); 6 a man with a swollen foot; 7 a man with a mustache; 8 a very stout woman—a sack within a sack. As for the number 87, what I see is a fat woman and a man twirling his mustache [Luria, 1968, p. 31].

However, S. was aided in his recall by another unusual quality of his mind, called *synesthesia.* Synesthesia is sensation removed from or different from the actual sense that was stimulated. As we noted, when S. experienced a sound, it was immediately converted into a visual impression. He sometimes also experienced a sense of taste and touch as well. Luria (1968, p. 28) gives us S.'s account of this synesthesic process:

> I recognize a word not only by the images it evokes but by a whole complex of feelings that image arouses. It's hard to express ... it's not a matter of vision or hearing but some over-all sense I get. Usually I experience a word's taste

and weight, and I don't have to make an effort to remember it—the word seems to recall itself. But it's difficult to describe. What I sense is something oily slipping through my hand . . . or I'm aware of a slight tickling in my left hand caused by a mass of tiny, lightweight points. When that happens I simply remember, without having to make the attempt.

We can see therefore that the converting of to-be-remembered items into visual images, which played such an important role in his ability to remember, was only a part of the synesthesia he experienced.

It would seem that S. had what we all want, an ability to remember practically everything. Was S. happy and successful? Luria's account shows us that his life was not particularly pleasant. The synesthesia he experienced interfered as he listened to people talking. Voices gave rise to such a blur of images that S. could not follow what was being said. His dependence on visual sensations, on translating the world around him into visual scenes, made it difficult for him to understand abstract concepts. As S. reported, he could understand only what he could see, and he had trouble understanding such ideas as *infinity, nothing,* or *eternity.* At one point in his life S. was tormented by another problem, his inability to forget. Earlier memories intruded on more recent memories. Further, the vivid visual impressions he produced sometimes left him wondering whether something had actually happened to him or whether he had imagined it. His life was disorganized, and he shifted from one job to another, eventually using a knowledge of Hebrew and Aramaic to read ancient sources in order to treat people with herbs.

We must admit to using this true story of Luria's friend and subject for its dramatic effect and because visual imagery played such an important role in this individual's ability to remember. As you will see in this chapter, visual imagery can be a powerful technique for aiding memory. However, we do not want to leave you with the impression that having a "perfect memory" need always produce the kinds of problems experienced by Luria's subject or that visual imagery is necessarily essential for an exceptional memory. Hunt and Love (1972) identified another person, who, although demonstrating an ability to remember not unlike that of Luria's subject, was apparently quite normal in other regards and, interestingly, claimed *not* to rely on visual imagery to perform his memory feats.

IMAGERY AS A MNEMONIC DEVICE

The exceptional memory of Luria's subject was obviously innate. The spontaneous nature of his rich visual imagery and the remarkable synesthesia are unlike anything most of us have experienced. Yet, as you will see, when we try to use visual imagery to encode to-be-remembered information, we can get some astounding results.

Converting to-be-remembered items into visual images is a powerful mnemonic device. However, for reasons we will discuss later, only in the last two decades have memory researchers investigated visual imagery systematically. Exactly how good a mnemonic visual imagery is can be illustrated by an experiment reported by Bower (1972). He asked two groups of college students to learn five paired-associate lists. Each list consisted of 20 pairs of concrete nouns (for example, *dog-bicycle*). Students had 5 seconds to view each word pair, and, after they had seen all pairs, students were immediately given a cued recall test. The left-hand member of each pair was presented and students attempted to recall the right-hand member. Following presentation and test of all five 20-pair lists, a final recall test was administered for all 100 pairs.

The only difference between the two groups of subjects in this experiment was the nature of the instructions given for associative learning. Half the subjects, the control group, were simply told to try to learn an association between the members of each pair so that they could recall the right-hand member when only the left-hand member was presented. The other subjects, the imagery group, were told to learn the pairs by creating a visual image of the two objects interacting. For example, if the pair was *dog-bicycle,* subjects might imagine a scene of a dog riding a bicycle. Level of recall in the two instructional groups, on both the immediate and final recall tests, is shown in Figure 13-1. Recall was about one and a half times greater for the subjects who used visual imagery than for the control subjects. As Bower (1972) pointed out, these results actually underestimate the effect of imagery on retention because interviews with subjects in the control group showed that some of them also used imagery to help encode the associations. When imagery instructions are compared with instructions simply to repeat the items in the pair (rote repetition), the results are even more dramatic, yielding recall that is sometimes three times greater for imagery than control subjects (Bower, 1972).

Imagery as a mnemonic device

Purpose
To demonstrate the effect of instructions to use mental imagery on retention of simple associations.

Materials
The experiment requires 40 concrete nouns. (See Table C in the Appendix.) The nouns are randomly arranged to form 20 pairs for presentation in the study list. The test list consists of the first word of each pair. Study and test

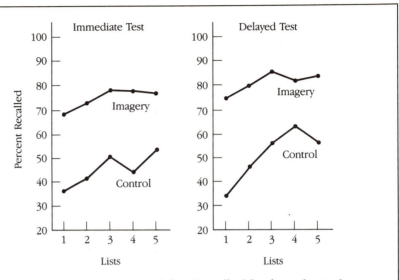

Figure 13-1. Immediate and delayed recall of five lists of paired associates with imagery or no imagery (control) instructions. *(From "Mental Imagery and Associative Learning," by G. H. Bower. In L. W. Gregg
(Ed.),* Cognition in Learning and Memory. *Copyright 1972 by John Wiley
& Sons, Inc. Reprinted by permission.)*

lists are presented in different random orders. So as to be conveniently presented to subjects, the 20 study pairs and 20 test items should be typed on
individual index cards. Subjects should be provided an answer sheet numbered 1 through 20.

Procedure

The 20 pairs of words are presented to two different groups of subjects. All
subjects are asked to learn an association between members of the pairs so
that when the first member of each pair is presented, they can recall the
second word. However, specific instructions vary between the two groups.
One group is given "imagery" instructions; the other group is given standard
"memory" instructions. Word pairs are each shown for 5 seconds. The retention test is conducted by presenting the first word of each pair for 5 seconds.
Subjects are told to write down the word that was paired with the test item
in the study list. Subjects are randomly assigned to receive either imagery or
memory instructions.

Instructions to Subjects

MEMORY

In this experiment I want you to try to learn a list of word pairs. I will show
you each pair for 5 seconds. Please study the word pairs so you will be able

to remember the second word in each pair if I show you only the first word. For example, if the word pair is *dog-bicycle,* you should study the pair so that if you saw the word *dog,* you would be able to recall the word *bicycle.* I will show you 20 word pairs before I give you a memory test. Are there any questions?

IMAGERY

In this experiment I want you to learn a list of word pairs. I will show you each pair for 5 seconds. Please study the word pairs so you will be able to remember the second word in each pair if I show you only the first word. I would like you to use a particular strategy when doing this task. For each pair of words I want you to try to visualize the two members of the pair interacting in some way. For example, if the word pair is *dog-bicycle,* you should try to visualize a *dog* and a *bicycle* together. You might imagine a dog riding a bicycle. I will show you 20 word pairs before I give you a memory test. Are there any questions?

TEST INSTRUCTIONS (BOTH GROUPS)

Now I will show you the first word in each of the pairs that you studied. As I do so, please try to write down the word that was paired with this word in the study list. Guess if you are not sure. Each word will be shown for 5 seconds.

Summary and Analysis

The dependent variable is the number of words subjects in the two groups correctly recall. A *t* test for independent groups (between subjects) can be used to test whether amount recalled is significantly different between the two groups.

Recommended Minimum Number of Subjects

Total of 32; 16 in each of two conditions.

Based on an experiment by Bower (1972).

The effect of imagery instructions on retention of simple associations is just as pronounced when subjects are asked to create images as part of an incidental learning task. In one experiment (Bower, 1972) subjects were told that the experimenter was interested in the vividness of the images they could produce. They were asked to create interacting images of pairs of objects and then to rate the vividness of their images. An unexpected recall test for the imaged pairs revealed that retention was similar to that of a group intentionally using visual imagery to learn the pairs. These results are another example of the effect that encoding activity, and not mere intent to learn, has upon retention (see Chapter 12). Imagery is clearly an important encoding activity for associative learning.

Not just any kind of visual imagery produces such amazing effects in associative learning. To be effective, the visual image must depict the to-be-remembered objects *interacting* in some manner (Bower, 1972; Wollen, Weber, & Lowry, 1972). For example, Bower (1972) compared the retention of subjects who created interacting images with another group that was told to create "separate" images. Recall of the group using "separated" images was almost half that of the "interactive" imagery condition and not much better than that found when rote repetition instructions were given. Figure 13-2 describes effective visual imagery when information is to be encoded for a later memory test.

Given such impressive findings, it stands to reason that people who seek to improve their memory or those who train people in mnemonic techniques frequently rely on visual imagery. We will look at some of the methods for improving memory that are based on visual imagery.

MNEMONIC SYSTEMS

Mnemonic devices are probably not new to you. If someone asks you how many days there are in October, you may find yourself thinking "Thirty days has September, April, June, and November. . . ." Many of us had taken only a few music lessons when we were told that knowing the first letter of each word in the phrase "Every good boy does fine" and the letters in the word *face* would help us remember the notes of the musical staff. Biology students are often heard to recite the ditty: "On Old Olympus' Towering Top a Finn and German Vault and Hop." The first letter of each word in the phrase is also the first letter of each of the 12 cranial nerves. Psychology students are sometimes aided in their memory for the colors of the visible spectrum by remembering Roy G. Biv, a name made by using the first letters of each color. How many times have you been confused when twice a year we must change the setting on our clocks until you remember "Spring forward, fall back"?

Arranging initial letters of to-be-remembered words to form a word or phrase are *first-letter mnemonics.* There are also *rhyme mnemonics.* First-letter and rhyme mnemonics are sometimes very useful in helping us remember something, but they are rather limited as general systems for remembering. Several more general mnemonic systems have been developed that can be used in many different situations (see Higbee, 1977). Visual imagery forms the basis for these major mnemonic systems. We will review four systems, beginning with one of the most ancient.

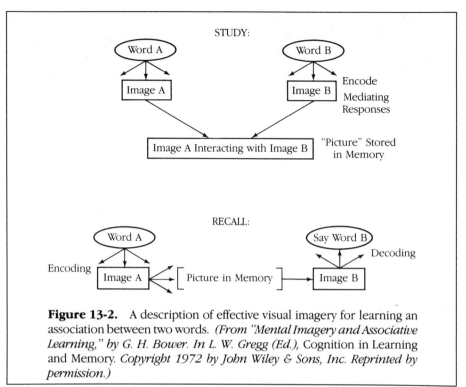

Figure 13-2. A description of effective visual imagery for learning an association between two words. *(From "Mental Imagery and Associative Learning," by G. H. Bower. In L. W. Gregg (Ed.), Cognition in Learning and Memory. Copyright 1972 by John Wiley & Sons, Inc. Reprinted by permission.)*

The method of loci

An ancient mnemonic system is that of "places and images" (in Latin, *loci et imagines*) or, as it is more popularly called, the *method of loci*. The inventor of this system of remembering is said to have been a poet named Simonides, who lived about 500 B.C. The method and its use in ancient times through the Middle Ages and the Renaissance is described in a beautifully written history, *The Art of Memory,* by Frances Yates (1966). The details of Simonides' discovery of the method of loci were related by Cicero in 55 B.C. Cicero (*De Oratore* 2.86) wrote as follows:

> I am grateful to the famous Simonides of Ceos, who is said to have first invented the science of mnemonics. There is a story that Simonides was dining at the house of a wealthy nobleman named Scopas at Crannon in Thessaly. . . . The story runs that a little later a message was brought to Simonides to go outside, as two young men were standing at the door who earnestly requested him to come out; so he rose from his seat and went out, and could not see anybody; but in the interval of his absence the roof of the hall where Scopas was giving the banquet fell in, crushing Scopas himself and his rela-

tions underneath the ruins and killing them; and when their friends wanted to bury them but were altogether unable to know them apart as they had been completely crushed, the story goes that Simonides was enabled by his recollection of the place in which each of them had been reclining at table to identify them for separate interment; and that this circumstance suggested to him the discovery of the truth that the best aid to clearness of memory consists in orderly arrangement. He inferred that persons desiring to train this faculty must select localities and form mental images of the facts they wish to remember and store those images in the localities, with the result that the arrangement of the localities will preserve the order of the facts, and the images of the facts will designate the facts themselves, and we shall employ the localities and images respectively as a wax writing tablet and the letters written on it.*

Simonides' memory system has three major steps. First, a series of locations is memorized. These places can be geographical locations, such as sites on a university campus, places along a well-known street, or even rooms in a familiar building. The second step involves using mental imagery to associate each of the to-be-remembered items with the locations. Suppose your list of loci began with the front steps of your house, followed by the inside hallway, and then the living room. Presented with the to-be-remembered items of *apple, rope,* and *dawn,* you might try to imagine a big red apple standing on your steps ringing the doorbell, a hangman's rope in the hallway, and the sun rising over the sofa in your living room. The third step comes at the time of recall. You "visit" each of the locations in a mental walk and identify the to-be-remembered item in your mental image.

The method of loci was an important topic for ancient students of rhetoric. Greek and Roman orators memorized their speeches with the aid of this mnemonic system by associating the key points or ideas in their oration with a series of mental locations. The teachers of rhetoric offered specific suggestions to their students concerning what locations would work best or the kind of mental images they should form. Locations to be selected were to be of moderate size, dissimilar, isolated, but not too dimly lighted. There was even a suggestion that a proper interval between the locations was about 30 feet. Appropriate imagery was to be striking, unusual, or even comic (see Yates, 1966). However, these suggestions for choosing locations are not particularly important and the locations chosen can even be imaginary (see Crovitz, 1971). Also, it is more important to form images in which the associated items are interacting in some manner than to form bizarre images (Wollen, Weber, & Lowry, 1972).

*From *De Oratore,* by M. T. Cicero. Translated by E. W. Sutton. Copyright 1959 by Harvard University Press. Reprinted by permission.

As Bower (1970, p. 498) commented, the whole idea of memorizing a series of locations and then creating images in order to associate items with locations strikes people as something that must have been "constructed by elves," and "magical and occult powers of mentation are required to use the system effectively." This, of course, is not the case. One need not have supernatural powers, or even the supernormal powers of someone like Luria's subject, to make this mnemonic system work. Although people often balk at the idea of "trying" to master a list of 20 or 30 locations, memorization of such spatial series is actually quite effortless. Ross and Lawrence (1968) described two experiments in which college students first had to learn a series of 52 locations. In one experiment a single subject was "instructed to select and commit to memory 52 loci in sequence along a walk through the grounds" of the university where the experiment was conducted. After only two mental walks the subject "could repeat the loci fluently in forward or backward order" (p. 107). In the second experiment a group of students learned 52 locations with no more than two practice trials. When presented lists of either 40 or 50 items to remember, subjects using the method of loci averaged better than 95% correct following only one study trial. You have to try it to believe it.

Peg systems

If you were to read one of the many popular books on memory improvement or were to take part in a workshop or course offered by a professional memory trainer, you would likely be introduced to some form of *peg system*. (For example, see *The Memory Book,* 1974, written by Harry Lorayne and the ex-basketball star, Jerry Lucas.) The "pegs" are a list of easily memorized items on which are "hung" the to-be-remembered items. As in the method of loci, visual imagery is generally used to associate an item with its peg. In fact, the method of loci can be considered one type of peg system, with mental locations being the pegs. More commonly, a peg system uses a list of easily memorized concrete words and often includes a method of numbering the pegs so that not only can you remember many items in order (either forward or backward), but you can retrieve specific items without reviewing the whole series. For example, it is not difficult for someone having mastered a peg system to memorize 100 items and then, often on request from persons in an audience, identify what was the 8th, 23rd, 67th, or any item in the series. Such demonstrations are very impressive. But it is something you could do knowing an appropriate peg system.

One frequently used peg system is based on a well-known children's rhyme: "One, two, buckle my shoe, three, four, shut the door. . . ." The peg system formed from this rhyme is as follows:

One is a bun
Two is a shoe
Three is a tree
Four is a door
Five is a hive
Six is sticks
Seven is heaven
Eight is a gate
Nine is wine
Ten is a hen

You will find this numbered list of pegs very easy to memorize. Once you have "got it," you can use mental imagery to associate the to-be-remembered items with the pegs. For example, suppose the first three items on a shopping list are *eggs, butter,* and *bread*. You might use this mnemonic technique by first imagining a dozen eggs inside a hot dog bun, then a shoe filled with melted butter, and then a tree with pieces of bread for leaves. Should you want to retrieve a particular item, such as the third one, you need only to remember "three-tree" and you'll recall the item without having to retrieve the whole list of pegs.

The "one is a bun" mnemonic works, of course, only for lists up to ten items. Other peg systems have been devised to facilitate retention of longer lists. One such system makes use of the 26 letters of the alphabet (see Higbee, 1977). Most of the 26 peg words rhyme (at least partially) with a different letter of the alphabet, as follows:

A-hay	G-jeep	L-el	Q-cue	V-veal
B-bee	H-hat	M-hem	R-oar	W-wig
C-sea	I-eye	N-hen	S-ass	X-ax
D-deed	J-jay	O-hoe	T-tea	Y-wire
E-eve	K-key	P-pea	U-ewe	Z-zebra
F-effigy				

The alphabet peg system permits you to remember 26 items but the system is without the convenient numbering device. This peg system does not allow direct retrieval of specific items, as does the "one is a bun" technique.

One of the most sophisticated peg systems is that based on the phonetic alphabet (see Higbee, 1977; Lorayne & Lucas, 1974). To use this system, a person must first associate ten different consonant sounds with the digits 0 through 9. There are actually mnemonics to help you with this stage of the system, and it is not as bad as it first seems. For example, the *t* or *d* consonant sound is associated with the number 1. You might remember this association because the letter *t* has only one downstroke. The *n* sound is associated with the number 2. Note that *n* has two downstrokes. A hissing sound, as found in saying the letter *z,* is associated with the number 0—*z* as in zero, of course. Similarly, other consonant sounds of English are associated with the remaining digits.

Once you've made the associations between the digits and the consonant sounds, you can construct a list of peg words in which the consonant sounds of each peg word denote a number and vice versa. For example, the first peg word could be *tie.* Note that *tie* has only one consonant sound, a *t.* A person using this system will come to think of the number 1 when hearing the word *tie* and the word *tie* when thinking of the number 1. The word *inn* could be used as the second peg word. The consonant sound is *n,* which stands for 2 in the peg system. *Tot* is the word for 11. Two *t* sounds, or 11. *Nose* is the word for 20. The number 100 is represented by the peg word *disease.* After mastering the associations between the consonant sounds and the 10 digits and memorizing a list of peg words whose consonant sounds represent various numbers, you can use this peg system in the same manner as the previous ones we have discussed. Mental imagery is used to associate each to-be-remembered item with its peg. Because each peg word represents a number and vice versa, the system allows ready retrieval for any numbered item in the list.

A potential problem with peg systems is that interference may arise when the same peg words are used over and over again. Note that when the pegs remain the same between successive lists and the to-be-remembered items change, the task can be described as A-B, A-C, and, as we saw in Chapter 6, interference can be expected (see also Wood, 1967). Nevertheless, most proponents of mnemonic peg systems suggest that the same set of locations, or the same list of concrete peg words, can be used repeatedly with little diminution of their effectiveness. An important variable may be the time interval between use of the peg system. Longer intervals should lead to less interference than shorter intervals because many of the to-be-remembered items will be forgotten at the longer interval. The peg list is not likely to be forgotten during the same interval because it will have been practiced many more times than was the list of to-be-remembered items. However, Higbee (1977) suggests that should you want to use a peg system frequently, it may be advisable to learn several different peg lists, perhaps having one for each day of the week.

Another potential problem with a system that relies on visual imagery is the memorization of abstract words. You can usually mentally visualize concrete words. But what about abstract words such as *life, liberty,* and *happiness?* To use a visual imagery mnemonic to learn abstract words or concepts, you must represent them with concrete symbols of some kind. You may imagine doctors operating on someone to save a *life;* the Statue of Liberty may be part of your visual imagery for the term *liberty;* and you could represent *happiness* by a "smile face" on a balloon. This technique sometimes results in a "decoding" problem. How do you know you are trying to remember *life* and not *patient, doctor,* or even *operation?* Nevertheless, you can use this method of substituting objects for abstract terms in many situations where you need to remember difficult-to-imagine concepts.

The link system

The *link system* and a related mnemonic system, the *narrative story,* are other examples of ways to improve memory through the use of mental imagery. Both these methods may be used in conjunction with a peg system to increase greatly the number of items handled. The link system consists of constructing a chain of mental images. The links in the chain are mental images of pairs of to-be-remembered items. Consider how you could use the link system to remember the following list of grocery items: *butter, milk, spaghetti,* and *ice cream.* First, create a mental image of the first two items in the list interacting in some manner. You might visualize a stick of butter having milk poured on it. Then form a visual association between the second and third items. Try imagining a carton of milk tied up with spaghetti. The next link would be an imaginal representation of spaghetti (the third item) and ice cream (the fourth item). How about a scoop of ice cream on top of a plate of spaghetti? Higbee (1977) reports that people have no difficulty using the link system with as many as 20 words, increasing their recall by 6 to 8 words on the average compared to recall attempted without the link mnemonic.

To use the narrative story technique, weave each item into a story, usually one you can visually imagine. It is perhaps not as easy to concoct stories using the names of grocery items as it is for other nouns, but a narrative story for the four grocery items might be as follows: There once was a stick of butter who proposed marriage to a carton of milk. Among the guests at the wedding was Mr. Spaghetti. The cake at the reception was good, but the ice cream was marvelous. You might try such a scheme on a list of unrelated words of your choice. There is substantial experimental support for the fact that the narrative story mnemonic can increase retention of word lists above that of an uninstructed control group (for example, Boltwood & Blick, 1970).

You can use either the link or narrative story mnemonic system in conjunction with a peg system to aid retention of lists containing more items than there are pegs. We noted you could use the "one is a bun" technique for only 10 items and an alphabet peg system permitted you to memorize as many as 26 items. Consider the possibilities when for each peg not 1 but 2, 3, or 10 words were linked together. In the simplest case, when 2 items are linked together at each peg, the simple 10-peg system based on the children's rhyme can now accommodate 20 items. The alphabetic system would permit a list of 52 items to be memorized if two items were linked to each peg. There appears to be little effect on recall performance of adding additional items to a peg. For example, Bower (1972) reported that recall was as good when subjects used 20 pegs to memorize 20 items (1 item per peg) as when they used 10 pegs (2 items per peg) or 5 pegs (4 items per peg).

The keyword method of language learning

Visual imagery mnemonics have also been used to aid foreign language learning (Atkinson, 1975). The mnemonic system is the *keyword method,* and laboratory findings show it to be effective in helping acquisition of foreign language vocabulary both for Romance languages such as Spanish (Raugh & Atkinson, 1975) and for a more difficult, non-Romance language such as Russian (Atkinson & Raugh, 1975).

The keyword method divides the study of foreign language vocabulary into two steps. In step 1 you form an association between the spoken foreign word and an English word (or phrase) that sounds approximately like it. The English word that is acoustically related to the foreign word is the *keyword.* An important characteristic of the keyword is that it is easily imaged. In step 2 you create a mental image in which the keyword and the English translation are interacting in some fashion. Therefore the keyword method establishes a "chain" between the foreign word and its English translation. There are two links in the chain; the first is based on an acoustic link (the foreign word *sounds* like the keyword), and the second link is an imagery link (the keyword is *imaged* with the English translation).

Consider how the keyword method might work when Russian is studied (see Atkinson & Raugh, 1975). Suppose the Russian word is *zvonók.* (Russian is written in the Cyrillic alphabet but is transliterated here into the Roman alphabet.) The Russian word is pronounced something like "zvahn-oak" and its English translation is bell. You can use the English word *oak* as the keyword. Therefore you first learn an association between the spoken Russian, "zvahn-oak," and the English *oak.* Then you link the keyword to the English translation using mental imagery. For example, you might imagine an oak tree with bells as leaves. Table 13-1 provides some examples of Russian words, their keywords, and English translations. These words are from a list of vocabulary items presented to Stanford University undergraduates as part of a test of the keyword method of language learning (Atkinson & Raugh, 1975). Students in the experimental group were instructed in the keyword method and given keywords for each of 120 Russian vocabulary items. Students in the control group learned any way they wished. Following three days of study, all the students were given a comprehensive test of the vocabulary items that had been presented. Students in the experimental (keyword training) group remembered about 26% more words on the average than did the students in the control group.

The keyword method appears to be particularly effective in aiding begin-

TABLE 13-1. Example of Russian Words, Keywords, and English Translations Selected from a List of Russian Vocabulary Items Students Learned by the Keyword Method

Russian	Keyword	Translation
vnimánie	[pneumonia]	attention
délo	[jello]	affair
západ	[zap it]	west
straná	[strawman]	country
tolpá	[tell pa]	crowd
linkór	[Lincoln]	battleship
rot	[rut]	mouth
gorá	[garage]	mountain
durák	[two rocks]	fool
ósen'	[ocean]	autumn
séver	[saviour]	north
dym	[dim]	smoke
seló	[seal law]	village
golová	[Gulliver]	head
uslóvie	[Yugoslavia]	condition
dévushka	[dear vooshka]	girl
tjótja	[Churchill]	aunt
póezd	[poised]	train
krovát'	[cravat]	bed
chelovék	[chilly back]	person

From "An Application of the Mnemonic Keyword Method to the Acquisition of a Russian Vocabulary," by R. C. Atkinson and M. R. Raugh. In *Journal of Experimental Psychology: Human Learning and Memory,* 1975, *1,* 126–133. Copyright 1975 by the American Psychological Association. Reprinted by permission.

ning language students' foreign language learning and among younger learners (for example, fifth graders) (Levin, Pressley, McCormick, Miller, & Shriberg, 1979). The method is also apparently more effective when the keywords are provided than when learners must construct their own (Atkinson & Raugh, 1975). For younger learners, a picture showing an interaction between the keyword and the translation can be provided rather than requiring the learners to generate their own visual images (Pressley, 1977).

MENTAL IMAGERY

Few people would deny the reality of the subjective experience of visual imagery. The success of visual mnemonics, like those we just reviewed, speaks to the ease with which most of us can produce mental images. But there is considerable debate as to exactly what a mental image is and how it functions in memory processing (for example, Anderson, 1978; Hebb, 1968; Pylyshyn, 1973; Shepard, 1978). Theoretical disputes over the concept of mental imagery are complex and a lengthy discussion of them would not be warranted given the goals of this textbook. However, in what follows we will describe something of the controversy surrounding mental imagery and discuss some of the reasons why mental imagery is such an effective mnemonic device. But, first, a little history.

History of the concept

Around the turn of the century the topic of mental imagery was quite popular (see Holt, 1964, for an informative historical review). The prevailing view of psychology during this period was structuralism, an approach to mental processes that had its origins in mid-19th-century Germany and with the founder of experimental psychology, Wilhelm Wundt. In the early part of the 20th century, E. B. Titchener, a student of Wundt, was the chief spokesman for structuralism in America. Generally speaking, structuralism defined the study of psychology as the investigation of the "mind" through the process of introspection. The structural psychologists sought to describe the contents of conscious experience. Subjective reports provided by laboratory observers furnished the data for this psychology. Mental images were often described in the process of introspection, and a significant amount of these psychologists' activities was devoted to the description and analysis of mental imagery.

Several events occurred to unseat structuralism as the dominant view of psychology and, as a result, to lead to the "banishment" from psychology of such concepts as "consciousness," "mind," and, of course, "imagery." One particularly important event was the *imageless thought controversy*. It turned out that introspection did not always succeed in delivering the processes of conscious experience. Operations associated with mental processes were found to be not always open to conscious inspection. As an example, try to introspect the processes that occur when you solve the following problem: $2 + 2 = ?$ That thought occurred in the absence of reportable images seriously questioned the method of introspection. Although Titchener argued that images were really present, if only fleetingly, others did not see it his way (Lieberman, 1979).

The problems with introspection, alone, would not have been enough to shove imagery and other mentalistic concepts from psychology's shelf. But the behavioristic movement was. In 1913, John B. Watson called for an objective science of psychology, like the natural sciences, and one that studied behavior exclusively. Watson (1913, p. 176) stated that psychology "needs introspection as little as do the sciences of chemistry and physics." For Watson the imageless thought controversy was just another example of what happens when a science is based on subjective reports. The time had come, argued Watson, when psychology "must discard all reference to consciousness" (p. 163). The whole concept of a centrally aroused mental image was questionable, and Watson (1913, p. 174, n. 2) referred to imagery as a "mental luxury" and "without any functional significance whatever." As most students of psychology know, behaviorism gripped American psychology for several decades following Watson's initial appeal, and only recently has this grip been loosened.

But if psychology was to abandon introspection and the analysis of conscious experience for the more objective, and as Watson claimed, more scientifically valid, behaviorism, how might questions of learning and memory be investigated? The answer had been provided by Hermann Ebbinghaus, who, as we have noted (see Chapter 4), published in 1885 the results of his experiments on memory. Ebbinghaus's systematic and highly controlled observations demonstrated that the scientific method could be applied to the study of learning and memory. Introspection and subjective reports played no role in this approach. The output of verbal items in a memory experiment could be treated like any other behavior, and objective measures—frequency and latency, for example—could be used as they were for other observable behaviors. (In fact, Watson assumed that thought processes were really implicit speech and simply motor habits associated with the speech musculature.) The Ebbinghaus tradition with its emphasis on rote verbal processes was acceptable in a psychology dominated by behaviorism, and the supposedly more subjective concept of mental imagery was not. (See Paivio, 1969, for an important review of the verbal tradition in the study of memory.)

The concept today

Although modern writers have sought to analyze the reasons for the recent "reemergence" of mental imagery as a topic in psychology (for example, Holt, 1964), there is no doubt that within the field of memory research a major factor has been the research and theory of Allan Paivio (1969, 1971, 1976). Paivio argued that imagery was no more subjective than the verbal mediators or implicit associative responses memory researchers often mentioned. More important, Paivio argued that *both* verbal and imaginal representation in memory is important and in fact necessary. In other words, imagery, Watson to the contrary, does have "functional significance." An often cited example of functional mediation using mental imagery is one given by Shepard (1966, p. 203): "If I am now asked the number of windows in my house, I find that I must *picture* the house, as viewed from different sides or from within different rooms, and then count the windows presented in these various mental images." That such examples are even necessary says something about the attitude of many regarding the concept of mental imagery.

Paivio (1969, 1971) presented a dual-code theory of memory, which, you may remember, we introduced in Chapter 10 as an explanation for picture superiority in recognition memory. The dual-code theory assumes that the human memory system uses both verbal and imaginal codes to represent information. Imagery, in this view, is a symbolic process linked to our experience with concrete objects and events. The greater the concreteness of a stimulus, the more likely it is to evoke an imaginal memory code. For example, the dual-code theory considers pictures to be more memorable than words because they can be represented in memory both imaginally and verbally (see Chapter 10). The dual-code theory assumes that involvement of both the verbal and imaginal coding systems will lead to better retention than when only one is involved, although it is possible that the imaginal code is somehow inherently superior to the verbal code (see Paivio, 1978). Much of the research supporting the dual-code theory has been directed toward demonstrating that pictures and concrete words are learned and remembered better than abstract words (see Paivio, 1971, for a review) and toward showing that the differences in memory for these items cannot be accounted for simply in terms of properties of the items themselves, such as association value or meaningfulness of words and verbal labels (for example, see Paivio, Yuille, & Rogers, 1969).

Propositional theory

However, visual imagery may not be what it seems to us, according to Zenon Pylyshyn (1973). Although a colleague of Paivio's at the University of Western Ontario, he holds a somewhat different view of mental imagery than does Paivio. Pylyshyn argues that we should not think of mental images as "pictures" in our mind, something many apparently assume when discussing mental imagery. For example, note that, when Shepard (1966) stated how he might determine the number of windows in his house, he referred to the "picture" he produced. The problem, says Pylyshyn, is that this concept of mental imagery is wrong. Concluding an important critique of the concept of mental imagery, Pylyshyn (1973, p. 22) stated that "the experience of imagery has no causal role."

Although this conclusion is reminiscent of Watson's condemnation of imagery more than 50 years ago, Pylyshyn actually means something very different. According to Pylyshyn, we do not perceive images as we do pictures. He suggests that for the brain to store literally all the images it receives through the senses would place an impossible burden on its capacity. How, Pylyshyn asks, would these images be retrieved? How could we possibly scan all the images our brain had stored in order to find the one we wanted? Another problem with thinking of images as pictures is that we can create and simultaneously make alterations in an infinite number of images. The mental image "behaves" more like a description of something than like a picture of it and seems to be more logically the product of some interpretive process rather than a picturelike entity. As Pylyshyn (1973, p. 5) stated,

> The need to postulate a more abstract representation—one which resembles neither pictures nor words and is not accessible to subjective experience—

is unavoidable. As long as we recognize that people can go from mental picture to mental words or vice versa, we are forced to conclude that there must be a representation (which is more abstract and not available to conscious experience) which encompasses both. There must, in other words, be some common format or interlingua. The problem is dramatized if we persist in using the common but utterly misleading metaphor of the "mind's eye," for then we have to account for the form of representation in the "mind's eye's mind" which clearly is not accessible to introspection.

The idea that both verbal and imaginal representations are based on a more abstract system is frequently referred to as a *propositional theory* (see Anderson, 1978). Bower (1972) used a propositional theory to explain imagery effects in memory—for example, when imagery mnemonics are used. Although it might be argued that imagery is an efficient code for remembering because it is more distinctive, longer lasting, or suffers less interference than verbal codes, Bower (1972) reminds us that *interactive* imagery is often best. It is possible that creating interacting images introduces meaning into the situation, not unlike the meaning that comes from processing a sentence. Bower (1972, p. 85) suggests that a "base grammar underlies our linguistic and pictorial analysis and generation." An associative connection between dog and bicycle is strengthened through the relational organization described by the proposition "The dog is riding the bicycle." Bower (1972) views the mnemonic value of interactive imagery as arising from the relational organization that is the product of the common generative grammar underlying the imaginal and verbal systems.

Summary

We began this chapter with a true story about a man with a phenomenal memory. He was able to achieve almost perfect recall due to the vivid visual impressions he formed and the synesthesia he experienced. In our attempts to improve our memory, we often utilize mnemonic devices that employ visual imagery. So, it appears, did ancient Greek and Roman orators. They frequently used a mnemonic system known as the method of loci, which entails mentally placing to-be-remembered items in a previously learned set of locations. At the time of test we take a mental walk through these locations to retrieve the items. The method of loci is similar to the more general peg systems, which memory "experts" often employ. Other techniques for improving memory are the link and narrative story methods. These systems can be used in combination with particular peg systems. The key to successful use of mental imagery is to create visual images that depict the to-be-remembered items interacting in some way. An important application of a mnemonic system is found in the keyword method of second language learning.

There is considerable debate as to the nature of visual imagery and its effect on retention. For instance, there are important reasons why we should not think of visual images as "pictures" in the brain. A propositional theory of visual imagery suggests that both verbal and imaginal representations are based on a yet more abstract memory system. This debate shows every evidence of continuing for some time, and research on this question offers exciting possibilities for learning how images are represented in memory.

Recommendations for further reading

An important review of research on mental imagery is found in Paivio's (1971) text, *Imagery and Verbal Processes*. The mnemonic techniques we discussed are reviewed in greater detail in an interesting book by Higbee (1977), *Your Memory: How It Works and How to Improve It*. The theoretical controversy over the concept of mental imagery has recently turned hot and heavy. Those who wish to enter the fray should begin with Pylyshyn's (1973) provocative article, "What the Mind's Eye Tells the Mind's Brain: A Critique of Mental Imagery." Having read that article, you will be prepared for several more recent theoretical papers, including those by Anderson (1978, 1979), Hayes-Roth (1979), Kosslyn (1981), Kosslyn and Pomerantz (1977), and Pylyshyn (1979, 1981).

14

Constructive and Reconstructive Processes in Memory

Introduction/overview

Have you ever gotten together with friends to reminisce about old times and found that not everyone remembers things the way you do? Was Harry really there? Was George with Harry? Who arrived first? Why didn't Mary go too? Sometimes when listening to someone describe an event that we also witnessed, we begin to wonder whether we experienced the same event. Errors or lapses in memory can be the source of mild disputes in social situations. In other situations an inability to remember the exact sequence of events or to identify who was present can have serious consequences, as when an eyewitness fails to remember that a particular person was present at the scene of a crime.

296

In this chapter we will examine some of the reasons recall of complex events may often be inaccurate and differ drastically from one person to another. The impetus for research in this area is the work of the English psychologist, Frederick C. Bartlett, who investigated the types of changes people introduce when attempting to reproduce lengthy verbal passages. Bartlett identified both constructive *and* reconstructive *processes in memory. Construction is associated with the processes of inference or integration, which frequently accompany our attempts to comprehend meaningful material. Suppose you're told the following: Johnny tripped over the chair and went into the pool. A reasonable inference is that the act of tripping caused Johnny to fall into the pool. But you need not construct the meaning of the sentence that way. The sentence could be describing Johnny's progress toward the pool, his tripping, in other words, occurring before he got to the pool. How you interpret the sentence will affect the way you remember it.*

How you remember information may also be affected by how you reconstruct it. Reconstruction is the process of inferring the past, rather than merely reproducing it on the basis of what was originally stored in memory. Reconstruction is assumed to be based on our general knowledge of the circumstances surrounding the original event, any general impressions or reactions we might have formed, and any details of the event we still remember when retention is tested. Assume again we are told that Johnny tripped over a chair and went into the pool. With the passage of time we can expect to forget details of the original information. We might later remember that Johnny tripped near a pool. He had to trip over something; so we might reasonably infer that it was a table because we know that tables can be found next to pools. Our reconstruction of the original sentence will involve Johnny tripping over a table. One of the hypotheses to be examined in this chapter is that reconstruction is affected by information we add after we experience an event. Suppose we learned afterwards that Johnny drowned while he was in the pool. Under these conditions would our memory for the original event be "changed" to accommodate this new information? Would we, for instance, be likely to remember that Johnny died because he tripped over a chair (or table), fell into the pool, and drowned? Research we review in this chapter suggests this might be the case.

The idea that memory is constructive as well as reconstructive has led psychologists to examine the structure and organization of knowledge and to identify possible ways knowledge might interact with information presented for a memory test. We will look briefly at some of the descriptions of the way knowledge is represented and illustrate how differences in prior knowledge can lead to differences in retention.*

---

*What we generally think of as "knowledge"—that is, our memory for abstract concepts, well-learned facts (who was the first president of the U.S.?), particular topics (geography, mathematics, football, sewing), meanings of words, and so forth—is sometimes referred to as *semantic* or *generic memory* (see Hintzman, 1978). This type of memory is generally devoid of spatial-temporal information. For instance, it is unlikely that you can remember exactly where or when you learned the name of the first

In the light of research findings regarding reconstructive processes in memory, we will examine the apparently widely held assumption that memory is permanent. Do we really retain all we experience in its original form or is memory malleable and capable of change as new information is accommodated? We begin with a review of Bartlett's important findings and a discussion of the hypotheses he offered to explain the distortions in our recall of everyday events.

BARTLETT'S EXPERIMENTS

Bartlett was originally interested in perception, but this led him to consider related factors—namely, the mental processes associated with imagery and recall. To investigate these processes, he set out on the course originally charted by Ebbinghaus (1885/1964) but soon found it less than satisfactory.

> Long before this, Ebbinghaus had introduced the "exact methods" of nonsense syllables into the Laboratory consideration of memory. As in duty bound, I followed his lead and worked for some time with nonsense material. The result was disappointment and a growing dissatisfaction. . . . The upshot was that I determined to try to retain the advantages of an experimental method of approach, with its relatively controlled situations, and also to keep my study as realistic as possible. I therefore built up, or selected, material which I hoped would prove interesting in itself, and would be of the type which every normal individual deals with constantly in his daily activities [Bartlett, 1932, p. v].*

Bartlett selected the very material that Ebbinghaus had rejected. Prose material, Ebbinghaus (1885/1964) had complained, was sometimes descriptive, sometimes reflective; it included various metaphors; it was occasionally humorous or pathetic; and the rhythm was never the same. This kind of material, he concluded, introduced a "multiplicity of influences which change without regularity and are therefore disturbing" (Ebbinghaus, 1885/1964, p. 23). Ebbinghaus felt that this could be avoided by using nonsense syllables. But prose

---

president of the U.S. or that 2 plus 2 is 4. These things are simply known. Following a distinction made by Tulving (1972), we can contrast semantic memory with *episodic memory*. This second type of memory refers to our memory for episodes in our lives (sometimes called remembrances). Episodic memory generally contains spatial-temporal information and is autobiographical—that is, it is an experiential record of our past. Your memory for what you ate for breakfast today or the last word in a list of words recently presented to you are instances of episodic memory. Although we have chosen not to emphasize the distinction between semantic and episodic memory in this book, it is an important one and we want you to be aware of it.

*From *Remembering: A Study in Experimental and Social Psychology*, by F. C. Bartlett. Copyright 1932 by Cambridge University Press. This and all other quotations from this source are reprinted by permission.

material is the stuff of everyday experiences and Bartlett set out to discover what people remember of such ordinary information.

Bartlett's experiments were simply performed. One method he used was called *serial reproduction*. This is similar to a party game known as "Telephone" or "Gossip" (depending on which part of the country you are from). One person tells a story or describes an event to another person. The second person relates the material to a third person, who relates the material to another person, and so forth. What the last person in the chain remembers is compared to the original version. Although we may identify this method with a children's game, it is nevertheless the way people have passed stories, jokes, and even gossip from one person or social group to another for thousands of years. A second method Bartlett relied on was *repeated reproduction*. He asked a person to read a passage or examine a picture and then on more than one occasion attempt to reproduce the original event. Bartlett usually asked for the first reproduction about 15 minutes after the material was presented. Later reproductions were requested at various intervals, after days, weeks, or even years. Bartlett intended both these methods to reveal the nature of recall and in particular the kinds of transformations people make when attempting to remember prose or picture material.

One of the verbal passages Bartlett used was a North American folk tale. The original version is as follows:

The War of the Ghosts

One night two young men from Egulac went down to the river to hunt seals, and while they were there it became foggy and calm. Then they heard war-cries, and they thought: "Maybe this is a war-party." They escaped to the shore, and hid behind a log. Now canoes came up, and they heard the noise of paddles, and saw one canoe coming up to them. There were five men in the canoe, and they said:

"What do you think? We wish to take you along. We are going up the river to make war on the people." One of the young men said: "I have no arrows." "Arrows are in the canoe," they said. "I will not go along. I might be killed. My relatives do not know where I have gone. But you," he said, turning to the other, "may go with them." So one of the young men went, but the other returned home.

And the warriors went on up the river to a town on the other side of Kalama. The people came down to the water, and they began to fight, and many were killed. But presently the young man heard one of the warriors say: "Quick, let us go home: that Indian has been hit." Now he thought: "Oh, they are ghosts." He did not feel sick, but they said he had been shot.

So the canoes went back to Egulac, and the young man went ashore to his house, and made a fire. And he told everybody and said: "Behold I accompanied the ghosts, and we went to fight. Many of our fellows were killed, and many of those who attacked us were killed. They said I was hit, and I did not feel sick."

He told it all, and then he became quiet. When the sun rose he fell down. Something black came out of his mouth. His face became contorted. The people jumped up and cried. He was dead [Bartlett, 1932, p. 65].

Bartlett had chosen a story containing elements foreign to the English culture from which he drew his subjects. He felt this material would be particularly likely to undergo transformation in his subjects' successive reproductions. It is also apparent from reading the story that parts of it do not seem connected to other parts. This, too, Bartlett (1932, p. 64) suggested, would provide an opportunity to observe changes as the subjects dealt with what he called a "lack of obvious rational order" in the story.

Typical of the recall Bartlett observed when the method of repeated reproductions was used is the following reproduction given by a subject several months after reading the original story. This was the subject's fourth recall attempt since reading the story.

The War of the Ghosts

Two youths went down to the river to hunt for seals. They were hiding behind a rock when a boat with some warriors in it came up to them. The warriors, however, said they were friends, and invited them to help them to fight an enemy over the river. The elder one said he could not go because his relations would be so anxious if he did not return home. So the younger one went with the warriors in the boat.

In the evening he returned and told his friends that he had been fighting in a great battle, and that many were slain on both sides. After lighting a fire he retired to sleep. In the morning, when the sun rose, he fell ill, and his neighbours came to see him. He had told them that he had been wounded in the battle but had felt no pain then. But soon he became worse. He writhed and shrieked and fell to the ground dead. Something black came out of his mouth. The neighbours said he must have been at war with the ghosts [Bartlett, 1932, p. 74].

Bartlett observed that several things were apparent and consistent in his subjects' reproductions. Perhaps the most obvious was that recall was rarely accurate in a literal sense. Subjects elaborated, omitted details, and even introduced new elements to the story. Further, repeated reproductions by the same subject revealed that a persistent outline or form emerged in the recall attempts. The story, in other words, became "stereotyped." Some of these changes Bartlett thought to be due to the use of visual imagery. Others he attributed to a subject's familiarity with a particular element, to personal preferences or interests, or to a process referred to as *rationalization*. This was defined as an attempt by the subject to make the material more readily understandable, comfortable, and "satisfying." For example, you may have noted that in the subject's reproduction just cited the word *boat* is substituted for *canoe*. Bartlett argued that his English subjects were more comfortable with the term *boat* than *canoe*.

Bartlett (1932, p. 213) summarized his findings as follows:

> Remembering is not the re-excitation of innumerable fixed, lifeless and frag-
> mentary traces. It is an imaginative reconstruction, or construction, built out
> of the relation of our attitude towards a whole active mass of organised past
> reactions or experience, and to a little outstanding detail which commonly
> appears in image or in language form.

We therefore find in Bartlett's experiments the basis for both a constructive and reconstructive hypothesis regarding changes in retention. The processing of prose material is seen as an active interaction between the learner's knowledge and the to-be-remembered text. This interaction is often constructive, leading to inferences or producing elaboration of the to-be-remembered material. Bartlett also considered memory to be largely reconstructive. He assumed that, as time passes, we rely more and more on our general knowledge and impressions of an event and less on memory for the original details. Therefore we would have to infer and reconstruct certain aspects of the original event on the basis of our general knowledge and impressions of the event. Memory was not, in other words, a literal reproduction of the past. In the following sections we will look more closely at these major hypotheses about retention of prose material. Before that, however, we will examine an important concept Bartlett introduced, that of *schemata*, and briefly mention its relation to more contemporary concepts.

SCHEMATA, SCRIPTS, AND FRAMES

Despite the significance of Bartlett's observations and his hypotheses about prose recall, for many years his contributions were generally unrecognized, particularly by American psychologists. His informal treatment of data and his interpretations in terms of visual imagery, attitude, and constructive and reconstructive processes did not find a ready acceptance in a psychology given to statistical treatment of verbal responses and explanations in terms of stimulus-response associations. Perhaps most unsettling to a psychology that had only recently abandoned introspection and the use of mentalistic concepts was Bartlett's notion of *schemata* (singular: schema). According to Bartlett (1932), schemata represent the mass of active organizations of past reactions or experiences. Any one schema presumably is the organized knowledge of a particular set of material or specific type of past experience. Bartlett assumed the changes he found in his subjects' reproductions of prose material reflected a dependence on schemata related to the story or into which the story mapped. As the retention interval increased, the subject relied more and more on these general schemata when attempting recall. Schemata, in other words, were the basis for reconstruction in memory. Consequently, there was a loss of detail in the subject's reproductions, some degree of elaboration, and an overall tendency to make the story comfortable or satisfying.

With the renewal of interest in memory for prose material that began in the late 1960s in American psychology, schemata were once again invoked as an explanatory device. According to Thorndyke and Hayes-Roth (1979, p. 82), "A memory schema, as it is typically conceptualized today, is a cluster of knowledge (a set of concepts and associations among the concepts) that defines a more complex and frequently encountered concept." Unfortunately, schema is not defined consistently from one researcher to another, and many researchers apparently use the term in a manner not that different from Bartlett's original and vague description. However, a wide variety of more specific definitions of our organized knowledge has been presented.

As suggested, a schema is generally used to refer to our knowledge structure for a fairly complex and general concept. Descriptions of possible substructures have also been offered. One frequently used concept is that of a *script*. Schank and Abelson (1977) have used a "script theory" to help explain the constructive elaboration of meaningful material. Scripts refer to our stereotyped knowledge for particular situations that most of us have encountered in life. Schank (1976, pp. 180–181) has elaborated on the meaning of a script as follows:

> A generalized episode is called a *script*. A script is a giant causal chain of conceptualizations that have been known to occur in that order many times before. Scripts can be called up from memory by various words in the correct context, by visual inputs, or by expectations generated through inferences. What a script does is to set up expectations about events that are likely to follow in a given situation. These events can be predicted because they have occurred in precisely this fashion before. Scripts are associated, then, with static everyday events such as restaurants, birthday parties, classrooms, bus riding, theater going, and so on.

Until recently, a script was likely to be based on researchers' intuitions regarding those events that might typically occur in a given situation. However, Bower, Black, and Turner (1979) collected descriptions of various events from students. The students were asked to list as many as 20 activities they associated with such events as going to a restaurant, visiting a doctor, or attending a lecture. There was substantial agreement among the students as to each of these scripts.

For example, when describing attending a lecture, most students listed enter room, find seat, sit down, take out notebook, listen to professor, take notes, check time, leave. Less frequently mentioned activities included such things as ask question, daydream, and look at other students. The researchers defined script elements in terms of their probability of being mentioned. The considerable agreement among the students in describing these episodes indicates that most of us possess stereotyped knowledge for these kinds of events. It is assumed that scripts will be invoked when attempting to comprehend a prose passage. For example, reading a story about a man going to a restaurant will likely lead us to rely on our script for activities in a restaurant in order to understand the story. It is possible that we will elaborate on the story in terms of our script for what "must have happened." Later in this chapter we will show how scripts may be a source of memory errors.

Script theory is a particular elaboration of a frame theory proposed by Minsky (1975; see also Bower, Black, & Turner, 1979). A *frame* is similar to a script except that it applies to our knowledge for a wider range of concepts, including stereotyping about people and knowledge about particular types of literature, games, architecture, or social situations. For instance, when we hear someone mention that she attended a cocktail party at a friend's split-level house in the suburbs, we presumably refer to our knowledge frames regarding cocktail parties, suburbs, and split-level houses and possibly to related frames such as living room, host, or hostess.

Schemata and the more specific scripts and frames are important explanatory devices to help us understand the effect of prior knowledge on memory for prose material. Numerous other concepts have been introduced, including themes, macrostructures, episodes, and grammars. As we mentioned, not everyone uses those terms consistently and there are considerable problems with providing operational definitions. An important step in clarifying the use of these terms is the collection by Bower, Black, and Turner (1979) of script norms. Now it is possible to use this term more precisely so that when a "restaurant script" is discussed, the meaning can be given in terms of the norms obtained. For the present we will avoid the many and subtle complexities found in the use of these concepts and refer, as Bartlett did, to our organized knowledge in terms of schemata, realizing that this concept is not clearly defined.

PRIOR KNOWLEDGE

It is not difficult to demonstrate that understanding (comprehension) of a verbal message, as well as our ability to remember it, can depend on our prior knowledge about the topic of the message. Both comprehension and remembering, in other words, are affected by our schemata for the contents of a passage.

Effect on comprehension

Measures of understanding or comprehension are generally nothing more than subjects' ratings of how well they understood something. Read the following passage.

> The procedure is actually quite simple. First you arrange items into different groups. Of course, one pile may be sufficient depending on how much there is to do. If you have to go somewhere else due to lack of facilities that is the next step, otherwise, you are pretty well set. It is important not to overdo things. That is, it is better to do too few things at once than too many. In the short run this may not seem important but complications can easily arise. A mistake can be expensive as well. At first the whole procedure will seem complicated. Soon, however, it will become just another facet of life. It is difficult to foresee any end to the necessity for this task in the immediate future, but then one never can tell. After the procedure is completed one arranges the materials into different groups again. Then they can be put into their appropriate places. Eventually they will be used once more and the whole cycle will then have to be repeated. However, that is part of life [Bransford & Johnson, 1972, p. 722].*

Using a seven-point scale where one equals difficult to understand and seven equals very easy to understand, how would you rate your understanding of the passage? Presumably, your rating would not be very high. Although all the words are familiar and any particular sentence is understandable, the passage as a whole does not seem to make much sense. Would it surprise you to learn that Bransford and Johnson (1972) presented this passage to college students and found they rated it fairly *easy* to comprehend? This is true, but these researchers also gave the students some additional information *before* they read the passage. Subjects were told that the passage describes washing clothes. Take another look at the passage with this information in mind. Subjects not given the information behaved as you likely did and rated the passage as difficult to understand. Further, when recall of the passage was tested, the students told what the passage was about before they read it remembered almost twice as much as students who read the passage without knowing the topic. Bransford and Johnson (1972) also found that giving the students the topic *after* they read the passage did not help comprehension or recall. These students rated their understanding of the passage no better than students given no information and both the no-information group and the information-after group recalled about

*From "Contextual Prerequisites for Understanding: Some Investigations of Comprehension and Recall," by J. D. Bransford and M. K. Johnson. In *Journal of Verbal Learning and Verbal Behavior,* 1972, *11,* 717–726. Copyright 1972 by Academic Press, Inc. Reprinted by permission.

the same amount. Apparently, a critical condition for understanding is the activation of appropriate prior knowledge patterns (schemata) at the time information is being processed.

The effect of prior knowledge on recall

Purpose
To show how prior knowledge of the semantic context of a verbal passage can influence memory for that passage.

Materials
All subjects in this experiment listen to *either* of the following passages.

> The procedure is actually quite simple. / First arrange things into different bundles depending on make-up. / Don't do too much at once. / In the short run this may not seem important, / however, complications easily arise. / A mistake can be costly. / Next, find facilities. / Some people must go elsewhere for them. / Manipulation of appropriate mechanisms should be self-explanatory. / Remember to include all other necessary supplies. / Initially the routine will overwhelm you, / but soon it will become just another facet of life. / Finally, rearrange everything into original groups. / Return these to their usual places. / Eventually they will be used again. / Then the whole cycle will have to be repeated. /

> Generally the atmosphere is not conducive to street clothing. / Proper attire lessens this worry. / It may also facilitate dexterity. / Awe-filled spectators surely provide extra motivation. / Hopefully they don't cause distractions. / Finesse and enthusiasm add a lot to the performance, / however, final results constitute the true measure of achievement. / Experiment with ways of throwing. / Making the thick pellets into thin skins is the aim. / You usually cannot select all the constituents. / Consumers choose much themselves. / Your task is to integrate the raw material. / Careful engineering of embellishment placement guarantees consistency of quality. / Once heated no changes can be made. / Consumption is imminent. / Quantity ultimately secures survival. /

Before hearing the passage, subjects are given one of two kinds of instructions. The different instructions define the experimental conditions. Written instructions can be used if the experiment is conducted in a large group and both conditions are tested simultaneously. Should subjects be seen individually or the two conditions tested in separate groups, instructions can be read aloud by the experimenter. Both passages can be used should the experimenter want to increase the generality of the results. The slashes that appear in the stories are for purposes of scoring recall and indicate where pauses should be made when reading the passage. All subjects need a pen or pencil and a blank sheet of paper to write down what they remember of the passage.

Instructions to Subjects

CONTEXT GROUP

In this experiment you will be asked to listen to a short passage that describes washing clothes [running a pizza parlor]. Please try to remember it as best you can. Later you will be asked to write down as much as you can remember from this passage.

NO-CONTEXT GROUP

In this experiment you will be asked to listen to a short passage. Please try to remember it as best you can. Later you will be asked to write down as much as you can remember from this passage.

Procedure

As the first passage says, the procedure is quite simple. Subjects are randomly assigned to either the no-context or the context condition. If subjects are tested in a large group, assignment to conditions can be accomplished by randomly distributing the two sets of written instructions. After subjects receive their instructions, the experimenter can present the passage. The passage should be read slowly with appropriate pauses at the end of clauses and between sentences (that is, where slashes appear in the passage). Immediately after hearing the passage, all subjects are asked to write down as much as they can remember from it. Five minutes is permitted for this recall test.

Summary and Analysis

Memory of the passage can be scored in either or both of two ways. Amount subjects in the two groups recall can be determined by finding the number of words or by recording the number of "idea units" each subject recalled. There are 106 words in each passage, with some words repeated (for example, *be* and *is*). In scoring number of words recalled, a word is considered correct if it appeared in the passage, and it can be scored correct as many times as there are repetitions of that word (for example, subjects can get credit for four *be*'s in the washing clothes passage). The slashes in the passages identify 16 "idea units." When recall is scored according to the number of idea units subjects remember, less attention is paid to the exact wording or to the number of words recalled. A good way to score for idea units is to have two people score each answer sheet and to see whether the two scorers agree. The percentage of times the two scorers agree should be reported.

A test of statistical significance of the difference in mean recall between the two groups can be carried out using a *t* test for independent groups. Statistical comparison can be made for either or both of the two measures of recall (words or ideas).

Recommended Minimum Number of Subjects
Total of 24; 12 in each of two conditions.

Based on an experiment by Bransford and Johnson (1972). The passages used in this experiment are from a dissertation by S. E. Nyberg, State University of New York at Stony Brook, 1975, entitled "Comprehension and Long-Term Retention of Prose Passages."

Effect on remembering

Other experiments have replicated these findings (Bransford & Johnson, 1973; Dooling & Lachman, 1971) and have added other important information about how schemata affect recall. First, it is clear that the effect of prior knowledge on retention is greater than mere repetition of the to-be-remembered material (Bransford & Johnson, 1972; Johnson, Doll, Bransford, & Lapinski, 1974). Bransford and Johnson (1972) found that students who read an "incomprehensible" passage twice still recalled less than half that recalled by students reading the passage only once but given the topic of the passage prior to reading it. This suggests that retention may at times be facilitated more by an effort spent toward understanding the contents of what must be remembered than spending time repeating the to-be-remembered information. A second consequence of prior knowledge is that it affects what particular information may be remembered (Bransford & Johnson, 1973; Dooling & Lachman, 1971). Bransford and Johnson (1973) had students read an ambiguous passage that could be meaningfully interpreted as either about watching a peace march from the fortieth floor or a space trip to an inhabited planet. Students omitted different details in the passage when recall was tested under the two different assumptions. Specifically, a sentence that mentioned that the atmosphere was such that no special suits had to be worn was more likely to be remembered when the theme was thought to be about space than when students considered it as a description of a peace march.

The aforementioned studies suggest that degree of prior knowledge is responsible for differences in remembering. In other words, just how much prior information one has about an event may affect not only whether one understands it but will determine how much and what details one remembers. The greater and more elaborate one's prior knowledge of a topic, the greater one's retention is likely to be. This was demonstrated by an interesting set of experiments by researchers at the University of Pittsburgh (Chiesi, Spilich, & Voss, 1979; Spilich, Vesonder, Chiesi, & Voss, 1979). Consider the following selection from a verbal passage presented to subjects in their experiment:

> Beck, the left-handed relief pitcher, is warming up in the bull pen. The next hitter for the Cougars is the right-hand hitting Carl Churniak, a .260 hitter who is known to hit well in the clutch. Claresen takes his sign, delivers, and Churniak takes the pitch for a ball. Claresen again is ready and pitches, and Churniak swings and hits a slow bouncing ball toward the shortstop. Haley comes in, fields it, and throws to first, but too late. Churniak is on first with a single. Johnson stayed on second [Spilich et al., 1979, p. 289].

Undoubtedly, most Americans would recognize this as a play-by-play description of their national pastime. However, people without prior knowledge about baseball would likely find this passage nearly as incomprehensible as the washing clothes passage was to those not given a description of its contents. Certainly, people possess different degrees of knowledge about baseball, the rules and actions of the game. The researchers at the University of Pittsburgh chose baseball passages for exactly that reason. They wanted to compare retention of baseball information for people with "low" and "high" baseball knowledge.

There was another and equally important reason for selecting baseball information for these experiments. To say that we possess schemata for an area of knowledge does not in any way help us to understand how these schemata might be organized. Within a particular domain of knowledge, for instance, how might our knowledge be organized and how might that organization affect the acquisition of new knowledge? It seemed to the researchers that baseball offered a knowledge domain that had a well-defined conceptual framework in which knowledge would be organized. A major goal of the research was to see if retention was related to such a framework.

The conceptual framework the researchers hypothesized to describe baseball knowledge is shown in Table 14-1. Knowledge of the game is assumed to consist first of *setting information*. This includes *general* information about who is playing, the inning, and so forth, as well as *specific* information about the records of the team and players and *enabling* information, which is information necessary to carry on the game, such as the pitcher is ready to pitch. Baseball also has a definite *goal structure*. The goal of baseball is to win the game. However, there are several subgoals (or *levels*), including scoring runs, getting runners on base, and "balls and strikes." The goal structure is identified in Table 14-1 as hierarchically organized in terms of these four levels. As you can see, this particular conceptual framework also includes a description of *values* that variables associated with the goal structure may take as well as

TABLE 14-1. Baseball Knowledge Structure

Setting	
General:	Teams playing, team at bat, team in field, inning, miscellaneous conditions
Specific:	Relevant: teams' records as related to goal structure, players' records as related to goal structure
	Irrelevant: team attributes, player attributes
Enabling:	Batter at bat and pitcher ready to pitch

Goal structure				
Team at bat	*Level*	*Variables*	*Values*	*Team in field*
Winning game	1	Game outcome	Win-lose	Winning game
Scoring runs	2	Score	Domain of game scores	Preventing runs from scoring
Getting runners on base and advancing runners	3	Pattern of base runners	Eight possible patterns	Preventing runners from getting on base or advancing by making outs
		Outs	0, 1, 2, 3	
Having "Balls," Avoiding "Strikes"	4	"Balls"	0, 1, 2, 3, 4	Getting "Strikes,"
		"Strikes"	0, 1, 2, 3	Avoiding "Balls"

Nongame actions
Relevant nongame actions
Irrelevant nongame actions

From "Text Processing of Domain-Related Information for Individuals with High and Low Domain Knowledge," by G. J. Spilich, G. T. Vesonder, H. L. Chiesi, and J. F. Voss. In *Journal of Verbal Learning and Verbal Behavior*, 1979, *18*, 275–290. Copyright 1979 by Academic Press, Inc. Reprinted by permission.

information in the goal structure related to the opposing team. Finally, as anyone who has seen a baseball game knows, there is also a lot of *nongame action* that has no direct effect on the outcome but must be considered in a complete description of baseball knowledge. The researchers distinguished between *relevant* nongame actions (for example, the catcher returns the ball to the pitcher) and *irrelevant* nongame actions (for example, the crowd yells).

Subjects in the baseball experiments were selected for their prior knowledge about the game. Specifically, a large number of students were given a 40-question baseball test. The test consisted of questions to evaluate a person's knowledge of the game, including terminology and principles of the game but not necessarily trivia information. On the basis of the pretest, high- and low-knowledge groups were defined. Despite the best efforts of the researchers at advertising the experiments, the high-knowledge group was nearly always all male and the low-knowledge group almost always completely female. The major question the researchers asked was how the degree of domain-related knowledge was related to retention of aspects of the game. In one experiment (Spilich et al., 1979) subjects listened to a half inning account of a fictitious baseball game (we presented a selection from that account earlier). The presentation lasted about 5 minutes and was presented auditorily. Afterwards subjects were asked to recall as much as they could and to answer 40 specific completion questions.

Retention of the baseball information was analyzed in terms of the theoretical framework described in Table 14-1. An analysis of subjects' recall suggested that the differential performance of high- and low-knowledge subjects could be explained by differences in knowledge of the relation between game actions and the goal structure and in differences in processing of sequences of game activities. In general the researchers found that high-knowledge subjects remembered more of the game description than low-knowledge subjects and that the quality of recall was different for the two groups. For example, the high-knowledge subjects were more likely to remember actions that produced changes in the more important aspects of the game—such as scoring and activity of runners. Interestingly, the two groups did not differ on information remembered about the highest goal structures: who won and what the score was.

That there is a relationship between degree of prior knowledge and retention should give students an appreciation for course prerequisites. The knowledge provided in many lower level courses is important in aiding comprehension and memory for more advanced topics. Presumably, someone required to take a course in introductory baseball would be able to comprehend and remember a play-by-play description better than someone without this course. The analysis of cognitive structures associated with domain-related knowledge, as exemplified by the baseball experiments, provides valuable insights into the organization of memory schemata. This analysis has important consequences for the construction of instructional prose. Types of knowledge that produce the greatest effect on understanding and retention can be identified and selected for particular emphasis. The results of these experiments also teach us that in planning instructional material it is important to take into account the level of the learner's prior knowledge. Material that is too advanced for the beginning student will have all the impact of a baseball play-by-play on the person with little or no knowledge of baseball.

MEMORY CONSTRUCTION

Comprehension is an active process. The interaction between the learner's knowledge and to-be-remembered prose will often lead the learner to construct meanings that add to the material presented. This is illustrated by experiments showing that people tend to confuse inferences constructed from to-be-remembered information with the originally perceived information. Consider an experiment performed by Bransford, Barclay, and Franks (1972). They asked students at the State University of New York at Stony Brook to listen to ten brief verbal passages. The passages described relationships between a series of items. One passage was "There is a tree with a box beside it, and a chair is on top of the box. The box is to the right of the tree. The tree is green and extremely tall" (p. 201). Following study of the passages, the students were given a recognition memory test for sentences from them. There were actually four types of recognition sentences. One type consisted of sentences actually heard during the study part of the experiment. Other sentences were permissible inferences (for example, "The chair is to the right of the tree"). A third type of sentence changed the spatial relationship described in the original passage (for example, "The box is to the left of the tree"). The fourth type of sentence changed both the spatial relationship and the subject noun of the sentence (for example, "The chair is to the left of the tree").

As you might expect, students most frequently recognized the original sentences as being those actually heard previously. However, the most frequent kind of error subjects made was to select a sentence that was a permissible inference from what was originally presented. The other two types of false sentences were seldom chosen as being part of the original passage. These results provide evidence that subjects use information in the passage to construct a meaningful description of the situation. Later it is difficult to remember whether information was actually presented or whether we constructed it on the basis of the information presented.

Memory errors based on inferences apparently constructed during comprehension of meaningful passages have been identified in many situations (Cofer, 1973; Johnson, Bransford, & Solomon, 1973; Sulin & Dooling, 1974). For example, Johnson, Bransford, and Solomon (1973) provided evidence for constructive processes in memory when subjects processed a series of simple stories. Subjects in the experiments were asked to listen carefully to the stories and be ready for a later retention test. The stories either allowed for inferences to be made ("When the man entered the kitchen, he slipped on a wet spot and dropped the delicate glass pitcher on the floor. The pitcher was very expensive, and everyone watched the event with horror.") or they did not encourage inferences ("When the man entered the kitchen, he slipped on a wet spot and just missed the delicate glass pitcher on the floor. The pitcher was very expensive, and everyone watched the event with horror.") (p. 204).

A recognition memory test followed, and as in other experiments of this type, the nature of the recognition alternatives was varied. One type of recognition sentence was, of course, exactly the same as contained in the original story. A second type of sentence used information from the original sentences but conveyed it in a manner that was inconsistent with the original story. The third type of sentence contained information reasonably inferred from the information in the original story ("When the man entered the kitchen, he slipped on a wet spot and broke the delicate glass pitcher when it fell on the floor."). Students who listened to stories that encouraged inferences were more likely to say that an inference was an original sentence than were students who listened to stories that did not encourage inferences.

Bower, Black, and Turner (1979) demonstrated that people will falsely recall and recognize actions that are based on the underlying scripts in a prose passage but are not actually stated in the passage. This effect increased as more passages that utilized the same script were read. Scripts, you will recall, are descriptions of our stereotyped knowledge for various commonly encountered events. Subjects in this experiment read many different stories that the experimenters assumed would elicit specific underlying scripts. When recall was tested, subjects were likely to recall unstated script actions, and, when recognition memory was tested, subjects were frequently found to falsely recognize an unstated script action.

The previous experiments provide substantial support for the constructive nature of memory, and this hypothesis, originally derived from the work of Bartlett, has gained wide support among psychologists (see Spiro, 1977, 1980). Bartlett's second hypothesis, that memory is largely reconstructive, has been more difficult to substantiate, as research reviewed in the next section suggests.

RECONSTRUCTIVE RECALL

In the previous section we saw that inferences or assumptions made when processing a verbal passage can become part of our memory for the passage. What is remembered, in other words, is partly our own construction. We assume that constructive processes are guided by schemata relevant to the topic or contents of the to-be-remembered passage. Yet schemata may have another role in remembering. Bartlett (1932) argued that recall was largely a reconstructive process. At the time of recall we are likely to remember some general impressions or perhaps the theme of the original prose passage as well as a few outstanding details. On this basis, Bartlett suggested that a memory is reconstructed. The original passage is recalled as "it must have been." In this view recall is not likely to be verbatim but will include paraphrases, inferences, and other distortions of the original passage that are consistent with the subjects' schemata. This is, of course, what Bartlett apparently found when his English subjects wrestled to reproduce the unfamiliar story of "The War of the Ghosts."

Recall was most often inaccurate in a literal sense, and an analysis of the kinds of recall errors subjects made appeared to provide evidence for reconstructive processes.

Problems with a reconstruction hypothesis

Subsequent research, however, has not been particularly supportive of Bartlett's reconstruction hypothesis. For example, many researchers have failed to observe the same degree of inaccuracy and distortion in recall as Bartlett saw (see Spiro, 1977). Further, when alterations or distortions are found, it is often difficult to determine their locus. Although a constructive hypothesis maintains that certain elements are incorporated into memory at the time of study, a reconstructive hypothesis holds that inaccuracies arise from processes operating at the time of recall. As an example of the problem in separating constructive and reconstructive processes, consider the reproduction of "The War of the Ghosts" one of Bartlett's subjects attempted. The subject recalled that one of the men in the story did not go with the others because his relations would be anxious if he did not return home. The original story does not mention that his relatives would be anxious. In the original story we hear the man say that he might be killed and his relatives do not know where he has gone. It is reasonable to infer that relatives would be anxious if the man did not return home. The subject could have made this inference when he read the passage. However, the distortion in the original passage may have occurred at the time of recall. It is possible that the subject had only a vague recollection that the man did not make the trip because his relatives did not know his whereabouts. The subject could be led to reconstruct the original story as it reasonably might have appeared—namely, that the relatives would be anxious if he did not return home. There is no way to decide on the basis of the subject's attempted reproduction whether the change was the result of processes occurring at time of study or at time of recall. However, the abundance of evidence for constructive processes in memory has led many researchers to suggest that such changes are more reasonably explained by processes at the time of study than at the time of recall.

Another problem with a reconstructive view of memory is that research has shown that whether or not evidence is obtained for reconstruction depends on how recall is requested. Hasher and Griffin (1978) asked subjects to read one of the two passages shown in Table 14-2. Each passage is an ambiguous description of either of two events. Passage A describes a man in the woods on a hunting trip or escaping from prison. Passage B describes a long voyage, either that of Columbus or an early manned space flight. All the subjects read one passage with one of the titles presented with the story.

TABLE 14-2. Ambiguous Stories Hasher and Griffin (1978) Used to Investigate Theme-Related Recall

Titles	Initial paragraph
Passage A	
Going Hunting An Escaped Convict	The man walked carefully through the forest. Several times he looked over his shoulder and scrutinized the woods behind him. He trod carefully, trying to avoid snapping the twigs and small branches that lay in his path, for he did not want to create excess noise. The gay chirping of the birds in the trees almost annoyed him, their loud calls serving to distract him. He did not want to confuse those sounds with the type he was listening for.
Passage B	
Columbus Discovers a New World First Trip to the Moon	The voyage was long and the crew was full of anticipation. No one really knew what lay beyond the new land that they were heading for. There were, of course, speculations concerning the nature of the new place, but this small group of men would be the only ones who would know the real truth. These men were participating in an event that would change the shape of history.

From "Reconstructive and Reproductive Processes in Memory," by L. Hasher and M. Griffin. In *Journal of Experimental Psychology: Human Learning and Memory,* 1978, *4,* 318–330. Copyright 1978 by the American Psychological Association. Reprinted by permission.

The experimental manipulation occurred after the subjects read the passage. In the presence of some of the subjects, the experimenter appeared to look over her records and notice that a mistake had been made, that the "wrong" title had been assigned to the passage. The subjects were told of the "mistake" and then given the "correct" (alternative) title. The purpose of this ruse was to convince the subjects that they should not rely on the original theme to help generate recall. Other subjects did not have the theme changed and therefore were presented the same theme at study and at test.

The researchers hypothesized that recall under the same-theme condition would lead to reconstructive errors in retention because subjects would reasonably rely on the theme to help them remember the passage. However, when the theme was changed, apparently through a mistake on the part of the experimenter, subjects should discard the theme when generating recall. Therefore the changed-theme subjects would make fewer reconstructive errors. In fact the researchers suggested that the changed-theme subjects would recall more of the actual material in the passage than the same-theme subjects. In other words the different theme subjects, realizing a "mistake" was made, would edit their recall carefully and also work harder to retrieve more details of the original passage because they could not use the original theme to generate recall. Both of the researchers' hypotheses were supported. Subjects in the changed-theme condition made fewer theme-related errors and recalled more of the original passage than did subjects receiving the same theme at study and test. The results indicate that subjects are capable of accurate recall of even complex events such as prose material but that whether recall is largely reconstructive or literally reproductive will depend on the demands made of the subjects when retention is tested.

The accommodative reconstruction hypothesis

Not all researchers are ready to consider reconstructive errors in retention as due merely to careless editing or overreliance on theme-related knowledge. Spiro (1977, 1980) has argued that if the conditions are right, memory will "change" to accommodate new information added after the original experience. Evidence for an "accommodative reconstruction" hypothesis comes from an interesting experiment that appears to escape the criticisms of other studies that have attempted to show reconstructive processes in memory. Subjects in Spiro's experiment were presented stories designed to tap their knowledge about how human relationships are affected by various kinds of events. The basic story described an engaged couple, Bob and Margie, and the fact that Bob did not want to have children. Two different versions of the story were constructed to provide subjects with a positive or negative expectation about the future of Bob and Margie's relationship. In one version Bob finds out that Margie also does not want children (positive expectation), and in the other version Bob finds out that she does (negative expectation).

Subjects read one of the two versions of the story. Then the experimenter casually informed the subjects that (1) Bob and Margie did get married and are living together happily or (2) Bob and Margie eventually broke off the engagement and have not seen each other since. The subsequent information about Bob and Margie is either consistent or inconsistent with expectations based on the previous story, depending on which version the subjects were presented. For example, knowing that Bob and Margie disagreed about the important issue of having children, one would not find it unreasonable for them to break off their engagement. On the other hand, that version of the story is not entirely consistent with the message that they got married. Similarly, knowing that Bob and Margie agreed about the child issue, one could reasonably expect them to get married. Less consistent with that version of the original story is the message that they broke off the engagement. According to Spiro (1980), if the accommodative reconstruction hypothesis is correct, then three types of information will be "blended" over time: details remembered from the original story, the subsequent message about Bob and Margie's present condition, and the subjects' general knowledge about interpersonal relations, courtship, and marriage. When the story and the subsequent message were "contradictory," it was hypothesized that accommodative processes would operate to increase coherence of the information presented. Specifically, recall errors in the contradictory conditions were expected to show reconciliation of the conflicting information. For example, the disagreement about children may be remembered as less severe than it really was when subjects later learned that Bob and Margie got married.

The results tended to support the accommodative reconstruction hypothesis. Accommodative errors occurred almost exclusively in the contradictory condition and the errors were in the direction of reconciliation of the conflicting information. This occurred even though subjects were told explicitly to recall as best they could and avoid giving personal reactions or feelings about the story. Accommodative errors also increased with time, with more errors observed after a three-week retention interval than after a two-day interval. Examples of recall errors that attempted to reconcile the original information are "They separated but realized after discussing the matter that their love mattered more" and "She was only a little upset at the disagreement" (Spiro, 1980, p. 91). Spiro (1980) obtained these results only when subjects believed that the purpose of the experiment was to investigate people's reactions to interpersonal relationships and not in the context of a standard memory experiment. Spiro argued that conventional laboratory studies of memory will not tend to reveal accommodative reconstruction because subjects usually isolate material learned in a memory experiment from their own general knowledge. Only when an experimental situation was created such that subjects were encouraged to use their general knowledge of the situation was evidence for accommodative reconstruction obtained. Further, the recall errors of subjects receiving conflicting information were not apparently fabrications or guesses based on theme-related information. When subjects in the conflicting conditions were asked to indicate their confidence that the remembered statements were actually part of the original story, statements indicative of accommodative errors were accorded at least as much confidence as were statements actually from the passage. In other words, the subjects were apparently confident that they were remembering the passage as originally presented. Under certain conditions a memory can be "changed" in order to accommodate new information. Before examining some of the possible implications of this view of memory, we will look at another situation and series of experiments that have also led researchers to conclude that memory can be changed as a consequence of new information.

Reconstruction in eyewitness reporting

It's usually over very quickly. Our attention is often drawn to it by a loud noise or unusual sight or sound. Later someone is apt to ask us what happened. We are talking about an event to which we are an "eyewitness." It may be a car accident, an apparent crime, or simply an everyday event we happened to observe. Our ability to remember details of the event may be critical in determining who was present and under what conditions the event occurred. Many times eyewitness reports have significant consequences for someone, as when a person is placed at the scene of a crime or the responsibility for a traffic accident is assigned. But just how good is our memory in these situations? In other words, what kind of eyewitness are we likely to be?

An interesting series of experiments performed by Loftus and her associates at the University of Washington has provided important and often surprising answers to these questions (Loftus, 1975, 1977, 1979b, 1979c; Loftus, Miller, & Burns, 1978; Loftus & Palmer, 1974). Her results also have provided evidence for reconstructive processes in remembering. The general methodology of the Loftus experiments is as follows. Subjects view an event such as a film of a car accident. They are then asked specific questions about what happened. An experimental variable is introduced at the time the subjects are questioned— that is, after they have viewed the event. Loftus has been chiefly interested in how information introduced after an event affects what people say they remember of the event. Consider the following experiment.

Loftus and Palmer (1974) showed that the wording of a question can influence what observers report about an event they have witnessed. In one experiment college students viewed a series of films, each depicting a traffic accident. After each film the students were asked to provide an account of what had happened and to answer specific questions in the form of a questionnaire provided by the experimenter. One of the questions was of particular interest. It asked about the speed the cars were traveling when the accident occurred. The general form of the question asked of all students was "How fast were the cars going when they _____ each other?" For different groups of students the missing word was one of the following: *smashed, collided, bumped, hit,* or *contacted.* The investigators found that the students' estimates of speed depended on the verb used in the question. The average speed reported by students reading *smashed* was 40.8 mph. Students seeing the exact same events but reading *contacted* reported that the cars were going 31.8 mph. Clearly, these results have important implications for the way an eyewitness is questioned. The results also suggest that our memory may be changed by information added after an event. Loftus and Palmer (1974) concluded that varying the nature of the verb in the question caused the subjects to remember the event as being more (or less) severe than it really was. In other words, they suggested that people's memory for an event was altered in accord with the information supplied by the verb in the sentence.

If memory is actually altered as a consequence of the phrasing of the question, then subjects might be expected to "remember" other things that are in line with this "new" memory. A second experiment by Loftus and Palmer

(1974) tested this possibility. They asked students to view a film of a multiple-car accident. The accident lasted about 4 seconds. As in the previous study, the students were asked to describe in their own words what happened and then to answer specific questions provided by the experimenter. Two groups of students were asked about speed of the cars. One group was asked using the verb *smashed;* the other group was asked using the verb *hit*. A third group of students did not receive a question about speed. All the students were dismissed and asked to return 1 week later. The critical question was presented on a second questionnaire given to the subjects when they returned. The question was "Did you see any broken glass?" There was actually no broken glass in the accident. As in the previous experiment, subjects gave different estimates of speed depending on the verb used: *smashed,* 10.46 mph; *hit,* 8.00 mph. The probability of saying yes to the question about broken glass also varied with the verb used. Of the subjects asked one week earlier about speed using the verb *smashed,* 32% said they saw glass. Only 14% of the subjects asked using the verb *hit* said they saw glass, and 12% of the subjects not receiving any question about speed answered the glass question positively. The investigators concluded that information added after the event—for example, the fact that the accident was one in which cars "smashed" together—produced a shift in the subject's memory in the direction of being more similar to the event the verb suggested. When cars smash together, broken glass can be expected. The students apparently remembered it that way.

In another set of experiments, Loftus (1975) showed that questions containing false presuppositions about an event can also influence what subjects say they remember. After viewing a traffic accident, subjects were asked "How fast was the white sports car going when it passed the barn while traveling along the country road?" There was in fact no barn in the film. One week later subjects who were asked this misleading question were more likely to say they remembered a barn than subjects who were not asked a question with the false presupposition. Another experiment demonstrated that even a direct question such as "Did you see a barn?" had an effect on what people said they remembered a week later. People who had been merely asked about whether an object was present were more likely to say they remembered that object than those not asked about the object.

According to Loftus, information added after the event literally changes the original memory. What is remembered is reconstructed on the basis of details that are remembered and information that has been since integrated with the original memory. Yet there is an alternative explanation for what we have seen so far, as perhaps you have detected. How do we know that subjects in these experiments are not simply conforming to the demands of the experimental situation? Suppose the subject, when asked about a barn in the film containing no barn, does not actually remember seeing a barn but does remember that the experimenter asked about one? This subject may respond that a barn was present even though he or she does not actually remember one. In a more recent series of experiments Loftus and her associates presented more convincing evidence that memory is actually altered, and they also designed an experiment to answer critics who say that subjects are merely conforming to the experimental situation.

Loftus, Miller, and Burns (1978) also asked subjects to witness a car accident and they also presented misleading information in the form of a question. In this experiment the events to be witnessed were on a sequence of 30 slides, which included pictures of a red Datsun hitting a pedestrian after turning at an intersection. Half the subjects in this experiment saw the car stopped at a stop sign before hitting the pedestrian. The other half saw the car stopped at a yield sign. After they viewed the slides, the subjects were given a series of questions. For half the subjects one of the questions was the following: "Did another car pass the red Datsun while it was stopped at the stop sign?" The other half received a similar question but it mentioned a yield sign. Remember that half the students actually saw a yield sign and half saw a stop sign. The critical question was presented so that half the subjects received consistent information (they saw a yield sign and the question mentioned a yield sign) and half the subjects got inconsistent information (subjects saw a yield sign and the question mentioned a stop sign).

Twenty minutes later the subjects were given a forced-choice recognition memory test. The test consisted of pairs of slides. Each pair contained one slide the subjects actually saw and another slide closely resembling the original scene. The critical pair showed a red Datsun stopped at the intersection at a stop sign and a red Datsun stopped at a yield sign. When the earlier question had presented consistent information (stop sign seen and stop sign mentioned), the subjects chose the correct slide 75% of the time when viewing the critical recognition pair. When the earlier question gave misleading information, only 41% of the students selected the correct slide. Given that the students were asked to select the scene that they actually remembered seeing, this result is rather convincing evidence that some of the subjects remembered the scene in accord with the information that was added after they viewed the original scene.

It is still possible, though, that subjects are conforming to the experimental situation and responding in a way that is cued by the experimental procedure. That is, subjects asked a question mentioning a stop sign may select a slide showing a stop sign, particularly if they are not really sure what the original sign was. To eliminate this alternative explanation for their results, the researchers carried out another experiment that was similar to the first but that gave subjects the chance to detect the experimental manipulation. After answering the questionnaire and receiving either consistent or misleading information, all subjects were told that some people had received a questionnaire that contained a question designed to make people believe they saw a different sign than had been presented. Subjects were invited to indicate whether the questionnaire they had received had the misleading item. Subjects, in other words, were asked to determine whether the questionnaire they had been given contained misleading or consistent information. The researchers reported that only 12% of the subjects receiving misleading information decided that they had indeed been given misleading information. Almost 90% of the subjects receiving misleading information felt that the information given them was consistent with what they remembered. These results, together with the results from the recognition memory experiment, provide convincing evidence that memory is altered by the addition of new information. This idea is consistent with the accommodative reconstruction hypothesis offered by Spiro (1980), which was discussed previously and, as we will see in the next section, challenges some popular views about the permanence of information stored in memory.

IS MEMORY PERMANENT?

None of us would deny the fact of forgetting. Information once learned can often, at a later time, not be recalled. However, we have seen on more than one occasion in this text (especially in Chapters 6 and 10) that forgetting need not mean that an event is no longer stored in memory. It is possible that a presently unrecallable event will, on a later test, when perhaps different retrieval cues are present, be recallable. Is it possible that *all* information we have learned is stored in the brain, that memory is actually permanent?

Two psychologists at the University of Washington recently conducted an informal survey of 169 people from all over the United States to determine what they thought about this issue. Loftus and Loftus (1980, p. 410) asked individuals with formal training in psychology and people without any psychology background (including lawyers and taxicab drivers) to say which of the following two statements best represented their views about human memory.

1. Everything we learn is permanently stored in the mind, although sometimes particular details are not accessible. With hypnosis, or other special techniques, these inaccessible details could eventually be recovered.

2. Some details that we learn may be permanently lost from memory. Such details would never be able to be recovered by hypnosis, or any other special technique, because these details are simply no longer there.

Loftus and Loftus (1980, p. 410) found that 84% of the 75 psychologists questioned agreed with the first statement; 14% agreed with the second statement;

and 2% gave some other answer. Sixty-nine percent of the nonpsychologists agreed with the first statement; 23% agreed with the second statement; and 8% were noncommittal. A sizable majority of both psychologists and nonpsychologists believed that memory is permanent.

What were the reasons for their choice? Most people opting for a permanent memory hypothesis mentioned the fact that they had experiences in which something had apparently been forgotten but was recovered spontaneously or was triggered by the right set of circumstances. Many persons with psychology training also mentioned the work of the neurosurgeon Wilder Penfield (see Penfield & Roberts, 1959). Penfield has published accounts of individuals who appeared to remember events long forgotten when brain stimulation was applied to parts of the temporal lobe. Penfield operated on epileptic patients whose conditions were serious enough that damaged areas of the brain had to be surgically excised to lessen the severity of their illness. In order to localize the damaged area, Penfield probed the surface of the cortex with a mild electric current prior to making an excision. Patients were conscious and capable of conversation with the surgeon during the operation. Penfield found that when certain areas of the temporal lobe were stimulated, the patients reported what appeared to be memories of past events. Penfield's procedure and results are widely cited in the psychology literature and often discussed in introductory psychology textbooks. One interpretation is that the brain acts like a "video-recorder" to store permanently all that is experienced. Only the right "switch" needs to be found to reveal what is stored in memory.

The respondents to the questionnaire also mentioned other reasons for believing in a permanent memory, including the apparent recovery of memory through hypnosis or psychoanalysis. Yet Loftus and Loftus (1980) are quite skeptical about the evidence for a permanent memory, including that presented by Penfield. They pointed out that Penfield himself admitted to obtaining evidence of "memory recovery" in only 40 out of the 1132 patients who were tested. Further, when these 40 cases are examined closely, Loftus and Loftus argue that the reported "memories" look more like reconstructions of an event. A similar reaction to these reports was given by Neisser (1967, p. 169) some years ago: "In short, the *content* of these experiences is not surprising in any way. It seems entirely comparable to the content of dreams, which are generally admitted to be synthetic constructions and not literal recalls. Penfield's work tells us nothing new about memory."

Loftus and Loftus (1980) also point out that there is evidence to indicate that under hypnosis people will construct memories merely to please the hypnotist. They describe an experiment (see Putnam, 1979) in which subjects viewed an automobile accident, then were hypnotized and asked to describe what happened in the original situation. The experimenter found that hypnotized individuals were more likely to be influenced by leading questions than people who were not hypnotized. As regards the often spontaneous or prompted recovery of memory that we all have experienced, Loftus and Loftus remind us that because one or even many memories are recovered does not necessarily imply that all memories can be recovered.

Despite the widespread belief in the permanence of memory, Loftus and Loftus find all the evidence lacking. Further, as you have seen in this chapter, there appears to be evidence for the contrary opinion, that memory is *not* permanent and that it is changed as a consequence of adding new information. The question will surely be debated for some years to come.

Summary

The English psychologist, Bartlett (1932), found that recall of prose material was rarely accurate in a literal sense and that successive reproductions of a story assumed a stereotyped form. His results provide evidence for an effect of prior knowledge on remembering and for both constructive and reconstructive processes in memory. Bartlett originally described our knowledge in terms of memory schemata. Contemporary researchers have attempted more precise definitions of the types of knowledge we might have and have introduced concepts such as scripts and frames.

The influence of prior knowledge on comprehension and remembering was nicely revealed in experiments by Bransford and Johnson (1972). They asked subjects to read a series of individually meaningful sentences describing a particular topic, for instance, washing clothes. Subjects who did not know the topic beforehand rated the passage as more difficult to comprehend and remembered significantly less of it than subjects who knew the topic before reading the passage. That degree of prior knowledge is related to performance on a memory test was also shown when retention of baseball information was compared for high- and low-baseball knowledge subjects. Analyses of recall for individuals of differing degrees of knowledge provide important information as to the way information is represented in memory.

Constructive and reconstructive processes are difficult to distinguish experimentally because similar errors in recall are expected on the basis of both these processes. In addition, research has shown that whether evidence for reconstruction or literal reproduction is obtained depends on how retention is tested. Recently, however, evidence has been found for accommodative reconstruction when subjects are presented information that conflicts with their generalized knowledge of the situation. Other evidence that memory might be "changed" by subsequent information comes from an interesting series of experiments conducted by Loftus. She showed that information added after a complex event has been witnessed can cause serious distortions in subjects' memory for that event. These results seem to contradict the apparently widely held view that memory is permanent.

In the past 10 to 15 years psychologists have turned increasing attention to our memory for meaningful kinds of events, such as memory for prose material or real-life scenes that are part of eyewitness reports. The results of these studies will have important implications for understanding how such information is represented in memory and may also have important practical consequences, as in the planning of curricula, presentation of prose material for learning and retention, and such critical activities as eyewitness testimony.

Recommendations for further reading

We recommended that all students of memory at some time read the classic work of Ebbinghaus (1885/1964), and we must recommend equally strongly that they read the work of Bartlett (1932). Bartlett's views are the starting point for most modern discussions of our memory for prose material. Contemporary models of cognitive structures, including descriptions of schemata, scripts, and frames, are found in many recently published volumes. An excellent introduction to this important area is *The Structure of Human Memory,* edited by Cofer (1976). Also informative are more advanced discussions found in Shaw and Bransford's (1977) *Perceiving, Acting and Knowing* and in Bobrow and Collins's (1975) *Representation and Understanding: Studies in Cognitive Science.* A frame theory is outlined by Minsky (1975), and a lengthy article by Bower, Black, and Turner (1979) provides an important demonstration of the role of scripts in our memory for meaningful material. Loftus's (1979a) *Eyewitness Testimony* offers a valuable lesson in the application of research on human memory to this very important problem. Finally, a recent article by Loftus and Loftus (1980) is a highly readable description of the controversial question of whether memory is permanent.

15

Individual Differences in Remembering

Introduction/overview

All of us have wondered at one time or another why our performance on a test of memory—a class examination, for example—was not as good as someone else's. We are, in other words, aware that there are likely to be wide individual differences associated with performance on cognitive tasks. Differences in performance are not only readily visible; they are sometimes the source of some embarrassment or discomfort, as when we miss the cutoff for a grade or fail to achieve some other form of recognition, such as a scholarship. Despite this apparent familiarity with human variation, students of learning and memory are frequently shocked to see the extent of individual differences within the data collected in a laboratory study investigating these processes. One reason for this surprise is that we are used to dealing with averages or overall proportions or percentages. Should you refer back to any of the numerous figures showing the results of memory experiments in this book, you will likely find that only the mean performance or overall proportion correct is shown. This emphasis on the "typical" performance in a group often leads us to overlook individual differences and even to assume falsely that everyone scored at or around the mean. Interest in performance among groups of individuals versus interest in individual variation within these groups has actually been somewhat separate within psychology.

Not too long ago scientific psychology was characterized as comprising two separate disciplines (Chronbach, 1957). One discipline was experimental psychology, a method of studying behavior and mental processes under rigidly controlled conditions. A treatment is introduced and its effect on some dependent variable is measured. Results are generally reported in terms of the mean or average performance of groups representing various levels of a particular treatment variable. A major goal of the experimental psychologist is finding general laws of behavior. This form of inquiry is frequently called nomothetic research, which means that statements of wide generality (universals) are sought.

The other discipline was identified as correlational psychology. This branch of scientific psychology also goes under the names of psychometrics, differential psychology, and individual psychology. Often concerned with test construction or developmental issues, psychologists in this discipline seek to account for those differences that the experimental psychologist has often tended to ignore. The experimental psychologist is generally interested in variation between groups. Individual differences in this approach can be a source of annoyance. Statistically, individual variation is represented as "error variance," and sizable amounts of it can reduce the chances of finding a statistically significant result in an experiment. Psychologists in the other discipline are interested in variation within groups. That is, their concern is with individual differences. Increasingly, the two disciplines are recognized as complementary. This is nowhere clearer than in the study of human learning and memory (see Carroll & Maxwell, 1979; Hunt, 1978; Osborne, Noble, & Weyl, 1978; Underwood, 1975). The growing partnership between these traditionally distinct disciplines is aimed at identifying fundamental processes in learning and memory through the study of individual differences (see Carroll & Maxwell, 1979). It is hoped the byproduct of this approach will be a better understanding of individual aptitudes and abilities and a strengthening of nomothetic theories.

In this chapter we examine the degree of individual variation likely to be found in learning and memory tests. Then we briefly review some of the possible sources of these differences in performance. Part of this discussion will take the form of reminding you of previous lessons you have learned while reading about the research reported in this book. In this chapter we also look more extensively at individual differences as they occur in two important areas of research: the investigations of memory span performance and of memory performance as a function of aging. Memory span is usually measured as part of standard intelligence tests, and there is some evidence that this particular test of memory reflects certain basic cognitive processes.

In the last section of this chapter we look at how an investigation of individual differences might help to construct a nomothetic theory. Having come nearly to the end of this survey of research and theory about human memory, perhaps you are ready to present a theory of your own. Information in this final section will help you with that task.*

INDIVIDUAL DIFFERENCES IN LABORATORY LEARNING AND MEMORY TASKS

The extent to which individual differences are present in laboratory tasks of learning and memory is illustrated by the results of a mammoth investigation carried out by Underwood, Boruch, and Malmi (1978) of Northwestern University. Over a two-year period these researchers advertised for undergraduate volunteers to serve as laboratory subjects in a learning and memory experiment. The volunteers were paid for their services, as well they should have been because they were asked to participate in ten 50-minute sessions spread over a 2-week period. Two hundred students volunteered for the experiment. During the experimental sessions each student was presented 24 different learning and memory tasks, including many of the tasks we have discussed in this book. A major purpose of this project was to look for possible correlations between performance on the many tasks. Would someone who is good at paired-associate learning also be good at serial learning? We will concern ourselves only with individual performance *within* these tasks.

Summary statistics obtained on seven of the tasks these investigators used are found in Table 15-1. You should recognize all these tasks from your reading of earlier chapters. With each task you will find a description of the dependent variable as well as two measures of central tendency (mean and median) and two measures of variation (range and standard deviation). The range identifies the difference between highest and lowest scores on a particular test; the standard deviation approximates the average distance of the scores from the mean. Because performance variation is most easily seen when results are presented pictorially, as in a frequency graph, we have presented the distribution of scores obtained for one of the tasks, that of free recall, in Figure 15-1. The results found in Table 15-1, together with the graphic presentation of free-recall scores in Figure 15-1, should help you to appreciate the extent to which individual

---

*Other than Chapter 1, this is the only chapter in the book that does not include a detailed description of an experimental demonstration. Any of the tasks described in previous chapters may be usefully employed to study individual differences in memory performance. In addition, the memory span task, which has often been associated with the study of individual differences, is described in some detail in the text of this chapter. A variation on the usual memory span task was also used to demonstrate the Hebb effect in Chapter 5.

differences in performance are present in laboratory tests of learning and memory. As you can see in Figure 15-1, even within this relatively homogeneous college population, free-recall performance yielded a nearly perfect "normal" distribution. However, not all the distributions obtained from these tasks were so symmetrical. In fact, performance was sometimes quite skewed (scores tending to be "bunched" at either the upper or lower regions of the scale).

One cannot help asking why scores vary so much. What causes one individual to remember only 4 words from a 24-item list presented for free recall and another to remember 18 from the same list? Potential sources of individual differences in remembering are the topic of the following discussion.

TABLE 15-1. Individual Differences on Standard Laboratory Learning and Memory Tasks

Task	Dependent variable	Mean	Median	Range	Standard deviation
Paired-associate learning	Number correct on a 12-pair list averaged over several study-test trials.	9.50	10.05	10.00	1.84
Serial learning	Number correct on 12-item serial list using the study-test method.	8.56	8.98	9.00	1.87
Verbal discrimination learning	Number correct on a single study-test sequence of 24 pairs.	20.30	20.67	10.25	2.16
Free recall	Number of words correctly recalled from 24-item list.	11.48	11.18	15.00	2.73
Digit span	Total number correct digits recalled from 8 strings of lengths 6, 7, 8, and 9 (see text).	222.10	225.00	70.00	15.52
Situational frequency judgments	Judgments of the number of times a word appeared in a lengthy word list were correlated with actual frequency. The correlations were transformed to z scores.	1.34	1.38	1.82	0.33
Recognition memory	Errors (misses plus false alarms) made in a continuous recognition memory task.	14.40	13.65	44.50	6.69

Note: Based on performance of 200 college students at a large midwestern university (see Underwood, Boruch, & Malmi, 1978). Data provided by Underwood.

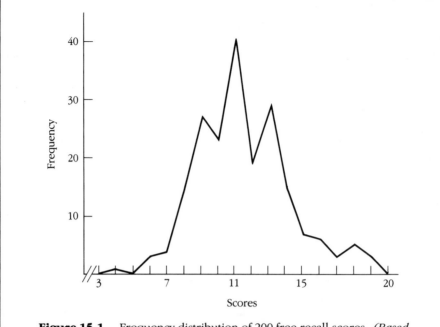

Figure 15-1. Frequency distribution of 200 free-recall scores. *(Based on data supplied by Underwood and on "Composition of Episodic Memory," by B. J. Underwood, R. F. Boruch, and R. A. Malmi. In Journal of Experimental Psychology: General, 1978, 107, 393–419. Used by permission.)*

Sources of individual differences

Individual differences in remembering are hypothesized to arise from four sources:

1. basic (mechanistic) processes,
2. knowledge of voluntary encoding strategies,
3. degree of topic-related knowledge, and
4. metamemory.

These categories are similar to those proposed by Flavell and Wellman (1977) to describe memory phenomena in general (see Chapter 11). They are also similar to those categories identified by Hunt (1978) as sources of variation in human cognition. He attributed individual differences in cognition to differences in mechanistic capability, knowledge, and the use of general information-processing techniques. The present organization suggests that two kinds of knowledge be distinguished: that associated with efficient encoding strategies, including mnemonics, and that of the topic or domain containing the to-be-remembered information. The fourth category, metamemory, is similar to what Hunt (1978) intended as his third source of individual variation. Hunt (1978) gives as an example the strategies of repeating names in order to remember them and of checking an answer after it has been developed but before publicly announcing it. These kinds of activities are associated with what has been called metamemory (see Chapter 11).

The most basic or mechanistic memory processes are those governing recognizing a stimulus, processing meaning, and holding, accessing, and manipulating information (see Hunt, 1978). Laboratory tasks designed to measure such capabilities show wide amounts of individual differences. For example, Hunt, Lunneborg, and Lewis (1975; see also Hunt, Frost, & Lunneborg, 1973) found that students identified as "high verbal" were superior to students classified as "low verbal" on a variety of information-processing tasks. Verbal ability was defined by performance on standard paper and pencil verbal aptitude tests. These tasks involved basic cognitive processes such as symbol recognition and manipulation and processing the meaning of sentences.

Variation in these basic processes may be expected on the basis of both "innate" and experiential factors. You have already been introduced to one individual whose unique memory ability was undoubtedly due to certain innate properties. The rich visual imagination of Luria's subject, and the synesthesia he experienced, were clearly not the product of experience (see Chapter 13). We can only speculate as to the source of his abilities. Although the subject could have inherited his talent, Luria's (1968) record of this individual gives us no evidence of this. We are told only that his father owned a bookstore and that his brothers and sisters were "conventional, well-balanced types" and "some were gifted individuals" (p. 8). It is conceivable that his unusual memory was related to brain abnormality or even brain pathology. For example, eidetic imagery (popularly referred to as "photographic memory") has been linked to brain injury (Gray & Gummerman, 1975).

Certain memory-related abilities may be biologically determined in the general population. For instance, females often do better than males on tests emphasizing verbal abilities; males tend to do better than females on tests of spatial ability (see Maccoby & Jacklin, 1974). There are many possible explanations for these differences, not the least of which are sociocultural factors that encourage development of different abilities in the two sexes. Nevertheless, there is some evidence to suggest that the brains of males and females are differentially organized for these cognitive tasks (see Witelson, 1976). It is known that the two hemispheres of the brain are differentially specialized for certain cognitive tasks, with most individuals showing left-hemisphere specialization for verbal abilities (speech and language processing) and right-hemisphere specialization for spatial abilities (shape and picture recognition) (Corballis & Beale, 1976; Nebes, 1974). Sex differences in the pattern and rate of maturation of cerebral specialization have been suggested (Levy & Levy, 1978; Waber, 1976). Therefore it is possible that differences in degree of brain lateralization may account for some of the verbal-spatial inequalities in male and female performance (McGee, 1979).

Differences in basic cognitive processes should not, however, be thought of as biologically fixed. Consider the fact that a beginning reader will be slower to recognize and process the meaning of a word than an experienced reader. Certain cognitive tasks, such as recognizing the meaning of a word, are the result of many hours of practice and many different kinds of experience. We should not overlook the role of extensive practice in individuals capable of exceptional cognitive processing. "Expert" abilities of any kind are likely to reflect a degree of experience and practice that is simply beyond the determination or interest of most of us. For example, the English psychologist Hunter (1978) has studied for many years the performance of "lightning calculators." These individuals are "experts" at performing mental calculations. They do numerical calculations at an astonishing rate. Consider the response of one lightning calculator Hunter (1978, p. 34) tested. He was asked how he quickly determined the decimal equivalent of the fraction 1/851:

> The instant observation was that 851 is 23 times 37. I use this fact as follows: 1/37 is 0.027027027 and so on repeated. This I divide mentally by 23. 23 into 0.027 is 0.001 with remainder 4. In a flash I can get that 23 into 4027 is 175 with remainder 2. And into 2027 is 88 with remainder 3. And into 3027 is 131 with remainder 14. And even into 14027 is 609 with remainder 20. And so on like that. Also, before I even start this, I know that there is a recurring period of sixty-six places.

As Hunter (1978) points out, these mental wizards acquired their skills only after years of experience and practice. His examination of the social history of three such expert calculators showed that they had each found an enjoyment and thrill working with numbers at an early stage and had spent years developing their competence. These individuals may have certain innate capabilities that fostered this interest and rewarded their effort, but, as you will see later in this chapter, extensive practice can lead to exceptional performance on a memory task.

Sources of individual differences arising from the three remaining categories listed at the beginning of this section have been documented by the research reviewed in previous chapters. Voluntary encoding strategies and their effect on retention were the major topics of Chapters 4 (rehearsal), 12 (levels of processing), and 13 (mnemonics). In Chapter 14 you saw the effect of prior knowledge on retention, and experiments contrasting high- and low-knowledge subjects were discussed. The topic of metamemory was discussed in Chapter 11. A major conclusion of that discussion was that differences between good and poor learners often depend on differences in metamemory skills.

In the next section we will examine individual differences in one of the most frequently performed tests of retention: measurement of an individual's memory span. Each of the four major sources of individual differences we have identified has at one time or another been implicated in the performance variation seen on this relatively simple task.

Individual differences in memory span

Very few individuals, when asked to recall a string of unrelated items, can remember in order more than ten of them. The average ordered recall of adult subjects is likely to be about seven items, a fact Miller (1956, p. 91) called to our attention: "Everybody knows that there is a finite span of immediate memory and that for a lot of different kinds of test material this span is about seven items in length."

Actually, there is substantial variation in memory span performance both among individuals and for different classes of to-be-remembered items. The average adult digit span is about eight (Chi, 1976), with 90% of the adult population able to recall at least five digits but not more than eight (Matarazzo, 1972). Adult digit span is about twice that of a 5-year-old. Memory span of adults is generally less than eight when the to-be-remembered items are letters or words. Word span decreases as the length of the to-be-remembered words increases (Baddeley, Thomson, & Buchanan, 1975) and is greater for high-frequency words than for low-frequency words (Watkins, 1977). And, as we saw in Chapter 3, the extent to which the to-be-remembered items form "chunks" is also an important factor in determining how much will be remembered in a memory span task.

Estimates of a person's memory span will also vary depending on the method used to measure it. A traditional definition of memory span is the number of items whose probability of ordered recall after a single presentation is .50. Memory span, in other words, is the number of items that can be successfully recalled on at least half the occasions that particular number of items is presented. To determine memory span using this definition, many strings of items, each of several different lengths, must be presented. One method of presenting strings is to increase the number of to-be-remembered items by one when recall is successful and to decrease the number by one when recall fails. This procedure continues until performance stabilizes at about the 50% level (see Watkins, 1977).

In practice there are many different ways to measure performance on a memory span task (see Woodworth & Schlosberg, 1954, for a discussion of one popular method). For example, the digit span test that is part of the Wechsler

Adult Intelligence Scale (WAIS) measures both forward and backward recall. Forward recall is tested by first presenting a string of three digits for recall, next a string of four digits, and so forth, until the subject fails to remember perfectly the order of the digits in the string. After the subject fails to recall a particular string, another string of the same length is given. If the subject is successful on this second attempt, the length of the string is increased by one and testing continues. If the second try is also missed, the subject's span is recorded as one less than the number of digits in the twice-failed string length. A similar method is used to test backward digit span, with subjects instructed to recall the digits in the reverse order in which they were given. Backward recall is much more difficult than forward recall. About 90% of the adult population can recall only four to six digits backwards (Matarazzo, 1972). An individual's score for the digit span component of the WAIS is the sum of the longest strings that could be recalled perfectly on the forward and backward tests (Wechsler, 1955).

Digits are often presented auditorily when memory span is measured. A typical presentation rate is 1 digit per second. However, presentation can be visual and the rate is sometimes as fast as 2 digits per second. Chiang and Atkinson (1976) reported that the average digit span of 34 Stanford University students (17 males and 17 females) was 7.3 (SD = .9), with individual performance ranging from 5.3 to 9.3. They presented items visually on a computer-controlled screen at the rate of 1 digit per second. First a string of 4 digits was presented, then a string of 6, followed by strings of 8, 10, and 12 digits. Each student was presented many different 5-string sets (4, 6, 8, 10, 12). To compute memory span, the longest string recalled perfectly in each 5-string set was determined. An individual's span was reported as the average of these perfectly correct strings across all the 5-string sets.

The extent to which individuals differ in memory span performance, even within a relatively homogenous college population, is revealed in the data of the Northwestern study referred to earlier. Memory span was measured by presenting visually strings of digits to small groups of subjects. Rate of presentation was 2 digits per second. Following practice on six strings of 5 digits, subjects were shown 8 strings of 6, 7, 8, and 9 digits. The number of correctly recalled digits for all 32 strings (8 strings times 4 different lengths) was determined. Performance could vary from zero to 240 (every digit in every string placed in the correct serial position). The distribution of scores when performance was measured in this way is shown in Figure 15-2. (The summary statistics associated with memory span performance are found in Table 15-1.) Forty-seven of the 200 students tested (23.5%) performed perfectly on all 32 strings. Yet, as you can see, there was considerable variation in memory span ability. Using a similar procedure but testing recall of unrelated letters rather than digits, the investigators found memory span performance to be lower and fewer students

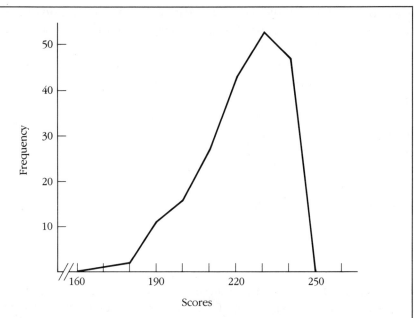

Figure 15-2.   Frequency distribution of 200 scores on a memory span task. *(Based on data supplied by Underwood and on "Composition of Episodic Memory," by B. J. Underwood, R. F. Boruch, and R. A. Malmi. In* Journal of Experimental Psychology: General, *1978, 107, 393–419. Used by permission.)*

(14.5%) capable of perfect performance on all strings. An analysis of memory span errors revealed that for all lengths and for both digits and letters errors were most frequently made on the next to the last item in the string (see also Chiang & Atkinson, 1976).

How are we to explain individual variation in memory span performance? We previously rejected the idea that memory span is a pure measure of the capacity of primary memory (see Chapter 3). You may recall that memory span performance is generally acknowledged to represent the product of both primary and secondary memory processes (see also Craik, 1968; Watkins, 1977). Therefore the number of items one might recall in a memory span task will necessarily be greater than the number that might represent strictly primary memory processes.

One widely held view is that individual memory span differences are due largely to processing strategy differences, such as rehearsal or chunking or grouping the to-be-remembered items (see Huttenlocher & Burke, 1976). Such a view would explain the large developmental differences in memory span performance as due to the emergence with age of these active encoding strategies (Belmont & Butterfield, 1971). The memory span of a 2½-year-old is about two items; that of a 16-year-old is seven to eight items (Huttenlocher & Burke, 1976). We have already noted that developmental differences on various memory tasks can often be explained by the fact that children are less aware of and less likely to perform various encoding activities, such as rehearsal, than are adults (see Chapters 4 and 11).

If differences in encoding strategies are mainly responsible for differences in memory span performance, then memory span would reasonably be expected to increase with practice. Several experiments have in fact found practice effects in a memory span task. One of the first was that of Gates and Taylor (1925), who compared the memory span of two groups of kindergarten children matched on various characteristics, including initial memory span performance. One group of these 4- and 5-year-olds was subsequently given 78 days of practice recalling digits. Digits were presented orally, and on each practice day a child was tested by beginning with a string that was shorter than the longest string recalled on the previous day. Several strings at each length were presented until the child failed in two of three attempts. The children receiving training increased their span an average of 2.07 digits, from an average of 4.33 to an average of 6.40 digits. The memory span of children in the unpracticed control group increased only an average of .73 digits, from 4.33 to 5.06, in the same time period. It is interesting to note that when the two groups were retested a little more than 4 months later, the trained group had lost its advantage over the untrained group. Although the researchers attributed the trained subjects' gains to "special techniques and mnemonic aids" (Gates & Taylor, 1925, p. 591), they were forced to admit the effects were transitory.

Under certain conditions adult subjects' memory span performance can change dramatically as a function of practice. Chase and Ericsson (1978, 1979; Ericsson, Chase, & Faloon, 1980) investigated the effect of extended practice on the memory span performance of several individuals. After 6 months of practice one subject increased his memory span from 7 digits to 38 digits, and following a year and a half of practice his memory span was almost 80 digits. Practice generally involved several hour-long sessions each week. Digits were presented auditorily at the rate of 1 per second with the length of a string determined by performance on the previous string. After perfect recall the string size was increased by one; following a mistake the string size was decreased by one. This individual was apparently able to increase his memory span by using various mnemonic techniques. He happened to be a long-distance runner and reported that he remembered short series of numbers by associating the numbers with the times of various races, such as the half mile, the marathon, and so forth. To remember 3492, he thought of "3 minutes and 49 point 2 seconds, near world-record mile time." He also associated numbers with dates, as 1944, "near the end of World War II," or with people's ages (893 was coded as "89 point 3, very old man"). In addition he developed a complex retrieval system using a hierarchical organization that permitted him to recall digits from various "levels" in the hierarchy (Ericsson, Chase, & Faloon, 1980, p. 1181).

To see whether the extended practice with digits had an effect on memory span performance in general, Chase and Ericsson (1978) switched their subject from recalling digits to recalling letters after 3 months of practice. Although his memory span for digits had improved substantially by this time, his memory span for letters immediately dropped to about six. The various encoding strategies he had developed to aid digit recall apparently could not be easily transferred to letters. Nevertheless, the findings based on this one individual suggest that with enough practice and by using appropriate mnemonics and a good retrieval system, truly impressive increases in retention are possible.

Chase and Ericsson (1978) also compared their subject's recall of a 50-digit matrix with the performance level of Luria's (1968) famous subject on the same task. Luria's subject relied primarily on visual imagery to perform his memory feats. The individual studied by Chase and Ericsson, following approximately 150 hours of practice, performed as well as Luria's subject had on the 50-digit matrix. His ability to recall apparently rested on his mnemonic technique of converting numbers into "running times" and not on the use of visual imagery. These results support Hunter's (1978) conclusion that mental "experts" come to their abilities largely through extensive practice.

Despite the fact that memory span may be shown to increase with practice, results of several recent investigations do *not* support the hypothesis that differences normally seen in memory span performance are completely explained by subject-controlled encoding strategies. Consider the hypothesis that memory span increases with age due to a concomitant increase in the ability to carry out rehearsal or to organize the to-be-remembered items. Huttenlocher and Burke (1976) reasoned that if this hypothesis was correct, two things should happen. First, differences in rehearsal should be reflected in the shape of the serial position curve that accompanies memory span performance. The primacy effect in recall is generally attributed to greater rehearsal of items from the beginning than from the middle or end of the list (see Chapter 4). Huttenlocher and Burke argued that a greater tendency to rehearse among older than younger children would be evidenced by differences in the primacy effect found in the recall of these different age groups. Second, if developmental differences in memory span are the result of subject-imposed grouping of the to-be-remembered items, experimenter-imposed grouping should have greater consequences for younger than for older children. Grouping the digits during presentation—for example, by introducing a short pause between groups of digits—is known to facilitate memory span performance relative to ungrouped presentation (Bower and Winzenz, 1969; Wickelgren, 1964). Because the organizational hypothesis says that older subjects are already benefiting from their self-imposed grouping strategies, experimenter-imposed grouping should help the younger children (who cannot organize well) more than the older children.

Huttenlocher and Burke (1976) sought evidence for the development of rehearsal or organizational strategies in the auditory memory span performance of children ranging in age from 4 to 11 years. These investigators found no significant differences in the primacy effects that accompanied the recall performance of these different aged children, tending to rule out rehearsal differences as an explanation for the increase in memory span seen with age. Nor did the researchers find that digit grouping favored one age group more than another, tending to exclude organizational strategies as an explanation. Huttenlocher and Burke did find that memory span was greater for grouped presentations than for ungrouped presentations, and, of course, they found sizable differences in memory span as a function of age. The average memory span of the nursery school children was about 2.25; that of fifth graders was 4.5 when presentations were ungrouped.

Lyon (1977) provided evidence that individual differences among adult learners are also not necessarily explained by differences in subject-imposed strategies. He reasoned that, if individual differences in memory span performance are due to rehearsal or grouping strategies, any situation that restricts persons' ability to carry out these operations should reduce individual differences. Specifically, Lyon suggested that there should be less opportunity for performances to vary when item presentation was faster than the normal rate. Lyon presented digits either slowly (1 digit per second) or quickly (3 digits per second). Although presentation rate affected performance, the fast rate leading to poorer performance than the slow rate, variability within the fast rate was not reduced, as the voluntary strategy hypothesis might predict. Because each subject in this experiment was tested under both slow and fast rates, Lyon was able to obtain correlations between subjects' performance under both conditions. The correlation was high (.82), suggesting that performance for both rates was reflecting the same processes. He concluded that the results argue against attributing individual differences in memory span performance to differences in rehearsal or grouping strategies.

What then are individual differences in memory span due to? Several investigators have argued that memory span performance reflects two basic kinds of remembered information: item information and order information (for example, Estes, 1972; Shiffrin & Cook, 1978). Therefore to understand individual differences in memory span, investigators might look for differences in subjects' ability to remember either of these types of information (see Chi, 1976; Huttenlocher & Burke, 1976). A major difference between the memory processing of children and that of adults is the speed with which they can identify a stimulus (Chi, 1976). Thus one possible explanation for the greater memory span performance of adults is that they can more efficiently process the to-be-remembered items, thereby producing better memory for item information (see also Dempster, 1981).

Martin (1978) presented evidence that individual differences in memory span are the result of differences in the ability to remember item order. She tested subjects on four types of tasks: immediate and delayed free recall of words, digit span, and ordered digit recall. All presentations were auditory. To test ordered digit recall, she presented each subject with several lists of 12 digits at the rate of 1 digit per second. Subjects attempted to identify the serial position of each digit they could remember. Responses were made by writing the digits in spaces corresponding to the different serial positions in the list. Martin (1978) calculated correlations between the subjects' performance on each of the four types of tasks. When free recall is immediate, number of items remembered from the recency part of the list has been a popular measure of primary memory capacity (see Watkins, 1974, and Chapter 4). Performance on the delayed free-recall test can be taken as a measure of long-term or secondary memory. She found that digit span performance did not correlate with performance on the recency part of the immediate free-recall list, and span did not correlate with amount of delayed free recall. On the other hand, digit span performance was significantly correlated with subjects' ability to remember item order. Martin concluded that order information is of primary importance in digit span tasks.

Such a conclusion does not, of course, help us to understand how item order information is encoded or why significant variation in this ability might appear developmentally or within particular age groups. Shiffrin and Cook (1978) have argued that memory for order information in a short-term memory task depends on the strength of "relational bonds" established during encoding. The reason individuals might differ in their ability to form these relational connections can at this time only be speculated upon. It may be that differences in this apparently fundamental process are the basis of individual differences in other cognitive processes (see especially Bachelder & Denny, 1977a, 1977b). We mentioned earlier a study by Hunt, Lunneborg, and Lewis (1975) that compared performance on a variety of cognitive tasks of persons scoring high on a verbal ability test and those scoring low on this test. In one experiment (Exp. 3) sensitivity to order information was measured. They found that the "high verbals" were superior to the "low verbals" in the "ability to retain in STM information about the order of stimulus presentation" (p. 223). Therefore although memory span can be increased through practice and with the use of special mnemonic techniques, memory span ability in general may depend on certain fundamental cognitive processes.

MEMORY AND AGING

Older adults often have more trouble remembering than do younger adults. These age-related effects on memory are considerably more likely to be seen on tests of long-term memory than on tests of short-term memory. If attention demands are not too great and if the task does not require reorganization of the to-be-remembered information, then marginal, if any, effects of age are found in short-term memory performance (Craik, 1977; Eysenck, 1977). For example, memory span for digits is not likely to differ between young and old adults. One recent study found performance on a digit span task to be somewhat better for old adults than for young adults (Till & Walsh, 1980). The average age of older adults in this study was 71.5 years (range 65–81); the average age of the younger adults was 18.8 (range 18–22). Once the amount of to-be-remembered material exceeds memory span, older adults are likely to perform more poorly than younger adults on a retention test.

Age-related effects on long-term retention are also usually greater when memory is tested by recall than by recognition. Indeed, some studies have reported no age effects when a recognition test is given (see Craik, 1977). You may recall from our discussion of frequency encoding in Chapter 8 that age-related effects are also often not found when memory for frequency of events is tested. That *both* recognition memory and memory for frequency do not show substantial changes with age is indirect support for the notion that the same processes underlie both these tasks (see Hasher & Zacks, 1979). This is exactly what the frequency theory of recognition memory suggests (see Chapter 10).

Retrieval-deficit versus processing-deficit hypotheses

That retention losses as a function of age are greater when memory is tested by recall than recognition can be interpreted as evidence for a *retrieval deficit* in elderly subjects. As Craik (1977, p. 402) has commented,

> Older subjects appear to be at the greatest disadvantage relative to younger groups when little retrieval information is provided by the experimental situation. In this case, they must rely on self-generated "reconstructive" activities ... to retrieve the items; it may be postulated that older people are less intellectually flexible and creative in these mental operations ... and thus their memory performance is impaired. By this analysis, age decrements should be greatest in free recall, where no retrieval cues are provided, and this seems to fit the observed facts. On the other hand, age decrements should be less in cued recall and in recognition where more retrieval information is provided by the situation and less need be generated by the subject; this is also borne out by the data.

Several experiments based on the levels-of-processing framework (which was discussed in Chapter 12) appear to support Craik's analysis.

Eysenck (1974) asked young (ages 18–30 years) and old (ages 55–65) subjects to perform several different orienting tasks on lists of 27 words before testing recall. The lists contained instances of nine semantic categories (three instances of each category) and all words were one syllable. Different groups of subjects performed two nonsemantic orienting tasks (counting, then record-ing, the number of letters in a word and finding a word that rhymed with the list word) and two semantic tasks (finding an appropriate adjective for each list word and forming an image of each word). Subjects doing the orienting tasks were not informed that a memory test would be given. Two additional groups of subjects (young and old) were given intentional learning instructions and no orienting tasks to perform for the same list of items. Mean recall of the young and old subjects is shown in Figure 15-3.

The results of Eysenck's experiment revealed an interaction between age and type of orienting task. Although there was no difference between the two

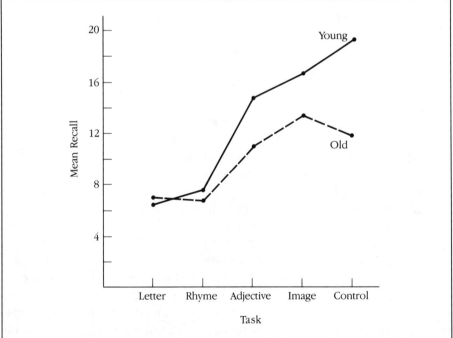

Figure 15-3. Mean recall of young and old adults as a function of type of orienting task. *(Based on data from "Age Differences in Incidental Learning," by M. W. Eysenck. In* Developmental Psychology, *1974,* 10, *936–941. Used by permission.)*

age groups when recall followed the nonsemantic orienting tasks, large differences were found following the semantic tasks. As can be seen in Figure 15-3, the young subjects also remembered more than the old subjects on the free-recall test when no orienting task was performed. Eysenck (1974) interpreted these results as supporting a *processing-deficit hypothesis* of age-related memory differences. He argued that younger people are better able to perform semantic or elaborative processing than are older people. The interaction shown in Figure 15-3 supports this hypothesis; age differences were found only for semantic processing or for intentional learning when it might be assumed that more meaningful kinds of encoding will be attempted. But there may be another explanation of these findings, as the results of a more recent experiment suggest.

White (see Craik, 1977) performed an experiment similar to that of Eysenck's, but with one important difference. She also examined retention of young and old adults following semantic and nonsemantic orienting tasks, but she tested retention using both a recall and a recognition test. When she tested recall, White found the same interaction as did Eysenck (1974); old and young adults did not differ following nonsemantic processing, but young adults did better following a semantic orienting task or after intentional instructions. However, when she tested recognition, there were no age differences following any of the orienting tasks, although retention was greater in both young and old groups for semantic than for nonsemantic processing activities. Craik (1977) took this pattern of results to be more supportive of a *retrieval deficit* than a processing deficit, as Eysenck (1974) had suggested. His argument was as follows: The fact that *recognition* memory performance following semantic processing did not differ for old and young adults is evidence that subjects at both ages processed the items equally well. But because differences in *recall* were found for young and old adults following semantic processing, it must be that the older people could not use their encoded information as well as the younger people when forced to retrieve the to-be-remembered items.

White reported another interesting finding. She found a sizable advantage for the young adults over the old adults when she tested recognition memory following intentional learning instructions and no orienting task. As we have noted, retention differences are often not found when recognition memory of old and young adults is tested, and certainly not to the same degree as when recall is tested, which was what White found. Craik (1977) suggested that this result would occur if older subjects, relative to younger subjects, are more likely to engage in nonsemantic processing unless otherwise led to do so by the orienting requirements. That is, it is not that they can't process semantically, as the processing-deficit hypothesis implies, but rather that older adults may not normally do so.

Failure to process spontaneously

Till and Walsh (1980) demonstrated that older subjects do not always spontaneously encode information to the same degree as younger adults. They used sentence materials rather than single words, making the task more like "real life." This is an important consideration when older subjects are tested. These people have likely been away from school for some time and thus away from the many demands on memory for "unrelated" items, such as lists of words. The experimenters tested retention for implicational sentences. These are sentences that entail information about objects or events that are not explicitly mentioned. Here are examples of several of the sentences and their implications.

1. The pupil carefully positioned the thumbtack on the chair.
   Implication: *prank*
2. The youngster watched the program.
   Implication: *television*
3. The chauffeur drove on the left side.
   Implication: *England*
4. The audience stood up and continued to clap loudly.
   Implication: *encore*

Till and Walsh (1980) presented implicational sentences to both young and old adults, once again under different orienting tasks with no mention that a memory test would be given. Retention was tested by both free and cued recall. In the case of cued recall the implications of each sentence were provided as cues for recall of the sentences. *Prank,* for example, was the cue for the first sentence. The results of this experiment revealed an interesting interaction between age and type of retention test (free or cued recall). In two experiments the younger subjects remembered more sentences under cued recall than free recall; the older subjects remembered *less* on the cued-recall test than they did when free recall was tested. As we have noted, age-related differences are generally less when young and old adults are compared on cued recall than on free recall. Till and Walsh's experiment showed just the opposite.

In another experiment using implicational sentences, Till and Walsh required both the young and old subjects to write down what they thought each sentence was about. Subjects were, in other words, required to attempt sentence comprehension. When this was done, there were no differences in the cued recall of young and old subjects. Apparently, the requirement to write down the meaning of the sentence led the older subjects to engage in processing that they would not normally have done. It can be suggested therefore that the implications did not serve as effective retrieval cues in the previous experiments because the older subjects did not think of them at the time of study. As we have seen, a cue is not likely to be effective in retrieving a memory unless it is present at both study and test (see the discussion of encoding specificity in Chapter 10).

Therefore the results to date suggest that an important source of age-related effects in secondary memory lies with differences in the extent to which semantic elaboration is carried out by young and old people. Unless led to do so by task demands, older adults appear less likely (though not necessarily less able) than younger adults to elaborate semantically on the to-be-remembered material. A similar problem appears to be present at the time of test. Older adults apparently fail to "work on" information in memory in the same way as younger adults. This may mean that they are less likely to reconstruct aspects of the initially encoded event (see Craik, 1977). Without this reconstructive effort, important retrieval cues will not be present at time of recall.

INDIVIDUAL DIFFERENCES AND NOMOTHETIC THEORY CONSTRUCTION

Underwood (1975, p. 130) has suggested that individual differences be used to assess the validity of a theory.

> Let me now state the generalized case. If we include in our nomothetic theories a process or mechanism that can be measured reliably outside of the situation for which it is serving its theoretical purpose, we have an immediate test of the validity of the theoretical formulation, at least a test of this aspect of the formulation. The assumed theoretical process will necessarily have a tie with performance which reflects (in theory) the magnitude of the process. Individuals will vary in the amount of this characteristic or skill they "possess." A prediction concerning differences in the performance of the individuals must follow. A test of this prediction can yield two outcomes. If the correlation is substantial, the theory has a go-ahead signal, that and no more; the usual positive correlations across subjects on various skills and aptitudes allow no conclusion concerning the validity of the theory per se. If the relationship between the individual-differences measurements and the performance is essentially zero, there is no alternative but to drop the line of theoretical thinking.

The logic of Underwood's argument goes something like this. We typically define a memory phenomenon in terms of the effect that some independent variable has on a retention measure. Often such observations lead us to theorize about some internal process that might "explain" the relationship we observed. You have, in the process of reading this book, been introduced to numerous examples of such theoretical processes. Multistore models often talk about "control processes"; dual-process theory suggests both verbal and imaginal codes; explanations of the spacing effect sometimes invoke an "attentional" mechanism; constructive theories of memory for prose emphasize inferences and script retrieval. Most theories include some form of intervening process to explain a particular relationship between an independent and dependent variable. You might remember that in Chapter 1 we introduced the notion of theory by examining how we might construct a theory to explain performance in a simple object-memory game. We were led in this process to consider "imagery" and "rehearsal" mechanisms as explanations for performance.

Having proposed some inferred mechanism or process to account for the results of an experiment, Underwood suggests that as a test of our theory we look for a measure that will demonstrate how individuals vary in this "ability." Consider the frequency theory of verbal discrimination learning we introduced in Chapter 8. It states that verbal discriminations are mediated by the subject's sensitivity to situational frequency. People, in other words, recognize differences in the situational frequency of verbal items and make decisions about correct and incorrect items on this basis. The theory, as you saw in Chapter 10, was extended to account for performance in recognition memory tasks. It can be assumed that old and new items presented in a recognition test differ in their situational frequency. Because they have appeared before, old items have frequency greater than one, whereas new items have zero situational frequency. The frequency theory posits some internal frequency mechanism that allows people to keep track of frequency. As with other cognitive processes, we can assume that people will differ in their ability to keep track of frequency. Therefore by finding a way to measure this ability, we have a test of the frequency theory of verbal discrimination and recognition memory. That is, people who are good at keeping track of frequency should also be good at discriminating between verbal items. This follows because the mechanism we are presumably measuring in our individual differences analysis (sensitivity to event frequency) is the same mechanism postulated to account for how people discriminate between items in verbal discrimination and recognition memory tasks.

As Underwood has pointed out, if a positive correlation is obtained, our theory is not necessarily proven, and in fact it may be wrong. Many abilities are correlated, and a positive relationship may be obtained because of some "third" variable that mediates performance in both tasks on which we are measuring performance. However, if the correlation turns out to be close to zero, we know that our theory must be wrong and we can start looking for another mechanism to explain performance. For instance, if people who are good at keeping track of frequency are not good at making verbal discriminations, then the frequency theory of recognition memory would have to be junked. Needless to say, strong positive correlations have been obtained between the ability to make frequency judgments and verbal discrimination performance (for example, Harris, Begg, & Mitterer, 1980; Underwood, Zimmerman, & Freund, 1971).

You likely did not recognize it at the time, but you saw a method similar to that described by Underwood (1975) used in this chapter. You will recall that Martin (1978) attempted to correlate performance on a memory span task with performance on the recency part of a free-recall task. Multistore theories have suggested that performance on these tasks measures the same thing—namely, a limited-capacity short-term store. The fact that performance did not correlate indicates that the multistore theory must be wrong about at least one of these tasks. At present it appears that performance on a memory span task and recall of the most recent items in a list presented for free recall are mediated by different processes (see also Baddeley & Hitch, 1974). On the other hand, the fact that Martin (1978) found a correlation between her subjects' ability to re-member item order and digit span performance supports (but does not prove) her theory that memory span largely depends on an ability to retain in memory the order in which events occur.

As you think about *your* theory for a particular memory phenomenon, you might consider Underwood's (1975) suggestion to use an individual differences analysis to give you the important "go-ahead" signal for the theory.

Summary

An investigation of individual differences in cognitive abilities complements the more traditional concern shown by memory researchers for nomothetic theory construction. In this chapter we saw the wide range of individual performances found in many standard memory tasks. We identified four major sources of individual differences: basic (mechanistic) processes, knowledge of voluntary encoding strategies, degree of topic-related knowl-edge, and metamemory. Evidence for the influences of these processes on memory performance has been shown in several previous chapters. There is the possibility that certain basic processes are biologically determined to some degree. On the other hand, there is clear evidence that extended practice can dramatically improve memory performance. For example, one individual increased his memory span from 7 to 80 digits through months of practice at recalling digits. Although memory span increases with practice, variation in memory span in the general adult population appears to reflect primarily differences in the ability to remember order information. Differ-ences in this apparently fundamental ability may be the basis for individual differences in other important cognitive tasks.

Age-related effects on retention are frequently observed. For instance, an adult's digit span is about twice that of a 5-year-old. Also, older adults are more likely to show retention deficits on tasks emphasizing information retrieval (for example, free recall) than are younger adults. It appears that older subjects do not always spontaneously encode information semantically or process information as actively as do younger adults.

Finally, we saw in this chapter how an analysis of individual differences can aid nomothetic theory construction when we have an independent measure of some internal process or mechanism postulated by our theory. Performance on this measure must be correlated with performance in those situations "explained" by our theory in order for the theory to be viable.

Recommendations for further reading

Eysenck's (1977) book, *Human Memory: Theory, Research and Individual Differences,* provides a fine summary of many areas in which individual differences have been investigated. Interesting reading are the papers by Hunt and his associates at the University of Washington, which we briefly discussed in this chapter (see especially Hunt, 1978). Further readings on individual differences in memory span ability can be found by consulting any of the numerous articles referenced in this chapter. Dempster (1981) has also reviewed the memory span literature. A recent article by Drewnowski (1980) is interesting reading because it provides an alternative approach to understanding memory span performance. The relationship between personality variables and memory task performance is the subject of an entire issue of the *Journal of Research in Personality* (December 1979). Many of the articles in that issue provide an important complement to the research we discussed in this chapter. An excellent review of memory and aging has been provided by Craik (1977). Underwood's (1975) article, "Individual Differences as a Crucible in Theory Construction," is worthwhile reading because we could not cover here many of the points he makes.

Appendix

A. Table of Random Numbers
B. Random Sample of 38 Low-Association Value (4–33%) Consonant Syllables (CCCs)
C. Random Sample of 120 Common Nouns
D. Random Sample of 24 Nonsense Syllables (CVCs) with Association Value 60–73%
E. Random Sample of 36 Two-Syllable Adjectives
F. Names of Famous and Not-So-Famous Male and Female Personalities
G. Alphabetized List of 150 High-Frequency Words
H. Alphabetized List of 150 Low-Frequency Words
I. General Information Questions and Multiple-Choice Alternatives

TABLE A. Table of Random Numbers

Line	(1)	(2)	(3)	(4)	(5)	(6)	(7)	(8)	(9)	(10)	(11)	(12)	(13)	(14)
1	10480	15011	01536	02011	81647	91646	69179	14194	62590	36207	20969	99570	91291	90700
2	22368	46573	25595	85393	30995	89198	27982	53402	93965	34095	52666	19174	39615	99505
3	24130	48360	22527	97265	76393	64809	15179	24830	49340	32081	30680	19655	63348	58629
4	42167	93093	06243	61680	07856	16376	39440	53537	71341	57004	00849	74917	97758	16379
5	37570	39975	81837	16656	06121	91782	60468	81305	49684	60672	14110	06927	01263	54613
6	77921	06907	11008	42751	27756	53498	18602	70659	90655	15053	21916	81825	44394	42880
7	99562	72905	56420	69994	98872	31016	71194	18738	44013	48840	63213	21069	10634	12952
8	96301	91977	65463	07972	18876	20922	94595	56869	69014	60045	18425	84903	42508	32307
9	89579	14342	63661	10281	17453	18103	57740	84378	25331	12566	58678	44947	05585	56941
10	85475	36857	53342	53988	53060	59533	38867	62300	08158	17983	16439	11458	18593	64952
11	28918	69578	88231	33276	70997	79936	56865	05859	90106	31595	01547	85590	91610	78188
12	63553	40961	48235	03427	49626	69445	18663	72695	52180	20847	12234	90511	33703	90322
13	09429	93969	52636	92737	88974	33488	36320	17617	30015	08272	84115	27156	30613	74952
14	10365	61129	87529	85689	48237	52267	67689	93394	01511	26358	85104	20285	29975	89868
15	07119	97336	71048	08178	77233	13916	47564	81506	97735	85977	29372	74461	28551	90707
16	51085	12765	51821	51259	77452	16308	60756	92144	49442	53900	70960	63990	75601	40719
17	02368	21382	52404	60268	89368	19885	55322	44819	01188	65255	64835	44919	05944	55157
18	01011	54092	33362	94904	31273	04146	18594	29852	71585	85030	51132	01915	92747	64951
19	52162	53916	46369	58586	23216	14513	83149	98736	23495	64350	94738	17752	35156	35749
20	07056	97628	33787	09998	42698	06691	76988	13602	51851	46104	88916	19509	25625	58104
21	48663	91245	85828	14346	09172	30168	90229	04734	59193	22178	30421	61666	99904	32812
22	54164	58492	22421	74103	47070	25306	76468	26384	58151	06646	21524	15227	96909	44592
23	32639	32363	05597	24200	13363	38005	94342	28728	35806	06912	17012	64161	18296	22851
24	29334	27001	87637	87308	58731	00256	45834	15398	46557	41135	10367	07684	36188	18510
25	02488	33062	28834	07351	19731	92420	60952	61280	50001	67658	32586	86679	50720	94953

TABLE A. Table of Random Numbers (cont.)

Line	(1)	(2)	(3)	(4)	(5)	(6)	(7)	(8)	(9)	(10)	(11)	(12)	(13)	(14)
26	81525	72295	04839	96423	24878	82651	66566	14778	76797	14780	13300	87074	79666	95725
27	29676	20591	68086	26432	46901	20849	89768	81536	86645	12659	92259	57102	80428	25280
28	00742	57392	39064	66432	84673	40027	32832	61362	98947	96067	64760	64584	96096	98253
29	05366	04213	25669	26422	44407	44048	37937	63904	45766	66134	75470	66520	34693	90449
30	91921	26418	64117	94305	26766	25940	39972	22209	71500	64568	91402	42416	07844	69618
31	00582	04711	87917	77341	42206	35126	74087	99547	81817	42607	43808	76655	62028	76630
32	00725	69884	62797	56170	86324	88072	76222	36086	84637	93161	76038	65855	77919	88006
33	69011	65795	95876	55293	18988	27354	26575	08625	40801	59920	29841	80150	12777	48501
34	25976	57948	29888	88604	67917	48708	18912	82271	65424	69774	33611	54262	85963	03547
35	09763	83473	73577	12908	30883	18317	28290	35797	05998	41688	34952	37888	38917	88050
36	91567	42595	27958	30134	04024	86385	29880	99730	55536	84855	29080	09250	79656	73211
37	17955	56349	90999	49127	20044	59931	06115	20542	18059	02008	73708	83517	36103	42791
38	46503	18584	18845	49618	02304	51038	20655	58727	28168	15475	56942	53389	20562	87338
39	92157	89634	94824	78171	84610	82834	09922	25417	44137	48413	25555	21246	35509	20468
40	14577	62765	35605	81263	39667	47358	56873	56307	61607	49518	89696	20103	77490	18062
41	98427	07523	33362	64270	01638	92477	66969	98420	04880	45585	46565	04102	46880	45709
42	34914	63976	88720	82765	34476	17032	87589	40836	32427	70002	70663	88863	77775	69348
43	70060	28277	39475	46473	23219	53416	94970	25832	69975	94884	19661	72828	00102	66794
44	53976	54914	06990	67245	68350	82948	11398	42878	80287	88267	47363	46634	06541	97809
45	76072	29515	40980	07391	58745	25774	22987	80059	39911	96189	41151	14222	60697	59583
46	90725	52210	83974	29992	65831	38857	50490	83765	55657	14361	31720	57375	56228	41546
47	64364	67412	33339	31926	14883	24413	59744	92351	97473	89286	35931	04110	23726	51900
48	08962	00358	31662	25388	61642	34072	81249	35648	56891	69352	48373	45578	78547	81788
49	95012	68379	93526	70765	10592	04542	76463	54328	02349	17247	28865	14777	62730	92277
50	15664	10493	20492	38391	91132	21999	59516	81652	27195	48223	46751	22923	32261	85653

From *Table of 105,000 Random Decimal Digits,* Statement No. 4914, File no. 261-A-1, Interstate Commerce Commission, Washington, D.C., May 1949.

TABLE B. Random Sample of 38 Low-Association Value (4–33%) Consonant Syllables (CCCs)

BMZ (33)	GKW (25)	LHD (33)	QCF (8)	WNQ (33)
BPF (33)	GJX (4)	LRB (33)	QKB (21)	WSZ (21)
CGW (25)	HFP (25)	MBD (33)	RJP (25)	XKH (4)
CJX (8)	HZP (33)	MQH (33)	RJX (17)	XMZ (13)
DJF (21)	JBW (21)	NWB (33)	SGC (25)	ZFK (8)
DLH (29)	JMC (29)	NZK (17)	SJF (13)	ZSB (21)
FQD (29)	KFH (21)	PNB (33)	TJQ (17)	
FZH (25)	KHF (17)	PXZ (21)	TZJ (21)	

Note: Items were sampled randomly with the restriction that no more than two items begin with the same letter. Numbers in parentheses are association values.

From "The Association Value of Three-Place Consonant Syllables," by L. R. Witmer. In *Journal of Genetic Psychology,* 1935, *47,* 337–360. Copyright 1935 by The Journal Press. Reprinted by permission.

TABLE C. Random Sample of 120 Common Nouns

One-syllable		Two-syllable			Three-syllable
aid	mass	anger	fashion	pattern	adventure
bar*	meal*	apple*	feature	police*	appearance
beach*	pie*	artist*	flour*	prayer	capital
bell*	plate	basket*	giant	prison*	committee
bond	ray	bottle*	habit	pupil*	companion
bone*	root	bottom	household	railway*	diamond*
bowl*	rope*	breakfast*	instance	relief	evidence
brain*	route	burden	justice	remark	expression
bread*	sheet*	cattle*	leather*	sailor*	factory*
breast*	shell*	chamber	lesson	secret	furniture*
breath	sin	coffee*	level	series	happiness
cheek*	speed	colonel*	lover	servant	hospital*
choice	stamp*	contract	marriage	statement	liberty
corn*	stroke	couple*	meaning	student*	library*
fault	sum	cousin*	message	substance	magazine*
flame*	teeth*	defense*	midnight	supper	memory
fur*	thread*	dozen	motion	ticket*	minister
goat*	throat*	effect	owner	tower*	passenger*
gun*	tongue*	empire	palacc*	vessel*	potato*
map*	tribe ‾	event	passion	witness	prisoner*

Note: Items were sampled randomly from the list of nouns compiled by Spreen and Schulz. Words marked by asterisks have ratings of high concreteness (imagery).

From "Parameters of Abstraction, Meaningfulness and Pronunciability for 329 Nouns," by O. Spreen and R. W. Schulz. In *Journal of Verbal Learning and Verbal Behavior,* 1966, *5,* 459–468. Copyright 1966 by Academic Press, Inc. Reprinted by permission.

TABLE D. Random Sample of 24 Nonsense Syllables (CVCs) with Association Value 60–73%

BAF (73)	JUV (73)	PIM (60)	SAH (60)	VAM (73)
BAP (67)	KES (60)	QAW (60)	SAQ (60)	VEN (67)
BEF (73)	NEM (60)	QIR (67)	SIM (67)	VEZ (60)
GIF (67)	NUM (67)	QOG (60)	SUC (73)	VOT (67)
HAB (67)	PEC (73)	ROL (67)	TAY (60)	

Note: Numbers in parentheses are association values.

From "The Association Value of Nonsense Syllables," by J. A. Glaze. In *Journal of Genetic Psychology,* 1928, *35,* 255-269. Copyright 1928 by The Journal Press. Reprinted by permission.

TABLE E. Random Sample of 36 Two-Syllable Adjectives

absurd	composed	entire	jocose	peevish	teeming
ancient	crabbed	flying	lifeless	prideful	unclear
anxious	cranky	gawky	mammoth	raging	unfit
artful	demised	genial	mulish	scornful	vagrant
cheerful	demure	holy	obscure	sloven	wicked
childish	depraved	hurting	oral	spiral	worldly

From "Synonymity, Vividness, Familiarity and Association Value Ratings of 400 Pairs of Common Adjectives," by C. H. Haagen. In *Journal of Psychology,* 1949, *27,* 453–463. Copyright 1949 by The Journal Press. Reprinted by permission.

TABLE F. Names of Famous and Not-So-Famous Male and Female Personalities

Famous females	*Not-so-famous females*
1. Jane Fonda	1. Anne Bancroft
2. Marilyn Monroe	2. June Allyson
3. Katherine Hepburn	3. Gloria DeHaven
4. Brigitte Bardot	4. Barbara Eden
5. Cheryl Tiegs	5. Lana Turner
6. Elizabeth Taylor	6. Veronica Lake
7. Farrah Fawcett	7. Loretta Young
8. Bette Davis	8. Dorothy McGuire
9. Vanessa Redgrave	9. Alexis Smith
10. Glenda Jackson	10. Lee Remick
11. Lily Tomlin	11. Greer Garson
12. Barbra Streisand	12. Stella Stevens
13. Julie Christie	13. Vivian Leigh
14. Liza Minnelli	14. Pamela Tiffin
15. Ali McGraw	15. Carole Lombard
16. Haley Mills	16. Elizabeth Montgomery
17. Natalie Wood	17. Judy Holiday
18. Faye Dunaway	18. Maureen Stapleton
19. Diane Keaton	19. Tippi Hedren
20. Carol Burnett	20. Barbara Harris

Famous males	*Not-so-famous males*
1. Clint Eastwood	1. Steve Forest
2. Peter Sellers	2. Beau Bridges
3. Alec Guinness	3. Anthony Hopkins
4. Paul Newman	4. Forrest Tucker
5. Warren Beatty	5. Burgess Meredith
6. Clark Gable	6. Alan Arkin
7. Richard Burton	7. Zero Mostell
8. Dustin Hoffman	8. Jack Hopkins
9. John Travolta	9. Sal Mineo
10. John Wayne	10. George Montgomery
11. Humphrey Bogart	11. Broderick Crawford
12. Jack Nicholson	12. Ernest Borgnine
13. Marlon Brando	13. Robert Young
14. Robert Redford	14. Audie Murphy
15. Jon Voight	15. Anthony Newley
16. Rock Hudson	16. Van Johnson
17. Cary Grant	17. Richard Crenna
18. James Stewart	18. Ronald Coleman
19. Woody Allen	19. Walter Brennan
20. Charlton Heston	20. Ben Johnson

Note: Labeling someone as famous or not-so-famous is clearly arbitrary and is undoubtedly relative to a particular population and even a certain month or year. Investigators may want to do some rearranging or substituting for the names in this table, depending on circumstances and the nature of the subject population in their experiment.

TABLE G. Alphabetized List of 150 High-Frequency Words

1. about	31. crown	61. head	91. paper	121. slight
2. above	32. dance	62. hero	92. part	122. slowly
3. afford	33. deal	63. history	93. peace	123. sold
4. allow	34. deed	64. hold	94. people	124. speed
5. alone	35. develop	65. hundred	95. percent	125. spite
6. angry	36. diamond	66. idea	96. pine	126. spoke
7. answer	37. disease	67. improve	97. place	127. stage
8. anyway	38. doubt	68. indicate	98. plane	128. strength
9. average	39. during	69. instant	99. pleasant	129. superior
10. bless	40. effect	70. instead	100. prayer	130. table
11. body	41. effort	71. intend	101. prepare	131. then
12. bury	42. eight	72. interest	102. profit	132. thirty
13. busy	43. else	73. into	103. purchase	133. thread
14. came	44. entirely	74. issue	104. purpose	134. tiny
15. camp	45. fact	75. jump	105. race	135. tonight
16. capital	46. faint	76. left	106. rate	136. training
17. careful	47. fence	77. lovely	107. regular	137. twelve
18. cast	48. flag	78. majority	108. relief	138. until
19. castle	49. fleet	79. match	109. religion	139. upon
20. chief	50. fold	80. may	110. request	140. upper
21. chosen	51. fool	81. measure	111. return	141. urge
22. coin	52. free	82. melt	112. room	142. utter
23. conclude	53. fruit	83. midnight	113. rose	143. very
24. contain	54. funny	84. month	114. save	144. want
25. content	55. game	85. moral	115. season	145. welcome
26. cool	56. gift	86. narrow	116. settle	146. where
27. corn	57. governor	87. only	117. shall	147. window
28. cotton	58. grave	88. original	118. shell	148. wine
29. country	59. hate	89. ought	119. single	149. worth
30. crime	60. have	90. pace	120. skin	150. yourself

Note: Words were randomly sampled from those words identified as appearing more than 50 times per million words of text (A and AA words in the Thorndike and Lorge norms). Only words of 4–9 letters were included in the sample.

Reprinted with permission of the publisher from *The Teacher's Word Book of 30,000 Words,* by Edward L. Thorndike and I. Lorge (New York: Teachers College Press, copyright © 1944 by Teachers College, Columbia University).

TABLE H. Alphabetized List of 150 Low-Frequency Words

1. accede	31. ellipse	61. intensify	91. perk	121. tankard
2. alkaloid	32. encumber	62. jumper	92. philology	122. tenfold
3. amass	33. erosion	63. laird	93. plumber	123. tidbit
4. appraise	34. escapade	64. layette	94. plural	124. tigress
5. athwart	35. ewer	65. leftover	95. poodle	125. tirade
6. bedspread	36. faery	66. liegeman	96. pounder	126. toboggan
7. beetling	37. falconer	67. louse	97. primacy	127. transpire
8. betimes	38. fancier	68. loyally	98. priority	128. trigger
9. betrayal	39. fiduciary	69. macaroon	99. prod	129. trinket
10. biennial	40. filth	70. malign	100. pshaw	130. tumbler
11. boarding	41. fitful	71. mania	101. rancher	131. ultra
12. boastful	42. fleck	72. marauder	102. reprieve	132. unpitied
13. bodyguard	43. flick	73. mediator	103. repudiate	133. upheaval
14. bowstring	44. forefront	74. missile	104. reversal	134. urgency
15. buttress	45. forsooth	75. monkish	105. revery	135. vehement
16. catbird	46. freakish	76. moralize	106. royally	136. villainy
17. cauldron	47. gaoler	77. muddle	107. rupture	137. visual
18. chard	48. gondola	78. munition	108. scaffold	138. voluble
19. clearness	49. gratis	79. nefarious	109. seaside	139. waffle
20. collide	50. habitable	80. northerly	110. shears	140. wallop
21. couplet	51. hellish	81. noxious	111. shotgun	141. wend
22. crock	52. helot	82. null	112. shrilly	142. whatnot
23. cryptic	53. hideously	83. numeral	113. signet	143. whiff
24. cumbrous	54. holly	84. oriole	114. sirrah	144. witchery
25. decoy	55. hothouse	85. outcast	115. skeletal	145. woefully
26. donate	56. hove	86. outweigh	116. slink	146. woody
27. drawback	57. iceberg	87. overseer	117. staccato	147. workable
28. duplicity	58. immune	88. overtop	118. stolid	148. yolk
29. ebon	59. incidence	89. painless	119. strainer	149. zebra
30. ecstatic	60. inorganic	90. pasturage	120. talc	150. zoology

Note: Words were randomly sampled from those words identified as appearing 1–4 times per million words of text. Only words of 4–9 letters were included in the sample.

Reprinted with permission of the publisher from *The Teacher's Word Book of 30,000 Words,* by Edward L. Lorge and I. Lorge (New York: Teachers College Press, copyright © 1944 by Teachers College, Columbia University).

TABLE I. General Information Questions and Multiple-Choice Alternatives

1. What is the minimum age allowed by law for a U.S. president?
   a. 25   b. 40   c. 30   **d.** 35

2. What movie actor played the lead role in the movie *The Ten Commandments?*
   a. Gregory Peck   b. Burt Lancaster   c. Otto Preminger   **d.** Charlton Heston

3. What is the capital city of Peru?
   a. Lima   b. Callco   c. Bogota   d. Trujillo

4. What is the chemical symbol for iron?
   a. Tb   b. I   **c.** Fe   d. Ir

5. With what singer is the song "Fire and Rain" usually associated?
   a. Jim Croce   **b.** James Taylor   c. Johnny Cash   d. Dolly Parton

6. What is the name of the longest river in the world?
   a. Amazon   b. Mississippi   **c.** Nile   d. Yangtze

7. In the Bible, who had the coat of many colors?
   a. Jacob   **b.** Joseph   c. Abraham   d. Peter

8. How many ounces are there in a pint?
   a. 16   b. 20   c. 10   d. 13

9. In what novel is the character Captain Ahab found?
   a. *Mutiny on the Bounty*   b. *Two Years Before the Mast*
   c. *Lord Jim*   **d.** *Moby Dick*

10. How many planets are there in our solar system?
    a. 10   b. 12   **c.** 9   d. 7

11. Who said "Go West, young man, go West"?
    a. Horace Greeley   b. Thomas Jefferson   c. Ben Franklin   d. Mark Twain

12. Abraham Lincoln, George Washington, Thomas Jefferson, and *what other president* are sculptured into Mount Rushmore?
    a. Theodore Roosevelt   b. Andrew Jackson   c. U. S. Grant   d. John Adams

13. Who was the first man to step on the moon?
    a. Edwin Aldrin   **b.** Neil Armstrong   c. Frank Borman   d. Alan Shepard

14. What did Little Jack Horner pull out of his pie?
    a. peach   b. apple   **c.** plum   d. cherry

15. Barbara Walters was co-anchorperson with which other newscaster?
    a. Walter Cronkite   b. Dan Rather   c. John Chancellor   **d.** Harry Reasoner

16. Who is considered to be the inventor of the radio?
    a. Thomas Edison   **b.** Guglielmo Marconi   c. Enrico Fermi   d. George Westinghouse

17. In what Shakespearean play was the following said: "Something is rotten in the State of Denmark"?
    a. *Macbeth*   b. *King Lear*   **c.** *Hamlet*   d. *Othello*

18. Who was the last horse to win racing's triple crown?
    a. Secretariat   b. Seattle Slew   c. Citation   **d.** Affirmed

19. What U.S. state is called the "Lone Star State"?
    a. Texas   b. California   c. Maine   d. Vermont

20. "Color My World" was popularized by what musical group?
    a. Cream   b. Kiss   **c.** Chicago   d. Queen

21. How many centimeters are there in an inch (to the nearest hundredth)?
    a. 2.54   b. 2.22   c. 2.47   d. 2.63

22. Who wrote *The Interpretation of Dreams?*
    a. James   b. Janet   c. Mesmer   **d.** Freud

23. Who wrote *The Origin of Species?*
    a. Freud   b. Mendel   c. Bacon   **d.** Darwin

24. Who painted the Sistine Chapel?
    a. Rembrandt   **b.** Michaelangelo   c. da Vinci   d. Raphael

25. What is the beer "that made Milwaukee famous"?
    a. Blatz   b. Pabst   c. Budweiser   **d.** Schlitz

26. Who founded the Standard Oil Company?
    a. E. Harriman   b. J. P. Morgan   c. C. Vanderbilt   **d.** J. D. Rockefeller

27. What airline is called "The Wings of Man"?
    a. TWA   b. Delta   **c.** Eastern   d. United

28. Who was the man Capone sought to kill on St. Valentine's Day?
    a. J. McGarn   b. D. O'Banion   **c.** G. Moran   d. J. Colosimo

29. How many feet are there in a mile?
    a. 6710   **b.** 5280   c. 2163   d. 3744

30. What city is the capital of Canada?
    a. Ottawa   b. Quebec   c. Montreal   d. Toronto

31. Who was voted the most valuable baseball player in 1977 in the National League?
    a. Pete Rose   **b.** George Foster   c. Tom Seaver   d. Reggie Jackson

32. Who wrote *Paradise Lost?*
    a. Milton   b. Byron   c. Brenning   d. Pope

33. What professional football team was the winner of the first Super Bowl?
    a. Kansas City Chiefs   **b.** Green Bay Packers   c. New York Jets   d. Baltimore Colts

34. In the comic strip "Peanuts" who is Lucy in love with?
    a. Linus   **b.** Schroeder   c. Franklin   d. Charlie Brown

35. What is the best known work of Cervantes?
    a. *Exemplary Novels*   b. *El Cid*   c. *Troilus and Cressida*   **d.** *Don Quixote*

36. On what river is the Hoover Dam?
    a. Missouri   b. Mississippi   c. Rio Grande   **d.** Colorado

37. Who first sailed around the world?
    a. Magellan   b. Balboa   c. Ponce de Leon   d. Cook

38. Who did Paul McCartney marry?
    a. Linda   b. Yoko   c. Mary   d. Bianca

39. What was the name of Lucy's neighbors on the television show "I Love Lucy"?
    a. Ricardo   B. Gillis   **c.** Mertz   d. Harmon

40. What sea does Syria border?
    a. Baltic   b. Arabian   **c.** Mediterranean   d. Red

Note: We were able to demonstrate the feeling-of-knowing phenomenon using these questions and recognition alternatives when subjects were students from a midwestern university. To find the same effect in other populations may require some changes in this list of questions. The letter of the correct alternative is boldfaced. Nelson and Narens (1980) have recently provided estimates of item difficulty, latency of recall, and average feeling-of-knowing ratings for 300 general information questions.

References

Abra, J. C. List differentiation and forgetting. In C. P. Duncan, L. Sechrest, & A. W. Melton (Eds.), *Human memory: Festschrift in honor of Benton J. Underwood.* New York: Appleton-Century-Crofts, 1972.

Adams, J. K., & Adams, P. A. Realism of confidence judgments. *Psychological Review,* 1961, *68,* 33–45.

Anderson, J. R. Arguments concerning representations for mental imagery. *Psychological Review,* 1978, *85,* 249–277.

Anderson, J. R. Further arguments concerning representations for mental imagery: A response to Hayes-Roth and Pylyshyn. *Psychological Review,* 1979, *86,* 395–406.

Anderson, J. R., & Bower, G. H. Recognition and retrieval processes in free recall. *Psychological Review,* 1972, *79,* 97–123.

Anderson, J. R., & Bower, G. H. *Human associative memory.* Washington, D.C.: Winston, 1973.

Anisfeld, M., & Knapp, M. Association, synonymity, and directionality in false recognition. *Journal of Experimental Psychology,* 1968, *77,* 171–179.

Appel, L. F., Cooper, R. G., McCarrell, N., Sims-Knight, J., Yussen, S. R., & Flavell, J. H. The development of the distinction between perceiving and memorizing. *Child Development,* 1972, *43,* 1365–1381.

Arbuckle, T. Y., & Cuddy, L. L. Discrimination of item strength at time of presentation. *Journal of Experimental Psychology,* 1969, *81,* 126–131.

Atkinson, R. C. Mnemotechnics in second-language learning. *American Psychologist,* 1975, *30,* 821–828.

Atkinson, R. C., & Raugh, M. R. An application of the mnemonic keyword method to the acquisition of a Russian vocabulary. *Journal of Experimental Psychology: Human Learning and Memory,* 1975, *1,* 126–133.

Atkinson, R. C., & Shiffrin, R. M. Human memory: A proposed system and its control processes. In K. W. Spence & J. T. Spence (Eds.), *The psychology of learning and motivation* (Vol. 2). New York: Academic Press, 1968.

Atkinson, R. C., & Shiffrin, R. M. The control of short-term memory. *Scientific American,* 1971, *225,* 82–90.

Attneave, F. Psychological probability as a function of experienced frequency. *Journal of Experimental Psychology*, 1953, *46*, 81–86.

Averbach, E. The span of apprehension as a function of exposure duration. *Journal of Verbal Learning and Verbal Behavior*, 1963, *2*, 60–64.

Averbach, E., & Coriell, A. S. Short-term memory in vision. *Bell System Technical Journal*, 1961, *40*, 309–328.

Ayres, T. J., Jonides, J., Reitman, J. S., Egan, J. C., & Howard, D. A. Differing suffix effects for the same physical stimulus. *Journal of Experimental Psychology: Human Learning and Memory*, 1979, *5*, 315–321.

Bach, M. J., & Underwood, B. J. Developmental changes in memory attributes. *Journal of Educational Psychology*, 1970, *61*, 292–296.

Bachelder, B. L., & Denny, M. R. A theory of intelligence: I. Span and the complexity of stimulus control. *Intelligence*, 1977, *1*, 127–150. (a)

Bachelder, B. L., & Denny, M. R. A theory of intelligence: II. The role of span in a variety of intellectual tasks. *Intelligence*, 1977, *1*, 237–256. (b)

Bacon, F. T. Credibility of repeated statements: Memory for trivia. *Journal of Experimental Psychology: Human Learning and Memory*, 1979, *5*, 241–252.

Baddeley, A. D. The trouble with "levels": A reexamination of Craik and Lockhart's framework for memory research. *Psychological Review*, 1978, *85*, 139–152.

Baddeley, A. D., & Hitch, G. Working memory. In G. Bower (Ed.), *The psychology of learning and motivation* (Vol. 8). New York: Academic Press, 1974.

Baddeley, A. D., Thomson, N., & Buchanan, M. Word length and the structure of short-term memory. *Journal of Verbal Learning and Verbal Behavior*, 1975, *14*, 575–589.

Baddeley, A. D., & Warrington, E. K. Amnesia and the distinction between long- and short-term memory. *Journal of Verbal Learning and Verbal Behavior*, 1970, *9*, 176–189.

Bahrick, H. P. Incidental learning under two incentive conditions. *Journal of Experimental Psychology*, 1954, *47*, 170–172.

Bahrick, H. P. Two-phase model for prompted recall. *Psychological Review*, 1970, *77*, 215–222.

Banks, W. P., & Barber, G. Color information in iconic memory. *Psychological Review*, 1977, *84*, 536–546.

Barnes, J. M., & Underwood, B. J. "Fate" of first-list associations in transfer theory. *Journal of Experimental Psychology*, 1959, *58*, 97–105.

Bartlett, F. C. *Remembering: A study in experimental and social psychology*. Cambridge, England: Cambridge University Press, 1932.

Belmont, J. M., & Butterfield, E. C. What the development of short-term memory is. *Human Development*, 1971, *14*, 236–248.

Bennett, R. W., & Bennett, I. F. PI release as a function of the number of prerelease trials. *Journal of Verbal Learning and Verbal Behavior*, 1974, *13*, 573–584.

Bilodeau, E. A. (Ed.). *Principles of skill acquisition*. New York: Academic Press, 1969.

Bilodeau, E. A., & Blick, K. A. Courses of misrecall over long-term retention intervals as related to strength of preexperimental habits of word association. *Psychological Reports*, 1965, *16*, 1173–1192 (Mongr. Suppl. 6).

Bilodeau, I. M., & Schlosberg, H. Similarity in stimulating conditions as a variable in retroactive inhibition. *Journal of Experimental Psychology*, 1951, *41*, 199–204.

Bisanz, G. L., Vesonder, G. T., & Voss, J. F. Knowledge of one's own responding and the relation of such knowledge to learning. *Journal of Experimental Child Psychology*, 1978, *25*, 116–128.

Blake, M. Prediction of recognition when recall fails: Exploring the feeling-of-knowing phenomenon. *Journal of Verbal Learning and Verbal Behavior*, 1973, *12*, 311–319.

Blumenthal, G. B., & Robbins, D. Delayed release from proactive interference with meaningful material: How much do we remember after reading brief prose passages? *Journal of Experimental Psychology: Human Learning and Memory,* 1977, *3,* 754–761.

Bobrow, D. G., & Collins, A. (Eds.). *Representation and understanding: Studies in cognitive science.* New York: Academic Press, 1975.

Boltwood, C. E., & Blick, K. A. The delineation and application of three mnemonic techniques. *Psychonomic Science,* 1970, *20,* 339–341.

Boring, E. G. *A history of experimental psychology.* New York: Appleton-Century-Crofts, 1950.

Bower, G. H. A multicomponent theory of the memory trace. In K. W. Spence & J. T. Spence (Eds.), *The psychology of learning and motivation* (Vol. 1). New York: Academic Press, 1967.

Bower, G. H. Analysis of a mnemonic device. *American Scientist,* 1970, *58,* 496–510.

Bower, G. H. Mental imagery and associative learning. In L. W. Gregg (Ed.), *Cognition in learning and memory.* New York: Wiley, 1972.

Bower, G. H. Selective facilitation and interference in retention of prose. *Journal of Educational Psychology,* 1974, *66,* 1–8.

Bower, G. H. Interference paradigms for meaningful propositional memory. *American Journal of Psychology,* 1978, *91,* 575–585.

Bower, G. H., Black, J. B., & Turner, T. J. Scripts in memory for text. *Cognitive Psychology,* 1979, *11,* 177–220.

Bower, G. H., Monteiro, K. P., & Gilligan, S. G. Emotional mood as a context for learning and recall. *Journal of Verbal Learning and Verbal Behavior,* 1978, *17,* 573–585.

Bower, G. H., & Winzenz, D. Group structure, coding and memory for digit series. *Journal of Experimental Psychology Monograph,* 1969, *80* (No. 2, Part 2).

Bransford, J. D., Barclay, J. R., & Franks, J. J. Sentence memory: A constructive versus interpretive approach. *Cognitive Psychology,* 1972, *3,* 193–209.

Bransford, J. D., Franks, J. J., Morris, C. D., & Stein, B. S. Some general comments on learning and memory research. In L. S. Cermak and F. I. M. Craik (Eds.), *Levels of processing and human memory.* Hillsdale, N.J.: Erlbaum, 1979.

Bransford, J. D., & Johnson, M. K. Contextual prerequisites for understanding: Some investigations of comprehension and recall. *Journal of Verbal Learning and Verbal Behavior,* 1972, *11,* 717–726.

Bransford, J. D., & Johnson, M. K. Considerations of some problems of comprehension. In W. G. Chase (Ed.), *Visual information processing.* New York: Academic Press, 1973.

Broadbent, D. E. *Perception and communication.* New York: Pergamon Press, 1958.

Broadbent, D. E. *Decision and stress.* New York: Academic Press, 1971.

Brooks, D. N., & Baddeley, A. D. What can amnesic patients learn? *Neuropsychologia,* 1976, *14,* 111–122.

Brown, A. L. The development of memory: Knowing, knowing about knowing, and knowing how to know. In H. W. Reese (Ed.), *Advances in child development and behavior* (Vol. 10). New York: Academic Press, 1975.

Brown, A. L. Knowing when, where, and how to remember: A problem of metacognition. In R. Glaser (Ed.), *Advances in instructional psychology* (Vol. 1). Hillsdale, N.J.: Erlbaum, 1978.

Brown, A. L., & Smiley, S. S. Rating the importance of structural units of prose passages: A problem of metacognitive development. *Child Development,* 1977, *48,* 1–8.

Brown, J. Some tests of the decay theory of immediate memory. *Quarterly Journal of Experimental Psychology,* 1958, *10,* 12–21.

Brown, R., & McNeill, D. The "tip of the tongue" phenomenon. *Journal of Verbal Learning and Verbal Behavior,* 1966, *5,* 325–337.

Burtt, H. E. An experimental study of early childhood memory: Final report. *Journal of Genetic Psychology,* 1941, *58,* 435–439.

Cain, L. F., & Willey, R. deV. The effect of spaced learning on the curve of retention. *Journal of Experimental Psychology,* 1939, *25,* 209–214.

Carey, S. T., & Lockhart, R. S. Encoding differences in recognition and recall. *Memory & Cognition,* 1973, *1,* 297–300.

Carroll, J. B., & Maxwell, S. E. Individual differences in cognitive abilities. *Annual Review of Psychology,* 1979, *30,* 603–640.

Carroll, J. B., & White, M. N. Word frequency and age of acquisition as determiners of picture-naming latency. *Quarterly Journal of Experimental Psychology,* 1973, *25,* 85–95.

Cermak, L. S., & Craik, F. I. M. (Eds.). *Levels of processing in human memory.* Hillsdale, N.J.: Erlbaum, 1979.

Chase, W. G., & Ericsson, K. A. Acquisition of a mnemonic system for digit span. Paper presented at the nineteenth annual meeting of the Psychonomic Society, San Antonio, Texas, November 1978.

Chase, W. G., & Ericsson, K. A. A mnemonic system for digit span: One year later. Paper presented at the twentieth annual meeting of the Psychonomic Society, Phoenix, Arizona, November 1979.

Chase, W. G., & Simon, H. A. Perception in chess. *Cognitive Psychology,* 1973, *4,* 55–81.

Chi, M. T. H. Short-term memory limitations in children: Capacity or processing deficits? *Memory & Cognition,* 1976, *4,* 559–572.

Chiang, A., & Atkinson, R. C. Individual differences and interrelationships among a select set of cognitive skills. *Memory & Cognition,* 1976, *4,* 661–672.

Chiesi, H., Spilich, G., & Voss, J. F. Acquisition of domain-related information in relation to high and low domain knowledge. *Journal of Verbal Learning and Verbal Behavior,* 1979, *18,* 257–274.

Chorover, S. L. An experimental critique of "consolidation studies" and an alternative "model-systems" approach to the biopsychology of memory. In M. R. Rosenzweig & E. L. Bennett (Eds.), *Neural mechanisms of learning and memory.* Cambridge, Mass.: MIT Press, 1976.

Chorover, S. L., & Schiller, P. H. Short-term retrograde amnesia in rats. *Journal of Comparative and Physiological Psychology,* 1965, *59,* 73–78.

Chow, S. L., & Murdock, B. B., Jr. The effect of a subsidiary task on iconic memory. *Memory & Cognition,* 1975, *3,* 678–688.

Chronbach, L. J. The two disciplines of scientific psychology. *American Psychologist,* 1957, *12,* 671–684.

Cicero, M. T. *De Oratore* (E. W. Sutton, trans.). Cambridge, Mass.: Harvard University Press, 1959.

Cofer, C. N. Constructive processes in memory. *American Scientist,* 1973, *61,* 537–543.

Cofer, C. N. (Ed.). *The structure of human memory.* San Francisco: W. H. Freeman, 1976.

Coltheart, M. Iconic memory: A reply to Professor Holding. *Memory & Cognition,* 1975, *3,* 42–48.

Coltheart, M. Iconic memory and visible persistence. *Perception & Psychophysics,* 1980, *27,* 183–228.

Connor, J. M. Effects of organization and expectancy on recall and recognition. *Memory & Cognition,* 1977, *5,* 315–318.

Conrad, R. Acoustic confusions in immediate memory. *British Journal of Psychology,* 1964, *55,* 75–84.

Coons, E. E., & Miller, N. E. Conflict versus consolidation of memory traces to explain "retrograde amnesia" produced by ECS. *Journal of Comparative and Physiological Psychology,* 1960, *53,* 524–531.

Cooper, E. H., & Pantle, A. J. The total-time hypothesis in verbal learning. *Psychological Bulletin,* 1967, *68,* 221–234.

Corballis, M. C., & Beale, I. L. *The psychology of left and right.* Hillsdale, N.J.: Erlbaum, 1976.

Corkin, S. Acquisition of motor skill after bilateral medial temporal-lobe excision. *Neuropsychologia,* 1968, *6,* 255–265.

Craik, F. I. M. Two components in free recall. *Journal of Verbal Learning and Verbal Behavior,* 1968, *7,* 996–1004.

Craik, F. I. M. The fate of primary memory items in free recall. *Journal of Verbal Learning and Verbal Behavior,* 1970, *9,* 143–148.

Craik, F. I. M. Age differences in human memory. In J. E. Birren & K. W. Schaie (Eds.), *Handbook of the psychology of aging.* New York: Van Nostrand, 1977.

Craik, F. I. M., & Jacoby, L. L. A process view of short-term retention. In F. Restle (Ed.), *Cognitive theory* (Vol. 1). Hillsdale, N.J.: Erlbaum, 1975.

Craik, F. I. M., & Levy, B. A. The concept of primary memory. In W. K. Estes (Ed.), *Handbook of learning and cognitive processes* (Vol. 4). Hillsdale, N.J.: Erlbaum, 1976.

Craik, F. I. M., & Lockhart, R. S. Levels of processing: A framework for memory research. *Journal of Verbal Learning and Verbal Behavior,* 1972, *11,* 671–684.

Craik, F. I. M., & Tulving, E. Depth of processing and the retention of words in episodic memory. *Journal of Experimental Psychology: General,* 1975, *104,* 268–294.

Craik, F. I. M., & Watkins, M. J. The role of rehearsal in short-term memory. *Journal of Verbal Learning and Verbal Behavior,* 1973, *12,* 599–607.

Crovitz, H. F. The capacity of memory loci in artificial memory. *Psychonomic Science,* 1971, *24,* 187–188.

Crowder, R. G. Prefix effects in immediate memory. *Canadian Journal of Psychology,* 1967, *21,* 450–461.

Crowder, R. G. *Principles of learning and memory.* Hillsdale, N.J.: Erlbaum, 1976.

Crowder, R. G. Mechanisms of auditory backward masking in the stimulus suffix effect. *Psychological Review,* 1978, *85,* 502–524.

Crowder, R. G., & Morton, J. Precategorical acoustic storage (PAS). *Perception & Psychophysics,* 1969, *5,* 365–373.

Dallett, K. M. "Primary memory": The effects of redundancy upon digit repetition. *Psychonomic Science,* 1965, *3,* 237–238.

Darwin, C. J., Turvey, M. T., & Crowder, R. G. An auditory analogue of the Sperling partial report procedure: Evidence for brief auditory storage. *Cognitive Psychology,* 1972, *3,* 255–267.

Deese, J. Frequency of usage and number of words in free recall: The role of association. *Psychological Reports,* 1960, *7,* 337–344.

Dempster, F. N. Memory span: Sources of individual and developmental differences. *Psychological Bulletin,* 1981, *89,* 63–100.

Deutsch, D., & Deutsch, J. A. *Short-term memory.* New York: Academic Press, 1975.

Dillon, R. F. Locus of proactive interference effects in short-term memory. *Journal of Experimental Psychology,* 1973, *99,* 75–81.

Dillon, R. F., & Bittner, L. A. Analysis of retrieval cues and release from proactive inhibition. *Journal of Verbal Learning and Verbal Behavior,* 1975, *14,* 616–622.

Dooling, D. J., & Lachman, R. Effects of comprehension on retention of prose. *Journal of Experimental Psychology,* 1971, *88,* 216–222.

Drachman, D. A., & Arbit, J. Memory and the hippocampal complex. *Archives of Neurology,* 1966, *15,* 52–61.

Drewnowski, A. Attributes and priorities in short-term recall: A new model of memory span. *Journal of Experimental Psychology: General,* 1980, *109,* 208–250.

Duncan, C. P. The retroactive effect of electroshock on learning. *Journal of Comparative and Physiological Psychology,* 1949, *42,* 32–44.

Durso, F. T., & Johnson, M. K. Facilitation in naming and categorizing repeated pictures and words. *Journal of Experimental Psychology: Human Learning and Memory,* 1979, *5,* 449–459.

Ebbinghaus, H. *Memory: A contribution to experimental psychology.* New York: Dover, 1964. (Originally published, 1885.)

Eckert, E., & Kanak, N. J. Verbal discrimination learning: A review of the acquisition, transfer, and retention literature through 1972. *Psychological Bulletin,* 1974, *81,* 582–607.

Egan, J. P. *Recognition memory and the operating characteristic* (Technical Note AFCRC-TN-58-51). Hearing and Communication Laboratory, Indiana University, 1958.

Eich, J. E. The cue-dependent nature of state-dependent retrieval. *Memory & Cognition,* 1980, *8,* 157–173.

Ekstrand, B. R. To sleep, perchance to dream (About why we forget). In C. P. Duncan, L. Sechrest, & A. W. Melton (Eds.), *Human memory: Festschrift in honor of Benton J. Underwood.* New York: Appleton-Century-Crofts, 1972.

Ekstrand, B. R., Wallace, W. P., & Underwood, B. J. A frequency theory of verbal discrimination learning. *Psychological Review,* 1966, *73,* 566–578.

Elliot, P. B. Tables of *d'.* In J. A. Swets (Ed.), *Signal detection and recognition by human observers.* New York: Wiley, 1964.

Engle, R. W., & Bukstel, L. Memory processes among bridge players of differing expertise. *American Journal of Psychology,* 1978, *91,* 673–689.

Ericsson, K. A., Chase, W. G., & Faloon, S. Acquisition of a memory skill. *Science,* 1980, *208,* 1181–1182.

Erlick, D. E. Effects of grouping of stimuli on the perception of relative frequency. *Journal of Experimental Psychology,* 1963, *66,* 314–316. (a)

Erlick, D. E. Effects of method of displaying categories on the perception of relative frequency. *Journal of Experimental Psychology,* 1963, *66,* 316–318. (b)

Estes, W. K. An associative basis for coding and organization in memory. In A. W. Melton & E. Martin (Eds.), *Coding processes in human memory.* Washington, D.C.: Winston, 1972.

Estes, W. K. The state of the field: General problems and issues of theory and metatheory. In W. K. Estes (Ed.), *Handbook of learning and cognitive processes* (Vol. 1). Hillsdale, N.J.: Erlbaum, 1975.

Eysenck, M. W. Age differences in incidental learning. *Developmental Psychology,* 1974, *10,* 936–941.

Eysenck, M. W. *Human memory: Theory, research and individual differences.* New York: Pergamon Press, 1977.

Eysenck, M. W. The feeling of knowing a word's meaning. *British Journal of Psychology,* 1979, *70,* 243–251.

Fischhoff, B., Slovic, P., & Lichtenstein, S. Knowing with certainty: The appropriateness of extreme confidence. *Journal of Experimental Psychology: Human Perception and Performance,* 1977, *3,* 552–564.

Fischler, I., Rundus, D., & Atkinson, R. C. Effects of overt rehearsal procedures on free recall. *Psychonomic Science,* 1970, *19,* 249–250.

Flavell, J. H. Developmental studies of mediated memory. In H. W. Reese & L. P. Lipsitt (Eds.), *Advances in child development and behavior* (Vol. 5). New York: Academic Press, 1970.

Flavell, J. H., & Wellman, H. M. Metamemory. In R. V. Kail, Jr., & J. W. Hagen (Eds.), *Perspectives on the development of memory and cognition.* Hillsdale, N.J.: Erlbaum, 1977.

Flexser, A. J., & Tulving, E. Retrieval independence in recognition and recall. *Psychological Review,* 1978, *85,* 153–171.

Galbraith, R. C., & Underwood, B. J. Perceived frequency of concrete and abstract words. *Memory & Cognition,* 1973, *1,* 56–60.

Gardiner, J. M., Craik, F. I. M., & Birtwistle, J. Retrieval cues and release from proactive inhibition. *Journal of Verbal Learning and Verbal Behavior,* 1972, *11,* 778–783.

Gardiner, J. M., & Klee, H. Memory for remembered events: An assessment of output monitoring in free recall. *Journal of Verbal Learning and Verbal Behavior,* 1976, *15,* 227–233.

Gardiner, J. M., Klee, H., Redman, G., & Ball, M. The role of stimulus material in determining release from proactive inhibition. *Quarterly Journal of Experimental Psychology,* 1976, *28,* 395–402.

Gates, A. I., & Taylor, G. A. An experimental study of the nature of improvement resulting from practice in a mental function. *Journal of Educational Psychology,* 1925, *16,* 583–592.

Ghatala, E. S., Levin, J. R., & Subkoviak, M. J. Rehearsal strategy effects in children's discrimination learning: Confronting the crucible. *Journal of Verbal Learning and Verbal Behavior,* 1975, *14,* 398–407.

Glanzer, M. Storage mechanisms in recall. In G. H. Bower & J. T. Spence (Eds.), *The psychology of learning and motivation* (Vol. 5). New York: Academic Press, 1972.

Glanzer, M., & Bowles, N. Analysis of the word frequency effect in recognition memory. *Journal of Experimental Psychology: Human Learning and Memory,* 1976, *2,* 21–31.

Glanzer, M., & Cunitz, A. R. Two storage mechanisms in free recall. *Journal of Verbal Learning and Verbal Behavior,* 1966, *5,* 351–360.

Glaze, J. A. The association value of nonsense syllables. *Journal of Genetic Psychology,* 1928, *35,* 255–269.

Glenberg, A. M. Component-levels theory of the effects of spacing of repetitions on recall and recognition. *Memory & Cognition,* 1979, 7, 95–112.

Glenberg, A., & Adams, F. Type I rehearsal and recognition. *Journal of Verbal Learning and Verbal Behavior,* 1978, *17,* 455–463.

Glenberg, A., Smith, S. M., & Green, C. Type I rehearsal: Maintenance and more. *Journal of Verbal Learning and Verbal Behavior,* 1977, *16,* 339-352.

Godden, D., & Baddeley, A. When does context influence recognition memory? *British Journal of Psychology,* 1980, *71,* 99–104.

Godden, D. R., & Baddeley, A. D. Context-dependent memory in two natural environments: On land and underwater. *British Journal of Psychology,* 1975, *66,* 325–331.

Graefe, T. M., & Watkins, M. J. Picture rehearsal: An effect of selectively attending to pictures no longer in view. *Journal of Experimental Psychology: Human Learning and Memory,* 1980, *6,* 156–162.

Gray, C. R., & Gummerman, K. The enigmatic eidetic image: A critical examination of methods, data, and theories. *Psychological Bulletin,* 1975, *82,* 383–407.

Greenberg, R., & Underwood, B. J. Retention as a function of stage of practice. *Journal of Experimental Psychology,* 1950, *40,* 452–457.

Greeno, J. G., James, C. T., & DaPolito, F. J. A cognitive interpretation of negative transfer and forgetting of paired associates. *Journal of Verbal Learning and Verbal Behavior,* 1971, *10,* 331–345.

Greenspoon, J., & Ranyard, R. Stimulus conditions and retroactive inhibition. *Journal of Experimental Psychology,* 1957, *53,* 55–59.

Gregg, V. Word frequency, recognition and recall. In J. Brown (Ed.), *Recall and recognition.* New York: Wiley, 1976.

Gude, C., & Zechmeister, E. B. Frequency judgments for the "gist" of sentences. *American Journal of Psychology,* 1975, *88,* 385–396.

Gunter, B., Clifford, B. R., & Berry, C. Release from proactive interference with television news items: Evidence for encoding dimensions within televised news. *Journal of Experimental Psychology: Human Learning and Memory,* 1980, *6,* 216–233.

Haagen, C. H. Synonymity, vividness, familiarity and association value ratings of 400 pairs of common adjectives. *Journal of Psychology,* 1949, *27,* 453–463.

Hagen, J. W., Hargrave, S., & Ross, W. Prompting and rehearsal in short-term memory. *Child Development,* 1973, *44,* 201–204.

Hall, J. F. Learning as a function of word frequency. *American Journal of Psychology,* 1954, *67,* 138–140.

Hall, J. W., Smith, T. A., Wegener, S. L., & Underwood, B. J. Rate and frequency as determinants of learning with complete and discrete list presentation. *Memory & Cognition,* in press.

Harris, G., Begg, I., & Mitterer, J. On the relation between frequency estimates and recognition memory. *Memory & Cognition,* 1980, *8,* 99–104.

Harris, R. L., Gausepohl, J., Lewis, R. J., & Spoehr, K. T. The suffix effect: Postcategorical attributes in a serial recall paradigm. *Bulletin of the Psychonomic Society,* 1979, *13,* 35–37.

Hart, J. T. Memory and the feeling-of-knowing experience. *Journal of Educational Psychology,* 1965, *56,* 208–216.

Hart, J. T. Methodological note on feeling-of-knowing experiments. *Journal of Educational Psychology,* 1966, *57,* 347–349.

Hart, J. T. Memory and the memory-monitoring process. *Journal of Verbal Learning and Verbal Behavior,* 1967, *6,* 685–691. (a)

Hart, J. T. Second-try recall, recognition, and the memory-monitoring process. *Journal of Educational Psychology,* 1967, *58,* 193–197. (b)

Hasher, L., & Chromiak, W. The processing of frequency information: An automatic mechanism? *Journal of Verbal Learning and Verbal Behavior,* 1977, *16,* 173–184.

Hasher, L., Goldstein, D., & Toppino, T. Frequency and the conference of referential validity. *Journal of Verbal Learning and Verbal Behavior,* 1977, *16,* 107–112.

Hasher, L., & Griffin, M. Reconstructive and reproductive processes in memory. *Journal of Experimental Psychology: Human Learning and Memory,* 1978, *4,* 318–330.

Hasher, L., & Johnson, M. K. Interpretive factors in forgetting. *Journal of Experimental Psychology: Human Learning and Memory,* 1975, *1,* 567–575.

Hasher, L., & Zacks, R. T. Automatic and effortful processes in memory. *Journal of Experimental Psychology: General,* 1979, *108,* 356–388.

Hayes-Roth, F. Distinguishing theories of representation: A critique of Anderson's arguments concerning mental imagery. *Psychological Review,* 1979, *86,* 376–382.

Healy, A. F., & Kubovy, M. The effects of payoffs and prior probabilities on indices of performance and cutoff location in recognition memory. *Memory & Cognition,* 1978, *6,* 544–553.

Hebb, D. O. *The organization of behavior.* New York: Wiley, 1949.

Hebb, D. O. Distinctive features of learning in the higher animal. In J. F. Delafresnaye (Ed.), *Brain mechanisms and learning: A symposium.* Oxford, England: Blackwell Scientific Publications, 1961.

Hebb, D. O. Concerning imagery. *Psychological Review,* 1968, *75,* 466–477.

Higbee, K. L. *Your memory: How it works and how to improve it.* Englewood Cliffs, N.J.: Prentice-Hall, 1977.

Hintzman, D. L. Apparent frequency as a function of frequency and the spacing of repetitions. *Journal of Experimental Psychology,* 1969, *80,* 139–145.

Hintzman, D. L. Effects of repetition and exposure duration on memory. *Journal of Experimental Psychology,* 1970, *83,* 435–444.

Hintzman, D. L. Theoretical implications of the spacing effect. In R. L. Solso (Ed.), *Theories in cognitive psychology: The Loyola symposium.* Hillsdale, N.J.: Erlbaum, 1974.

Hintzman, D. L. Repetition and memory. In G. H. Bower (Ed.), *The psychology of learning and motivation* (Vol. 10). New York: Academic Press, 1976.

Hintzman, D. L. *The psychology of learning and memory.* San Francisco: W.H. Freeman, 1978.

Hintzman, D. L., & Block, R. A. Repetition and memory: Evidence for a multiple-trace hypothesis. *Journal of Experimental Psychology,* 1971, *88,* 297–306.

Hintzman, D. L., Block, R. A., & Inskeep, N. R. Memory for mode of input. *Journal of Verbal Learning and Verbal Behavior,* 1972, *11,* 741–749.

Hintzman, D. L., & Rogers, M. K. Spacing effects in picture memory. *Memory & Cognition,* 1973, *1,* 430–434.

Hintzman, D. L., & Stern, L. D. Failure to confirm Elmes, Greener, and Wilkinson's findings on the spacing effect. *American Journal of Psychology,* 1977, *90,* 489–497.

Hintzman, D. L., Summers, J. J., Eki, N. T., & Moore, M. D. Voluntary attention and the spacing effect. *Memory & Cognition,* 1975, *3,* 576–580.

Hitch, G. J. The role of attention in visual and auditory suffix effects. *Memory & Cognition,* 1975, *3,* 501–505.

Holding, D. H. Sensory storage reconsidered. *Memory & Cognition,* 1975, *3,* 31–41.

Holt, R. R. Imagery: The return of the ostracized. *American Psychologist,* 1964, *19,* 254–264.

Hopkins, R. H., Edwards, R. E., & Cook, C. L. Presentation modality, distractor modality, and proactive interference in short-term memory. *Journal of Experimental Psychology,* 1973, *98,* 362–367.

Howell, W. C. Representation of frequency in memory. *Psychological Bulletin,* 1973, *80,* 44–53.

Howes, D. On the interpretation of word frequency as a variable affecting speed of recognition. *Journal of Experimental Psychology,* 1954, *48,* 106–112.

Hunt, E. Mechanics of verbal ability. *Psychological Review,* 1978, *85,* 109–130.

Hunt, E., Frost, N., & Lunneborg, C. Individual differences in cognition: A new approach to intelligence. In G. H. Bower (Ed.), *The psychology of learning and motivation* (Vol. 7). New York: Academic Press, 1973.

Hunt, E., & Love, T. How good can memory be? In A. W. Melton & E. Martin (Eds.), *Coding processes in human memory.* Washington, D.C.: Winston, 1972.

Hunt, E., Lunneborg, C., & Lewis, J. What does it mean to be high verbal? *Cognitive Psychology,* 1975, *7,* 194–227.

Hunter, I. M. L. The role of memory in expert mental calculations. In M. M. Gruneberg, P. E. Morris, & R. N. Sykes (Eds.), *Practical aspects of memory.* New York: Academic Press, 1978.

Huttenlocher, J., & Burke, D. Why does memory span increase with age? *Cognitive Psychology,* 1976, *8,* 1–31.

Hyde, T. S., & Jenkins, J. J. Differential effects of incidental tasks on the organization of recall of a list of highly associated words. *Journal of Experimental Psychology,* 1969, *82,* 472–481.

Hyde, T. S., & Jenkins, J. J. Recall for words as a function of semantic, graphic, and syntactic orienting tasks. *Journal of Verbal Learning and Verbal Behavior,* 1973, *12,* 471–480.

Jacoby, L. L. Context effects on frequency judgments of words and sentences. *Journal of Experimental Psychology,* 1972, *94,* 255–260.

Jacoby, L. L. Test appropriate strategies in retention of categorized lists. *Journal of Verbal Learning and Verbal Behavior,* 1973, *12,* 675–682.

Jacoby, L. L. On interpreting the effects of repetition: Solving a problem versus remembering a solution. *Journal of Verbal Learning and Verbal Behavior,* 1978, *17,* 649–667.

Jacoby, L. L., Bartz, W. H., & Evans, J. D. A functional approach to levels of processing. *Journal of Experimental Psychology: Human Learning and Memory,* 1978, *4,* 331–346.

Jacoby, L. L., & Craik, F. I. M. Effects of elaboration of processing at encoding and retrieval: Trace distinctiveness and recovery of initial context. In L. S. Cermak & F. I. M. Craik (Eds.), *Levels of processing in human memory.* Hillsdale, N.J.: Erlbaum, 1979.

Jacoby, L. L., Craik, F. I. M., & Begg, I. Effects of decision difficulty on recognition and recall. *Journal of Verbal Learning and Verbal Behavior,* 1979, *18,* 585–600.

James, W. *Principles of psychology* (Vol. 1). New York: Henry Holt, 1890.

Jenkins, J. G., & Dallenbach, K. M. Obliviscence during sleep and waking. *American Journal of Psychology,* 1924, *35,* 605–612.

Jenkins, J. J. Can we have a theory of meaningful memory. In R. L. Solso (Ed.), *Theories in cognitive psychology: The Loyola symposium.* Hillsdale, N.J.: Erlbaum, 1974.

Jenkins, J. J. Four points to remember: A tetrahedral model of memory experiments. In L. S. Cermak and F. I. M. Craik (Eds.), *Levels of processing in human memory.* Hillsdale, N.J.: Erlbaum, 1979.

Jevons, W. S. The power of numerical discrimination. *Nature,* 1871, *3,* 281–282.

Johnson, M. K., Bransford, J. D., & Solomon, S. K. Memory for tacit implications of sentences. *Journal of Experimental Psychology,* 1973, *98,* 203–205.

Johnson, M. K., Doll, T. J., Bransford, J. D., & Lapinski, R. H. Context effects in sentence memory. *Journal of Experimental Psychology,* 1974, *103,* 358–360.

Johnson, M. K., & Raye, C. L. Reality monitoring. *Psychological Review,* 1981, *88,* 67–85.

Johnson, M. K., Raye, C. L., Wang, A. Y., & Taylor, T. H. Fact and fantasy: The roles of accuracy and variability in confusing imaginations with perceptual experiences. *Journal of Experimental Psychology: Human Learning and Memory,* 1979, *5,* 229–240.

Johnson, M. K., Taylor, T. H., & Raye, C. L. Fact and fantasy: The effects of internally generated events on the apparent frequency of externally generated events. *Memory & Cognition,* 1977, *5,* 116–122.

Johnston, W. A., & Uhl, C. N. The contributions of encoding effort and variability to the spacing effect on free recall. *Journal of Experimental Psychology: Human Learning and Memory,* 1976, *2,* 153–160.

Kahneman, D. *Attention and effort.* Englewood Cliffs, N.J.: Prentice-Hall, 1973.

Kalbaugh, G. L., & Walls, R. T. Retroactive and proactive interference in prose learning of biographical and science materials. *Journal of Educational Psychology,* 1973, *65,* 244–251.

Kausler, D. H. *Psychology of verbal learning and memory.* New York: Academic Press, 1974.

Keppel, G. Facilitation in short- and long-term retention of paired associates following distributed practice in learning. *Journal of Verbal Learning and Verbal Behavior,* 1964, *3,* 91–111.

Keppel, G. A reconsideration of the extinction-recovery theory. *Journal of Verbal Learning and Verbal Behavior,* 1967, *6,* 476–486.

Keppel, G. Retroactive and proactive inhibition. In T. R. Dixon & D. L. Horton (Eds.), *Verbal behavior and general behavior theory.* Englewood Cliffs, N.J.: Prentice-Hall, 1968.

Keppel, G. Forgetting. In C. P. Duncan, L. Sechrest, & A. W. Melton (Eds.), *Human memory: Festschrift in honor of Benton J. Underwood.* New York: Appleton-Century-Crofts, 1972.

Keppel, G., Postman, L., & Zavortink, B. Studies of learning to learn: VIII. The influence of massive amounts of training upon the learning and retention of paired-associate lists. *Journal of Verbal Learning and Verbal Behavior,* 1968, *7,* 790–796.

Keppel, G., & Underwood, B. J. Proactive inhibition in short-term retention of single items. *Journal of Verbal Learning and Verbal Behavior,* 1962, *1,* 153–161.

Kihlstrom, J. F., & Evans, F. J. (Eds.). *Functional disorders of memory.* Hillsdale, N.J.: Erlbaum, 1979.

King, J. F., Zechmeister, E. B., & Shaughnessy, J. J. Judgments of knowing: The influence of retrieval practice. *American Journal of Psychology,* 1980, *93,* 329–343.

Kinney, L. B., & Eurich, A. C. A summary of investigations comparing different types of tests. *School and Society,* 1932, *35,* 540–544.

Kinsbourne, M., & George, J. The mechanism of the word-frequency effect on recognition memory. *Journal of Verbal Learning and Verbal Behavior,* 1974, *13,* 63–69.

Kinsbourne, M., & Wood, F. Short-term memory processes and the amnesic syndrome. In D. Deutsch & J. A. Deutsch (Eds.), *Short-term memory.* New York: Academic Press, 1975.

Kintsch, W. Models for free recall and recognition. In D. A. Norman (Ed.), *Models of human memory.* New York: Academic Press, 1970.

Kintsch, W. *Memory and cognition.* New York: Wiley, 1977.

Kirkpatrick, E. A. An experimental study of memory. *Psychological Review,* 1894, *1,* 602–609.

Klee, H., & Gardiner, J. M. Memory for remembered events: Contrasting recall and recognition. *Journal of Verbal Learning and Verbal Behavior,* 1976, *15,* 471–478.

Kolers, P. A., & Palef, S. R. Knowing not. *Memory & Cognition,* 1976, *4,* 553–558.

Koriat, A., Lichtenstein, S., & Fischhoff, B. Reasons for confidence. *Journal of Experimental Psychology: Human learning and memory,* 1980, *6,* 107–118.

Koriat, A., & Lieblich, I. What does a person in a "TOT" state know that a person in a "don't know" state doesn't know? *Memory & Cognition,* 1974, *2,* 647–655.

Kosslyn, S. M. The medium and the message in mental imagery: A theory. *Psychological Review,* 1981, *88,* 46–66.

Kosslyn, S. M., & Pomerantz, J. R. Imagery, propositions, and the form of internal representations. *Cognitive Psychology,* 1977, *9,* 52–76.

Kreutzer, M. A., Leonard, C., & Flavell, J. H. An interview study of children's knowledge about memory. *Monographs of the Society for Research in Child Development,* 1975, *40* (1, Serial No. 159).

Kucera, H., & Francis, W. N. *Computational analysis of present-day American English.* Providence, R.I.: Brown University Press, 1967.

Landauer, T. K., & Bjork, R. A. Optimum rehearsal patterns and name learning. In M. M. Gruneberg, P. E. Morris, & R. N. Sykes (Eds.), *Practical aspects of memory.* New York: Academic Press, 1978.

Landauer, T. K., & Streeter, L. A. Structural differences between common and rare words: Failure of equivalence assumptions for theories of word recognition. *Journal of Verbal Learning and Verbal Behavior,* 1973, *12,* 119–131.

Lee, A. T., Tzeng, O. J. L., Garro, L. C., & Hung, D. L. Sensory modality and the word-frequency effect. *Memory & Cognition,* 1978, *6,* 306–311.

Levin, J. R., Pressley, M., McCormick, C. B., Miller, G. E., & Shriberg, L. K. Assessing the classroom potential of the keyword method. *Journal of Educational Psychology,* 1979, *71,* 583–594.

Levy, J., & Levy, J. M. Human lateralization from head to foot: Sex-related factors. *Science,* 1978, *200,* 1291–1292.

Lewis, D. J. Sources of experimental amnesia. *Psychological Review,* 1969, 76, 461–472.

Lewis, D. J. Psychobiology of active and inactive memory. *Psychological Bulletin,* 1979, *86,* 1054–1083.

Lewis, D. J., Miller, R. R., & Misanin, J. R. Control of retrograde amnesia. *Journal of Comparative and Physiological Psychology,* 1968, *66,* 48–52.

Lewis, D. J., Miller, R. R., & Misanin, J. R. Selective amnesia in rats produced by electroconvulsive shock. *Journal of Comparative and Physiological Psychology,* 1969, *69,* 136–140.

Lichtenstein, S., & Fischhoff, B. Do those who know more also know more about how much they know? *Organizational Behavior and Human Performance,* 1977, *20,* 159–183.

Lichtenstein, S., Fischhoff, B., & Phillips, L. D. Calibration of probabilities: The state of the art. In H. Jungermann & G. deZeeuw (Eds.), *Decision making and change in human affairs.* Dordrecht, Holland: D. Reidel, 1977.

Lichtenstein, S., Slovic, P., Fischhoff, B., Layman, M., & Combs, J. Judged frequency of lethal events. *Journal of Experimental Psychology: Human Learning and Memory,* 1978, *4,* 551–578.

Lieberman, D. A. Behaviorism and the mind: A (limited) call for a return to introspection. *American Psychologist,* 1979, *34,* 319–333.

Light, L. L., & Carter-Sobell, L. Effects of changed semantic context on recognition memory. *Journal of Verbal Learning and Verbal Behavior,* 1970, *9,* 1–11.

Light, L. L., Kimble, G. A., & Pellegrino, J. W. Comments on "Episodic Memory: When Recognition Fails," by Watkins and Tulving. *Journal of Experimental Psychology: General,* 1975, *1,* 30–36.

Lippman, L. G., & Kintz, B. L. Group predictions of item differences of CVC trigrams. *Psychonomic Science,* 1968, *12,* 265–266.

Lockhart, R. S., & Murdock, B. B., Jr. Memory and the theory of signal detection. *Psychological Bulletin,* 1970, *74,* 100–109.

Loftus, E. F. Leading questions and the eyewitness report. *Cognitive Psychology,* 1975, *7,* 560–572.

Loftus, E. F. Shifting human color vision. *Memory & Cognition,* 1977, *5,* 696–699.

Loftus, E. F. *Eyewitness testimony.* Cambridge, Mass.: Harvard University Press, 1979. (a)

Loftus, E. F. Reactions to blatantly contradictory information. *Memory & Cognition,* 1979, *7,* 368–374. (b)

Loftus, E. F. The malleability of human memory. *American Scientist,* 1979, *67,* 312–320. (c)

Loftus, E. F., & Loftus, G. R. On the permanence of stored information in the human brain. *American Psychologist,* 1980, *35,* 409–420.

Loftus, E. F., Miller, D. G., & Burns, H. J. Semantic integration of verbal information into a visual memory. *Journal of Experimental Psychology: Human Learning and Memory,* 1978, *4,* 19–31.

Loftus, E. F., & Palmer, J. C. Reconstruction of automobile destruction: An example of the interaction between language and memory. *Journal of Verbal Learning and Verbal Behavior,* 1974, *13,* 585–589.

Lorayne, H., & Lucas, J. *The memory book.* New York: Stein & Day, 1974.

Lorge, I. Influence of regularly interpolated time intervals upon subsequent learning. *Teachers College. Contributions to Education,* 1930, No. 438.

Luh, C. W. The conditions of retention. *Psychological Monographs,* 1922, *31* (3, Whole Number 142).

Luria, A. R. *The mind of a mnemonist.* New York: Basic Books, 1968.

Lyon, D. R. Individual differences in immediate serial recall: A matter of mnemonics? *Cognitive Psychology,* 1977, *9,* 403–411.

Maccoby, E. F., & Jacklin, C. N. *The psychology of sex differences.* Stanford, Calif.: Stanford University Press, 1974.

Macey, W. H., & Zechmeister, E. B. Test of the multiple-trace hypothesis: The effects of temporal separation and presentation modality. *Journal of Experimental Psychology: Human Learning and Memory,* 1975, *4,* 459–465.

MacLeod, C. M. Release from proactive interference: Insufficiency of an attentional account. *American Journal of Psychology,* 1975, *88,* 459–465.

Mactutus, C. F., Riccio, D. C., & Ferek, J. M. Retrograde amnesia for old (reactivated) memory: Some anomalous characteristics. *Science,* 1979, *204,* 1319–1320.

Maki, R. H., & Hasher, L. Encoding variability: A role in immediate and long-term memory? *American Journal of Psychology,* 1975, *88,* 217–231.

Malmi, R. A. Context effects in recognition memory: The frequency attribute. *Memory & Cognition,* 1977, *5,* 123–130.

Mandler, G. Recognizing: The judgment of previous occurrence. *Psychological Review,* 1980, *87,* 252–271.

Mandler, J. M., Seegmiller, D., & Day, J. On the coding of spatial information. *Memory & Cognition,* 1977, *5,* 10–16.

Martin, E. Stimulus meaningfulness and paired-associate transfer: An encoding variability hypothesis. *Psychological Review,* 1968, *75,* 421–441.

Martin, E. Verbal learning theory and independent retrieval phenomenon. *Psychological Review,* 1971, *78,* 314–332.

Martin, E. Generation-recognition retrieval theory and the encoding specificity principle. *Psychological Review,* 1975, *82,* 150–153.

Martin, E., & Greeno, J. G. Independence of associations tested: A reply to D. L. Hintzman. *Psychological Review,* 1972, *79,* 265–267.

Martin, M. Memory span as a measure of individual differences in memory capacity. *Memory & Cognition,* 1978, *6,* 194–198.

Masur, E. F., McIntyre, C. W., & Flavell, J. H. Developmental changes in apportionment of study time among items in a multitrial free recall task. *Journal of Experimental Child Psychology,* 1973, *15,* 237–246.

Matarazzo, J. D. *Wechsler's measurement and appraisal of adult intelligence* (5th ed.). Baltimore: Williams & Wilkins, 1972.

McCloskey, M., & Watkins, M. J. The seeing-more-than-is-there phenomenon: Implications for the locus of iconic storage. *Journal of Experimental Psychology: Human Perception and Performance,* 1978, *4,* 553–564.

McCormack, P. D. Recognition memory: How complex a retrieval system? *Canadian Journal of Psychology,* 1972, *26,* 19–41.

McGee, M. G. Human spatial abilities: Psychometric studies and environmental, genetic, hormonal, and neurological influences. *Psychological Bulletin,* 1979, *86,* 889–918.

McGeoch, J. A. Forgetting and the law of disuse. *Psychological Review,* 1932, *39,* 352–370.

McGeoch, J. A. *The psychology of human learning.* New York: Longmans, Green, 1942.

McGeoch, J. A., & Irion, A. L. *The psychology of human learning.* New York: David McKay, 1952.

McGovern, J. B. Extinction of associations in four transfer paradigms. *Psychological Monographs,* 1964, *78* (16, Whole No. 593).

Melton, A. W. Implications of short-term memory for a general theory of memory. *Journal of Verbal Learning and Verbal Behavior,* 1963, *2,* 1–21.

Melton, A. W. The situation with respect to the spacing of repetitions and memory. *Journal of Verbal Learning and Verbal Behavior,* 1970, *9,* 596–606.

Melton, A. W., & Irwin, J. M. The influence of degree of interpolated learning on retroactive inhibition and the overt transfer of specific responses. *American Journal of Psychology,* 1940, *53,* 173–203.

Meyer, G. An experimental study of the old and new types of examination: I. The effects of the examination set on memory. *Journal of Educational Psychology,* 1934, *25,* 641–661.

Meyer, G. An experimental study of the old and new types of examination: II. Methods of study. *Journal of Educational Psychology,* 1935, *26,* 30–40.

Meyer, G. E., & Maguire, W. M. Spatial frequency and the mediation of short-term visual storage. *Science,* 1977, *198,* 524–525.

Miller, G. A. The magical number seven, plus or minus two: Some limits on our capacity for processing information. *Psychological Review,* 1956, *63,* 81–97.

Miller, R. R., & Marlin, N. A. Amnesia following electroconvulsive shock. In J. F. Kihlstrom & F. J. Evans (Eds.), *Functional disorders of memory.* Hillsdale, N.J.: Erlbaum, 1979.

Miller, R. R., & Springer, A. D. Recovery from amnesia following transcorneal electroconvulsive shock. *Psychonomic Science,* 1972, *28,* 7–8.

Minsky, M. A framework for representing knowledge. In P. H. Winston (Ed.), *The psychology of computer vision.* New York: McGraw-Hill, 1975.

Misanin, J. R., Miller, R. R., & Lewis, D. J. Retrograde amnesia produced by electroconvulsive shock after reactivation of a consolidated memory trace. *Science,* 1968, *160,* 554–555.

Morris, C. D., Bransford, J. D., & Franks, J. J. Levels of processing versus transfer appropriate processing. *Journal of Verbal Learning and Verbal Behavior,* 1977, *16,* 519–533.

Morton, J., Crowder, R. G., & Prussin, H. A. Experiments with the stimulus suffix effect. *Journal of Experimental Psychology,* 1971, *91,* 169–190.

Murdock, B. B., Jr. The retention of individual items. *Journal of Experimental Psychology,* 1961, *62,* 618–625.

Murdock, B. B., Jr. The serial position effect of free recall. *Journal of Experimental Psychology,* 1962, *64,* 482–488.

Murdock, B. B., Jr. *Human memory: Theory and data.* Hillsdale, N.J.: Erlbaum, 1974.

Murdock, B. B., Jr., & Metcalfe, J. Controlled rehearsal in single-trial free recall. *Journal of Verbal Learning and Verbal Behavior,* 1978, *17,* 309–324.

Nebes, R. D. Hemispheric specialization in commissurotomized man. *Psychological Bulletin,* 1974, *81,* 1–14.

Neisser, U. *Cognitive psychology.* New York: Appleton-Century-Crofts, 1967.

Nelson, D. L. Remembering pictures and words: Appearance, significance, and name. In L. S. Cermak & F. I. M. Craik (Eds.), *Levels of processing in human memory.* Hillsdale, N.J.: Erlbaum, 1979.

Nelson, D. L., Reed, V. S., & McEvoy, C. L. Learning to order pictures and words: A model of sensory and semantic encoding. *Journal of Experimental Psychology: Human Learning and Memory,* 1977, *3,* 485–497.

Nelson, T. O. Savings and forgetting from long-term memory. *Journal of Verbal Learning and Verbal Behavior,* 1971, *10,* 568–576.

Nelson, T. O. Repetition and depth of processing. *Journal of Verbal Learning and Verbal Behavior,* 1977, *16,* 151–171.

Nelson, T. O. Detecting small amounts of information in memory: Savings for non-recognized items. *Journal of Experimental Psychology: Human Learning and Memory,* 1978, *4,* 453–468.

Nelson, T. O., Fehling, M. R., & Moore-Glascock, J. The nature of semantic savings for items forgotten from long-term memory. *Journal of Experimental Psychology: General,* 1979, *108,* 225–250.

Nelson, T. O., & Narens, L. Norms of 300 general-information questions: Accuracy of recall, latency of recall, and feeling-of-knowing ratings. *Journal of Verbal Learning and Verbal Behavior,* 1980, *19,* 338–368.

Nelson, T. O., & Rothbart, R. Acoustic savings for items forgotten from long-term memory. *Journal of Experimental Psychology,* 1972, *93,* 357–360.

Noble, C. E. Age, race, and sex in the learning and performance of psychomotor skills. In R. T. Osborne, C. E. Noble, & N. Weyl (Eds.), *Human variation: The biopsychology of age, race, and sex.* New York: Academic Press, 1978.

Nyberg, S. E. Comprehension and long-term retention of prose passages. Unpublished doctoral dissertation, State University of New York at Stony Brook, 1975.

O'Neill, M. E., Sutcliffe, J. A., & Tulving, E. Retrieval cues and release from proactive inhibition. *American Journal of Psychology,* 1976, *89,* 535–543.

Osborne, R. T., Noble, C. E., & Weyl, N. (Eds.). *Human variation: The biopsychology of age, race and sex.* New York: Academic Press, 1978.

Oscar-Berman, M. Neuropsychological consequences of long-term chronic alcoholism. *American Scientist,* 1980, *68,* 410–419.

Osgood, C. E., Suci, G. J., & Tannenbaum, P. H. *The measurement of meaning.* Urbana: University of Illinois Press, 1957.

Owings, R. A., Petersen, G. A., Bransford, J. D., Morris, C. D., & Stein, B. S. Spontaneous monitoring and regulation of learning: A comparison of successful and less successful fifth graders. *Journal of Educational Psychology,* 1980, *72,* 250–256.

Paivio, A. Mental imagery in associative learning and memory. *Psychological Review,* 1969, *76,* 241–263.

Paivio, A. *Imagery and verbal processes.* New York: Holt, Rinehart & Winston, 1971.

Paivio, A. Imagery in recall and recognition. In J. Brown (Ed.), *Recall and recognition.* New York: Wiley, 1976.

Paivio, A. Mental comparisons involving abstract attributes. *Memory & Cognition,* 1978, *6,* 199–208.

Paivio, A., Yuille, J. C., & Rogers, T. B. Noun imagery and meaningfulness in free and serial recall. *Journal of Experimental Psychology,* 1969, *79,* 509–514.

Palermo, D. S., & Jenkins, J. J. *Word association norms: Grade school through college.* Minneapolis: University of Minnesota Press, 1964.

Pasko, S. J., & Zechmeister, E. B. Temporal separation in verbal discrimination transfer. *Journal of Experimental Psychology,* 1974, *102,* 525–528.

Pavlov, I. P. *Conditioned reflexes.* New York: Dover, 1960. (Originally published, 1927.)

Penfield, W., & Roberts, L. *Speech and brain mechanisms.* Princeton, N.J.: Princeton University Press, 1959.

Penney, C. G. Modality effects in short-term verbal memory. *Psychological Bulletin,* 1975, *82,* 68–84.

Penney, C. G. Interactions of suffix effects with suffix delay and recall modality in serial recall. *Journal of Experimental Psychology: Human Learning and Memory,* 1979, *5,* 507–521.

Peterson, L. R., & Peterson, M. J. Short-term retention of individual verbal items. *Journal of Experimental Psychology,* 1959, *58,* 193–198.

Peterson, L. R., Saltzman, D., Hillner, K., & Land, V. Recency and frequency in paired-associate learning. *Journal of Experimental Psychology,* 1962, *63,* 396–403.

Peterson, L. R., Wampler, R., Kirkpatrick, M., & Saltzman, D. Effect of spacing of presentations on retention of a paired associate over short intervals. *Journal of Experimental Psychology,* 1963, *66,* 206–209.

Peterson, M. J., Thomas, J. E., & Johnson, H. Imagery, rehearsal, and the compatibility of input-output tasks. *Memory & Cognition,* 1977, *5,* 415–422.

Petrich, J. A. Storage and retrieval processes in unlearning. *Memory & Cognition,* 1975, *3,* 63–74.

Postman, L. Choice behavior and the process of recognition. *American Journal of Psychology,* 1950, *63,* 576–583.

Postman, L. The generalization gradient in recognition memory. *Journal of Experimental Psychology,* 1951, *42,* 231–235.

Postman, L. Short-term memory and incidental learning. In A. W. Melton (Ed.), *Categories of human learning.* New York: Academic Press, 1964.

Postman, L. A pragmatic view of organization theory. In E. Tulving & W. Donaldson (Eds.), *Organization of memory.* New York: Academic Press, 1972.

Postman, L. Tests of the generality of the principle of encoding specificity. *Memory & Cognition,* 1975, *3,* 663–672. (a)

Postman, L. Verbal learning and memory. *Annual Review of Psychology,* 1975, *26,* 291–335. (b)

Postman, L. Interference theory revisited. In J. Brown (Ed.), *Recall and recognition.* New York: Wiley, 1976.

Postman, L., & Burns, S. Experimental analysis of coding processes. *Memory & Cognition,* 1973, *1,* 503–507.

Postman, L., & Gray, W. D. Response recall and retroactive inhibition. *American Journal of Psychology,* 1978, *91,* 3–22.

Postman, L., & Gray, W. D. Does imaginal encoding increase resistance to interference? *American Journal of Psychology,* 1979, *92,* 215–233.

Postman, L., & Keppel, G. Conditions of cumulative proactive inhibition. *Journal of Experimental Psychology: General,* 1977, *106,* 376–403.

Postman, L., & Kruesi, E. The influence of orienting tasks on the encoding and recall of words. *Journal of Verbal Learning and Verbal Behavior,* 1977, *16,* 353–369.

Postman, L., & Parker, J. F. Maintenance of first list associations during transfer. *American Journal of Psychology,* 1970, *83,* 171–188.

Postman, L., & Rau, L. Retention as a function of the method of measurements. *University of California Publications in Psychology,* 1957, *8,* 217–220.

Postman, L., & Stark, K. Role of response availability in transfer and interference. *Journal of Experimental Psychology,* 1969, *79,* 168–177.

Postman, L., Stark, K., & Burns, S. Sources of proactive inhibition on unpaced tests of retention. *American Journal of Psychology,* 1974, *87,* 33–56.

Postman, L., Stark, K., & Fraser, J. Temporal changes in interference. *Journal of Verbal Learning and Verbal Behavior,* 1968, *7,* 672–694.

Postman, L., Thompkins, B. A., & Gray, W. D. The interpretation of encoding effects in retention. *Journal of Verbal Learning and Verbal Behavior,* 1978, *17,* 681–705.

Postman, L., & Underwood, B. J. Critical issues in interference theory. *Memory & Cognition,* 1973, *1,* 19–40.

Pressley, M. Children's use of the keyword method to learn simple Spanish vocabulary words. *Journal of Educational Psychology,* 1977, *69,* 465–472.

Putnam, B. Hypnosis and distortions in eyewitness memory. *International Journal of Clinical and Experimental Hypnosis,* 1979, *27,* 437–448.

Pylyshyn, Z. W. What the mind's eye tells the mind's brain: A critique of mental imagery. *Psychological Bulletin,* 1973, *80,* 1–24.

Pylyshyn, Z. W. Validating computational models: A critique of Anderson's indeterminacy of representational claim. *Psychological Review,* 1979, *86,* 383–394.

Pylyshyn, Z. W. The imagery debate: Analogue media versus tacit knowledge. *Psychological Review,* 1981, *88,* 16–45.

Quartermain, D., McEwen, B. S., & Azmitia, E. C., Jr. Recovery of memory following amnesia in the rat and mouse. *Journal of Comparative and Physiological Psychology,* 1972, *79,* 360–370.

Raskin, D. C., Boise, C., Rubel, E. W., & Clark, D. Transfer tests of the frequency theory of verbal discrimination learning. *Journal of Experimental Psychology,* 1968, *76,* 521–529.

Raugh, M. R., & Atkinson, R. C. A mnemonic method for learning a second-language vocabulary. *Journal of Educational Psychology,* 1975, *67,* 1–16.

Raye, C. L., Johnson, M. K., & Taylor, T. H. Is there something special about memory for internally generated information? *Memory & Cognition,* 1980, *8,* 141–148.

Reitman, J. S. Mechanisms of forgetting in short-term memory. *Cognitive Psychology,* 1971, *2,* 185–195.

Reitman, J. S. Without surreptitious rehearsal, information in short-term memory decays. *Journal of Verbal Learning and Verbal Behavior,* 1974, *13,* 365–377.

Roediger, H. L., III, Knight, J. L., Jr., & Kantowitz, B. H. Inferring decay in short-term memory: The issue of capacity. *Memory & Cognition,* 1977, *5,* 167–176.

Rosenzweig, M. R., & Bennett, E. L. (Eds.). *Neural mechanisms of learning and memory.* Cambridge, Mass.: MIT Press, 1976.

Ross, J., & Lawrence, K. A. Some observations on memory artifice. *Psychonomic Science,* 1968, *13,* 107–108.

Rothkopf, E. Z. Incidental memory for location of information in text. *Journal of Verbal Learning and Verbal Behavior,* 1971, *10,* 608–613.

Rowe, E. J., & Rose, R. J. Effects of orienting task, spacing of repetitions, and list context on judgments of frequency. *Memory & Cognition,* 1977, *5,* 505–512.

Rozin, P. The psychobiological approach to human memory. In M. R. Rosenzweig & E. L. Bennett (Eds.), *Neural mechanisms of learning and memory.* Cambridge, Mass.: MIT Press, 1976.

Rubin, D. C. The subjective estimation of relative syllable frequency. *Perception & Psychophysics,* 1974, *16,* 193–196.

Rundus, D. Analysis of rehearsal processes in free recall. *Journal of Experimental Psychology,* 1971, *89,* 63–77.

Rundus, D. Maintenance rehearsal and single-level processing. *Journal of Verbal Learning and Verbal Behavior,* 1977, *16,* 665–681.

Rundus, D., & Atkinson, R. C. Rehearsal processes in free recall: A procedure for direct observation. *Journal of Verbal Learning and Verbal Behavior,* 1970, *9,* 99–105.

Russ-Eft, D. Proactive interference: Buildup and release for individual words. *Journal of Experimental Psychology: Human Learning and Memory,* 1979, *5,* 422–434.

Russell, W. R., & Nathan, P. W. Traumatic amnesia. *Brain,* 1946, *69,* 280–300.

Sakitt, B. Locus of short-term visual storage. *Science,* 1975, *190,* 1318–1319.

Sakitt, B. Iconic memory. *Psychological Review,* 1976, *83,* 257–276.

Sakitt, B., & Long, G. M. Relative rod and cone contributions in iconic storage. *Perception & Psychophysics,* 1978, *23,* 527–536.

Salter, D., & Colley, J. G. The stimulus suffix: A paradoxical effect. *Memory & Cognition,* 1977, *5,* 257–262.

Salzberg, P. M. On the generality of encoding specificity. *Journal of Experimental Psychology: Human Learning and Memory,* 1976, *2,* 586–596.

Schank, R. C. The role of memory in language processing. In C. N. Cofer (Ed.), *The structure of human memory.* San Francisco: W.H. Freeman, 1976.

Schank, R. C., & Abelson, R. P. *Scripts, plans, goals and understanding: An inquiry into human knowledge structures.* Hillsdale, N.J.: Erlbaum, 1977.

Schneider, A. M., Tyler, J., & Jinich, D. Recovery from retrograde amnesia: A learning process. *Science,* 1974, *184,* 87–88.

Schulman, A. I. Word length and rarity in recognition memory. *Psychonomic Science,* 1967, *9,* 211–212.

Schulman, A. I. Memory for words recently classified. *Memory & Cognition,* 1974, *2,* 47–52.

Schulman, A. I. Memory for rare words previously rated for familiarity. *Journal of Experimental Psychology: Human Learning and Memory,* 1976, *2,* 301–307.

Scoville, W. B., & Milner, B. Loss of recent memory after bilateral hippocampal lesions. *Journal of Neurology, Neurosurgery, and Psychiatry,* 1957, *20,* 11–19.

Seamon, J. G., & Gazzaniga, M. S. Coding strategies and cerebral laterality effects. *Cognitive Psychology,* 1973, *5,* 249–256.

Shapiro, B. J. The subjective estimation of relative word frequency. *Journal of Verbal Learning and Verbal Behavior,* 1969, *8,* 248–251.

Shaughnessy, J. J. Verbal discrimination learning and two-category classification learning as a function of list length and pronunciation instructions. *Journal of Experimental Psychology,* 1973, *100,* 202–209.

Shaughnessy, J. J. Persistence of the spacing effect in free recall under varying incidental learning conditions. *Memory & Cognition,* 1976, *4,* 369–377.

Shaughnessy, J. J. Subjective rating scales and the control of encoding in incidental learning. *Bulletin of the Psychonomic Society,* 1979, *14,* 205–208.

Shaughnessy, J. J. Memory monitoring accuracy and modification of rehearsal strategies. *Journal of Verbal Learning and Verbal Behavior,* 1981, *20,* 216–230.

Shaughnessy, J. J., Zimmerman, J., & Underwood, B. J. Further evidence on the MP-DP effect in free-recall learning. *Journal of Verbal Learning and Verbal Behavior,* 1972, *11,* 1–12.

Shaw, R. E., & Bransford, J. D. *Perceiving, acting and knowing.* Hillsdale, N.J.: Erlbaum, 1977.

Shepard, R. N. Learning and recall as organization and search. *Journal of Verbal Learning and Verbal Behavior,* 1966, *5,* 201–204.

Shepard, R. N. Recognition memory for words, sentences, and pictures. *Journal of Verbal Learning and Verbal Behavior,* 1967, *6,* 156–163.

Shepard, R. N. The mental image. *American Psychologist,* 1978, *33,* 125–137.

Shepard, R. N., & Teghtsoonian, M. Retention of information under conditions approaching a steady state. *Journal of Experimental Psychology,* 1961, *62,* 302–309.

Shiffrin, R. M. Information persistence in short-term memory. *Journal of Experimental Psychology,* 1973, *100,* 39–49.

Shiffrin, R. M. Capacity limitations in information processing, attention, and memory. In W. K. Estes (Ed.), *Handbook of learning and cognitive processes* (Vol. 4). Hillsdale, N.J.: Erlbaum, 1976.

Shiffrin, R. M., & Cook, J. R. Short-term forgetting of item and order information. *Journal of Verbal Learning and Verbal Behavior,* 1978, *17,* 189–218.

Shulman, H. G. Semantic confusion errors in short-term memory. *Journal of Verbal Learning and Verbal Behavior,* 1972, *11,* 221–227.

Simon, H. A. How big is a chunk? *Science,* 1974, *183,* 482–488.

Slamecka, N. J., & Graf, P. The generation effect: Delineation of a phenomenon. *Journal of Experimental Psychology: Human Learning and Memory,* 1978, *4,* 592–604.

Smiley, S. S., Oakley, D. D., Worthen, D., Campione, J. C., & Brown, A. L. Recall of thematically relevant material by adolescent good and poor readers as a function of written versus oral presentation. *Journal of Educational Psychology,* 1977, *69,* 381–387.

Smith, S. M. Remembering in and out of context. *Journal of Experimental Psychology: Human Learning and Memory,* 1979, *5,* 460–471.

Smith, S. M., Glenberg, A., & Bjork, R. A. Environmental context and human memory. *Memory & Cognition,* 1978, *6,* 342–353.

Spear, N. E. Experimental analysis of infantile amnesia. In J. F. Kihlstrom & F. J. Evans (Eds.), *Functional disorders of memory.* Hillsdale, N.J.: Erlbaum, 1979.

Sperling, G. The information available in brief visual presentations. *Psychological Monographs,* 1960, *74* (Whole No. 498).

Spilich, G. J., Vesonder, G. T., Chiesi, H. L., & Voss, J. F. Text processing of domain-related information for individuals with high and low domain knowledge. *Journal of Verbal Learning and Verbal Behavior,* 1979, *18,* 275–290.

Spiro, R. J. Remembering information from text: The "state of schema" approach. In R. C. Anderson, R. J. Spiro, & W. E. Montague (Eds.), *Schooling and the acquisition of knowledge.* Hillsdale, N.J.: Erlbaum, 1977.

Spiro, R. J. Accommodative reconstruction in prose recall. *Journal of Verbal Learning and Verbal Behavior,* 1980, *19,* 84–95.

Spoehr, K. T., & Corin, W. J. The stimulus suffix effect as a memory coding phenomenon. *Memory & Cognition,* 1978, *6,* 583–589.

Spreen, O., & Schulz, R. W. Parameters of abstraction, meaningfulness and pronunciability for 329 nouns. *Journal of Verbal Learning and Verbal Behavior,* 1966, *5,* 459–468.

Squire, L. R., Slater, P. C., & Chace, P. M. Retrograde amnesia: Temporal gradient in very long term memory following electroconvulsive therapy. *Science,* 1975, *187,* 77–79.

Standing, L., Conezio, J., & Haber, R. N. Perception and memory for pictures: Single-trial learning of 2500 visual stimuli. *Psychonomic Science,* 1970, *19,* 73–74.

Stein, B. S. Depth of processing re-examined: The effects of the precision of encoding and test appropriateness. *Journal of Verbal Learning and Verbal Behavior,* 1978, *17,* 165–174.

Strand, B. Z. Change of context and retroactive inhibition. *Journal of Verbal Learning and Verbal Behavior,* 1970, *9,* 202–206.

Sulin, R. A., & Dooling, D. J. Intrusion of a thematic idea in retention of prose. *Journal of Experimental Psychology,* 1974, *103,* 255–262.

Thompson, R. F. The search for the engram. *American Psychologist,* 1976, *31,* 209–227.

Thomson, D. M., & Tulving, E. Associative encoding and retrieval: Weak and strong cues. *Journal of Experimental Psychology,* 1970, *86,* 255–262.

Thorndike, E. L., & Lorge, I. *The teacher's word book of 30,000 words*. New York: Columbia University Teachers College, 1944.

Thorndyke, P. W., & Hayes-Roth, B. The use of schemata in the acquisition and transfer of knowledge. *Cognitive Psychology,* 1979, *11,* 82–106.

Till, R. E., & Jenkins, J. J. The effects of cued orienting tasks on the free recall of words. *Journal of Verbal Learning and Verbal Behavior,* 1973, *12,* 489–498.

Till, R. E., & Walsh, D. A. Encoding and retrieval factors in adult memory for implicational sentences. *Journal of Verbal Learning and Verbal Behavior,* 1980, *19,* 1–16.

Treisman, A. Monitoring and storage of irrelevant messages in selective attention. *Journal of Verbal Learning and Verbal Behavior,* 1964, *3,* 449–459.

Tulving, E. Episodic and semantic memory. In E. Tulving & W. Donaldson (Eds.), *Organization of memory*. New York: Academic Press, 1972.

Tulving, E. Ecphoric processes in recall and recognition. In J. Brown (Ed.), *Recall and recognition*. New York: Wiley, 1976.

Tulving, E. Relation between encoding specificity and levels of processing. In L. S. Cermak & F. I. M. Craik (Eds.), *Levels of processing in human memory*. Hillsdale, N.J.: Erlbaum, 1979.

Tulving, E., & Bower, G. H. The logic of memory representations. In G. Bower (Ed.), *The psychology of learning and motivation* (Vol. 8). New York: Academic Press, 1974.

Tulving, E., & Donaldson, W. *Organization of memory*. New York: Academic Press, 1972.

Tulving, E., & Madigan, S. A. Memory and verbal learning. *Annual Review of Psychology,* 1970, *21,* 437–484.

Tulving, E., & Osler, S. Effectiveness of retrieval cues in memory for words. *Journal of Experimental Psychology,* 1968, *77,* 593–601.

Tulving, E., & Psotka, J. Retroactive inhibition in free recall: Inaccessibility of information available in the memory store. *Journal of Experimental Psychology,* 1971, *87,* 1–8.

Tulving, E., & Thomson, D. M. Encoding specificity and retrieval processes in episodic memory. *Psychological Review,* 1973, *80,* 352–373.

Tulving, E., & Watkins, O. C. Recognition failure of words with a single meaning. *Memory & Cognition,* 1977, *5,* 513–522.

Tulving, E., & Wiseman, S. Relation between recognition and recognition failure of recallable words. *Bulletin of the Psychonomic Society,* 1975, *6,* 79–82.

Tversky, A., & Kahneman, D. Availability: A heuristic for judging frequency and probability. *Cognitive Psychology,* 1973, *5,* 207–232.

Tversky, A., & Kahneman, D. Judgment under uncertainty: Heuristics and biases. *Science,* 1974, *185,* 1124–1131.

Tversky, B. Encoding processes in recognition and recall. *Cognitive Psychology,* 1973, *5,* 275–287.

Tversky, B., & Sherman, T. Picture memory improves with longer on time and off time. *Journal of Experimental Psychology: Human Learning and Memory,* 1975, *1,* 114–118.

Tyler, S. W., Hertel, P. T., McCallum, M. C., & Ellis, H. C. Cognitive effort and memory. *Journal of Experimental Psychology: Human Learning and Memory,* 1979, *5,* 605–617.

Underwood, B. J. Interference and forgetting. *Psychological Review,* 1957, *64,* 49–60.

Underwood, B. J. Ten years of massed practice on distributed practice. *Psychological Review,* 1961, *68,* 229–247.

Underwood, B. J. False recognition produced by implicit verbal responses. *Journal of Experimental Psychology,* 1965, *70,* 122–129.

Underwood, B. J. Individual and group predictions of item difficulty for free learning. *Journal of Experimental Psychology,* 1966, *71,* 673–679.

Underwood, B. J. Attributes of memory. *Psychological Review,* 1969, *76,* 559–573.

Underwood, B. J. A breakdown of the total-time law in free-recall learning. *Journal of Verbal Learning and Verbal Behavior,* 1970, *9,* 573–580.

Underwood, B. J. Recognition memory. In H. H. Kendler & J. T. Spence (Eds.), *Essays in neobehaviorism: A memorial volume to K. W. Spence.* New York: Appleton-Century-Crofts, 1971.

Underwood, B. J. Are we overloading memory? In A. W. Melton & E. Martin (Eds.), *Coding processes in human memory.* Washington, D.C.: V. H. Winston, 1972.

Underwood, B. J. The role of the association in recognition memory. *Journal of Experimental Psychology, 1974, 102,* 917–939.

Underwood, B. J. Individual differences as a crucible in theory construction. *American Psychologist, 1975, 30,* 128–134.

Underwood, B. J., Boruch, R. F., & Malmi, R. A. Composition of episodic memory. *Journal of Experimental Psychology: General, 1978, 107,* 393–419.

Underwood, B. J., & Ekstrand, B. R. An analysis of some shortcomings in the interference theory of forgetting. *Psychological Review,* 1966, *73,* 540–549.

Underwood, B. J., & Freund, J. S. Errors in recognition learning and retention. *Journal of Experimental Psychology,* 1968, *78,* 55–63. (a)

Underwood, B. J., & Freund, J. S. Two tests of a theory of verbal-discrimination learning. *Canadian Journal of Psychology,* 1968, *22,* 96–104. (b)

Underwood, B. J., & Freund, J. S. Relative frequency judgments and verbal discrimination learning. *Journal of Experimental Psychology,* 1970, *83,* 279–285. (a)

Underwood, B. J., & Freund, J. S. Retention of a verbal discrimination. *Journal of Experimental Psychology,* 1970, *84,* 1–14. (b)

Underwood, B. J., & Freund, J. S. Word frequency and short-term recognition memory. *American Journal of Psychology,* 1970, *83,* 343–351. (c)

Underwood, B. J., & Humphreys, M. Context change and the role of meaning in word recognition. *American Journal of Psychology,* 1979, *92,* 577–609.

Underwood, B. J., Jesse, F., & Ekstrand, B. R. Knowledge of rights and wrongs in verbal-discrimination learning. *Journal of Verbal Learning and Verbal Behavior,* 1964, *3,* 183–186.

Underwood, B. J., Kapelak, S. M., & Malmi, R. A. The spacing effect: Additions to the theoretical and empirical puzzles. *Memory & Cognition,* 1976, *4,* 391–400.

Underwood, B. J., Patterson, M., & Freund, J. S. Recognition and number of incorrect alternatives presented during learning. *Journal of Educational Psychology,* 1972, *63,* 1–7.

Underwood, B. J., & Postman, L. Extraexperimental sources of interference in forgetting. *Psychological Review,* 1960, *67,* 73–95.

Underwood, B. J., & Schulz, R. W. *Meaningfulness and verbal learning.* Philadelphia: Lippincott, 1960.

Underwood, B. J., & Schulz, R. W. Studies of distributed practice: XX. Sources of interference associated with differences in learning and retention. *Journal of Experimental Psychology,* 1961, *61,* 228–235.

Underwood, B. J., & Zimmerman, J. The syllable as a source of error in multisyllable word recognition. *Journal of Verbal Learning and Verbal Behavior,* 1973, *12,* 701–706.

Underwood, B. J., Zimmerman, J., & Freund, J. S. Retention of frequency information with observations on recognition and recall. *Journal of Experimental Psychology,* 1971, *87,* 149–162.

Waber, D. P. Sex differences in cognition: A function of maturation rate? *Science,* 1976, *192,* 572–573.

Wallace, W. P. Verbal discrimination. In C. P. Duncan, L. Sechrest, & A. W. Melton (Eds.), *Human memory: Festschrift in honor of Benton J. Underwood.* New York: Appleton-Century-Crofts, 1972.

Wallace, W. P., & Sawyer, J. J. Verbal discrimination reversal in a whole/part re-pairing transfer paradigm. *Memory & Cognition,* 1974, *2,* 367–371.

Walsh, D. A., & Jenkins, J. J. Effects of orienting tasks on free recall in incidental learning: "Difficulty," "effort," and "process" explanations. *Journal of Verbal Learning and Verbal Behavior,* 1973, *12,* 481–488.

Warrington, E. K., & Weiskrantz, L. Amnesic syndrome: Consolidation or retrieval? *Nature,* 1970, *228,* 628–630.

Watkins, M. J. Concept and measurement of primary memory. *Psychological Bulletin,* 1974, *81,* 695–711.

Watkins, M. J. The intricacy of memory span. *Memory & Cognition,* 1977, *5,* 529–534.

Watkins, M. J., & Todres, A. K. Suffix effects manifest and concealed: Further evidence for a 20-second echo. *Journal of Verbal Learning and Verbal Behavior,* 1980, *19,* 46–53.

Watkins, M. J., & Tulving, E. Episodic memory: When recognition fails. *Journal of Experimental Psychology: General,* 1975, *104,* 5–29.

Watkins, M. J., Watkins, O. C., Craik, F. I. M., & Mazuryk, G. Effect of nonverbal distraction on short-term storage. *Journal of Experimental Psychology,* 1973, *101,* 296–300.

Watkins, O. C., & Watkins, M. J. Buildup of proactive inhibition as a cue-overload effect. *Journal of Experimental Psychology: Human Learning and Memory,* 1975, *1,* 442–452.

Watson, J. B. Psychology as the behaviorist views it. *Psychological Review,* 1913, *20,* 158–177.

Waugh, N. C. On the effective duration of a repeated word. *Journal of Verbal Learning and Verbal Behavior,* 1970, *9,* 587–595.

Waugh, N. C., & Norman, D. A. Primary memory. *Psychological Review,* 1965, *72,* 89–104.

Weaver, G. E. Effects of poststimulus study time on recognition of pictures. *Journal of Experimental Psychology,* 1974, *103,* 799–801.

Wechsler, D. *Manual for Wechsler Adult Intelligence Scale.* New York: Psychological Corporation, 1955.

Weingartner, H., Adefris, W., Eich, J. E., & Murphy, D. L. Encoding-imagery specificity in alcohol state-dependent learning. *Journal of Experimental Psychology: Human Learning and Memory,* 1976, *2,* 83–87.

Wellman, H. M. Tip of the tongue and feeling of knowing experiences: A developmental study of memory monitoring. *Child Development,* 1977, *48,* 13–21.

Wells, J. E. Strength theory and judgments of recency and frequency. *Journal of Verbal Learning and Verbal Behavior,* 1974, *13,* 378–392.

White, S. H., & Pillemer, D. B. Childhood amnesia and the development of a socially accessible memory system. In J. F. Kihlstrom & F. J. Evans (Eds.), *Functional disorders of memory.* Hillsdale, N.J.: Erlbaum, 1979.

Whitlow, J. W., Jr., & Estes, W. K. Judgments of relative frequency in relation to shifts of event frequencies: Evidence for a limited-capacity model. *Journal of Experimental Psychology: Human Learning and Memory,* 1979, *5,* 395–408.

Whitten, W. B., II, & Bjork, R. A. Learning from tests: Effects of spacing. *Journal of Verbal Learning and Verbal Behavior,* 1977, *16,* 465–478.

Wickelgren, W. A. Size of rehearsal group and short-term memory. *Journal of Experimental Psychology,* 1964, *68,* 413–419.

Wickelgren, W. A. Acoustic similarity and intrusion errors in short-term memory. *Journal of Experimental Psychology,* 1965, *70,* 102–108.

Wickelgren, W. A. Chunking and consolidation: A theoretical synthesis of semantic networks, configuring in conditioning, S-R versus cognitive learning, normal forgetting, the amnesic syndrome, and the hippocampal arousal system. *Psychological Review,* 1979, *86,* 44–60.

Wickens, D. D. Encoding categories of words: An empirical approach to meaning. *Psychological Review,* 1970, *77,* 1–15.

Wickens, D. D. Characteristics of word encoding. In A. W. Melton & E. Martin (Eds.), *Coding processes in human memory.* Washington, D.C.: Winston, 1972.

Wickens, D. D., Born, D. G., & Allen, C. K. Proactive inhibition and item similarity in short-term memory. *Journal of Verbal Learning and Verbal Behavior,* 1963, *2,* 440–445.

Wickens, D. D., & Clark, S. Osgood dimensions as an encoding class in short-term memory. *Journal of Experimental Psychology,* 1968, *78,* 580–584.

Winocur, G., & Weiskrantz, L. An investigation of paired-associate learning in amnesic patients. *Neuropsychologia,* 1976, *14,* 97–110.

Witelson, S. F. Sex and the single hemisphere: Specialization of the right hemisphere for spatial processing. *Science,* 1976, *193,* 425–427.

Witmer, L. R. The association value of three-place consonant-syllables. *Journal of Genetic Psychology,* 1935, *47,* 337–360.

Wollen, K. A., Weber, A., & Lowry, D. H. Bizarreness versus interaction of mental images as determinants of learning. *Cognitive Psychology,* 1972, *3,* 518–523.

Wood, G. Mnemonic systems in recall. *Journal of Educational Psychology,* 1967, *58,* 1–27, Pt. 2.

Woodward, A. E., Jr., Bjork, R. A., & Jongeward, R. H., Jr. Recall and recognition as a function of primary rehearsal. *Journal of Verbal Learning and Verbal Behavior,* 1973, *12,* 608–617.

Woodworth, R. S., & Schlosberg, H. *Experimental psychology.* New York: Holt, Rinehart & Winston, 1954.

Yarmey, A. D. I recognize your face but I can't remember your name: Further evidence on the tip-of-the-tongue phenomenon. *Memory & Cognition,* 1973, *1,* 287–290.

Yates, F. A. *The art of memory.* London: Routledge & Kegan Paul, 1966.

Zacks, R. T. Invariance of total learning time under different conditions of practice. *Journal of Experimental Psychology,* 1969, *82,* 441–447.

Zechmeister, E. B. Orthographic distinctiveness. *Journal of Verbal Learning and Verbal Behavior,* 1969, *8,* 754–761.

Zechmeister, E. B. Orthographic distinctiveness as a variable in word recognition. *American Journal of Psychology,* 1972, *85,* 425–430.

Zechmeister, E. B., Christensen, J., & Rajkowski, B. *What is known about what is known?: Predicting recall without prior test trials.* Paper presented at the fifty-second annual meeting of the Midwestern Psychological Association, St. Louis, May 1980.

Zechmeister, E. B., Curt, C., & Sebastian, J. A. Errors in a recognition memory task are a U-shaped function of word frequency. *Bulletin of the Psychonomic Society,* 1978, *11,* 371–373.

Zechmeister, E. B., & Gude, C. Instruction effects in recognition memory. *Bulletin of the Psychonomic Society,* 1974, *3,* 13–15.

Zechmeister, E. B., King, J. F., Gude, C., & Opera-Nadi, B. Ratings of frequency, familiarity, orthographic distinctiveness and pronunciability for 192 surnames. *Instrumentation & Psychophysics,* 1975, *7,* 531–533.

Zechmeister, E. B., & McKillip, J. Recall of place on the page. *Journal of Educational Psychology,* 1972, *63,* 446–453.

Zechmeister, E. B., McKillip, J., & Pasko, S. Verbal discrimination learning of items read in textual material. *Journal of Experimental Psychology,* 1973, *101,* 393–395.

Zechmeister, E. B., McKillip, J., Pasko, S., & Bespalec, D. Visual memory for place on the page. *Journal of General Psychology,* 1975, *92,* 43–52.

Zechmeister, E. B., & Shaughnessy, J. J. When you know that you know and when you think that you know but you don't. *Bulletin of the Psychonomic Society,* 1980, *15,* 41–44.

Zimmerman, J. Free recall after self-paced study: A test of the attention explanation of the spacing effect. *American Journal of Psychology*, 1975, *88,* 277–291.

Zimmerman, J., & Underwood, B. J. Ordinal position knowledge within and across lists as a function of instructions in free-recall learning. *Journal of General Psychology*, 1968, *79,* 301–307.

Zipf, G. K. The meaning-frequency relationships of words. *Journal of General Psychology*, 1945, *33,* 251–256.

Name Index

Subject Index